Gift of the Devil

Other titles in the *Perspectives on Underdevelopment* series

Gift of the Devil

A History of Guatemala

Jim Handy

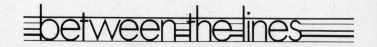

Published in Canada by Between The Lines,
427 Bloor St. West,
Toronto, Ont.

Between The Lines is a joint project of Dumont Press Graphix and the Development Education Centre.

Typeset by Dumont Press Graphix, Kitchener, Ont.

Printed in Canada at Gagne Printing Ltd.

Cover design by Goodness Graphics

Maps used with permission of Oxfam America and the World Bank

Canadian Cataloguing in Publication Data

Handy, Jim, 1952-
  Gift of the devil

(Perspectives on underdevelopment)
Includes bibliographical references and index.
ISBN 0-919946-42-9 (bound). - ISBN 0-919946-43-7 (pbk.).

1. Guatemala - History. 2. Guatemala - Politics and government. 3. Peasant uprisings - Guatemala.
I. Title. II. Series.

F1466.H35 1984   972.81   C84-099684-5

To my parents

For it is beautiful
to love the world
with the eyes
of those not yet born

Por es bello
amar el mundo
con los ojos
de los que no han nacido todavia

— Otto René Castillo,
    Guatemalan poet

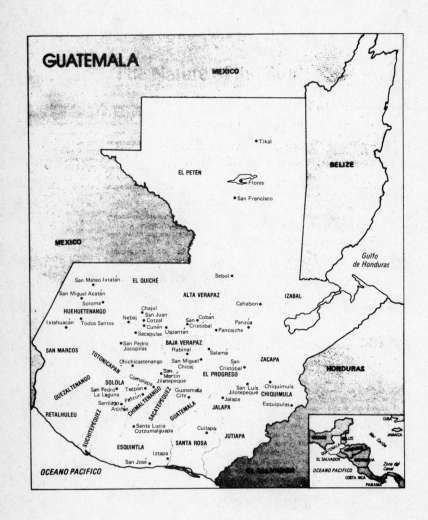

GUATEMALA

MEXICO

• Tikal

BELIZE

EL PETÉN

Flores

• San Francisco

MEXICO

Gulfo
de Honduras

San Mateo Ixtatán   EL QUICHÉ   Sebol •

San Miguel Acatán   ALTA VERAPAZ   Cahabon •   IZABAL
  Soloma •   Chajul
HUEHUETENANGO   San Juan   Cobán
              Nebaj • Cotzal   San • Cristóbal   Panzós •
Ixtahuacán Todos Santos •   Cunén   Cristóbal   Pancajche •
             Sacapulas Uspantan

             • San Pedro   BAJA VERAPAZ
SAN MARCOS   Jocopilas   Rabinal •   San •   ZACAPA
         TOTONICAPAN Chichicastenango San Miguel   Salamá San •
                         Chicaj   Cristóbal   HONDURAS
              SOLOLA   Comalapa • San •   EL PROGRESO
QUEZALTENANGO   Martín
                 Tecpan • Jilotepeque   Chiquimula •
        San Pedro •   Patzún   Guatemala   San Luis
RETALHULEU La Laguna   City   Jilotepeque Jalapa   CHIQUIMULA
       Santiago •   SACATEPEQUEZ   • Jalapa
        Atitlán CHIMALTENANGO   JALAPA   Esquipulas •
                        GUATEMALA
                 • Santa Lucia   Cuilapa •
         SUCHITEPEQUEZ Cotzumalguapa   JUTIAPA
           ESQUINTLA   SANTA ROSA
                  Iztapa
OCEANO PACIFICO   San José •

EL SALVADOR

Table of Contents

Topographical Regions

1 *Petén and Caribbean Lowlands*
2 *Central Highlands*
3 *Cuchumatanes Paramo and High Mountain Peaks*
4 *Southeastern Valleys, Plains, and Mountains*
5 *Cobán and Zona Reina Hills and Valleys*
6 *Western Huehuetenango Hills and Valleys*
7 *Upper Pacific Piedmont*
8 *Lower Pacific Piedmont*
9 *Pacific Coastal Plain*

AREAS OF THE REGIONS AND
PERCENTAGES OF TOTAL AREA

REGION 1 - 50,277 Sq.Km.- 46.0%;
REGION 2 - 20,072 Sq.Km.- 18.4%;
REGION 3 - 1,423 Sq.Km. - 3.3%;
REGION 4 - 14,904 Sq.Km. - 7.3%;
REGION 5 - 6,200 Sq.Km. - 5.7%;
REGION 6 - 1,583 Sq.Km. - 1.4%;
REGION 7 - 4,217 Sq.Km. - 2.3%;
REGION 8 - 3,715 Sq.Km. - 3.4%;
REGION 9 - 6,731 Sq.Km. - 6.2%.

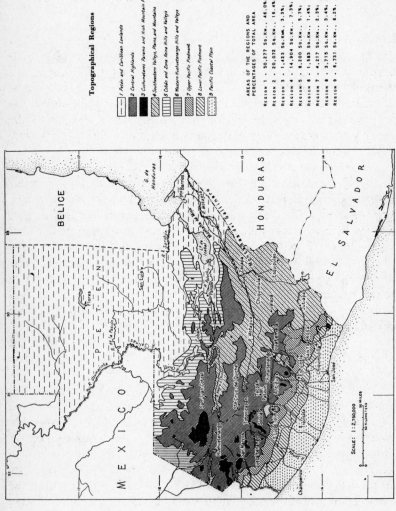

Preface and Acknowledgements

THE IDEA OF WRITING a general history of Guatemala first occurred to me in 1980, when I was working as the Central American co-ordinator for Amnesty International, Canada. This was during the administration of Romeo Lucas García, a horrible period for labour unionists, peasants and reform politicians in Guatemala. Much of my time was spent trying to explain the human rights situation in the country to a variety of very different audiences in university lecture halls and church basements.

The scope of the human tragedy in Guatemala made the story compelling and gripping. But what proved difficult was to make Guatemala comprehensible, to make understandable the very real, palpable terror I had felt during frequent visits to the Guatemalan highlands. For most audiences the all-encompassing brutality that typified the Lucas García regime was, at heart, unbelievable.

At the same time, I was completing research for my doctoral thesis in history. My thesis topic, the reform administrations in Guatemala from 1945 to 1954, prompted a broad investigation into the earlier periods of Guatemalan history. I was struck by how so much of the current unrest in Guatemala was rooted in earlier history, stretching back to the three long centuries of colonial rule. This book is an attempt, then, to make the Guatemala of the 1980s understandable through an examination of its history.

Two assumptions have remained constant in my approach to Guatemalan history. The first is that Guatemalan history is *not* best explained through a study of American foreign policy. While U.S. governments and business interests have always had an important influence on the way events unfold in Guatemala, they do not control them. The United States has never been able simply to shape Guatemala for its own interests. The second assumption is that the roots for the current brutal nightmare in Guatemala stretch far back into history. To explain contemporary Guatemala it is necessary to trace those roots back into the depths of colonial society where the underpinnings of the existing society were established, and to follow them through the course of Guatemala's complex, often fascinating history.

There are a number of people I would like to thank here for their assistance in the preparation of this book. Liisa North, David Raby, Tim Draimin, Ken Epps, Jamie Swift and Al Berry read parts of earlier versions and made valuable suggestions. Kris Inwood also deserves thanks for constantly feeding my curiosity, listening with interest to reports on my progress and questioning with intelligence my assumptions and theories. Kathryn Jones read and reread many chapters of the manuscript, made numerous suggestions and was constantly encouraging and understanding. And Robert Clarke of Between the Lines patiently reworked much of my copy and gently brought me back to earth when this book threatened to extend beyond any manageable size. Finally, through numerous trips to Guatemala I was taught and befriended by innumerable people from Guatemala City to tiny villages in the Cuchumatán mountains. They will always have my gratitude for making me love Guatemala and for inspiring me to finish this book.

J.H.
October 1984

— 1 —
Introduction: Indians and the Colonial Legacy

The year having come,
Was the beginning of the arrival of Christianity
here;
Bloody vomit
Painless death;

Time of death.
Time of locusts;

Pustule fever
Was the burden of misery.

The gift of the Devil
White Crown
— *Book of Chilam Balam,* a Mayan account of the conquest

NIGHT WAS FALLING as we entered San Miguel Uspantán in Guatemala's Quiché department. The town was welcome after four hours of gruelling travel over almost non-existent roads but, as we turned the first corner, the sense of welcome faded. At irregular intervals along the street, huddled in doorways or talking around sandbag barricades, stood seemingly hundreds of soldiers, automatic rifles at the ready. Light shone from metal as khaki clothing and dark faces merged into the shadows left by smouldering lanterns. We slowly wound our way along a maze of back streets, looking for an exit not barred by military checkpoints. The sense of being lost in an ever deepening labyrinth with danger at every corner heightened until finally we turned one more corner and the town was behind us, the road slowly deteriorating as we moved farther from the village.

It was April of 1983 and I was in the western highlands of Guatemala. General Ríos Montt had come to power a little over a year earlier and was yet to be overthrown in the coup of August 1983. These villages had just gone through the most brutal period of an often brutal history. Rebel forces had been challenging the government for two decades, and in the last few years they had successfully incorporated many highland Indian peasants into the struggle. Government counter-insurgency had, since 1978, struck back indiscriminately at a variety of sectors of popular protest. Since Ríos Montt had come to power through a military coup in 1982, the bulk of the government repression had been aimed with ferocious brutality at these peasants.

An untold number of villages, many isolated in the rugged highlands, had been destroyed by government troops. Thousands of peasants, men, women and children, had been killed. However, by April, during my visit, the counter-insurgency that had decimated Indian villages had entered a new phase. The government claimed the highlands had been secured; the guerrilla forces of the Guerrilla Army of the Poor (EGP) were reportedly scattered, reduced to pockets on the Mexican border. Every town was patrolled by civil guards (militias of local residents under the control of the local army commander), and all the larger towns, like Uspantán, hosted sizable garrisons of Guatemala's conscript army.

I was in the highlands visiting as many of these villages as possible in the limited time available at the end of a research trip to the capital. What I found was a tale of despair and hope, of terror and perseverance. An old Mam woman in one small village told of how the village had been deserted for almost seven months and described what it had been like to hide in the mountains for that amount of time. Another woman in another town, while showing some native clothing pointed to a burned corner and sadly spoke about how the house once there had been set on fire. In the gathering darkness one evening I drove past darkened burnt shells of adobe huts.

Another day I searched for the site of yet another reported massacre, walking past closed and shuttered homes, eventually to be forced back by darkness and the eerily silent hills. Through this and five earlier visits to the highlands between 1978 and 1983 I had become accustomed to many of the habits that terror had engrained on the population. In one town in Huehuetenango I had noticed how the conversation would almost naturally stop when a truck went by on the road outside. One could almost hear the silent prayers that the truck not stop outside their home this night. It was surprising how quickly I began to do the same thing; how quickly terror sank into the consciousness. In another town in the Quiché highlands I listened while one proud Indian peasant, a marvelous painter-artist had pleaded with me to find some way to get his family out of the highlands. Soldiers had killed three men in the town the night before, and the army was expected back that night, as it had been almost every night that month. These were the tiny glimpses afforded a visitor of the sorrow and terror that has engulfed the Indian in the highlands.

But I also found villages resettled after many months of emptiness. Land that hadn't been planted for two years was again being worked by the hoe. A patient family baked adobe in the sun to repair their home. I listened to an army commander, in a moving speech, explain to peasants that a soldier's family grieves the death of a son, just as they do; I watched as thoughtful Indians listened to his words being translated into Ixil. The terror remained, palpable, but mixed with it was an equally palpable resolution that the last decade of suffering would not be in vain, a determination to effect significant, structural change. I found people prepared to talk about the future, if only in hushed tones and with many backward glances.

Revolution and Repression

THE LATE 1970s and the early 1980s were a time of revolution and bloody repression in Central America. Guerrilla organizations had operated sporadically in Nicaragua, El Salvador and Guatemala for many decades, but in the 1970s and 1980s they succeeded in overthrowing one government of corrupt and rapacious landowning elites and were poised to challenge another two. In 1979 the United States administration had failed to prop up the faltering dictatorship of Anastasio Somoza in Nicaragua but seemed determined, no matter the cost, to reverse the revolution there and prevent the governments of El Salvador and Guatemala from falling to popular forces which seemed clearly to represent the majority of the population. U.S. attempts to destabilize the Sandinistas in Nicaragua and U.S. involvement in supporting the military in El Salvador ensured that events in those two countries dominated coverage in the North American news media.

But to anyone familiar with Central American history, Guatemala remained the key to the region. Guatemala contained over one-third of the region's population, had the most powerful and dynamic economy and boasted the most efficient and well-trained military. While the U.S. State Department and the Pentagon were more intimately involved in supporting the El Salvadorean military, State Department officials occasionally made it clear that for them the "last line" in Central America was in Guatemala.

The stability of the rightist, military-controlled governments that had dominated Guatemala for the last three decades became a serious question for U.S. foreign policy in the early 1980s. Four guerrilla organizations had developed a powerful, co-ordinated opposition, which enjoyed the support of much of the nation's Indian majority.

Guerrilla successes in the highlands were matched by the fragmentation of the conservative political parties and the military that together dominated Guatemalan politics. A military coup in spring 1982 and another in August 1983 did little to strengthen the position of the Guatemalan elite. While a brutal counter-insurgency campaign had temporarily weakened the guerrilla movements, their organization remained intact and their popular support, athough subdued by the counter-insurgency, smouldered beneath the surface.

It was clear that the same type of unresponsive and repressive government that had predominated in Guatemala for the last three decades could not continue to rule or provide any sort of stability in the country. Yet, it was equally clear that the Guatemalan elite had demonstrated no willingness to compromise with the popular forces and initiate long overdue reforms. The revolutionary path to structural economic and social change had clearly become the only viable alternative.

The path that had led Guatemala to this seeming impasse had followed a tortuous route through over four and a half centuries of a frequently violent, occasionally inspiring history. History makes itself evident in Guatemala in sometimes startling, sometimes subtle ways: in the huge immense ruins of churches in colonial Antigua, in the words of a young *ladino** whose solution for Guatemala's problems was the extermination of the Indian, in the complex relationship between the military and the political parties, and in the guarded statements of the U.S. embassy's political officers. But most compellingly, it becomes evident in the strong faces of Indian peasants and the tiny, dusty plots of land from which they eke miserable livings. It is hard to fully grasp the lives of the Indians of Guatemala; their poverty and centuries of repression and racism wrap them in a cocoon of suffering and mistrust. It is a cocoon that must be penetrated if we hope to understand Guatemala.

The Colonial Heritage

THE GUATEMALAN HISTORIAN, Severo Martínez Paláez, in his superb study of colonial Guatemala, *La Patria del Criollo*, sums up the colonial period as a "regimen of terror for the Indians".

> What we must recognize [is that] the cruel treatment of the Indian was not a sporadic phenomenon, but . . . inherent in the social structures of the colony, absolutely necessary to maintain subjected to incredible

---

* *Ladino* refers to people of mixed blood and western culture, and is also used in Guatemala to refer to Indians who have adopted western costume and culture.

forms of exploitation a mass of serfs with enormous numerical superiority.[1]

This heritage of cruelty, of exploitation and oppression, is apparent in all aspects of Guatemala today. The institutions designed or used to exploit Indian labour or land during the colonial period are at the heart of the still-prevailing systems of land ownership and labour recruitment. The heritage of the conquest and attempts to defend themselves against the incessant demands of their colonial masters prompted Indian groups to withdraw into suspicious, closed communities. The early and powerful influence of the Catholic church and its subsequent partial withdrawal from Indian villages helped form a blend of native and Catholic beliefs that still provides the basis for both religious and political organization in the villages.

Perhaps most importantly, the general perception of Indians during the colonial period as a reluctant, but necessary, source of labour that needed to be compelled to work by a number of legal and illegal coercive measures has continued to shape the treatment of labour in Guatemala. The colonial period laid the basis of a society moulded principally by the need for extensive terror and force as a means of social control.

The violence and repression that this spawned lasted throughout the colonial period. It endured through the anarchy immediately following independence in 1821 and the successful peasant revolt of Rafael Carrera in the 1830s. It was heightened during the liberal regimes of Barrios, Barrillas and Cabrera as the demand for labour and native land again dominated the Guatemalan economy. While the subsequent dictatorship of Jorge Ubico was noted for rigidly maintained law and order and, in some areas, reduced pressure on peasants, the basic, repressive, rural power structure survived.

Ten years of "revolutionary" government following World War II had begun to alter the tenor of Guatemalan society when the government was overthrown by a coalition of traditional conservative elements and the U.S. Central Intelligence Agency. The governments that followed reversed many of that decade's gains and subsequently did little to disturb the traditional, rural power-holder's control over Indian labour and the vast bulk of the agricultural land.

Throughout it all, the Guatemalan peasantry has shown a propensity for effective organization in defence of its rights and land. Quite often this defence has taken the shape of armed revolt. While at times successful in pressing for specific demands, these revolts have failed to alter the repressive nature of Guatemalan society. This is the context for the current political and social unrest in Guatemala.

The Geographic Setting

GUATEMALA, THE SIZE OF THE STATE of Ohio or the island of New-foundland with slightly over 42,000 square miles, nonetheless offers incredible diversity in climate, terrain and culture.[2] Its geography is best described as a backbone of mountain ridges framed on both sides by a piedmont, which diminishes in height until it meets a low, flat coastal plain. The backbone — the highlands — is formed by a series of mountain ranges and is usually considered to be divided into distinct parts: the central (or western); and the less rugged eastern area. In the midst of these ranges are 30 volcanic peaks. The highest, most rugged section is in the extreme northwestern region — the Cuchamatán Mountains. The highlands, which gradually flatten out as they extend southeastward towards the border with El Salvador, constitute approximately one-third of the total area of the country.

These highlands and the slopes of the upper piedmont have been at the centre of Guatemalan life. It is amidst the broken topography, the isolated valleys, the high plateaus of the western highlands and pockets of the piedmont, such as the area around Lake Atitlán, where the bulk of Indians — who still make up almost 50 per cent of the country's 7.2 million people — live. There they scratch out a living from a seemingly timeless cycle of corn and bean cultivation. Tiny villages are linked by innumerable paths trodden deep into the sides of the surrounding hills. On these paths there is constant traffic. Often, the figures gathering firewood from diminishing forest-cover, walking to a neighbouring market or returning from an isolated field bear the distinctive dress of their native *municipio* (township). Whether dressed in native clothing or not, the Indians carry with them the imprint of their native village wherever they go.

The rugged terrain helps isolate their land and their *municipio*, fostering local identification and inhibiting national awareness. The descendants of the Maya who live in these highlands are grouped into six major linguistic affiliations and speak 23 different dialects.[3] Here their Mayan ancestors seem real and palpable and guard against any attack on tradition or any threat to the ancient culture.

The sense of isolation in the *municipios* is constantly present. The American anthropologist Sol Tax offered an assessment of Guatemalan townships in 1941. Besides distinctive costumes, dialects, customs and practices, Tax found:

> The Indians of the *municipios* think of themselves as distinct groups of peoples, biologically and socially. . . . Each *municipio* tends to have its own economic specialties, sometimes its own economic and social values and even its own different standard of living. Each *municipio* has a

politico-religious system of public service; each has its own saints, and its own fiestas for them, and its own annual religious calendar.[4]

In the 40 years since Tax recorded these impressions the process of national integration has progressed steadily. Improved transportation and communications, a more extensive school system, increasing numbers of Indians who work for brief or extended periods outside of the community and the increased authority and presence of the national government — apparent through political parties and the military — have all played their roles. Nonetheless, the village remains the primary reference point and focus of loyalty for all but a few of the highland Indian peasants.

With minor exceptions, the rest of Guatemala is *ladino* dominated. As the severity of terrain diminishes in the eastern highlands, the rural villages are increasingly populated by *ladino* farmers and the farm plots grow slightly larger in size. While still important, corn and beans give way to a number of other crops. Identification with the national government and its institutions is more prevalent.

To the south and west of the highlands lies Guatemala's true agricultural heartland. The upper slopes of the highlands, as they wend their way to the Pacific plain (usually called the upper Pacific piedmont), are the centre of Guatemala's coffee production. With rich, volcanic soils, a regular and moderate rainy season (May to November) and a perfect climate for growing, this area produces some of the best, most expensive coffee in the world. While still containing a significant Indian population, most of the productive land is controlled by large *fincas* (farms) given over to coffee production.

The next area, the lower Pacific littoral, similarly enjoys rich fertile soil, adequate rainfall and a beneficial climate. Higher temperatures mean the region's coffee is not as good as the upper piedmont's. However, the area was the scene of considerable agricultural expansion in the 1950s and 1960s; cotton, corn, sugarcane and cattle ranching have all developed to dominate the region. For many years the fastest growing part of Guatemala, the Pacific littoral has seen significant urbanization, with large centres at Retalhuleu and Escuintla.

Guatemala's other regions — the coastal plain, the Cobán and Petén, the southeastern valley plains and mountains, the Caribbean lowlands — are less favoured agriculturally. The Petén is Guatemala's vast, tropical frontier where precious wood and chicle is harvested and oil exploration carried out. The Cobán is perhaps most notable for the Franja Transversal del Norte, a strip being rapidly developed to provide transportation to the oil fields of the Petén. It also hosts resource development in the form of large hydroelectric projects and nickel mining, and harbours an increasing number of large cattle ranches.

Indian and *ladino* communities in this zone have come under increasing land pressure in recent years. The Caribbean lowlands are dominated by banana production, with control for the first half of the twentieth century resting almost entirely in the hands of the United Fruit Company.

Pre-colonial Society: Warring Kingdoms

BY THE TIME OF THE CONQUEST by Pedro de Alvarado beginning in the 1520s, the Guatemalan highlands had become the centre of a large population. The great Mayan ceremonial centres of the Petén and Chiápas lowlands had long since been abandoned. The population of these areas had migrated north to the drier Yucatan peninsula and southwest to the Guatemalan highlands. At a later date, by the middle of the 13th century, the revived Mayan-Toltec cities of Chichen-Itza and environs had also declined. It appears that Toltec groups from these centres migrated to the Meso-American highlands and over a period of years conquered the resident Maya. The new conquerors, though, were absorbed by Mayan culture and while they constituted a dominant elite and influenced architecture, warfare and ceremony, highland Guatemalan society remained predominantly Mayan.

Under the direction of their Toltec rulers a number of rival empires developed, based on linguistic differentiation and situated around large ceremonial centres. The first and most powerful of these empires was the Quiché, which came to dominate highland and Pacific Guatemala from Soconusco on the Chiápas coast to Alta Verapaz, with perhaps one million inhabitants subject to the Quichean king.

However, Quichean dominance began to be challenged by subject groups in the 15th century and by 1470 Cakchiquel, Rabinal, Mam, Tzutzuhil and other sub-groups successfully revolted and became rivals to the Quiché.

The major groups, the Tzutzuhil, Cakchiquel and Quiché, were able to join together to defeat an Aztec army sent by emperor Alhuitzotl in the late 15th century. Nevertheless, by the time of the Spanish conquest, these three kingdoms were locked in bitter rivalry.[5]

The population of the preconquest highlands has never been determined exactly. The chronicles of conquistadors and written Mayan records from immediately following the conquest indicate a population in excess of one million people. Major population centres, such as the Quiché town of Utatlán, would have had between 10 and 20 thousand people at their height shortly before 1520.[6]

It has been speculated that the populations had reached the upper limit of the capacity of the land. Land pressure appears to have been extreme, helping prompt the continuing bitter battles between the various kingdoms. Historian Murdo MacLeod has argued that by the early years of the 16th century the Guatemalan highlands "offered signs of having reached ... a grave Malthusian crisis of population and food supply. There is some justification for saying that if 14th century Europe was ripe for disaster (shortly before the great plagues), then Meso-America was overripe."[7]

The Conquest: Disease and War

DISASTER CAME IN THE FORM of the conquest, heralded and abetted by horrific epidemics of previously unknown diseases. Even before the Spanish entered Meso-America, great European diseases had rampaged before them, spreading from New Spain (Mexico) to engulf Central America. The first great pandemic was probably a combination of smallpox, influenza and bubonic plague, which swept through the highlands in 1520.[8]

It is almost impossible to imagine the tremendous disruption caused by the rapid spread of unfamiliar disease. Inexplicable deaths in huge numbers rent the social and economic fabric of the kingdoms apart. The best description of the period comes from the *Annals of the Cakchiquels,* the sacred book of history written shortly after the conquest:

> It happened that during the twenty-fifth year the plague began, oh my sons! First they became ill of a cough, they suffered from nose-bleeds and illnesses of the bladder, it was in truth terrible the number of dead there were in that period. ... The people could not in any way control the sickness. Great was the stench of the dead. After our fathers and grandfathers succumbed, half the people fled to the fields. The dogs and vultures devoured the bodies. The mortality was terrible. Your grandfathers died and with them died the son of a king and his brothers and kinsmen. So it was that we became orphans, oh my sons! So we became when we were young. All of us were thus. We were born to die.[9]

Up to one-third of the population of the highlands died in this one pandemic alone.[10]

Smallpox, influenza and bubonic plague were followed by pulmonary plague epidemics in 1545 to 1548 and in 1576 to 1581. These epidemics, combined with the bloody conquest and the effects of the new system of forced labour, reduced the population of the Meso-American highlands by between 70 to 90 per cent in the first century after the conquest. The immensity of this loss of life can be more easily grasped in light of the assertion by French demographer Channu that in 1490 what is today Latin America accounted for 20 per cent of the world's population, most of this centred in New Spain, Meso-America and the Andes. Less than a century later it comprised under 3 per cent.[11]

The terrible toll of disease was augmented by an incredibly brutal conquest led by Cortés' former lieutenant Don Pedro de Alvarado. Unlike New Spain, the kingdoms of Central America were not co-ordinated by a centralized empire. Thus, the conquest could not be accomplished by one fierce battle directed at the heart of the empire. Conquest came through a series of bloody wars, beginning in 1524 with the arrival of Don Pedro and not ending in the highlands until the defeat of the more isolated Pokoman, Mam and Ixil Indians in the 1530s. Indeed, the Ketchi of Alta Verapaz proved so difficult to con-quer that Don Pedro eventually gave the task over to the church.

The death and destruction of the time were heightened by the character of both the conquest and the conquistadors of Guatemala. Don Pedro de Alvarado was the archetype of conquistadors. A hand-some, blond man, he was overwhelmingly physical, consumed by rest-less energy that never allowed him to settle and enjoy the fruits of his exploits. Often displaying immense personal courage and physical endurance, he waged devastating wars against the Maya-Toltec of Guatemala. Taking advantage of the rivalries between the competing Mayan kingdoms, he faced fierce resistance from the Quiché and Tzutzuhil in 1524, but used the Cakchiquel as allies. In the initial battle between the Quiché and the invaders, 30,000 Quichean war-riors reportedly took part; most of them were slain.[12] Mayan accounts of the battle suggest there was a personal duel between Alvarado and the Quichean king, in which Alvarado triumphed. Alvarado himself claimed to have fought for hours pinned to his saddle by an arrow, an injury that affected his walk for the rest of his life. Quichean sources describe the battle graphically: "There were so many Indians that they killed, that they made a river of blood. . . . all the water became blood and also the day became red on account of the great bloodshed."[13]

By 1526 the former allies, the Cakchiquel, revolted in response to Spanish demands for warriors, tribute and, perhaps, Alvarado's designs on the wife of a Cakchiquel noble. Further battles followed for over a decade. Conquered natives were continually being drafted to provide fodder for the continuing wars. Others fled to the more iso-lated mountains, leaving abandoned villages behind. The *Annals of the Cakchiquel* tell how they "scattered in the forests; all our towns were taken; oh my children we were slaughtered by Tunatiuh [Alvarado]. . . . From that time the Castilians were hated by the Cak-chiquels."[14]

The conqueror of New Spain, Hernan Cortés, had quickly shown a propensity for administration after the initial conquest. Alvarado did not demonstrate a similar aptitude. From 1524 until his death in 1541, he ruled Guatemala like a personal fiefdom. While on occasion he turned his tremendous energies to one economic pursuit or another, they were brief respites between further expeditions meant to find a field for himself as potentially wealthy as New Spain. He rewarded his followers with free domain over conquered Indians and drove enormous numbers of conscripts to work in the Honduran mines to outfit his expeditions.

The Spanish crown, attempting to curb the most blatant abuses and to control the power of Alvarado, required that Indians not be enslaved unless they resisted Spanish authority. Henceforth, all natives would be given the opportunity to submit to God and the crown before war could be made on them. If they submitted they were not to be molested. The *requerimiento* or law in effect offering this choice was to be read to every non-subject group.

Alvarado, while dutifully proclaiming the *requerimiento,* did so in such a way as to ensure non-acceptance; allowing him to take slaves freely. In fact, Alvarado enslaved Guatemalan Indians so freely that he provoked complaints from Mexico where, it was asserted, slaves sold for 40 *pesos* each, while in Guatemala they could be had for but two.[15]

Colonial Society:
Encomienda, Repartimiento, and Reducción

THE DEATH OF ALVARADO in 1541, while he was away from Guatemala on one of his many adventures looking for new spoils, came at roughly the same time as the Spanish crown demonstrated determined intent to assert dominion over its subjects in the New World and to some extent curb the abuses that were gaining notoriety in Spain. The new colonial institutions that emerged at this time, including the New Laws of 1541, were designed along one common theme. Whatever wealth the New World offered, whether it be in the form of precious metals or agricultural exports, was of little worth if not accompanied by access to Indian labour. The New Laws were designed to regulate and reassert crown control over this valuable commodity.

As American anthropologist Eric Wolf points out, much of this impulse came from a fear that the men in the colonies would become too independent:

> If Indian labor made the wheels turn in this New Spain, then whoever was lord and master of Indians would also be lord and master of the land. With unlimited access to Indian energy, the colonists would soon have no need of Spain nor King; hence the crown had to limit this access, supervise it, curtail it.[16]

The *encomienda* (literally, a "commission" from the crown to an individual) set up by the New Laws of 1541 was only partially successful in this endeavour. First used in the New World in 1503, the *encomienda* has been described as "an artifice to transfer the riches of the Indian to the hands of the Spanish in a procedure that was more ordered than a frank plundering of booty".[17] In simple terms it was the transfer of the crown's right to tribute to an individual as a reward for service to the crown. The *encomienda* had been used liberally by Alvarado to reward his cohorts and by subsequent governors to gain support, and by the end of the 16th century there were 200 *encomenderos,* Spaniards who had received these grants, in the Audiencia of Guatemala.*[18]

In the early years following the conquest many *encomenderos* enjoyed almost total dominion over those Indians included in the *encomienda* grant. Labour was freely exacted and abuse was common. The New Laws restricted the Spaniard's rights somewhat, theoretically limiting the Indians' obligations to tribute alone and providing for a host of protective measures for the Indians against abuse by the *encomendero.* According to the New Laws, the Spaniards were to enjoy their grant for only two generations before the tribute again reverted to the crown.

However, as Severo Martínez Paláez points out, the Spanish elite in Guatemala employed "diverse tricks" to ridicule measures intended to protect the Indian.[19] The Spaniards were free to demand tribute in a particular product — most notably, cacao — which in effect forced Indians to work on coastal plantations. The restriction to two generations was not rigidly adhered to, particularly in the case of large grants, many of which were maintained generation after generation.

Nevertheless, the New Laws did provide the crown with greater control over the granting of *encomiendas.* By late in the 16th century many of the original conquistadors no longer controlled the *encomienda* because better allotments of Indians were being made to new arrivals with closer connections to the governor. Most of the grants with highest potential were given out in the late 16th century, during the heyday of the cacao boom in Guatemala.[20]

As the colonial period progressed, however, the *encomienda* became less important. The institution persisted until the 18th century, but most grants in the later years were small, serving primarily as pensions for long-term residents with declining incomes.

* The Audiencia of Guatemala was comprised of what is now Guatemala, Honduras, El Salvador, Costa Rica, Nicaragua and Chiápas (now part of Mexico).

The New Laws of 1541 also refined the system of *repartimiento* (literally, an "allotment" or "assessment"). All Indians, with only a few exceptions, were subject to this system of forced labour, which could take away up to one-quarter of the inhabitants of any village at any one time. These workers, paid one *real* (one-eighth of a *peso*) per day, were allotted by colonial officials to petitioning landowners. While various ordinances regulated the duration of the labour, enforcement of these regulations was lax. Many Indians were required to travel long distances to the site of their forced labour, time not paid for or considered as part of their required service.

Martínez Paláez calls the *repartimiento,* which continued until close to the end of the 18th century, "the key piece of the colonial economic system":

> The base of that structure was the regimen of work: the *repartimiento,* the obligatory labour of the natives, the rigorous control of the Indians in their villages, from which they were sent periodically to work on the *haciendas* of the Spanish . . . for the three colonial centuries. This regimen imposed the basis and determined the character of colonial Guatemalan society. . . . The *repartimiento* was . . . the mechanism that guaranteed [the Indians'] subjugation and exploitation and hence their position of inferiority.[21]

One of the elements of the New Laws that eventually assisted in the regulation of the *repartimiento* was the crown's agreement to the church's policy of *reducción.* The severe population decline and attempts by Indians to avoid the demands of slavery, *encomienda* and *repartimiento* by retreating to more isolated areas had resulted in a marked dispersal of the Indian population. The isolation of these pockets of Indians made it difficult to extend crown and church control. Thus, beginning in 1543, the Dominicans, with the help of civil authorities, commenced to "reduce" the scattered population into larger, more centralized towns. The Dominicans argued that the reduction was a means to both help stop illegal oppression of the Indians and assist in conversion. Consequently, between 1543 and 1600 — although the process was largely complete by 1550 — the remnants of the original Mayan population were congregated into 700 towns.

While the initial impulse for the *reducción* might have been to control exploitation and to assist in conversion, it did not remain so. The result of the *reducciones* was to free up Indian land for confiscation by the Spanish and to assist in the effective operation of the *repartimiento.*

It soon became apparent to colonial officials that the *reducciones* had simplified the arrangement of *repartimiento.* By 1601 the crown openly attested to that relationship by demanding that any new Indian village be created near *haciendas,* or estates, to provide a labour force.

While these new towns were provided with land, it was in reduced amounts. According to one scholar, the amount of land given to these new, amalgamated towns was usually less than that enjoyed previously by each individual hamlet.[22] Spanish residents took advantage of the *reducciones* to lay claim to the best of the now empty land.[23] Although land was an abundant commodity in the depopulated highlands throughout most of the colonial period, the usurpation of the best land in the early years laid the basis for the growth of the *hacienda* and the intense land scarcity felt later by highland Indians.

Colonial Products:
Cacao, Indigo and the Growth of the Hacienda

COLONIAL GUATEMALA WAS A DISAPPOINTMENT for its Spanish conquistadors and settlers. Despite early hopes for great wealth based on the existence of a numerous population and the accumulated treasure of generations of Mayan rulers, it soon became apparent that Guatemala provided few opportunities for quick accumulation of wealth. The treasures of the Mayan rulers were soon exhausted. While gold panning was pursued with Indian labour and helped build some fortunes, it soon petered out in all but the Tegucigalpa region of Honduras. The newly arrived Spaniards hunted elsewhere for sources of wealth. They soon turned to agriculture.

Guatemala's first agricultural export of any consequence was cacao, a favoured drink of both the Mayan and Aztec ruling class before the conquest. Soon after the conquest, Spanish *encomenderos* gained control of the cacao produced in the prime growing area on the Soconusco coast of Chiápas. The market for the crop also increased dramatically, as its use spread to commoners.

In the early years the crown and *encomenderos* interfered little in production of the crop, leaving the fields in the hands of native owners. They did, however, continually demand increasing levels of tribute in the form of cacao. The demand soon impoverished those potentially wealthy natives who owned cacao land. At the same time, Spaniards who did not enjoy *encomiendas* in the cacao-growing areas began to demand their tribute in the form of cacao, forcing natives to travel to the coastal fields to labour. The climatic change involved took its toll. One colonial official called the area around Soconusco "a general sepulchre for all those Indians who come to it, for great numbers of them die".[24]

Along with cacao other crops were attempted in colonial Guatemala, including balsam and sarsaparilla (used to treat syphillis and other ailments), but the market and production opportunities for these were limited. The only export crop of note that was consistently exploited throughout the colonial period was indigo.

A blue dye obtained from the leaves of the xiquilite plant, indigo was produced primarily along the Pacific coastal plain. Although the plant is native to Guatemala, it first began to be cultivated for indigo production and export in the mid-16th century. From that point until the end of the colonial period, indigo producers constantly complained about the paucity of labour and continually schemed to avoid the various crown restrictions on recruitment of Indian labourers. Although the xiquilite harvest lasted only two months, the processing of indigo from the leaves was also labour intensive. The leaves were steeped in large vats of water, which induced fermentation, thus releasing the dye from the plant. At this stage the water was drained into another vat and beat rapidly to promote the coagulation of the dye. This lump of semi-liquid dye was then left to dry in the sun for periods of up to 40 days.[25]

This process required numerous workers and was also considered unhealthy. The fermenting mass of xiquilite left in the vats attracted clouds of flies, infecting both workers and animals. Because of this concern, the crown, from the mid-16th century on, banned the use of Indians in the processing of indigo. Despite numerous efforts to have it repealed, the restriction persisted until 1738.

Theoretically, indigo producers were restricted to using "free" *ladino* labourers or black slaves. However, indigo producers were frequently able to skirt government restriction to obtain labour. The most common trick was to subcontract Indians to perform certain tasks for fraudulent wages. Often, *ladinos* were contracted by the owner of the indigo dye-works, who in turn hired Indians to do the work at a tiny fraction of the amount paid them. There were also numerous instances of Indians simply being coerced by threats of force or demands for tribute to work on the production.

Planters and dye-works owners continually complained that non-Indians, usually *ladinos*, were freely hired and accepted advances but failed to show for work. Finally, in 1723, in response to civil attempts to restrict the use of Indian labour in church dye-works, an ecclesiastical judge claimed the civil *alcalde* (mayor) held no jurisdiction over the church and declared the production of indigo "morally impossible" without Indian labour.[26] From that point impediments to the use of Indians in indigo production were swept aside. Indians could, henceforth, be contracted to work in indigo production.

This was not enough to satisfy the producers, who demanded that Indians from the *repartimiento* also be forced to participate. Finally, in 1784, in an effort to end the "scandalous idleness" of the Indians a system not unlike the *repartimiento,* with conscripts from each village, was initiated to ease the labour problems of indigo growers.

Described in 1723 as "the most precious product this realm possesses" and in 1799 as the "principal and almost the only article of export which sustains the commerce of Guatemala with Europe", indigo did little to provide Guatemalan planters with huge fortunes. A few substantial planters developed large estates based on the production of indigo and were able to integrate marketing and production successfully. However, fully two-thirds of the crop came from small-scale producers who were at the mercy of and continually in debt to Guatemala City and Spanish merchant houses. The formation of the Indigo Grower's Association in 1782 did little to ameliorate their condition.

By the turn of the century, indigo production in the Audiencia began to decline steadily: a decline that continued past independence. Continual disruptions in trade and increased competition prompted a fall in export from 1.3 million lbs. in the peak year of 1797 to less than one-fifth that in 1818, shortly before independence.[27]

Despite the constancy of indigo as an export crop from the late 16th century to the early 19th, the Audiencia of Guatemala suffered through almost 100 years of depression from 1570 to the 1660s. During the early days after the conquest, the Spanish always expected to find some new crop, or some rich strike, which would make the Audiencia profitable. By late in the 16th century this optimism had begun to fade. Confidence, exports and internal trade all began to dwindle as the economy, tied to a similar stagnation in Spain itself, sank deeper into depression. Tiny pockets of intense activity like a new cacao area on the south coast did not alleviate the effects. At the heart of the depression in the Audiencia was the continued reduction of the Indian labour force, the base of all wealth. Population levels reached their lowest point in the mid-17th century.[28]

This depression had particular effects on colonial society. Spaniards who had enjoyed sufficient income from tribute during the first half of the 16th century saw that income continually decline as their Indian tributaries died off. It is probably for this reason that the *encomienda* began to lose significance and few were granted in the first half of the 17th century. By the mid-century the crown was again awarding *encomiendas* but they were, by and large, smaller than their earlier counterparts, being viewed as a kind of pension for old *criollos* (Spanish descendants born in Central America). The majority of the large *encomiendas* were no longer held by residents of the Audiencia, but by nobles closer to the court who appointed agents to ensure that their tribute was collected.[29]

As income levels declined the holders of diminished *encomiendas*, no longer able to afford town life, began to retire to estates in the countryside. While there was no direct link between the *haciendas* and the possession of Indians in *encomiendas,* it does appear that many *encomenderos* obtained land near the villages from which they received tribute, in order to assure themselves of labour. As Martínez Paláez describes it: "Land without Indians wasn't worth anything, but the great worth of the Indians as creators of wealth counselled the acquisitions of great extensions of land."[30]

Whether the *encomenderos* retired to a large or small *hacienda,* the generally depressed economy and the lack of available labour prompted a slow collapse into self-sufficiency, with owners attempting to tie Indian labourers to their land through debt-bondage or share-cropping arrangements. Generally speaking, however, the Indian was a valuable, scarce commodity "carefully rationed out" to landowners through a variety of colonial structures, principally the *repartimiento*.[31]

The "century of depression" had lasting effects on Guatemalan society. Diminished internal trade helped fragment the Audiencia into a number of smaller regions with jealously guarded, local power centres. In addition, the former white townsman now became a rural landowner, lord of a *hacienda*, jealous of his privileges and his hold over Indian labourers who he attempted to tie to his property through a variety of non-economic, almost feudal constructs. Even within the various regions, loyalty devolved to the largest landowner who often held a number of *ladinos* in his employ and who dominated the economic and political life of the area. These local *caudillos* thwarted the extension of crown control and even more effectively, the extension of national institutions following independence.

Colonial Society: The Indians

THREE CENTURIES OF COLONIAL rule fundamentally altered the political, social and religious organization of the Maya. Every native felt the demands of the crown and colonial government in some manner. Most were forced to work for the government, for Spaniards with *encomiendas* or for other planters through the *repartimiento*. Almost all were required to pay tribute to the crown or to an *encomendero*. Most were forced into the larger villages created by the Dominican *reducción* and were baptized by the church. Many lost the right to land they had traditionally used.

Colonial society also altered internal relationships within native communities by fostering, first, a powerful group of *caciques* (or village chiefs) who were to a large extent free from colonial demands and, later, an "elected" town council (*ayuntamiento*), which eventually challenged and overcame the influence of the *cacique*. The theocratic basis of power in pre-conquest Mayan society was to a certain extent maintained, although in altered circumstances. But, by the end of the colonial period the authority of the village rulers was derived, partly, from a record of service in a church at least partially Christian and Catholic.

Two decades of brutal conquest and rapacious adventurism had shattered the Quiché, Tzutzuhil, Cakchiquel and other Indian kingdoms. The "royalty" of pre-conquest Guatemala had either been killed in battle or denied position by the Spanish conquerors. The always tenuous cord that had tied individual villages to a larger Indian empire had been decisively cut. The highest native figure of authority that remained was the *cacique*.

The Spanish conquerors tolerated the *caciques* as a means of maintaining internal order within the native community and gave them a number of privileges normally denied Indians. They were permitted to ride horses, own land, wear Spanish clothing, bear arms and were often exempt in practice from the demands of the *repartimiento*. According to Charles Gibson, the foremost historian of the early colonial period in New Spain, these privileges were afforded the *caciques* to prompt them "to function as cooperative, puppet bosses in their communities".[32] The *caciques* were responsible for ensuring that tribute was collected and that the proper number of workers appeared for the *repartimiento*. During the *reducciones* of the 16th century they were also used by the Dominicans to help forcibly collect labour for the construction of churches.

All of these activities served to rob the *caciques* of their traditional authority. Often appointed to their places by colonial officials who could and did remove recalcitrant *caciques*, they were forced to perform the function of interpreting crown demands in the village. In the process, they became increasingly associated with the colonial rather than native society and resented by the villagers.

The colonial government also fostered the spread of town councils along the Spanish model. The English Dominican, Thomas Gage, who lived in Guatemala from 1625 to 1637, described the process:

> From the Spanish [they] have borrowed their civil governments and in all towns they have one or two *alcaldes,* with more or less *regidores* (who are aldermen or jurists amongst us) and *alguaciles,* who are as constables to execute the orders of the *alcalde* (who is a mayor) with his

brethren. . . . These are changed every year by new elections, and are chosen by the Indians themselves, who take their turns by the tribes or kindreds whereby they are divided.[33]

In some villages, the *caciques* gained election to the posts of this *ayuntamiento* or council. But in those *municipios* where their traditional authority had already been sufficiently undermined, a battle developed between the *caciques* and the new, "elected" *ayuntamiento:* a battle eventually won by the elected body.

The Indian *alcaldes* had strictly limited powers, however. According to the decree of Felipe III in 1618, the village chief was given jurisdiction:

> Only to make investigations, to arrest and to bring delinquents to Jail of the Spanish Pueblo of that district; but they shall be able to punish with one day in prison, six to eight lashes, the Indian who misses Mass on the day of the Fiesta, or who becomes intoxicated or commits similar faults; and in the case of habitual drunkenness they may punish the offender with more severity.[34]

Throughout the long period of depression the influence and control of the crown and the church on the more isolated areas steadily diminished. Even minor government positions were hotly pursued by *criollos* desiring a steady income — and the more enticing chance for graft. However, the crown's ability to extend the tentacles of centralized direction, which had been so apparent during the *reducciones* in the middle of the 16th century, was substantially reduced throughout much of the 17th. At the same time the clergy, which had been so powerful in all of the amalgamated villages formed by the *reducción,* was by the 17th century no longer quite so ubiquitous. With less political power in Spain and a marked absence of missionary fervour, the religious orders found it increasingly difficult to find brothers to man the more isolated parishes in the highlands.

This had a twofold effect on Indian villages in the highlands. Many who had been forced into the 700 towns dispersed to outlying *municipios,* repopulating sites of older villages and creating new ones. The reduced pressure of government officials allowed villagers greater freedom in shaping internal political and social relationships. Elements of the old hierarchy reinvigorated themselves and many villages began to establish a kind of treasury to assist the village in emergencies. Most notably this was used on occasion to help pay tribute and to ensure continued possession of land through paying legal and registration fees.

The paucity of priests in these more isolated villages also allowed pre-conquest Mayan religious practices to creep back into the religious ceremonies of the village. A complex syncretism of Mayan and Catholic religious custom eventually dominated most villages in the highlands. The *cofradía* — a body of followers in charge of caring for and organizing celebrations honoring each important village saint — became an integral part of religious organization. In many villages unique figures were beatified; the most common was Maximon or San Simeon, who may have represented both Judas and the *ladino* vices. In many communities throughout the highlands this became the most important "saint" and thus service in his *cofradía* was an important step in the progression through the ranks of the hierarchy. As political organization again began to reflect the theocratic roots of preconquest Maya, service in the *cofradía* also became the most important stepping stone in political progression.

The election of officials for the *ayuntamiento* was retained, but now the candidates were most often chosen by the traditional hierarchy, and the civic posts of the *alguaciles, regidores,* and even *alcaldes* were but steps on an alternating civic-religious ladder. The most influential decision-makers were *principales,* or the cluster of old men who had obtained prestige through their service in both political affairs and religion, and had consequently earned the right to "retire" from this costly (in time and money) service.

Native Defence of Community

BY THE MIDDLE OF THE 18TH CENTURY many Indian villages had developed a reinvigorated hierarchy and a strong sense of community, and had demonstrated a determined hold on their communal lands. As the political, religious and economic basis of these villages began to be threatened by the Bourbon reforms in the latter part of the century, by increased church involvement and more constant encroachment on their land, these villages explored a number of avenues to protect their autonomy. When other means failed, they frequently took up arms against the crown's agents.

The abuse of Indians by *criollo* officials heightened the Indians' bitterness. During the 17th and 18th centuries virtually the only sure way for *criollos* to obtain an adequate living was to secure a government position. However, the bulk of the major government posts were allocated to more recent arrivals from Spain and denied *criollos*. The most a *criollo* without substantial influence at court could hope for was a minor post, usually for a limited period of time. The most common of these posts was the *corregidor* — the crown's representative in the Indian township — and it became accepted practice for *corregidores* to milk the highest possible income from their limited time in this post. They could do this most readily by abusing the Indians under their charge.

The most common means of abuse was the *corregidores'* virtual economic monopoly over the Indian village. They consistently bought Indian products at below market price and resold them for substantial profit. In addition the *corregidores* had the right to introduce into Indian villages certain products they considered "beneficial". *Corregidores* routinely used this right to "impose excessive amounts of unwanted articles at arbitrary prices". According to colonial historian C.H. Haring, "The tyranny of the *corregidores* was notorious."[35] Martínez Paláez has called the *corregidor* "the functionary most given to maltreat and rob the Indians".[36]

In the early 18th century the Catholic church began to reassert its authority over Indian villages and began a campaign against the "pagan" practices that had become mixed with Catholic ceremony. The most famous instance of this was an attempt by the bishop of Chiápas to banish "pagans" among the Tzotzil Indians near the town of San Cristóbal. The Indians rose up under the inspiration of a young woman who claimed she had been told by the Virgin to eliminate the Spanish. Two thousand Indians eventually joined the revolt which was put down only with difficulty. Similar campaigns in other areas had less dramatic but roughly equivalent effects.[37]

In the mid-18th century, the Bourbon Spanish crown introduced a series of reforms designed to reassert the crown's authority and to provide higher levels of taxes and tribute to help pay for defence against Britain. These reforms had a number of effects on colonial society. While the Audiencia retained its central authority, a number of *intendentes* were posted in Honduras, El Salvador, Nicaragua and Chiápas to provide for closer supervision. These semi-autonomous governing districts helped accentuate the fragmentation of the Audiencia. Further reforms checked the church's power, exiled the Jesuits from the New World in 1767 and broke down trading monopolies that had been enjoyed throughout the colonial period. Many of these reforms were deeply resented by Guatemalan *criollos*, fostering a dual image of Spain in which the "old" Spain was glorified, while the "new" Spain of "scheming officials" was reviled.

In highland villages, these reforms were felt primarily as increased demands of tribute and increased "white" interference in local affairs. These heightened demands prompted a number of revolts, which continued until the time of independence. The most famous of these was the revolt of the Quichean "King and fiscal King" in the department of Totonicapán in 1820[38] (see also chapter 2).

In addition to these pressures, as Indian, *criollo* and *ladino* populations increased, there was heightened conflict over land. *Hacienda* owners were constantly accused of expanding beyond the confines of their property to incorporate Indian land. Many of the complaints involved *hacienda* cattle that were allowed to roam onto Indian land, damaging crops. The American anthropologist Robert Carmack describes one such conflict in the highlands in which a *hacienda* owner was accused of robbing sheep from Indians, whom he had thrown in jail when they complained. He also allegedly extorted funds from the village. The natives brought a case against him in the colonial courts and won, but were eventually forced to sell their communal land to pay increased levels of tribute.[39]

Ladinos had also been spreading to rural areas, obtaining Indian land through a variety of measures. At the same time the increased native population caused the restricted communal lands of some villages to become notably insufficient. Indian response to these pressures was varied. It became quite common for native communities to argue land cases in front of colonial courts, using village priests or legal advisors from Guatemala City. The courts often found in favour of the village community but when they did not, the only effective response was armed revolt. Consequently the highlands became the scene of numerous revolts in the late 18th and early 19th centuries.

Throughout the colonial period, but increasingly evident in the last part of the 18th century, native villages demonstrated a vigorous response in defence of their rights and customs. Having recovered from conquest and disease, they were, by the end of the colonial era, often effective defenders of their position. Robert Carmack, in concluding a study of a village in the highlands he calls "Tecpanoca", suggests:

> It is interesting to observe that the Tecpanoca Indians were not simply peons at the hands of the Spanish or the criollos. Although very exploited by them, they were not left without defences or power. They lost land, but they were able to stop the expansion of the criollos' haciendas. . . . They resisted the Spanish religious reform and even in actuality were able to retain a large part of their 'pagan' religion. They rebelled on numerous occasions without the criollos being able to control them. Especially notable is their success in getting the Crown to turn against the criollos in various cases of litigation. . . . [The villages] resisted the criollos with collective force at times, with sporadic factional organization [at others] but always with intelligence and power.[40]

Those Indians were not alone. Rebellions were recorded in Ixtahuacán (1748), Santa Lucía de Utatlán (1760), Tecpán (1764) and Cobán (1770 and 1803). In 1811 in Santa Cruz del Quiché, a group of Indian peasants attempted to take back lands that had been claimed by the church. As the editors of a compilation of Guatemalan historical documents conclude: "History refutes the notion of a fatalistic Indian population: the persistence of Indian uprisings since 1524 demonstrates the existence of a significant number of angry and active Indians in every generation."[41]

The Legacy of the Colonial Period

THE LONG COLONIAL PERIOD shaped much of modern Guatemala. The roots of independence sprouted in the ever increasing antagonism between *criollos* and Spanish. The Audiencia of Guatemala was already demonstrating the factionalism which would later doom hopes for a Central American union. Most importantly, the society was divided into three very distinct, mutually antagonistic sectors: *criollos,* Indians and, perched tentatively between them, a rapidly increasing number of *ladinos.*

The fixation with rapid accumulation of wealth among the *criollos,* left over from the early days of the conquest, helped promote a rapacious economic outlook, while determining that economic growth would always be viewed as the search for one profitable export after another. The necessity of controlling large amounts of scarce Indian labour created a number of institutions that lasted throughout most of the colonial era and tempered a society that forced a reluctant majority to create wealth for a racially-defined minority. The resulting society was one ruled by terror, violence and coercion.

Indian communities had responded effectively to the colonial regime. Recovering from the terrible losses of conquest and disease, they created for themselves their own religion and a political and social system that helped reinforce group solidarity in defence of encroachment from the outside. While sometimes able to protect themselves from *criollo* demands through appealing to the crown, this defence was never very secure.

In the less isolated area of the country — much of the Pacific piedmont — Indians had been unable to defend their villages or their separate identities successfully. With valuable land gobbled up by *haciendas* and plantations, Indians became attached to estates and subject to the demands of the *hacendado.* The Indian community lost much of its distinctiveness. However, in the highlands native communities were able to retire to valleys and hillsides and defend these communities through a variety of means.

The terror of the colonial regime left its mark on highland Indian communities. They were closed, suspicious, isolated places. Community structures were designed to exclude outsiders, to ensure a continuation of tradition through the selection of elders with a demonstrated attachment to that tradition. The village government acted mainly as an intermediary between the village and colonial society, buffering the community from its demands. Perhaps most importantly, the colonial era created guarded individuals, seemingly docile, humble and outwardly obedient to authority — yet harbouring bitterness and distrust. The long colonial oppression also made Indians quick to revolt to defend their homes. The colonial regime forged a society rife with deep fractures and laden with mistrust and resentment.

— 2 —
Revolt from the Mountains: Rafael Carrera and the 1838 Uprising

> I believed that they were playing upon the ignorance and prejudices
> of the Indians, and, through the priests, upon their religious
> fanaticism; amusing them with fêtes and Church ceremonies,
> persuading them that the Liberals aimed at a demolition of churches,
> destruction of the priests, and hurrying back the country into
> darkness, and in the general heaving of the elements there was not a
> man of nerve enough to rally around him the strong and honest men
> of the country, reorganize the shattered republic, and save them from
> the disgrace and danger of truckling to an ignorant, uneducated
> Indian boy.
> — John L. Stephens, on a diplomatic trip to Guatemala, 1839

ON FEBRUARY 1, 1838, the rebel forces of Rafael Carrera marched into
Guatemala City. One chronicler at the time noted that the peasants of
Carrera's army, "all with green bushes in their hats", looked like "a
moving forest" — or like "4,000 barbarians" invading Rome: "rude,
half-naked, drunk and elated". According to this writer, "The swell of
human voices filled the air and made the breasts of the inhabitants
quake with fear."[1]

Carrera's victory was indeed a shock to the white inhabitants of
Guatemala City. Prepared by exaggerated polemic and their own ill-
formed perceptions of the Indian and *ladino* masses, they expected the
worst. To the "gentle folk" of Guatemala City, Carrera's host of
peasant supporters led by "an ignorant, brutal, fanatically religious,
21 year old Indian"[2] seemed to portend their worst fear: a successful
peasant revolt that would deal harshly with the landowning masters. It
was a revolt long anticipated and dreaded. To many Guatemalan
politicians at the time, the victory of the "reactionary" peasant masses
marked the end of what has been described as a "gallant Liberal
experiment".[3]

The peasant revolt of 1837-39 has most often been portrayed as a
conservative reaction to measures taken by the ruling Liberal Party

against the power of the Catholic church. The story goes that local priests convinced illiterate, superstitious peasants that a series of natural disasters and a cholera epidemic were "a whip from God" and used this to inspire an irrational, violent reaction led by a series of ignorant *caudillos.*

However, there was much more to the revolt of *"los montañeses".* In many ways the revolt was an inevitable reaction to the previous decade's independence from first Spain and then Mexico, a development thrust upon a stratified and unprepared Central American society. While there were some admirable aspects to the Liberal program following independence, at the village level it was most clearly seen as an ever increasing load of taxes borne on the backs of poor peasants and, most importantly, an attack on their land: the very basis of village life. At the same time *ladinos,* long a persecuted and shunned part of Guatemalan society, finally broke the chains of discrimination which had kept power in the hands of a tiny, white elite. Joined by Indian peasants, long simmering resentments rose to the surface as the effects of the liberal "experiment" began to be perceived in mixed *ladino* and Indian villages.

Independence: The Federation of Central America and Liberal Control

IN 1823, TWO YEARS AFTER gaining independence from Spain, the Federation of Central America (comprised of the old Audiencia of Guatemala) ended its allegiance to Emperor Augustín Iturbide's short-lived Mexican monarchy, finally achieving complete independence. Free at last (the Liberals felt) from the fetters of monopoly and special privilege under which they had chafed for centuries as a colony of Spain, the Liberals saw the future as holding only promise. Simon Bolivar, in his *Jamaican Letter,* gave voice to their expectations:

> The States of the Isthmus from Panama to Guatemala will perhaps form a confederation. This magnificent location between the two great oceans could in time become the emporium of the world. . . . Its canals will shorten the distance throughout the world, strengthen commercial ties with Europe, America and Asia and bring that happy region tribute from the four quarters of the globe.[4]

José Cecilio del Valle, Central America's most noted intellectual of the period, predicted that there would be a flowering of culture in the region: "America will not walk a century behind Europe, at first it will keep pace, later, America will advance, and finally [will be] the area most illuminated by its science as it is most illuminated by the sun."[5] Nor was the prosperity to be achieved, as it had been in the past, for only the few at the cost of the many. The Liberal Century, the 19th, was to be a "friend of man". All people were to benefit from the economic prosperity and all were to be equal before the law.[6] According again to del Valle:

> Free, under a protecting government: Equal in one just and impartial legislation, without restriction in their choice of work, or oppression in the enjoyment of their products, rich with the progressive development of new sources of prosperity, Americans will finally know that they are men: feel all the dignity of their being, know that rich and poor, wise and ignorant, titled and those without title, Newton and the Indian, are sons of one family, individuals of one species. . . . The Indians will not be a being degraded so that in the furrows of their own forehead are manifest the signs of the humiliation.[7]

There was, however, much to do; the uncertainty and disruption of the struggle for independence, the quick breakdown of Iturbide's empire and an internecine battle between Liberal and Conservative parties in Central America had all disrupted order and the struggle for progress.

In addition, production of Guatemala's only major export, indigo, had declined drastically. Faced with competition from new, more profitable areas, total exports from Central America had fallen from over one million pounds in 1793 to just over 300 thousand in 1818. The situation was particularly distressing for Guatemala, which had seen the bulk of this reduced production shift to El Salvador.[8]

For Central America, independence came not as a victory in a bitter battle against a commonly perceived oppressor (as it had in other parts of Spanish America). Rather, it was the culmination of a series of incidents that prompted almost universal acceptance of the need for breaking ties with Spain, but which did little to determine the shape politics would take in the region. Aggravated by rivalries between the various provinces of the Federation and, in some areas, a bitter contest for supremacy between various towns, Central America was torn into a myriad of warring factions.

On the threshold of the 19th century Central America remained, as it had been throughout much of the colonial period, a segregated, racist society. According to an estimate made in 1810, of the approximately one million souls in the Audiencia de Guatemala, only 40 thousand were white.[9] Nonetheless, this minority dominated all wealth and position in the society. Moreover, within this dominant minority dwelled a tiny elite of Spanish-born bureaucrats, landowners and merchants who enjoyed the fruits of monopoly and privilege enforced by the weight of the Spanish crown. By far the wealthiest and most powerful family within this magic circle were the Ayicenas who owned, in 1819, seven large estates and accounted for one-sixth of all Central America's indigo product.[10]

The advantages this oligarchy enjoyed were bitterly envied by those whites (primarily native born) who were left outside of the flow of official favours. Estate owners, many descendants of the original conquistadors, saw themselves slipping into what they considered a genteel poverty. Together with merchants unable to obtain a royal licence, they vehemently protested the oligarchy's privilege. Perhaps most resented was the monopoly on government positions held by Spanish-born whites as opposed to Guatemalan-born whites, or *criollos*.

Early in the 19th century, this elite's control over colonial society was threatened by events in Spain. When the Spanish king Ferdinand VII was forced from the throne by Napoleon's adventurism in the Iberian peninsula, Spanish Liberals took advantage of their powerful position in the forefront of the defence of the nation to impose a new, liberal constitution in 1812, which did away with many of the government monopolies and implemented a brief period of relatively free trade for the colonies. When the danger from the French was overcome and Ferdinand was securely on the throne once again, the "liberal" provisions of the constitution were left unimplemented.

Central America during this period was under the strong arm of the reactionary Captain-General José de Bustamente, who refused to put through any of the reform measures. As a result, Bustamente faced a number of revolts led by Liberals. The political struggles produced two discernible factions. The Conservatives (known as *serviles* or *bacos* — drunkards — to their opponents) were primarily either estate owners or merchants who benefited from government monopolies. Their Liberal opponents (alternatively *fiebres* or *cacos* — pickpockets) opposed the Conservative clique and espoused a philosophy of free trade, modernization and anti-clericalism. A bitter feud developed between the two groups, heightened by attacks in two opposing newspapers: *El Editor Constitutional* (Liberal) and the more moderate *El Amigo de la Patria* edited by José Cecilio del Valle.[12]

In 1820 Ferdinand VII, faced with opposition at home, reinstated many of the Liberal measures of the 1812 constitution, causing considerable apprehension amongst Central American Conservatives, who feared for their privileges. By 1821, confronted by a chaotic situation in Spain, both Liberals and Conservatives had accepted the need for independence. At that time José Cecilio del Valle expressed what may have been a common sentiment: "The American turned his eyes to his mother country and saw in her a chaos of darkness, separated from the world which could give her light."[13]

This common acceptance of the idea of independence did little to determine the form of the prospective nation, however. According to historian Louis Bumgartner, the Conservatives accepted the concept of separation from Spain only as a means to "maintain their position of power and influence: they had to place themselves in the vanguard of the drive for independence so they could manipulate it for their own ends."[14] For these Conservatives salvation lay in an alliance with Colonel Augustín Iturbide's newly emerging Mexican empire. Early in 1821, Colonel Iturbide, given the task of confronting rebels against the crown in Mexico, turned on his colonial masters and declared independence from Spain, with himself at the head of a constitutional monarchy. The opportunistic Captain-General of Guatemala quickly followed suit, declaring independence in September of that year. Guatemala, dominated by the conservative Ayicenas and José Cecilio del Valle, pledged allegiance to Mexico. It was a move bitterly opposed by the more radical Liberals, one of whom berated the Central American congress with a tirade: "Ignorant men ... do you not have eyes to see the advantages of a country which until now has been frustrated by tyranny? Cowards, without the heart to have and defend a fatherland."[15]

This bitter denunciation was joined by armed revolt in El Salvador, led by José Manuel Arce. The Salvadorean rebels, threatened by Mexican troops, even suggested annexation to the United States. Finally, with Iturbide's empire unravelling from within through internal opposition and from without through rebellion on the periphery, the Central American congress declared for absolute independence in 1823.

The intense rivalry was far from over, however. Arce won the first election to the presidency of Central America, narrowly defeating Cecilio del Valle and using rather suspect political manoeuvering. From 1823 to 1825, there was constant struggle for prominence in the Federation between the various provinces. Guatemala dominated the Federation by its size and commercial power. However, with the Marquis de Ayicena as the governor, the Federation was suspect to Liberals. Even within the provinces, factionalism predominated. In Nicaragua, the towns of León and Granada, locked in commercial rivalry, engaged in armed combat over which should be the seat of the provincial government. That struggle quickly took on a Liberal/Conservative aspect as these factions supported rival towns. Finally, in 1829, Arce was overthrown by a Honduran and adamant Liberal, Francisco Morazán, who beat the perennial also-ran Cecilio del Valle in the subsequent elections. Morazán, a much better field commander than Arce, was able to extend federal dominance over the recalcitrant provinces and to curtail the power of the Conservatives. The seat of the federal government was moved to San Salvador from Guatemala City and Liberal policies were implemented throughout the isthmus.

In Guatemala, Mariano Galvéz, a radical Liberal, was installed as governor, and that province quickly became the leading light in constituting Liberal policy.

The decade of turmoil had done more than settle the question of independence and prove the pre-eminence of Liberal party adherents. The years of struggle had inspired a deeply seated hatred between two opposing factions, which would help doom the Liberal experiment in Guatemala. A British diplomat living in Guatemala during the period observed that these rivalries were "not caused by a desire to support any defined system of government, to promote principles or enforce the observance of recognized laws". According to him they simply served "as a pretext for the gratification of passions and interests of individual members of the community".[16] The conflicts rent deep chasms in Central American society. Nonetheless, by the late 1820s the Liberals were securely in power in Guatemala.

The Liberal Program

THE INSPIRATION FOR MANY of the economic and social ideas of the Central American liberals stemmed from 18th-century enlightenment thinking, which had dominated the University of San Carlos in Guatemala during the latter part of the century, and from the Spanish liberals in the Cortes of Cadiz set up to oppose Napoleon's ambitions in Spain. These concepts were transplanted to Guatemala in the form of revolutionary legislation.

Slavery was abolished. Governor Mariano Galvéz, believing "an educated people can never be enslaved nor can an ignorant people be virtuous",[17] placed great emphasis on education, on taking control out of the hands of the church and on expanding access. The University of San Carlos was secularized, scholarships provided for a few Indian students and plans made for the introduction of the Lancasterian system, which focused on literacy using teams of semi-trained teachers and soldiers for educators. According to the English visitor, F. Crowe, "The very barracks were converted into classrooms and the barefoot Indian soldiers were taught the rudiments of knowledge by their officers."[18]

Equally dear to Galvéz were provisions for a comprehensive judicial system. Feeling that "Society was born to provide justice,"[19] Galvéz introduced the Livingstone Codes to Guatemala. Prepared by Edward Livingstone in Louisiana, the codes had proved too radical for the United States but became the basis of the Guatemalan legal system. They provided for habeas corpus, trial by jury and a host of other legal protections. Greeted with enthusiasm by the Liberals, they were to "guarantee that peace and harmony will flower forever". The port of Livingstone was established to commemorate the adoption of the codes and, ironically, populated with Indians arrested in various tax revolts and forced there *en masse*.[20]

As laudable as a few of these measures appear, they were felt primarily by the urban white population and had little positive impact on the rest of the nation.

Colonial Society: Indians and Ladinos

ENTERING THE 19TH CENTURY and prior to independence, Guatemala was a deeply divided, stratified society. One estimate in 1810 suggested that of the one million people in Central America, almost two-thirds were Indians and close to one-third *ladino*, leaving only a relative handful of white residents in whose hands rested all economic and political power.[21]

Guatemala, which contained over half of the Federation's population in 1824,[22] was the most divided of the provinces. It was both heavily populated with Indian descendants of the Maya, and a larger population of *ladino* inhabitants. The white population held nervous control, continually frightened of the potential Indian revolt that would destroy the society Europeans had created. Dependent on Indian labour for the wealth they enjoyed, whites nonetheless feared Indians and held them in contempt.

Yet there were two elements that had, to some extent, mitigated the effects of the constant and systematic oppression of Indians in Guatemala: crown protection and an abundance of land. The Spanish crown had always been perched in an ambiguous position with regard to Indians. It realized its debt to the conquistadors and their descendants who had extended Spanish dominion throughout the New World; it was aware that the prosperity and loyalty of the colonial societies depended on Indian labour. However, the crown had also been thrust into the role of defender and protector of the Indian, and at times was forcefully reminded of that position by the powerful Spanish clergy.

Consequently, throughout the colonial period the Spanish crown had issued proclamations designed, at least to some degree, to protect Indians. Decrees issued in never-ending streams from Madrid: establishing working conditions, setting tribute levels, providing a legal framework for defence of Indians and their land, and providing for their spiritual salvation. While many of these were barely acknowledged by colonial officials and easily circumvented by colonial landowners, they did, at certain times and in certain areas, provide a minimal measure of protection. In Guatemala the most important colonial laws protected Indian land. By the 18th century village authorities had become accustomed to petitioning crown officials over land disputes with neighbouring landowners. Village priests and, increasingly, *procurados* (legal advisors from Guatemala City) were employed to press village claims. The crown often decided on behalf of the villagers.

The second element that had to some extent alleviated Indian oppression was of a more horrendous character: a severe population decline. In the years immediately following the conquest, war losses, periodic epidemics of European diseases and the effect of forced labour had decimated the Indian populations. In some areas less than 10 per cent of the pre-conquest population was left intact.

While horrible in its nature, the result of this sharp decline in numbers was to relieve land pressure throughout most of the colonial period. However, a steady resurgence in native population throughout the 18th century had by the early 19th century caused severe land shortages in some villages and led to "squatters" moving on to neighbouring village lands. It was partially this increasing pressure on land that led to heightened conflict in the late colonial period. Disputes and open revolt multiplied as peasants saw their access to land curtailed.

The second stratum of the societal pyramid in colonial Guatemala society, the *ladinos,* was perhaps the most volatile. As the product of Spanish-Indian liaisons, their existence provided daily evidence of a commonplace but nonetheless embarrassing 'sin'. Partly as a consequence, *ladinos* had no place in colonial society. Generally feared by Indians and reviled as the most obvious local oppressor, they were equally shunned by Spanish society. Prevented by law from settling in Indian villages and unable to obtain land, they were pushed into the most loathsome, dangerous and ill-paying jobs. While colonial laws at least theoretically provided Indians with some measure of protection from abuse, none existed to protect *ladinos*. Forbidden from holding public office, shunned on all sides, they formed a disgruntled, often desperate and large segment of colonial society.

By the end of the 18th century *ladinos* were a portion of society increasingly difficult to ignore. In the early 19th century José Cecilio del Valle — always a lonely apostle of reason in the Guatemala of his day — had empathized with their lot, describing them as the constant companions of "poverty, misery, nakedness, hunger and thirst" and calling out for measures on their behalf.[23]

The prevailing view was one of mistrust and loathing, of misunderstanding brought about by fear. Dr. Antonio Larrazábal, in an account of the colonial economy written for the Cortes of Cadiz, described how he perceived a large portion of the *ladinos:*

> Never working, in order to subsist they live at the expense of the robbery of cattle and fruit that are grown in the haciendas, from the plantains that they find abandoned on the banks of rivers and from plundering and robbing the people, with which they pass their life playing dice, drinking, wounding and killing each other inhumanly, and seeking shelter at the walls and gates of the towns and the outskirts of the capital, inspiring fear in their honourable and laborious neighbours.[24]

Despite official proscription, by the coming of independence many *ladinos* had insinuated themselves into native villages. Settling on abandoned land, becoming petty merchants working on the sides of colonial roads or buying and selling at a variety of Indian markets, they provided the primary link between Indian and Spanish society, fitting completely into neither.

In addition, following their example, a number of Indians — small in number but important in influence — had begun to adopt Spanish (or at least *ladino*) customs: leaving behind the land as the sole means of support, setting themselves up as merchants; some became literate. They were the harbingers of important changes in native communities. Rebelling against the traditional authority of the village *principales,* or elders, they established a newer, active, non-traditional centre of authority. By the end of the colonial period a number of predominantly Indian villages even had *ladino alcaldes* or mayors and, particularly in the eastern districts where native population density was lower, many villages were clearly mixed *ladino*-Indian. It was these more European-influenced Indians and resident *ladinos* who would be most active in inspiring peasant revolt in the early 19th century.

Given this segregated society, the "noble" aspects of the Liberal program had little effect on that part of the population outside the white "civilized" minority. According to historian Louis Bumgartner there was not even any intent to extend these ideas throughout the population. The whites "knew that outside of the capital and the major cities of the provinces they were foreigners in their own land. . . . As foreigners they stood in fear, not only of the Indians but of the 'uneducated and unmannered'."[25] Moreover, the other elements of the Liberal program, including prohibitions against the church, tax reform and an aggressive economic policy based on land, contained considerable import for village life, threatening to shatter a system kept intact for over three centuries.

To the Galvéz government the peculiar mix of Indian religious beliefs engulfed the populace in shackles of superstition and illiteracy: shackles held firmly in place by the church. The church's role in impeding progress was heightened by its large landholdings and demands on the public purse. In 1818, the Catholic church in Central America owned 914 *haciendas* and 910 sugar mills.[26] According to George Thompson, a British traveller, fully twice as much was being spent on the maintenance of the Catholic faith throughout Central America as on the various levels of government.[27] Consequently, one of the first concerns of Liberals in Central America was to reduce the power of the Catholic church.

The Liberal party allowed full religious freedom in 1832. It substituted a land tax for the tithe, limited church holidays, allowed nuns to leave the convent, declared marriage to be a civil contract and permitted divorce, took over the operation of the University of San Carlos and laid plans for public education outside of the control of clerics. As church opposition developed, the government also exiled the archbishop, curtailed the appointment of village priests and restricted the activity of the most radical of the church hierarchy.

Ironically, beginning in 1830 Central America was the scene of a bewildering series of natural disasters, which many peasants linked to the Liberal measures against the church. That year the worst earthquakes since 1773 shook Guatemala. In 1833 the Volcano Atitlán erupted and portentous meteor showers were seen. However, the most spectacular event was the eruption of Volcano Cosigüina in Nicaragua in 1835; ash fell up to 1,500 miles away and the sun was hidden for seven days. In Nicaragua, "Priests wandered in the streets giving the last rites to passers by. Domestic animals were mad with terror and wild animals roamed the streets of the towns."[28]

In 1837, a cholera epidemic rampaged through the Guatemalan highlands, devastating peasant villages in its wake. Lt. Colonel Juan Martínez, an official in the department of Chiquimula, described how "entire families have disappeared within 24 hours".[29] The fact that larger urban centres were relatively untouched only lent credence to the belief held by rural peasants that the government was poisoning the water to steal their land.

While one church official declared that the calamities were "a whip from heaven for the punishment of sin" and many local curates used these occurrences to stir up opposition to the Galvéz government, a number of other prominent churchmen helped publicize scientific explanations for the epidemic, assisted the campaign against the disease and, in general, supported the Liberal government.

Despite the opposition of local curates, the natural catastrophes that afflicted Guatemala would not have prompted the revolt of *los montañeses* were it not for the perceived attack on rural villages through tax measures and an aggressive land policy.

To Governor Galvéz, as to most liberals in Guatemala, economic development was, in his own words, "an exact science based on concrete facts and figures".[30] In Guatemala this science of economic development was intimately linked to the growth of the agricultural sector, following the precepts set down by the Spanish economist, Caspar Melchor de Jovellanos. In 1795 in a report to the Spanish Agricultural Society, Jovellanos stressed that Spain's future lay in a dynamic agricultural sector. He decried the "non-utilization of potential land resources" due to its control by "special interests who ignored economic productivity". Jovellanos believed that agriculture had a "natural tendency toward perfection" and legislators should only endeavour to "remove the hindrances that retard its progress".[31] Jovellanos' *Informe de Ley Agraria* became the "economic bible" of Latin American liberals.

Jovellanos' criticisms were directed, at least partly, at large Spanish estates. In Guatemala the large estates of hacienda owners were also notoriously inefficient. The lack of a truly profitable export crop, the stunted local market for agricultural produce and a view of land that saw it of equal value as a tool for social prestige ensured that much estate land was put to little productive use. One English traveller described a large Guatemalan estate in 1821. The estate, about 20 miles in circumference, was made up of mostly "excellent, well watered land". It "partook of the character of park scenery, and in every direction furnished the most agreeable walks". The whole estate supported only a small herd of cattle and horses.[32]

Despite these conditions, Liberal adherents tended to identify a variety of other hindrances to the rational use of agricultural land, rather than attacking large estates. They pointed to a number of evils in the way of Guatemala's economic development: an excess of empty lands *(tierras baldias),* a too heavy reliance on monoculture based on indigo, a paucity of infrastructure that would allow exploitation of isolated areas and, most importantly, inadequate agricultural practice on the part of Guatemalan peasants.

For Central American Liberals, correcting each one of these evils involved an attack on Indian land or village structure. The Guatemalan legislature argued that the "rural economy lies in a state of abandonment" not because of the practices of the landowners but because of the "indolence and vices of rural labourers" and in that way justified further compulsory labour laws.[33] The lack of roads and services to agriculture was not to be met by increased taxes on the wealthy but by handing out huge tracts of land, some of it already occupied by native communities, to foreign entrepreneurs, and by taxing peasant villages. In their quest for economic development of a particular type, the Liberal government simply pushed aside any consideration of the needs of the majority of the population. For most white Guatemalans, "The Indian was a beast of burden who would be treated with animal brutality in order to preserve society."[34]

The Effect of Liberal Measures on Peasant Villages

DESPITE THREE CENTURIES OF PRESSURE by Spanish colonial administration, Guatemalan Indian communities had been able to retain a surprising degree of autonomy. Colonial officials had been imposed in the form of *corregidores*, the crown's representatives who held almost unbridled local authority, often even a monopoly on local trade. The colonial government had even redefined the physical boundaries of villages through forced relocation in the 16th century. Yet, through it all, local authority remained in the hands of a traditional political-religious hierarchy. Village communities were ruled, to some degree as they are today, by an intermixture of civic and religious offices held by village elders who reached their position through a continuity of service. By the early 19th century a few of the political offices in some villages were being filled by *ladinos* who had worked their way into the village society. The religious procession was permeated by a mixture of Catholic and Mayan belief and custom. Nonetheless, the basic concept of rule by a council of proven elders had remained intact. The village curate was integrated into and yet situated somewhere on the margin of this semi-theocratic government.[35]

The core of village life revolved around the land, which provided not only sustenance and security but also connected Indians to their gods. This identification with the land carried with it an emotional intensity and, according to anthropologist Robert Naylor, "Life for the most part continued in harmony with the ancient rhythms that had shaped the daily existence of the highland Indian for centuries."[36]

For *ladino* and Indian peasants alike, primary allegiance was owed to the village. It was the source of security and identification. The village hierarchy and structure impinged at every instance whereas the national society was rarely felt.

Village lands were divided into private plots and farmed by individual families, but were "owned by the ancestors" and allotted by the village. Most villages were surrounded by *tierras baldias*. Although formally empty, these areas had always been used without title by a number of families and relied upon by the whole village for pasturage, wood and forage. They were jealously guarded.

In the Mita district of eastern Guatemala, where the revolt of *los montañeses* was spawned, Indian and *ladino* farmers relied upon a mixture of crops: tobacco, grain, cotton and rice along with the holy trinity of corn, beans and squash. A number of farmers, *ladino* and Indian, had grown indigo and were joining the shift to cochineal as indigo became increasingly unprofitable. A significant number manufactured cotton and wool cloth, which they peddled throughout Guatemala, establishing widely spread contacts. The district was dominated by a number of large Indian and mixed villages: Santa Rosa with a population of 1,720, Cuajiniqua with 2,000, Mataquescuintla with 554 and Gualán with 1,821, among others.[37]

By the 1830s the Galvéz government was in desperate need of money. The Liberal program demanded significant expenditure for salaries of officials and teachers, transportation facilities, two levels of bureaucracy (the federal and Guatemelan governments) and incentives for the diversification of agricultural production. All of these demands fell upon a government singularly unable to meet them. In the latter years of the colonial empire Spain had spent more on the *Audiencia de Guatemala* than it had received from customs duty. This source of funds was removed at the same time as production of the region's largest export, indigo, experienced a severe decline. Moreover, Guatemala's largest source of income, the government monopoly on tobacco, had been pledged to the federal government in San Salvador.

While some of the state's requirements were met through the sale of confiscated church property in 1838, or through the occasional special contribution demanded of wealthy individuals and a hastily implemented income tax, the full weight of tax measures was felt by peasants. In rapid succession the Liberal government imposed a direct tax on individuals, a land tax to replace the abolished tithe, plus taxes on slaughtered meat and on the harvesting of certain crops. Many peasants unable to pay these taxes lost their land or were forced into labour for local landowners. The most onerous and contentious of the government tax measures, however, were the charges against the community funds. These village funds had been an important element in ensuring the security of the community and had long been considered sacrosanct.

A few of Galvéz's Liberal cronies opposed the charges. José Francisco Barrundía opined, "These community funds are the product of the sweat of the Indian and for the emergencies of his family and villages" and Dr. Pedro Molina warned that state use of these funds "would leave no memory other than greater misery for the villagers and a hatred for the vexations they must suffer".[38] Nevertheless, in desperation, Galvéz persisted.

The villages responded to these moves with resistance which, as we've seen (chapter 1), was nothing new. During the 18th and early 19th century, Guatemalan villages repeatedly opposed increased taxation and threats to their land with violent protest, creating a long string of uprisings. Although the rebellions erupted in often widely separated villages, they were not dissimilar and were linked by common complaints. The majority were the result of simmering outrage at land dispossession, increased levels of taxation and, more generally, encroachment on traditional authority by local officials. For example, in 1803 in Cobán, a protest was sparked when the *criollo alcalde* ordered five *principales* to receive 20 public lashes as punishment for complaining to officials in Guatemala City about the *alcalde*'s arbitrary decisions. In response both to the indignity offered to traditional authority and the continuation of the *alcalde*'s unfair decrees, Indians rose in a revolt that for a time threatened to engulf all of the sizable department of Verapaz.

By far the most active area of unrest was the partido de Totonicapán, part of the larger Alcadía Mayor de Totonicapán. An area of high population density, the *partido* had in the early 19th century approximately 30,000 people, primarily Quiché Indians, mostly resident in relatively large villages. In 1811 one village, Momostenango, burst into brief revolt against increased tribute and abuses by local authorities. Although the uprising was quickly quelled, complaints continued, leading to another revolt in 1819. In 1813, villagers in Totonicapán complained about being deprived of common land they had traditionally cultivated. In the ensuing dispute the *ladino alcalde* struck one of the petitioning Indians, prompting a small armed revolt. The lawyer who defended one of the Indian leaders at his subsequent trial argued that the Indian was rightfully looking to protect the village's communal interests, stating, "The land is the only patrimony of these miserables."[39]

Neighbouring villages rose in rebellion throughout the decade but by far the largest was a revolt led by Atanasio Tzul in 1820. Protesting the reinstitution of tribute, and joined by rebels in other villages, his followers seized control of the whole district of Totonicapán. They expelled the colonial officials and crowned Atanasio the "king and fiscal king" and his adviser, Lucas Aquilar, president. Although the reign of the Quichean king lasted only 29 days, it was an indication of the unrest in the highlands and a portent of more to come. Throughout the next decade active protest would ebb and flow, until the peasants joined in the successful revolt of *los montañeses* under Rafael Carrera.[40]

While Guatemala had experienced numerous native uprisings in the almost three centuries of colonial rule, this period from the beginning of the 19th century on was especially active. The reasons for this were manifold: the attempt by the Spanish crown, strapped for money, to extract a higher level of tribute; land scarcity prompted by population increase and encroachment on Indian land as more *ladinos* moved into native areas; in addition, *ladinos* and *criollos,* beginning with the Bourbon reforms of the 1780s, interfered more often and more seriously with traditional village decision-making. Influenced by the example of resident *ladinos* and European-influenced Indians, native villages were becoming more divided and thus more volatile. Villagers were more ready to take action against the colonial officials.

Despite the implicit warning this level of unrest would have afforded any prudent government, the Liberal administration after independence continued to augment the levels of taxation in peasant villages and introduce policies that were seen as attacks on village land.

One of the primary tenets of the Liberal program was the attraction of foreign colonists: immigrants with the proper attitude to work. The Galvéz government carried this policy to extremes. Hoping both to attract settlers and prompt the construction of transportation facilities in the lightly populated east, the Guatemalan government dangled the vision of "wilderness empires" in front of foreign lumber barons. In a measure of dubious legality, Galvéz handed out large plots of land to three entrepreneurial companies, which "within six months . . . stripped the state of virtually its entire public domain".[41] These contractors, intent on harvesting mahogany and not on promoting settlement, were given extended periods of time to fulfill settlement requirements but were allowed to cull the forests immediately. Guatemala received little benefit from the contracts while the grantees were able to export large quantities of valuable hardwood.

The most extensive and controversial of these grants went to the partnership of Marshall Bennet and Carlos Meany in the departments of Chiquimula and Totonicapán. The grant encompassed many of the villages in the Mita district. While villages were allowed to retain some land, the grant impinged on the *tierras baldias* traditionally used by the Indians. Declaring that the grant "would result only in national disaster", making Gualán the "most unfortunate and ruinous area of the state", the villagers of Gualán and surrounding area kept up a continuous protest directed at Guatemala City politicians.[42]

While these measures had created considerable tension within the villages it was, finally, the rationalization of communal land and *tierras baldias* that set off the revolution. Declaring that "agriculture is the first fountain of public riches", in 1825 and 1829 the Guatemalan legislature passed land acts that called for the public sale of *tierras baldias* and the eventual transfer of common land to private hands.

The 1829 act declared that it was necessary "to remove the obstacles that obstruct the industry and betterment of all individuals"; those obstacles if allowed to continue "would cause the total ruin of farming and misery for all the population".[43] Consequently the government began a decade-long process of forcing Indians off any land they could not prove title to. This included many people who had been farming *tierras baldias* for generations; their crops and huts were burned to ensure compliance. In addition, village after village lost communal land enjoyed for centuries.

In the face of widespread protest in 1835, the legislature allowed peasants who had been farming land without title to obtain the necessary document by paying one-half the value of that land. For destitute Guatemalan peasants, this was hardly a compromise. A particularly galling aspect of the land seizures was that some of the peasants arrested for not evacuating their land were sold to the Bennet-Meany company as indentured labourers.[44]

However, the most serious threat to highland peasants came from the wealthy landowners who denounced communal land as *tierrras baldias* and thus were able to transfer land to their own hands. With their access to the legislative mechanism and courts, the landlords were usually able to override Indian and *ladino* protest. Even on the rare occasions when peasants were able to stop legal usurpation of their land, powerful landowners simply forced their will. After numerous litigations over their land claims, the Indians of Escuintla in desperation petitioned the government, declaring "The Indians . . . have always been oppressed by the whites. . . . We have won many government decisions . . . but the whites always were able to suppress the decisions in our favour."[45] Even the half-hearted protection given Indians by colonial legislation had been swept away.

Thus, in an atmosphere of intense unrest caused by a bewildering series of natural disasters that seemed linked to Liberal measures against the church, intensified by two years of rampaging cholera, the peasants of the eastern highlands felt confronted on all sides. Their village autonomy was attacked, their security challenged through loss of communal funds. Their land was systematically alienated from them. As had happened increasingly in the three decades previously, village after village rose up under local leaders. Repressive government measures to control the uprisings only served to stimulate a greater conviction that the government threatened their very existence. Eventually the revolt coalesced around the figure of Rafael Carrera.

Rafael Carrera and the Revolt of 1838

RAFAEL CARRERA, BORN in a Guatemala City slum in 1814, in many ways typified the disadvantaged *ladino* in Guatemalan society. Prevented by colonial legislation from owning land in Indian villages and excluded from holding public office, *ladinos* scrambled for a living on the fringes of both Indian and white society. Making miserable wages as craftsmen, becoming minor traders to Indians or squatting on any land they could find, they were by necessity rootless.

Carrera found some stability in joining the ragtag military of the period. Having fought with Arce's troops against Morazán, he settled in the village of Matasquescuintla after Arce's defeat in 1829. There he became a swine dealer, a prominent position in a Guatemalan village. He married an Indian woman and developed close ties with the village priest.

Matasquescuintla had been involved in unsuccessful litigation to protect its land for a number of years. Throughout the 1820s villagers had complained about the cattle of wealthy estate owners ruining their crops. Following the Galvéz government's measures to "rationalize" communal land, the wealthiest neighbouring landowner laid claim to almost all the common land and, purportedly, backed up this claim by making criminal threats against the villagers.[46] By the 1830s the majority of the villagers were in active opposition to the local elite and the government, which could not control them.

During a campaign to put down one of the numerous small revolts in the area, Morazán's troops had burned down Carrera's buildings and some soldiers had brutally raped his wife. Incensed, Carrera, with a "quiet but dominating personality, a will and a talent for power", was easily able to take command of the revolt in his village. Demonstrating both a "shocking and brutal degree of personal courage" and phenomenal skill as a guerrilla leader, "He soon won the allegiance of insurgent leaders in other villages as the flames of revolt raced across the highlands."[47]

Galvéz warned the assembly of white politicians in Guatemala City that they teetered on the "crater of a volcano . . . facing a race war", inspired by "the enemies of reform . . . using the fears of men of barbarism and ignorance",[48] and called for solidarity in facing this threat. However, the bitter state of party politics, an inheritance of the struggle for independence and the civil war between the Liberals and Conservatives, doomed this request for unity. Through the 1820s, the two political parties had increasingly used *ladinos* in their battles. Henry Dunn, an English traveller, commented that the opposing political parties had "appealed to arms, exicted the passions and called forth the energies of a dangerous ally in the coloured population. Happy will it be for the disputants of either side if these dissensions shall have subsided before this third party, powerful enough to extirpate both, wash out their differences in mingled blood."[49]

Some minor concessions to conservatives by Galvéz failed to win their support and instead prompted increasing opposition from the more radical faction of liberals (the *Oposición*). Already leery of what they considered to be arbitrary acts, *Oposición* members labelled Galvéz a "militaristic tyrant" and prepared to oppose his government.

Meanwhile, revolution spread throughout the highlands and Carrera consolidated his power, staying one step ahead of Galvéz' troops. The *Oposición* liberals, hoping to take advantage of the unrest, planned an attack on Guatemala City from their stronghold in Antigua. They enticed Carrera into an alliance, expecting to be able to dominate the "peasant boy". However, faced with the endless stream of Carrera's followers, they allowed him to take charge of the battle. Similarly impressed, government forces put up little resistance and on Feb. 1, 1838, Carrera entered Guatemala City, victorious, while the frightened inhabitants cowered behind their doors.

Oposición liberals had hoped to ride Carrera's coat-tails to power and at first they seemed successful. Content with certain promises from the politicans, including an offer of the position of commander of the Mita District, 10,000 *pesos* for his troops and 1,000 for himself, Carrera left the capital and the government to the politicians. *Oposición* member Pedro José Valenzuela presided over a mixed Liberal-Conservative assembly, but one dominated by *Oposición* members. Saved from the pillage, rape and bloodshed they felt certain awaited them, the relieved citizens of Guatemala City accompanied the departure of Carrera's surprisingly well-behaved troops with accolades and plaudits.

Conflict between Carrera and the radical *Oposición* liberals was inevitable. Carrera continued to insist on the fulfillment of his demands concerning protection of peasant land and the reappointment of village priests. He strenuously opposed measures directed against the villages. When the new government refused to take these demands seriously, or to temper Liberal policies, Carrera and his peasant army again took to the field. This time he was supported by the Conservatives, who found they could not co-operate with the radical liberals who had quickly dominated congress.

The president of congress, José Valenzuela, so recently put into office by Carrera, declared: "The ferocity and barbarism of the bandits led by Rafael Carrera at last can be seen totally.... They want the destruction ... of the society of men."[50] *Oposición* liberals — this time supported by Mozazán's federal troops — and Carrera were at war.

By 1839 Carrera returned triumphantly once again to Guatemala City. He deposed the Morazán appointee, allowed the conservative Rivera Paz to take over the position of president, and withdrew Guatemala from the Central American federation. This time Carrera remained in Guatemala City. Exercising increasing control over the legislature as minister of war, he reversed previous decisions and, at one point furious with assembly members, chased the distinguished Rivera Paz and council members over the roofs of Guatemala City.

John Lloyd Stephens, an American diplomat in Guatemala in 1839, was appalled at the turn of events in Central America. He felt the conservatives were "consorting with a wild animal which might at any time turn and rend them into pieces". In one conversation, Carrera told Stephens about the sacrifices he had made for the country, saying he had been wounded in eight places and still had three bullets in his body. Stephens afterwards provided this assessment of Carrera:

> So young, so humble in his origin, so destitute of early advantages, with honest impulses perhaps, but ignorant, fanatic, sanguinary and the slave of violent passions, wielding absolutely the physical force of the country and that force entertaining a natural hatred to the whites.[51]

Finally, in 1844, after dissolving the constituent assembly, Carrera took over the presidency, retaining that position (with the exception of a brief period during which a short-lived revolt forced him from the country in 1850) until his death in 1865.

Carrera's opposition to Liberal policies, his increasing personal wealth, which distanced him from peasant concerns, and his insistence on the restoration of some of the church's powers have led to his portrayal as a tool of conservative forces. This is misleading. While Conservatives did seek an alliance with him against the Liberals (as the radical liberals did against Galvéz), they feared him as much as the Liberals did. The conservative press had, in fact, portrayed him as "a cannibal thirsting for blood".[52]

At times Carrera did allow the Conservatives their way in enacting legislation, reinstituting the Consulado de Comercio trading monopoly, rigorously opposing British colonization and even bringing back laws allowing forced labour. There is little doubt that his substantial wealth affected the direction of his government in subsequent years and prompted much of its repressive nature.

Nevertheless, throughout much of Carrera's regime, government reflected his concern for maintaining the integrity of village communities and their lands. This "ignorant, fanatic" boy understood the country and the people living outside of the tiny circle of privileged whites much better than the Liberal legislators. And the constituent assembly over which he ruled, whose manner carried Stephens "back to the dark ages and seemed a meeting of inquisitors", often passed laws more appropriate and fair than all the liberal legislation borrowed from other countries.

Carrera's allegiance to the church is best seen as a preference for the simple village curate over the church hierarchy. While much of his legislation indicated a retreat to past paternalism, Carrera believed that the Liberals had mistreated and exploited the peasant "under the pretext of equal treatment for all". He argued that while colonial regulations "had compelled [peasants] to work, to provide public service; it also gave them protection against the influential and powerful in their land claims".[53] This was something the Liberal regime had failed to do.

Until Carrera's death in 1865, peasant land, while still occasionally under pressure from neighbouring landowners, was more secure. Although Carrera was less intent on forcing economic development, he did not try to finance this development from the toils of peasants or by robbing village funds.

The early Liberal experiment in Guatemala had many noble aspects. Imbued with concepts of equality and justice, Liberals had a perception of a socially progressive and economically dynamic federation. But their vision and concerns — and power — were only shared by a tiny minority of the population. In the deeply stratified society of Guatemala in the early 19th century they had little thought for Indian and *ladino* peasants who, while a majority, existed only on the fringes of white society. There was no place in the Guatemala they were planning for the native cultures that thrived in the highlands. In their haste to emulate the "liberal" nations of England and the United States, Guatemalan Liberals took little notice of their own society. When they did, they "concluded that... national aspirations necessitated breaking down the surviving Indian cultures which hovered on the periphery of the small national society".[54]

For *ladino* peasants, the struggle which developed became one of securing for themselves a niche in the emerging nation, a niche long denied them in colonial society. For Indians, it was a struggle for survival.

The revolt's success, achieved through effective coordination under a powerful *caudillo* and through taking advantage of deeply rooted animosities among the white politicians in the capital, marked the only time in Guatemalan history that peasants, *ladino* and Indian, have been able to significantly alter national legislation and press their interests. Their inability to defend these interests against the later regime of Justo Rufino Barrios was to result in a further retreat into isolation by peasant villages — and would set the stage for continued struggle over the country's major source of wealth: land.

— 3 —
Barrios and the Coffee Economy: Order, Progress and the Assault on Indian Land

But it must not be forgotten that the author of *progress*
is General Barrios; the supporter of *liberty*, General Barrios;
the son of the people, father of the people, the grandfather
of the people, General Barrios; and finally, the man of democracy.
— from the diary of Enrique Gúzmán, circa 1884

The agro-exporters of Guatemala,
ignore the limits of their 'latifundia',
The resident worker
doesn't know the flavour of coffee.
— Luis Sam Colop, "Refuges Sentimentales", *Versos sin refugio*

SHORTLY AFTER THE DEATH of Rafael Carrera in 1865, a new generation of Liberals surged to power in Guatemala. Although they shared
many of the ideals of their earlier counterparts who had ruled
Guatemala before Carrera's successful revolt, they also demonstrated
a significantly different approach to government. If the Liberals of the
early 19th century had ignored the desires of the majority of the
population, they were also driven by the contradictory dreams of
justice and *equality*. By the latter half of the same century Liberals or
positivists throughout Latin America concentrated only on *progress*
— and imposed order to achieve it. The most prominent Liberal rulers
of Guatemala, Justo Rufino Barrios (1873-1885) and Manuel Estrada
Cabrera (1898-1920), developed dictatorships singularly devoid of
liberty and justice.

The Liberal regimes are often credited with ushering Guatemala
into the modern era, with developing a dynamic new export crop, with
initiating monetary and transportation facilities and with establishing
the basis for a modern bureaucracy and military. The particular type
of progress they fomented ensured vast fortunes for members of the

elite, both foreign and indigenous. However, it also curtailed any more equitable type of economic development and demanded a wholesale assault on Indian land. Their vision of progress wedged Guatemala into an economic and social position that ensured incomplete development of the internal market and worked against domestic production of alternate crops. Perhaps of more importance, they forced the retreating peasant villages into a cocoon of mistrust and apprehension.

The Liberal Revolt: Economic Demands and a Struggle for Power

THE COMBINED LIBERAL forces of Miguel García Granados and Justo Rufino Barrios overthrew the Conservative regime in 1871. It was a revolt much different from Carrera's of 30 years earlier. There was no charismatic figure leading hordes of peasant supporters, no fear of pillage and plunder, no talk of the end of civilized society, of "cannibals thirsting for blood". The Liberal revolt pitted members of the Guatemalan elite against each other: two small groups of opposing whites, still surrounded by a sea of ladinos and Indians, quarrelling over economic incentives on a newly developing export crop, coffee.

The Liberal rebels complained that "the oligarchic and tyrannical government" was made intolerable by "repeated arbitrary and cruel acts and by the daily violation of the fundamental laws of the Republic".[1] But at the heart of the revolt was the retooling of Guatemalan agriculture from the production of cochineal to coffee.

For most of his years in power Rafael Carrera had benefited from an economic alliance that helped insure internal peace and the continuation of his "monarchy without a king".[2] The foundation of the economic alliance rested with cochineal, a dye-stuff produced from insects that feed off the nopal plant. Cochineal had begun to replace indigo as Guatemala's major export in the 1830s. In 1840, $500,000 worth of cochineal was exported. By 1850 exports had increased to $600,000 and in 1854 the largest harvest was recorded, worth $1,757,300. By the mid-1850s, over 300,000 manzanas* of land were being used for the production of cochineal.[3]

Cochineal production was the preserve of small, peasant producers. Victor Solórzano, Guatemala's best known economist, described how "in the house of every peasant [was] a small nopalera, and so in all the zones of production one wouldn't find a large plantation."[4] The bulk of these cochineal producers were ladinos, newly arrived in the highlands in the 19th century. Cash-cropping cochineal

* 1 manzana equals 1.7 acres.

provided an economic outlet for *ladino* energies and had to some extent provided the niche in Guatemalan society they had sought since the colonial period. More than one prominent Guatemalan considered that this outlet had "aided in consolidating internal peace" by "satisfying [*ladino*] aspirations".[5]

Just as importantly, the development of cochineal had protected Indian lands from encroachment and reduced the demand for Indian labour. As cochineal was best grown on small holdings, there existed little economic incentive for the development of large plantations that would have threatened Indian land. In addition, because the families of peasant producers worked their own plots and dye-works, there was little demand for Indian labour. While Carrera had legally reinstated a levy of forced labour from each village, it was seldom used during his administration and the burden on Indian villages was slight. While cochineal was the particular preserve of *ladino* peasants, many Indians had seen the economic advantages of cochineal cultivation and had joined in production.

These peasant cultivators formed part of an economic alliance centred around powerful cochineal exporters who marketed their product. Made up of the largest merchant houses in Guatemala City, the exporters enjoyed access to government circles and oligarchic powers over the economy through the Consulado de Comercio. It was this "alliance of aristocracy in the capital with a strong rural mass dedicated to the cultivation of cochineal" that provided the most important political support for the Carrera regime.[6]

By the mid-1850s this economic alliance was unravelling as cochineal production declined, confronted by falling prices and drastically reduced markets due to the development of synthetic analine dyes in Europe. In 1862, Rafael Carrera petitioned members of congress to search diligently for a substitute for cochineal. A brief flirtation with cotton (19 per cent of Guatemalan exports in 1865) failed in the face of U.S. competition after cessation of the American Civil War.[7] Coffee seemed a god-send. It had long been grown in Guatemala as a decorative plant and for household consumption. The Liberal government of Mariano Galvéz had briefly encouraged production by promising bonuses to planters who harvested over 100 *quintales** worth. However, it wasn't until Manuel Aquilar, impressed with Costa Rican coffee-growing, published a pamphlet in 1845 urging cultivation and the government agreed to purchase coffee at fixed prices, that the crop began to play a significant part in the Guatemalan economy. By 1866 coffee constituted 23 per cent of

* 1 *quintales* equals 101.4 pounds or about 46 kilograms

Guatemalan exports.[8] However, the Carrera government was unwilling or unable to provide the full range of economic reforms that coffee planters felt necessary. Heading their list of demands was a more dependable supply of labour, along with monetary reforms that would make it easier to raise capital for investment in coffee production.

Spearheading the Liberal assault on the Conservative regime's economic foundations was a group of powerful politicians, members of the Sociedad Económica. Prominent among them were Miguel García Granados and Marco Aurelio Soto. This group pushed Carrera to a few minor reforms, reducing the power of the Consulado de Comercio somewhat and providing incentives for coffee production. However, Carrera had done little to appease them before his death in 1865.

His successor, Vincente Cerna, a former military commander under Carrera, felt the full weight of Liberal agitation. In an atmosphere of increasing opposition, Cerna won re-election in 1869 by a margin of only two votes over his Liberal opponent — despite Conservative control of the rudimentary electoral machinery. Finally, in 1870, the Sociedad Económica, led by Marco Aurelio Soto, presented a plan for monetary and credit reform that the Liberal coffee planters felt necessary to fully stimulate the spread of coffee cultivation. The plan complained, in part: "Land which we should esteem as the most valuable of the country's riches, is among us almost without importance. It is necessary that national credit put into circulation this dead value, deliberately mobilizing property."[9]

While Cerna accepted some of the provisions, passing a new monetary law the same year, he did little to satisfy the demands of the Liberals. Thus, this progressive cadre went from pushing for economic reforms to supporting an armed revolt led by one of their members, Miguel García Granados, and a rural property owner and notary public, Justo Rufino Barrios. In 1871 the revolutionaries published a call to arms, the Actá de Patzicía, which described the Cerna government as "intolerable", arguing that it had destroyed the public treasury. The act declared, "Citizens have not only the right but the obligation to resist tyranny" and called on them to support the revolution.[10] These rebels, linked as they were to the most dynamic and aggressive economic clique in the capital, were easily able to overthrow Cerna.

The New Liberalism: Order and Progress

THE LIBERAL ADMINISTRATIONS that followed the overthrow of Vincente Cerna were guided by a unifying philosophy. Like that of the earlier Liberals, this political philosophy grew out of a vigorous debate centred in the University of San Carlos. Again the Liberals attempted to adapt foreign social ideas to the Guatemalan environment.

The new Liberalism, closely linked to positivism, sprang primarily from the writings of the French mathematician-philosopher Auguste Comte. Rejecting the unbridled freedoms championed by earlier French philosophers linked to the French revolution, Comte in his *Cours de philosophie positive* in 1838 argued that order and progress

> were two equally indispensable conditions, their intricate and insoluble combination is henceforth the fundamental difficulty and at the same time the principal resource of every true political system . . . no progress can be accomplished if it does not lead finally to the consolidation of order.[11]

Embellishing Comte with ideas taken from English philosopher Herbert Spencer and the worst aspects of Social Darwinism, Guatemalan positivists developed their own concept of society. With the clear lesson of the chaos and unrest that had accompanied the earlier Liberal regimes following independence, they were determined to temper their search for progress with substantial doses of stability. In the end they erred on the side of order. Under the Liberal regime, as the party newspaper *El Porvenir* declared, the new religion of the state was the "religion of duty, the religion of work".[12] All the means at the disposal of the new government would be used to ensure the widespread acceptance of the new faith.

The first new president of the "liberal" era was the aging patriarch of Liberal congressmen, Miguel García Granados. García Granados, coming from a family of well-connected and well-established merchants, was by nature a moderate, cautious man. Nonetheless, he had been one of the principal backers of the Liberal candidate in the 1869 elections and was subsequently forced to flee the country. From his exile in Mexico, he had become the leading figure in the Liberal movement.

García Granados carried this moderate bent into the presidency with him. As the Guatemalan historian García Laguardia has pointed out, García Granados was "surrounded by friends of his generation, many of them old servants of the overthrown conservative regime".[13] Any reforms introduced by this group would be cautious and tentative.

The mercurial Barrios, García Granados' major lieutenant in the rebellion, was not even in this cabinet. However, Barrios had reserved for himself the position of commander of the Los Altos district of Guatemala. Finally, by the end of 1872, as he and other Liberals bristled at the inactivity of the government, Barrios led his Los Altos army into Guatemala City. While not directly threatening the government, Barrios settled his army in the San José barracks and waited, ominously. Three days later García Granados resigned, calling for elections which Barrios easily won.

There was nothing moderate or cautious about Justo Rufino Barrios. Half García Granados' age, he was given to dramatic swings in mood. According to his Guatemalan biographer, Jesús Carranza, Barrios dominated those about him through a "powerful magnetic force".[14] Described as a typical local *caudillo* of the period, Barrios had taken a circuitous route to rebellion. Raised in a provincial landowning family, he settled down to a comfortable if drab life as the notary public in the small town of Zelaya after a not-too-distinguished career at university. He was saved from this stifling future by being caught in the bedroom of the daughter of the *corregidor*. Forced to flee town, Barrios retired to his *finca,* which conveniently straddled the Mexican-Guatemalan border. From this advantageous position, Barrios led numerous revolts against the Conservative regime before aligning himself with the Liberal cause and forcing his way to the presidency.

According to García Laguardia, there existed between the young Barrios and the cautious elder García Granados "a chasm . . . of temperament and, possibly, ideology".[15] This chasm was quickly reflected in the government and legislation of Barrios.

Two pet liberal ideas received immediate attention. The education system was reorganized and the power of the church attacked. Barrios called education "the cement and base that must sustain the new edifice begun by the revolution over the ruins of the old regime", and complained that the education system provided by the religious orders was woefully inadequate:

> It has been more than three centuries that [Guatemala] has been governed under the oligarchic-theocratic regimen. The government has been retrograde and despotic; the clergy has enjoyed the highest preeminence and meddled in everything; it has been maintained in its opulence and in the enjoyment of luxury by the sweat of the people. And what have they been given in compensation for so much sacrifice? Nothing, absolutely nothing! Here are some eight hundred thousand men, women and children who can't read or write, who can't understand the religion they profess and that for them is reduced to mere superstitious formulas. They go without shoes, almost naked, and work transformed into beasts of burden.[16]

Barrios revised levels of schooling to inculcate "the ideas of liberty, equality, fraternity, order, progress, Central American Union . . . love for work and in general all those ideals that elevate moral sentiments and are the basis for any well-organized society".[17] He saw to a wide range of measures against clerics and church dominance. The University of San Carlos was again secularized and divided into modern faculties. Some orders were expelled; clerics were forbidden to wear religious garb and to hold religious processions in public. When the church responded by excommunicating Barrios, he expelled the archbishop.

To stifle opposition to these dramatic measures, Barrios grasped tyrannical control over most aspects of Guatemalan society. Concentrating on developing a professionalized military as a political base he not only ruled Guatemala with a strong arm but also set up Liberal cronies in Honduras and El Salvador.

Assuring Liberal friends that he knew "how far respect for individual guarantees should go, how far tolerance can be carried and to what extent all the liberties of conscience, speech, press and action should be permitted", Barrios presided over what the British consul called "one of the most cruel despotisms the world has ever seen".[18]

Enrique Gúzmán, a Nicaraguan Liberal visiting Guatemala, recorded:

> The secret police is a veritable institution here . . . such is the uneasiness and distrust which the vile instruments of tyranny disseminate in society, that they make difficult, almost impossible, frank relationships, sincere expansions of personality, intimate confidences. One is always afraid of encountering in the best companion and even in the woman one courts a secret agent of Don Martin Barrundía [the chief of police] . . . even drunk men are prudent here.[19]

Like Carrera before him, undoubtedly much of the impulse for the repressive nature of the Barrios regime stemmed from the increasing wealth he and his cohorts were able to accumulate, fed from the constantly flowing springs of corruption. The British consul claimed that Barrios himself had a share "more or less large in every profitable enterprise in Guatemala". Five to ten years after coming to power, many of his associates had risen from being "penniless adventurers" to millionaires, according to the American representative, George Williamson. Immediately after his death, Barrios' family left Guatemala to live in one of his splendid New York homes, taking "all the spare cash of the government with them".[20] On one level the Liberal revolt had only substituted one set of elites for another. As the wealth of the nation increased dramatically with the spread of coffee cultivation, the share for those with access to government office and favours increased accordingly.

The Growth of the Coffee Economy

BARRIOS' GREATEST EFFORTS were reserved for promoting the spread of coffee cultivation. Having removed the restrictions engendered by the monopolist Consulado de Comercio, he established a Ministry of Development, which provided greater incentives and helped grant credit through the Bank of Guatemala, established in 1871, and the International Bank, Bank of Columbia and Bank of the West, all established by 1881.

While coffee had comprised 50 per cent of Guatemalan exports when the Liberal revolt succeeded in 1871, by 1876 the quantity exported had almost doubled and by 1884 quintrupled.[21] Guatemalan coffee won gold medals in European competition in 1888 and dominated the German market. Production could barely keep up to demand. A Mexican planter trying to promote coffee cultivation in the Mexican state of Chiápas in 1875 observed:

> In order to appreciate what coffee could do for this coast it is enough to record what Guatemala was like twenty years ago and what it is like now. Land which was totally despoiled has been converted into well-cultivated fields, cities and towns in decay have been lifted up and enriched in growing proportions. . . . There is work for all.[22]

Guatemalan Exports

	Cochineal %	Cotton %	Coffee %	Total (in millions of pesos)
1840-1850 (average)	93			.7
1850-1855 (average)	79			1.2
1856-1860	81		1	1.5
1861	71		5	1.1
1862	61		9	1.4
1863	57	1	13	1.5
1864	44	15	12	1.6
1865	53	19	17	1.8
1866	57	5	23	1.7
1867	57	6	22	1.9
1868	41	1	36	2.2
1869	51		32	2.5
1870	34		44	2.6
1871	33		50	2.7

(R.L. Woodward, *Central America: A Nation Divided*, p. 131)

Expanded trade demanded more adequate means of transportation than the ragged cartroads that were still the norm in Carrera's time. The government embarked on an ambitious program of port and railroad construction. Ports were established or expanded along the

Pacific Coast in Puerto San José, Ixtapa and Champerico, all designed to facilitate the transportation of coffee to external markets. Railroad construction reflected this bias even more obviously. The first railway, constructed in 1880, ran from Escuintla (a major coffee-trading centre) to Puerto San José. This line was later linked to Guatemala City, while other routes were constructed from the coffee growing areas on the western piedmont to Pacific ports in the northwest.

All of these lines, built by foreign investors with substantial loans from the government, returned handsome profits to North American and European entrepreneurs. The Barrios government repeatedly ignored bids, often at substantially better terms, from local developers, reflecting "the common Liberal presupposition of the superiority of imported skill and capital".[23] Nevertheless, they served their purpose and between 1870 and 1900 the volume of Guatemala's international trade increased 20 times.

The Coffee Economy and Indian Labour

THE DRAMATIC INCREASE in the cultivation of coffee had far-reaching effects on Guatemalan society. The elite had found a motor force for the economy, one desperately sought but never truly encountered since the early days of colonial rule. The particular manner in which positivist thought interacted with the spread of coffee cultivation prompted a wholesale assault on Indian land and intensified the demand for Indian labour.

The positivist-dominated regimes of the late 19th and early 20th centuries despaired of the "clogged blood" and "natural propensity to indolence" of the Guatemalan *ladino* and Indian populace. To them, despite the obvious example of quick peasant response to the value of cochineal production, the greatest obstacle to economic development lay in the apathy and stupidity of peasants, particularly Indian communities.

The first response to this was a series of measures designed to encourage the immigration of white settlers from Europe and North America, reminiscent of the earlier colonization schemes of the Galvéz government. Generous immigration stipulations, paid passage and the promise of land were all used to attract settlers. Few came.

The government had hoped to use the example of foreign labourers on the soon aborted Northern Railroad "to maximize the beneficial influence upon the indigenous population of the foreigners' superior application and morality".[24] However, even in the depressed American south of the 1880s, the minuscule wage offered failed to attract any but, as even the Ministry of Development admitted, the "most vicious, depraved and incapable of work".[25] Still, the government thought those few a sufficiently instructive example to offer them 30 acres each if they could be induced to fulfill their contract. Not many stayed long enough to collect their land.

Similar schemes showed equally poor results. Responding to the latest government advertisement for immigrants, the American chargé, George Williamson, expressed the sincere desire that no Americans would be foolish enough to venture to this "social atmosphere ... impregnated with the odor of superstition and immoralities". It was his opinion that the Barrios government was looking for immigrants to support "a vicious dictatorship which opposed the majority".[26]

The generous conditions and profitable business atmosphere provided by the Liberal governments did succeed in attracting a small cadre of foreign, primarily German, planters enticed by the possibilities opened up by coffee. Given numerous advantages by the positivist administrations, the Germans quickly came to dominate coffee production. By 1913, although German planters only owned 170 coffee *fincas* (compared to 1,657 controlled by Guatemalans) they produced 358,000 of the 525,000 *quintales* of coffee — two-thirds of Guatemala's total crop.[27] This incestuous clique developed into a tightly woven economic and political network, which until 1940 virtually controlled the Department of Alta Verapaz as well as much of the economic life in the capital. They borrowed from German banks, owned their own transport facilities and fully integrated marketing and distribution networks. Few gave up their German citizenship or integrated into Guatemalan life. They formed a "tight cohesive subculture" set apart from Guatemalan society.[28]

Designed to lure a "large exemplary working [force]", the welcome offered by the Liberal regime led rather to the creation of an "arrogant class of merchants and planters".[29] This foreign elite, allied with elements of the Guatemalan upper class, dominated Guatemalan society and controlled the direction of the economy until the middle of the 20th century.

Unable to attract a white labour force, the Guatemalan elite was left with a vast reservoir of Indians whom they felt needed to be trained to the habits and rigour of labour and thus be made useful for work.[30] The Carrera government had reintroduced the colonial institution of forced labour whereby the *jéfe politico* of each district was to ensure that each Indian village gave up a specified number of workers for a certain period each year. But one of the complaints of the coffee growers against both the Carrera and Cerna governments had been their ineffectual measures to ensure a work force. In 1870, a year before the Liberal revolt, the magazine of *Sociedad Económica* had complained of "the laziness of workers who don't agree or come forward to lend their services or contracts in San Marcos, Santa Rosa, Quezaltenango and Sololá". Because of this, estate owners who had started to plant coffee found themselves, as the magazine put it, "obliged to give loans to the Indians, by which has spread demoralization among them, as they spend their advances and make debts with other *fingueros*."[31]

After coming to power, Barrios responded to these complaints by applying the system of forced labour with a vengeance. In 1876, Barrios ordered all *jéfe politicos* to lend "strong and energetic aid" to planters searching for labourers, "else all their efforts will be doomed to failure due to the deceit of the Indian". They were to ensure that "'Indian villages in your jurisdiction be forced to give the number of hands to the farmers that the latter ask for".[32] Justifying this forced labour with the need for "inculcating the habits of work" and prompting the Indian to take part "if only in small ways in the development of the general wealth", the positivist government made increasingly onerous demands upon Indian villages. Up to one-quarter of the males in any village could be parcelled out to landowners for periods from one week to one month. According to one Indian in the village of San Andrés, "The labourer had to comply. It was not important if he had a harvest, if he was sick, if he didn't have money or could not stand the sadness of his family."[33]

Despite the increased use of institutionalized forced labour, landowners still had to resort to other practices to ensure an adequate supply of workers. The most common of these practices was a form of debt bondage. Labour contractors would comb the highlands, loaning small sums to peasants in return for a contract to work off these debts during harvest time. The labour contractor would then sell these contracts to various *finca* owners, returning to the highlands to round up his human cargo for the harvest. The debts carried usurious interest rates and the charge-book recording the amount of debt was controlled by the planter or his foreman. Once hooked, labourers seldom got free of debt and were forced to return to the plantation year after year. While there they were virtual prisoners, and the full weight of the law descended on them should they refuse to work. The *finca* owners not only secured the lifelong labour of men, but of their children as well.

Debt peonage rapidly spread throughout the highlands. By the 1920s virtually all of the men in many villages were weighted with a sizable, ever increasing debt to an estate owner.[34]

Still, landowners complained of the paucity of labour and suggested the forcible moving of whole villages to coffee-growing regions to ensure a resident labour force. The *jéfe politico* of Alta Verapaz complained that the Indians had moved from his department to escape forced labour and that "it is very difficult to collect hands for agriculture."[35] In 1881, Barrios suggested, "One of the gravest obstacles which opposes the development of agriculture is the lack of punctual fulfillment on the part of day labourers of their contracts with *finca* owners." He demanded that the authorities lend their most effective co-operation in ensuring peasant compliance.[36] But despite the most active co-operation of the government, *finca* owners were bedevilled with insufficient labour. The minuscule wages (two to four cents a day in the highlands in 1900, ten cents in the lowlands, and by 1916, still only ten cents a day)[37] and miserable working conditions were not attractive to peasants who could survive from the produce of their own land. For peasant villagers there was little or no inducement to leave their land, other than the compulsive measures imposed by the government.

The Coffee Economy and Indian Land

IN RESPONSE, THE POSITIVIST regimes embarked on what historian D. McCreery describes as "a massive assault upon Indian land", aimed at destroying the autonomy of the highland villages.[38] As early as 1873, the Barrios government took communal land from the village of Samalá, decrying the tiny harvests produced there and declaring that the government would pass the lands over to "an entrepreneur who will exploit them . . . for the general benefit of agriculture".[39] In 1874, the *jéfe politico* of Totonicapán began a similar action in the village of Momostenango. According to anthropologist Robert Carmack, during this period almost all the fertile land was taken out of Indian hands.[40]

In 1877, this piecemeal process was organized with the passage of a law ostensibly to rationalize common land, that is, to provide for those villages that lacked sufficient land by taking 'excess' land from neighbouring municipalities.

The bill expanded the practice of forced labour and required that all village communal land be sold. Those peasants using village land were required to pay for their plot within six months or forfeit it. When it was forfeited, the common land was to be sold at public auction, with the funds going to the national government, which in turn paid the community 4 per cent interest annually. The result was a cataclysmic alteration of village land structure. Peasant land controlled by the community for centuries was snatched away; the villages received only a small annual payment in return.

While Barrios did take small amounts of land from some of the largest *haciendas* shown to be not using their land profitably, this was a rare occurrence, more often linked to feuds than to a desire to increase production. In some even rarer instances, villages that were particularly destitute before the passage of the law ended up with increased common land.[41] However, the law was primarily used to attack village lands.

Tens of thousands of peasants lost access to land. Although the figures are incomplete, it is estimated that in the first year alone 23,427 lots were registered, which brought the government 206,823 pesos. In addition, from 1871 to 1883, the government sold 8,839 caballerias* of land designated as tierras baldias.[42] While undoubtedly some peasants were able to scrape together the money to purchase their lot, the majority were simply dispossessed and their land sold to ladinos with either connections to the government or the cash to purchase the property. For example, in 1882 the villagers of Bueñhabaj had their tierras baldias sold to ladinos who had assisted the Barrios government in putting down a local revolt. The municipio of San Antonio Ilotenago lost 139 caballerias of land between 1877 and 1905, most of it going to five prominent ladinos who had denounced the land as baldia.[43]

Indian peasants in the highlands were under constant pressure. With increased demands to prove that village land was not idle, they were forced from their villages for long periods due to the heightened demands of the forced labour system or a self-perpetuating debt contract. They would often return to their villages to find their land sold out from under them. The forced labour, the debt contracts, the forced sale of village common land and the confiscation of tierras baldias had the desired effect. In combination they broke down the autonomy of the highland villages, impoverished peasant agriculture and drove increasing numbers of peasants to labour on the developing coffee fincas.

Peasant Communities Respond: Indian Revolt in the Late 19th Century

FACED WITH THIS CONTINUAL PRESSURE, highland villages responded forcefully as they had to similar pressure a half century earlier. But Guatemala had changed in the meantime and, as it turned out, the possibilities for success were limited.

A revolt that started in 1875 in the village of Momostenango is illustrative. It had similarities to the early stages of Carrera's uprising. It was led by a ladino with significant influence in the village, and other villages in the area joined in the rebellion. Soon more than 500 rebels were in arms and the uprising began to take on a national

* 1 caballeria equals 109.8 acres or 64.4 manzanas.

character as Conservative politicians gingerly tested the waters of counter-revolution.[44]

The successful uprising of 50 years earlier could not be re-enacted, however. In the intervening years, Indian peasants' control over the local power structure had been seriously eroded by increasing encroachment and local influence exercised by *ladinos* with national connections. In addition, the enemy the peasants faced, the national government, was no longer the disorganized crew of Liberals headed by Galvéz, but a powerful national government rapidly extending its control throughout the countryside.

No longer controlled by colonial legislation that restricted their access to land in peasant communities, *ladinos* had, during the Carrera period, consolidated positions of local power. As in the case of Momostenango, some of the local *ladinos* shared peasant concerns and helped lead their protest. However, many of the most powerful *ladinos* in village areas were linked to the national government through ties of patronage and had benefited personally from the Liberal land measures. The Barrios government designed measures to increase this influence. In more and more villages, formal local government and the traditional hierarchy fell under the control of men with connections to the national government.

Of particular importance were government measures to reform the military and militia. One of Barrios' most pressing concerns was to establish a modern military, well-trained, well-organized and responsive to the national government, rather than relying on mercenaries loyal to a string of local *caudillos*, as the previous governments had done. Barrios created the Escuela Politécnica military academy, designed to inculcate attitudes of professionalism and loyalty. By 1903, it was overseen by a French military adviser and was the model for similar schools in Central America. The military soon became the preserve of *ladinos* who used the military career as a means of social mobility denied in the otherwise rigid social atmosphere.

Military reorganization had important effects locally. Barrios' professional army was more than a match for peasant insurgents. As the uprising in Momostenango continued into 1877, for example, Barrios' troops were easily able to overrun insurgent areas and burn peasant houses. At the same time, Barrios' control over his troops was sufficient to prevent theft of livestock and acts of outrage against the non-combatants in the area, which might have spread the revolt further.

Of equal importance was the reorganization of the militia. During the Carrera government, local militias were loose organizations informally controlled by Indian villages, with the command loosely integrated into the traditional village hierarchy. Under Barrios, command was given to trusted *ladinos* and Indians were gradually weeded out of the militias. Soon the regular militia in most areas was composed almost exclusively of *ladinos,* most of whom were indebted in some manner to the commander. Indians were pressed into service only at times of emergency.

Another example, cited by anthropologist Robert Carmack from a village he calls Tecpanoca, also illustrates this increasing control. After years of Liberal administration the local government of Tecpanoca was in the hands of Teodoro Cienfuegos, a general with influence in the national government and who had fought in military campaigns for Barrios. In 1895 he consolidated his influence as one of the major landowners in the region by getting himself appointed the *alcalde major* of "Totonicapán". Cienfuegos kept his hands tightly clenched around the reins of local power through a complex system of *ladinos* resident in smaller communities and acting as his agents. The Liberal administrations allowed him to arm local *ladinos,* who often forced "unruly" peasants from the community. Through a "mixture of violence and paternalism" Cienfuegos gained control over the Indian representatives in the formal local government, many of whom he had named to office.[45]

Many of the Liberal regimes' land and labour policies helped break down the authority of the traditional village hierarchy. Ricardo Falla, in one of the most complete studies of a Quichean village's history, has pointed out that *alcaldes,* both *ladino* and Indian, who during the time of Carrera most often truly reflected the wishes of the community, lost this position as they were forced to implement Liberal measures on the local level. Especially when they helped round up workers for forced labour, they began to be perceived as "mere instruments of the estate owners and of the *jéfe politico*". They lost influence in the village and no longer had sufficient moral authority to provide effective organization or even to arbitrate internal conflict.[46]

When local village authorities did support peasant concerns, they often faced incredible brutality as a result. On Sept. 4, 1884, every village official in Cantel was shot by federal troops. It appears that the village authorities had been vigorously defending village lands which were being taken over by a newly established textile factory.[47]

Thus it was during this period that the basic structure of highland village politics, which continued to exist through much of the 20th century, was created. Power and influence percolated down from the national government to local *caudillos,* landowners mostly, who maintained their control through favours and patronage passed out on the local level and through the brutal repression of any challenge to their authority. Allegiance was fostered by a deliberately inspired racial separation. Power was held in *ladino* hands while the formal structure of peasant authority was used primarily to interpret national demands upon the village. Within the community this formal structure lost authority, which gradually devolved more completely on the informal authority of village elders and *cofradía*.

Throughout the late 19th century and early 20th century, highland villages rose up in revolt against the Liberal demands on their labour and land. This time, however, the national government's dominance through a modern military, the militia and indirect control of the formal structure of local government was sufficient to ensure that the revolts remained isolated and unsuccessful. Perhaps most importantly, *ladinos* had been a persecuted sector of Guatemalan society before the Carrera revolt in the 1830s, and had joined in his uprising against the white minority. But by the 1870s the division between white and *ladino* had eroded. The Liberal measures benefited aggressive *ladinos*, who increased the size of their holdings at the expense of Indian peasants. While class allegiance prevailed in some villages and *ladino* peasants joined Indian villagers in revolt, by and large *ladino* peasants did not feel threatened by Liberal reforms and used their own new power to thwart rebellion.

To the national government, these peasant revolts only served to demonstrate "the near impenetrable stupidity" of the Indian and strengthened a resolve to break down Indian autonomy. Seizures of Indian land continued unabated as increasing numbers of peasants were driven to the coast to feed the coffee plantations' voracious appetite for labour.

While some confiscated village land was promptly put into the production of coffee and other crops, much of it remained idle, as it has done for most of the 20th century. Seen from the perspective of the overwhelming need for wage labour, the rationale, from the planters' point of view, is quite apparent. By and large, village land was not coveted solely to allow landowners to extend their cultivations (although many eventually did that) but to break down the autonomy of villages and to create a sufficiently large labour force for the few months of harvest every year.

Given the land base of the peasant cultivator, the only alternative means of enticing them towards wage labour would have been to offer sufficiently attractive salaries. This would have, in all probability, led to a gradual movement away from the land for a significant percentage of the peasants in the highlands, allowing the remaining ones to enlarge their holdings sufficiently to make their farms more labour productive. This would have, however, entailed a dramatic increase in the wage costs of the planters and a consequent reduction in profits; something the autocratic measures of the Barrios and Cabrera administrations ensured would not occur. Also, with no opposing pressure group within the society (such as an indigenous manufacturing sector) there was no incentive to expand the rural market or to resist "efforts to depress rural living standards".[48]

Stymied at armed revolt, with no alternative, village communities turned inward. While Guatemalan peasants had always been to some extent defensive due to the long history of exploitation under colonial rule, this posture had ebbed and flowed according to the demands placed on them by government and elites. During the early part of the 19th century they had shown a noted propensity to respond to the market opportunities presented by cochineal. While maintaining village integrity, they willingly embraced participation in the national economy. The concerted attack on village lands by the positivist regimes throughout the latter third of the 19th and first half of the 20th century left them no opportunity to do so with coffee. The "twin goals of resource alienation and social policies designed to ignore or crush evidence of Indian cultures" drove these communities to an increasingly defensive, hostile posture.[49] A process of economic differentiation and native economic initiative was stifled. In many villages the decline in native harvest due to the demands of forced labour and confiscation of land forced native merchants, who had previously sold their foodstuffs outside the community, to rely on wage labour. Villages become more "tightly organized" and Indians developed a passive resistance to the national society.

The Coffee Economy and Economic Growth

BY THE 1880s THE COFFEE economy showed signs of internal weakness. The beginning of coffee production in Brazil saturated what had been until then an ever-increasing market. International prices fell dramatically, from 23 cents per pound in 1876 to 9 cents by 1885. Prices continued to drop through the 1890s.

The government briefly promoted agricultural diversification, offering to exempt cotton cultivators from military service and promising a bonus for production. Similar types of incentives were provided for sugar producers.[50] In 1907, each department was given a quota of basic foodstuffs. Meeting these quotas was the responsibility of the *jéfe politico* and for a few years they were able to pressure landowners to increase this type of production.[51] However, by 1912 coffee prices began to revive and the efforts at diversification were largely abandoned. Coffee remained king in Guatemala.

Prices and Quantity of Guatemalan Coffee Exports

	Quantity (lbs.)	Price (cents)
1871	11,322,900	13
1872	13,322,900	18
1873	15,050,600	20
1874	16,158,300	22
1875	16,195,900	20
1876	20,534,600	23
1877	20,788,500	21
1878	20,728,500	18
1879	25,201,600	17
1880	28,976,200	16
1881	26,027,200	14
1882	31,327,100	12
1883	40,406,900	11
1884	37,130,600	11
1885	51,516,700	9

(D.McCreery, "Financiado el desarrollo en la America Latina del siglo XIX: el caso de Guatemala: 1871-1885", *Revista del Pensamiento Centro Americano* [Abril-Junio, 1975], p. 2)

As it had in much of Central America, coffee had provided Guatemala with an unprecedented boom. Abetted by the measures of the positivist governments it had lent an air of dynamic economic development and modernization to the "Liberal" regimes. In the process, however, a number of distortions within the society and economy were accentuated: distortions that continue to plague Guatemala.

The export of coffee came to completely dominate the Guatemalan economy. All other aspects of development were secondary or forgotten. Transportation links connected coffee producing areas to export centres with little attempt to facilitate internal communication. A tiny pocket of foreign planters with ties to European exporting houses, allied with a circumscribed, indigenous elite, drove the economy and determined government policy. Avenues for the development of a middle class or medium-sized, owner-operated farms were restricted.

Most importantly, an embryonic process of economic growth which had begun in the rural areas among *ladino* and Indian rural cultivators in the mid-1800s was truncated. If they had been encouraged to respond to the opportunities presented by coffee cultivation, the economic and social structure of Guatemala would have been drastically different.

Instead, Liberals used "the impoverished masses as the manpower to provide the material advances of the regimes".[52] Unable to attract a modern white working force to bleach out the lower classes, at even substantially higher wages than that offered indigenous workers, they employed a number of techniques to drive the peasants to wage labour. Ensuring that labour costs were kept at minuscule levels, they ultimately forced peasants to work by depriving them of sufficient land to subsist. This served a dual purpose; it impelled the peasant to leave the village for wage labour during harvest, but their reduced plots of land provided an existence — miserable as it might be — for the rest of the year. This relieved the plantation owner of the responsibility of ensuring their subsistence throughout that part of the year during which their labour was not needed.

In the process, this type of labour recruitment, while guaranteeing huge profits, reinforced an apparent "duality" within the economy and society. The Guatemalan economy was built on peasant, primarily Indian backs. However, peasant interaction with the society outside of the highland village became increasingly constricted. Outside of the few months of the year spent labouring on *fincas,* the villagers subsided into a collective isolation of mistrust and hostility. Tolerating government officials only when forced to, they retreated further into the old forms of theocratic self-government, viewing with increasing and entirely warranted apprehension any encroachment. The Liberal measures, as D. McCreery concludes, "produced an indigestible, culturally hostile core of corporate Indian communities."[53]

Karl Schmitt's description of Mexico during this period fits Guatemala equally well.

> The positivist peace was an armed peace; the Positivist order was an imposed order; ... Positivist prosperity was a prosperity for the few. Exploitation of natural resources proceeded apace with the exploitation of the masses, more brutalized than ever before.[54]

— 4 —
Banana Empire: U.S. Intervention and the Ubico Dictatorship

I spent thirty-three years [in the Marine Corps]... most of the time
being a high class muscleman for big business, for Wall Street and
bankers. In short, I was a muscleman for capitalism. I helped purify
Nicaragua... I helped make Mexico... safe for oil interests. I
brought light to the Dominican Republic for sugar interests in 1916.
I helped make Haiti and Cuba a decent place for the National City
Bank boys. I helped in the rape of a dozen Central American
republics for the benefit of Wall Street.
— General Darlington Smedley Butler, *New York Times*, 1931.

THE FIRST PART OF THE 20TH century marked the beginning of the
intrusion of U.S. capital into the Central American region. While Liberal
dictators extended their reign over the republics of Central
America and battled over succession to office, foreign entrepreneurs
developed powerful economic empires. One of these, Minor C. Keith,
president of the International Railways of Central America and vice-president
of the United Fruit Company, became so powerful one
chronicle called him "the uncrowned king of Central America".[1] By
the end of World War I, through a variety of means, U.S. interests had
pushed aside the British and Germans to predominate in the region.

The aggressive, arrogant and manipulative attitude of the large
American corporations that predominated in the region prompted significant
anti-American feeling and a variety of nationalistic attempts
to win back control of the economies. The manner in which these
threats were dealt with clearly demonstrates the close links between
U.S. capital and the U.S. State Department. American presidents were
emphatic about where their interests lay. In 1912, President William
Howard Taft declared, "Intervention is justified when it was made
necessary to guarantee the capitals and markets of the United States."[2]
Throughout Central America the United States placed diplomatic, economic
and military pressure on recalcitrant nationalist leaders.

When withholding diplomatic recognition, recalling and preventing
further loans and other forms of subtle and not so subtle meddling
occasionally proved ineffective, Washington readily resorted to direct

military intervention. U.S. troops were used "to protect American property and interests" in Cuba, Haiti, the Dominican Republic, Nicaragua and Honduras in the first two decades of the 20th century. As the comments of people like General Darlington Smedley Butler demonstrate, it was clear for whom these actions were taken. Only Central American presidents who maintained the proper attitude towards U.S. capital and respect for U.S. entrepreneurs were capable of holding on to power. Despite rhetoric to the contrary, the most blatant tyrannies were tolerated by U.S. administrations if those countries could ensure order and a healthy investment climate.

In Guatemala, U.S. capital was primarily represented by the "unholy trinity" of the United Fruit Company (UFCo), International Railways of Central America (ICRA) and the United Fruit Steamship Company. Acting together, these concerns dominated the Guatemalan economy and, in alliance with U.S. diplomatic representatives, determined much of Guatemala's politics. While Guatemala avoided the more direct forms of military pressure placed on the neighbouring republics of Honduras and Nicaragua, all Guatemalan presidents were influenced and controlled to some degree by the U.S. mission and companies. The connection between favourable contacts with the United Fruit Company and its appendages on the one side, and U.S. support for political leaders on the other, is apparent throughout the first half of the 20th century; but is most clearly seen in the career of the archetype of Guatemalan dictators, General Jorge Ubico.

The Unholy Trinity: Early Days

THE UNITED FRUIT COMPANY'S empire in Central America developed with astonishing rapidity. Emerging in the waning years of the 19th century, the empire controlled vast expanses of land as well as marketing and distribution networks, railways, Caribbean shipping and many Central American governments. By the 1930s the company's domain and power appeared limitless.

For over three decades in the early twentieth century, UFCo's fortunes were tied to the drive and ambition of one man, Minor Cooper Keith. Keith, a short slim man of unflagging ambition, became so powerful that Miguel Angel Asturias, the great Guatemalan novelist, labelled him the "Green Pope", who "says a word and a republic is bought. He sneezes and president, whether general or lawyer, falls. . . . He rubs his behind on his chair and a revolution breaks out."[3]

Contracted to build the Pacific Railway from San José, Costa Rica, to the Pacific Coast, Keith and his associates ran into serious financial difficulty. Searching for a commercially viable crop that would provide transport revenue for the railway, he began to grow bananas in

1878-79 on land granted to the railroad concession. Banana cultivation quickly proved so profitable that even the Costa Rican president, Tomas Guardía, soon joined Keith in developing plantations.

Hoping to monopolize banana production and marketing, in 1899 Keith merged his Tropical Trading and Transport Company with his only serious competitor, Andrew Preston's Boston Fruit Company, to form the United Fruit Company. While Preston was named president of the new firm, Keith was the most active and dominated Central American operations. Expanding from its relatively modest start in Costa Rica, by 1930 UFCo had assets of over $242 million, possessed more than three million acres of land throughout the world and controlled a long list of subsidiaries. Through an accumulation of shipping companies, UFCo's "Great White Fleet" controlled over 100 ships and in the early years of the 20th century marketed 80 to 90 per cent of banana imports to the United States. By 1952, it was shipping out 51.6 million bunches of bananas annually.[4] United Fruit Company holdings became so extensive that a 1954 anti-trust suit in the United States stated (probably exaggeratedly) that excluding Ecuador, UFCo "leases or otherwise controls 85 per cent of land in the American tropics suitable for banana cultivation."[5]

UFCo quickly moved into Guatemala. It signed its first contract for the purchase of banana land in 1901, but it did not begin to dominate the Guatemalan economy until the incorporation of Guatemala's major railroad: a process that began in 1904 when President Estrada Cabrera, attempting to complete the long delayed Northern Railway, granted a contract to Minor Keith and William Van Horne, of Canadian Pacific fame, to finish the remaining miles.

The Northern had been started in the early years of Barrios' dictatorship and alternately espoused as the key to Guatemala's economic future and worked on feverishly — or left to rust in the lowland jungle by succeeding regimes. By 1904, the government had spent over $8 million on construction.[6] The railway ran 136 miles, from the newly completed Caribbean port of Puerto Barrios to a tiny settlement called El Rancho. Only 61 miles separated it from the capital, however.

In 1904, Van Horne and Keith incorporated the Guatemalan Railway Company, deposited a bond of $200 thousand in a New York Bank, invested close to $4 million raised on a bond issue and completed the road to Guatemala City. Cabrera was more than generous to the new Guatemalan Railway Company. The previously completed miles of track were handed over to the company, along with Puerto Barrios. The company was granted a 100-foot right of way across most of the country; 4,600 *caballerias* of land; a monopoly on rail transport to the Caribbean; free use of material such as stone and lumber on all public land along the railway; exemption from most taxes for 99 years; and exemption from taxes on the export of agricultural products (except coffee) for 35 years. The railway was given the right to control water that encroached on railway lands. The $4 million investment was in fact raised by the government, which guaranteed 5 per cent interest on the bonds issued by the company. Most importantly, the company was to exercise "the sole and exclusive government on the railway and will never be subject to the intervention of the government."[7] The railway's accounts could not, by law, be inspected by the government.

In 1912, the company was granted ownership of the over-600 miles of track already built in western Guatemala and serving Pacific ports and coffee growing areas. The company acquired both a new name — International Railways of Central America — and a complete monopoly of rail transit (indeed of any cost efficient commercial transport) in Guatemala.

IRCA, the United Fruit fleet and the United Fruit Company established a powerful triumvirate that dominated the Guatemalan economy. Despite the continued predominance of coffee as an export crop, UFCo, through transport appendages and company stores, controlled an estimated 40 per cent of the Guatemalan economy by the 1930s.[8]

This economic preponderance brought with it significant political clout. Government contracts with the United Fruit Company in 1924, 1930 and 1936 demonstrated increasingly favourable terms for the company. The 1924 agreement granted the company a 25-year lease of all unoccupied lands stretching 25 miles along both sides of the Rio Motagua, for $6,000 a year. The company was exempted from taxes for 25 years and an addendum to the contract declared that the company would not be bound by laws decreed by the government if those laws were not first settled by negotiation between the two.

The Rio Motagua area was the subject of a long-simmering dispute between Honduras and Guatemala, prompted by competition for the prime banana-growing land along the river. A conflict between UFCo and the Cuyamel Banana Company, headed by the American Samuel Zemurray, propelled Guatemala and Honduras into a vicious dispute, which for a period of 15 years threatened to erupt in war. In 1910 Zemurray had allegedly orchestrated the overthrow of the Honduran president to insure a reduction in import duties. He consequently exerted an inordinate influence on the Honduran government he had helped install. He was determined to forestall UFCo control of these banana lands and was easily able to prompt the government to press its claims for the river area. UFCo exerted similar influence on the Guatemalan government. The dispute continued from 1915 to 1929 when UFCo eliminated yet another competitor by merging the two companies, buying out Zemurray for $31.5 million in stock. Although he briefly retired, Zemurray emerged during the depression as president of the company.

UFCo and the Banana Economy

LARGE-SCALE BANANA cultivation on the depressed Caribbean coast could have proved a tremendous economic boon for Guatemala. The hot, humid lowlands had been avoided by Indian and *ladino* peasants and for the most part were empty and barren. Attempts since independence to develop flourishing economic activity in any part of the region had been consistently fruitless, with the exception of some minor natural harvesting of rubber, chicle and hardwood. The nascent ports along the Caribbean had for decades lain in a tropical stupor, the climate's ubiquitous moisture attacking the few wood buildings that remained from the earlier Liberal government attempts to develop ports. Until the completion of the railways, potential settlers were frightened away by the formidable transportation costs to the inhabited highlands and, more importantly, by the threat of tropical diseases.

Banana plantations and the completion of the IRCA line put an end to this seemingly endless torpor. According to the company historians: "Tropical swamps and jungles soon blossomed into immense plots of luscious green plants. . . . Whole communities sprang up almost overnight."[9] The company began to export millions of bananas every year. The U.S. embassy estimated that in 1941 more than 25,000 people in Guatemala earned their livelihood directly from the banana industry.[10] When ships of the Great White Fleet docked, Puerto Barrios hummed with activity. The once almost deserted coast was, in places at least, almost unrecognizable. In the process of this settlement, campaigns to eradicate many of the most debilitating diseases, particularly malaria, proved enormously successful.

Yet the benefit that accrued to Guatemala from the development of the banana industry did not come without heavy costs. The prejudicial contracts that the company was able to wring from a congress dominated by tyrannical and obsequious (to UFCo) dictators ensured that Guatemala received only limited returns from the golden harvest, while UFCo stockholders were continually blessed with remarkable profits from their investment. The UFCo's economic empire held the Guatemalan economy in a stranglehold — a noose fashioned securely from the ribbons of IRCA tracks.

Even after the imposition of an export tax in 1912, the returns to Guatemala from its banana wealth remained minuscule. The various agreements that prevented the inspection of company and railway books ensured that the government had an incomplete idea of exactly how many bananas were being shipped. In 1946 the International Monetary Fund estimated that UFCo exported over Q10 million* worth of bananas whereas the company only declared Q8.5 million. The following year, when the Fund estimated an increase to Q19 million, the company's declared export was only slightly over Q11 million.[11] There is no way of ascertaining what percentage of actual exports the company declared before 1946. However, even on the amount declared, by 1928 the company averaged a tax of only 1.97 per cent of the export value of its bananas, while coffee exporters were being charged 8.7 per cent.[12]

The inability of the Guatemalan economy to benefit significantly from banana cultivation was so obvious that the British Overseas Trade Officer, in his 1937 report, suggested that despite an export of 3.5 million bunches in 1936, "They are not of corresponding importance to the country since the entire export is in the hands of the United Fruit Company."[13]

By 1934 UFCo controlled an immense amount of land: over 3.5 million acres of which it cultivated slightly less than 115,000 acres.[14] The company argued that large expanses of land were required for the construction of buildings and irrigation systems. More importantly, land needed to be kept fallow for a number of years in areas where the major banana diseases struck. Nevertheless, a great amount of potentially valuable banana land lay unused and Guatemalan planters eager to get into the business were thwarted by the fruit company's grip.

In addition to the lands granted by government contracts, the company was easily able to force the sale to itself of desired, independently-owned land. It often used the right of way and control over water supplies granted in the railway contract to put pressure on private owners. Writing in the 1930s, former company employee David Kepner observed:

> Recently in buying lands to round out its estate in western Guatemala, the UFCo has been faced by many who did not wish to give up the lands which they had held for years.... In such situations the company's policy was to buy the surrounding cultivation plots, to fence them in, to take advantage of all local laws such as those regarding the wandering

---

* The *quetzal* replaced the *peso* as Guatemala's principal monetary unit in 1925. Like the *peso*, it was worth about $1.00 U.S.

of stray cattle, and in every way possible to molest the landowner until he was willing to get rid of his holdings.[15]

During the 1920s and 1930s the company began to purchase an increasing percentage of its exports from contract banana growers rather than grow them on its own plantation land. It maintained a near feudal control over the products of these independent producers. There was nobody else to sell to and the company reserved the right to reject or accept at will bananas delivered to dockside. Often a contract planter would find more than half his crop rejected at the dock, with no return for those rejected. This tactic was used most frequently against independents involved in politics or those active in forming growers' associations to combat the monopoly power of the company. The company purchased the bulk of its bananas on contract in areas where the land was becoming less fertile. In these areas bunches generally were short of the "full" size of nine stems, in which case the company had a severely sliding scale of payment. Even at the best of times, shortly before the depression when prices were highest and contract planters were farming relatively new, thus fertile, ground, a banana contracter could expect little more than a $20 return on an acre of banana land. Given the small size of the holdings of most private contractors, the income would be singularly meagre.

The company determined price, amount and conditions of delivery and could easily force independent producers out of business. When contractors attempted to bypass the UFCo monopoly and sell their crops to smaller distributors, they found it impossible to avoid the tentacles of *"el pulpo"* (the octopus).

Wage labourers suffered worse hardships. UFCo salaries were relatively generous: between $1 and $2 a day in the eastern lowlands and 65 cents to 70 cents on plantations in the more heavily populated and healthier western littoral. This compares favourably with the minuscule wages offered on coffee *fincas* but conditions were much worse for the plantation workers. Costs of basic necessities, such as corn and black beans, were 60 to 90 per cent higher on the Atlantic coast, according to the Guatemalan director-general of statistics. The work was unpleasant, often carried out during the torrential rainy season, and during harvest workers were driven at an unceasing, relentless tempo. Housing conditions were abysmal; whole families lived in 12-foot square huts, with inadequate water and sanitary facilities. Malaria was a constant threat.[16] In addition, as in the coffee *fincas,* workers were kept in debt to the company through easy credit available in the network of company stores. Indeed, at times the only wages offered were in the form of credit notes to be used at these stores.

Partly in protest against these stores, a series of bloody strikes broke out against the company during the 1920s. Most such strikes were obligingly and brutally squashed by quickly dispatched soldiers or private security forces. In the words of A. Bauer Paiz, a Guatemalan lawyer and politician, "The company administered its possessions as a feudal patrimony. . . . It did not bother to comply with labour laws . . . but used the forces of police and military to trample and persecute its workers."[17]

The most common complaint against the company, however, was the way in which the various appendages of *el pulpo* functioned together. Nominally separate, UFCo and the Great White Fleet worked in close co-ordination to prejudice operations against non-company products. The most obvious example of this was the distorted freight rates within the country.

IRCA obviously had a vested interested in ensuring continual traffic through its port at Puerto Barrios, both to increase revenue from docking charges and because this traffic would be handled by the allied Great White Fleet. Pacific ports were serviced by its competitor, Grace Steamship Lines. Consequently, IRCA set distorted freight rates that ensured the bulk of Guatemalan exports would be funnelled through Puerto Barrios. The cost of shipping coffee to Puerto San José on the Pacific averaged .097 cents per ton per mile, while to Puerto Barrios it was only .026 cents.[18] Similarly, goods imported through Pacific ports had hefty surcharges levied on the cost of their subsequent transport over IRCA tracks. As a consequence, although the bulk of Guatemalan coffee was grown in proximity to these Pacific ports, only 28 per cent was exported through them in 1930.[19]

United Fruit Company ships, that "great fleet of white corpses" in the words of Guatemalan novelist Miguel Angel Asturias, similarly benefited from and augmented the power of the diverse elements of the empire. The fleet charged higher rates for shipping coffee that had not been taken to port on the railway. It gouged exorbitant shipping rates from Guatemalan coffee growers and used its gains to subsidize lower rates when faced with competition. During the 1930s, it cost as much to ship coffee from Guatemala to New Orleans as it did from Brazil to New Orleans. Throughout Central America, the fleet used its monopoly position to harass competing growers by delaying the loading of their bananas until the fruit was past peak ripeness and spoiled for the U.S. market. UFCo used the Great White Fleet as a "fighting arm of the banana empire, capable of defending other parts of the empire from the attacks of competitors."[20]

The heart of the octopus, of course, lay with UFCo's banana plantations, and the railway helped ensure continued profits in this part of the operation. IRCA's rates for the transport of UFCo bananas were ridiculously low: For a full carload moved to Puerto Barrios from the Pacific plantation, it charged $60. In 1955, a group of the railway's minority American stockholders were granted $5.5 million by the U.S. courts as compensation for the forgone income they would have received had IRCA charged the fruit company a more competitive rate. Subsidizing its heaviest user, UFCo, IRCA operated at a profit by charging inflated prices for the transport of other goods, thus increasing costs to Guatemalan consumers and producers.

The disadvantages to Guatemala of this oppressive monopoly became readily apparent to certain elements of the Guatemalan elite. In 1930 the President of the Confederation of Agriculture Associations of Guatemala warned congress: "The railroad company, the owners of the farms situated in the interior . . . and the United Fruit Steamship Company are intimately bound together and everything which is conceded to them without stipulating anything in favour of the agriculture of the country conduces to strengthen the monopoly of the exploitation of the bananas."[21]

All of UFCo's machinations were of course designed to ensure a continuous rate of profit and growth for the company. In this the company was uniquely successful. Between 1900 and 1930 its assets multiplied 14 times, from a book value of $16.9 million to over $242 million.[22] Those who purchased stock in the original issue in 1899 would have received an average return of 17.75 per cent per annum by 1933 (three years into the depression) solely on the increased value of stock through stock divisions and without any calculations for dividends. David Kepner, at the conclusion of his two-volume study of the United Fruit Company in the 1930s, charged that the company: "Intrenched [sic] behind monopolistic concessions, holding in the same hand control of transportation facilities and banana production, being able to a large extent to dictate terms to planters and labourers, having greater income, influence and power than many governments . . . is able to amass larger profits."[23]

The UFCo, Minor Keith and Samuel Zemurray used their powerful influence on Guatemalan politics freely, always watchful to maintain the company's dominant position in the economy and intent on wringing whatever concessions they could from a weakened congress and accommodating dictators. UFCo's intervention in politics was, in the words of Guatemalan academic and politician Luis Cardoza y Aragon, "constant, open and bloody".[24]

American Intervention

THE EARLY 20TH century was a time of political turmoil in Central America, a period when the few attempts made at democratic government were quickly overthrown by competing elites. The region was ruled by a series of tyrants, mostly inept. Faced with a constant struggle to remain in power, the dictators grasped at all means of support. This often meant a heavy reliance upon the good will of the U.S. administration and the cultivation of American diplomatic representatives.

The consequences of not doing so were generally dramatic. The early 20th century presents a litany of U.S. military involvement in the Caribbean region, with administration after administration that could not guarantee order or that adopted a belligerent attitude to U.S. interests being overthrown in rapid succession. Before the 1920s the views of influential Americans towards Central America were remarkably consistent. In 1904 Theodore Roosevelt declared, "Sooner or later it is inevitable that the United States will . . . regulate life in the republics of the Caribbean."[25] In 1912 Elihu Root, a one-time lawyer for the UFCo and an influential lobbyist in Washington, was even more explicit. "It is only a matter of time," he declared, "until Mexico, Central America and the islands that we don't possess in the Caribbean will fall under our flag. . . . By 1950, the frontiers of the United States will encircle the entire continent."[26]

The "Big Stick" bullying of Theodore Roosevelt (1904-1908), the "Dollar Diplomacy" of William Taft (1908-1912) and even the "Presbyterian morality turned foreign policy" of Woodrow Wilson (1912-1920) were all translated into remarkably similar policies in Central America and the Caribbean. U.S. marines landed in Cuba, Panama, Haiti, the Dominican Republic, Nicaragua and Honduras under these administrations. They were used freely to quell rebellions, pressure distasteful presidents and protect U.S. interests. A notable figure in many of these interventions was Darlington Smedley Butler, who worked his way up the ranks of the marine corps by being the U.S. State Department's enforcer in Mexico, Nicaragua, Haiti and even China. In Haiti, U.S. troops killed 3,250 Haitian rebels in 1916 and Colonel Butler was awarded the congressional Medal of Honor.[27]

During the 1920s the American approach became often more subtle, if no less effective. The Harding administration, like Wilson's before it, expressed an abiding fondness for constitutional government. In 1923 Warren Harding pressured the Central American nations into signing the Treaty of Peace and Amity in Washington. The treaty bound Central American governments to respect the territorial integrity of neighbouring nations and to pledge non-interference in their internal affairs. The part of the treaty that would be most heavily applied affirmed that governments that came to power unconstitutionally would not be recognized by the other signatories. Although the United States did not sign the treaty, Washington was to be its unofficial watchdog.

Whatever the intentions of the treaty, subsequent decisions by U.S. administrations made it painfully clear that there were many "exceptions" making non-constitutional governments more palatable than their constitutional alternative. Perhaps the most obvious example was the U.S. recognition of General Maximiliano Hernández Martínez in El Salvador after he had proved so effective in subduing "communist peasants" in the 1933 uprising and massacre.[28]

In Guatemala, American involvement with the various administrations did not (until 1954) take the form of military intervention. However, there are plenty of examples where the influence of American business was sufficient to prompt strenuous diplomatic intervention. Throughout this period, until well into Ubico's long dictatorship, U.S. representatives played kingmaker between competing elites. The goals of U.S. business interests and U.S. diplomatic representatives were often inseparable.

Despite his dictatorial nature, Manuel Estrada Cabrera enjoyed the full support of the American legation throughout most of his regime (1898-1920). His ability to impose rigid order was viewed with favour. He severely restricted union organization and implemented other pro-business legislation. Generous contracts with the UFCo and IRCA prompted significant goodwill. Most important was Cabrera's compliance in the forced sale of the European-owned company Emprésa Electríca to American interests.

That sale was part of a pattern in which U.S. capital used the opportunity presented by World War I to expand foreign operations at the expense of European interests. During the hostilities, restrictions placed on European capital and the rapidly expanding American economy fostered American predominance, and the U.S. State Department was most vigorous in pressing its interests on Latin American economies. In Guatemala, the U.S. War Board continually pressured the government to reduce its reliance on German capital, always the most active of European economies in Guatemala. The Americans were finally able to force the sale of Emprésa Electríca (with its monopoly of electrical generation in the country) to the U.S. Electric Bond and Share Company. Guatemalan economist Alfonso Bauer Paíz asserts that due to U.S. pressure the company was picked up by Electric Bond and Share for a fraction of its value.[29]

However, Estrada Cabrera became increasingly intransigent towards the major American corporations and refused to go as far as the State Department urged in restricting German interests in Guatemala. In addition, his rigid administration proved unable to respond effectively to a monetary and economic crisis that confronted the country in 1919. The State Department gradually extricated itself from its former close allegiance. In 1920 Estrada Cabrera was ousted in a coup. His subsequent attempt to shell Guatemala City into submission and force his will upon the now hostile congress only served to demonstrate how completely he had lost the support of the elite and certain members of the military.

It is clear that the attitude of the American legation was instrumental in the overthrow of Cabrera. According to historian R.L. Woodward: "Wilson abandoned his dedication to the preservation of constitutional governments in the case of Guatemala when it became apparent that the Estrada Cabrera government was no longer the best protector of U.S. interests. The U.S. State Department's intimation that it would not oppose the overthrow of Estrada was a major factor in his ouster."[30]

U.S. business interests were quickly disillusioned with Cabrera's successor. Carlos Herrera rose to power with a coalition of conservative and liberal politicians dubbed the Unionist Party because it also wished to work towards a reconciliation of Central American Republics. Despite Herrera's refusal to resort to oppressive tyranny to squelch opposition and his obvious attachment to constitutional measures and even a form of democracy, he quickly angered U.S. interests. He was particularly opposed by Electric Bond and Share and IRCA because of his attempts to cancel a number of disadvantageous contracts with them.[31] Consequently, despite the rhetoric of attachment to constitutionalism, the United States immediately recognized General José Maria Orellano when he overthrew Herrera and the Unionist Party in December 1921.

After this brief hiatus with a more democratic system, Guatemalan politics were flung back into a familiar mode. Orellano, a typical *caudillo* with extensive connections in the Liberal party, employed the familiar tactics of tyranny and concessions to foreign entrepreneurs. On one hand, General Jorge Ubico, Orellano's Minister of War, dealt harshly with unrest, killing perhaps 290 political opponents before Orellano's death in 1926. On the other, Orellano reversed all restrictions Herrera had placed on foreign capital in Guatemala. In May 1922 Orellano granted Electric Bond and Share its former monopoly concession and a year later generously broadened the existing concessions to IRCA.[32]

Orellano's heart attack In 1926 prompted an electoral battle between the Liberal Lázaro Chacón and Jorge Ubico, who fronted a Liberal Progressive Party. Ubico, perceived to be radical, frightened the traditional Liberal Party machine and Chacón easily obtained the presidency.

Chacón and the Liberal congress immediately proved amenable to the increasingly powerful U.S. interests in Guatemala. In February 1926, congress passed a complicated bill which, in effect, made it impossible to strike. But the allegiance between Chacón and U.S. interests was most obvious in dealings with the United Fruit Company. In 1930, Chacón forced the European-controlled Guatemalan Plantations Ltd. to sell its extensive holding on the Pacific Coast to UFCo's Pacific subsidiary, the Agricultural Company of Guatemala, at very generous terms. In return, UFCo was to expand and operate a port at San José on the Pacific Coast.

As the United Fruit Company monopoly became more and more obvious throughout the 1920s, elements of the indigenous business elite fought its growing dominance. While Chacón maintained friendly relations with Minor Keith, congress was stiffening opposition to UFCo's western expansion. Chacón's administration, according to historian Kenneth Grieb, was characterized by a "sea of indecision . . . and by progressive disintegration within its womb."[33] It was unable to force its will on the recalcitrant congress and a cadre of indigenous elite who opposed the fruit company. The campaign by Chacón and the UFCo together to push the company's western expansion fostered growing enmity. When Dr. Eduardo Aquire Velasquez, influential owner of the Guatemala newspaper *El Excelsior,* criticized the proposed contract, he became a target for UFCo machinations. The fruit company forced a bank from which Aquire had drawn a longstanding loan to demand immediate repayment. Aquire was unable to do so, the bank foreclosed and the paper shut down.[34]

With opposition to both Chacón and UFCo domination growing, the president suffered a permanently incapacitating stroke in 1930. This fortuitous occurrence allowed for the imposition of General Jorge Ubico as president and, through his vigorous domination of all political life in the country over the next 13 years, the stifling of opposition to the banana empire and its west coast expansion.

The Rise of General Jorge Ubico Casteñada

GENERAL JORGE UBICO Casteñada was intimately connected to the traditional elite in Guatemalan society. As the product of a wealthy landowning family, he enjoyed the patronage of his godfather, Justo Rufino Barrios. Although not a particularly distingushed student in the military academy, his connections helped him to get a commission under Cabrera. Ubico served well and became a full colonel by the age of 28.

While *jéfe politico* of Alta Verapez, Ubico implemented a number of impressive reforms, particularly in expanding transportation networks in the department. However, attempts to increase his control over the district brought him into conflict with the powerful cadre of German coffee planters. Influenced by the German planters, Cabrera removed Ubico from the department.

It was as *jéfe politico* of Retalhuleu and, later, as head of the National Sanitation Drive that Ubico demonstrated his genius for organization, caught the attention of American diplomats and was catapulted to national prominence. In the border district of Retalhuleu, Ubico imposed stringent law and order decrees, ostensibly to prevent the spread of unrest that was engulfing neighbouring Mexico. Ubico's campaign resulted in the death of hundreds of Mexican refugees fleeing to Retalhuleu, only a tiny few of whom could possibly have been the bandits he was obsessed with. He also initiated a variety of measures to encourage agricultural diversification and better marketing of products. His term as *jéfe* of Retalhuleu demonstrated the attributes that would later determine the temper of his years as president: a brutal obsession with stability and a penchant for administrative detail.

His vigorous measures to eradicate the spread of epidemic diseases while chairman of the National Sanitation Drive brought him to the attention of the American legation, which was impressed with his efficiency. It also helped develop a following for him among university students who were searching for political alternatives to the incompetent administrations that had predominated for the previous decade.

Although Ubico was not involved in the coup that overthrew Herrera, Orellano chose the rising star as his minister of war. Enjoying widespread support among officers, he demonstrated his customary efficiency and brutality before resigning from the Orellano government in a dispute over the military budget.

Ubico then began to court the political sympathies of a new generation of University of San Carlos students and formed the Liberal Progressive Party from among leading student politicians. After Orellano's heart attack in 1926 Ubico translated this support into an effective campaign to succeed him, declaring that the Progressive Party would replace the older Liberal and Conservative parties, which were "deaf to the loud incessant voices of evolution".[35] Ubico built the Progressive Party around an organization of student reformers called "the generation of 1920", which traced its origins to outrage at the lack of governmental assistance to those stricken by the 1917-18 earthquake, which "not only shook the earth but jolted consciences".[36] Their outrage went only so far, however, as to advocate a number of mild reforms. Influenced by the work of José Vasconceles, the Mexican education reformer, they started the Normal School for Indians and the Popular University of Guatemala to spread literacy among Indians and urban masses. Many promoted some form of land reform; others criticized foreign dominance and were viewed by the most reactionary of landowners as "Leninism brought to the tropics".

Most of these hesitant reformers held a traditional view of Guatemalan society, particularly of the role of Indians in that society. Most agreed with one American attaché's advice that "illiterate Indians ... who go to the polls without the faintest idea as to what they were doing and for whom they are voting" be disenfranchised.[37] Leading lights of the generation, such as Jorgé García Granados and Miguel Angel Asturias, argued a variety of remedies for Guatemala's social ills. While García Granados believed that much of Guatemala's history stemmed from the fact that the Spanish "had buried [Guatemala] ... in an immense tomb sprinkled with a few drops of holy water", he also urged the government to take away all communal land from Indians and "transport them in mass to the wilds of Petén".[38] Asturias' *El Problema Social del Indio* became the blueprint for a whole generation's assessment of the Guatemalan Indian. Asturias' perception of the "Indian problem" had changed little from that espoused by Liberals since independence. The Indian was "dirty, slow, barbaric and cruel", a condition resulting from "irredeemable debasement at the hands of conquerors". Miscegenation was a "wide door" that would allow the Indian to traverse from "his primitive social state to European civilization". It was also believed that this mixing of blood would result in a continual process of decline for the *ladino*. This defilement and the subsequent sad consequences for Guatemala could only be reversed by the immigration of large numbers of Europeans, particularly Swiss, Germans and Belgians.[39]

Accepted and repeated by a whole generation of professionals and students, this solution to the perceived problem of a large Indian population was remarkably similar to mainstream traditional liberal precepts. Thanks partly to the inability to break with prejudices long established in Guatemalan society, the theories of positivism — of Comte, Darwin and Spencer — "continued to enjoy favour in Guatemala ... long after they had become anachronistic in the rest of the world".[40]

Despite these solid roots in the tradition of positivist thought, the "generation of 1920" was held suspect by the landowning elite that dominated the Liberal party. The most reactionary Liberals saw Ubico surrounded by "apostles from the steppes of Siberia".[41] While a minority of the Liberal party was attracted to the ideas of the "generation", the students were sufficiently alarming to ensure a loss of support for Ubico and the appointment of Chacón as president.

After losing the 1926 election, Ubico retired to his *finca*. While he had attracted significant support from the University of San Carlos because of his reputation for honesty and administrative efficiency, his subsequent actions were to demonstrate clearly that he had no lasting commitment to student ideals. Hoping to translate the generation's new ideas into political power, he had made a colossal political blunder. After the election, he conscientiously reaffirmed his connections with the mainstream of Liberal adherents while remaining aloof from the increasingly inept Chacón government.

By the time of Chacón's stroke, Ubico had again floated to the top of an increasingly confused political cauldron. He had also carefully cultivated the approval of U.S. representatives in Guatemala. A consistently pro-American stance and a blossoming personal friendship with U.S. ambassador Sheldon Whitehouse meant significant support in his quest for residence in the Casa Crema.

Guatemala had a complex system of three presidential delegates who were to take power in a predetermined order upon the incapacitation of the president. But with Chacón's stroke, the first delegate was passed over and congress appointed the second. The latter, a conservative, was quickly overthrown by a number of military officers led by General Mariano Orellano. Orellano's claim to be acting solely in the interests of the first delegate could not be tested as this politician was killed in the coup: a death that allowed Orellano to press his own claim to the presidency.

Orellano ran into trouble seeking U.S. recognition. Faced with the steadfast opposition of the American ambassador, Orellano was eventually forced to accept congress' appointment of a new interim president, José María Reina Andrade, who called for elections to be held a month after his appointment. On American insistence, all those who had participated in the Orellano coup were not permitted to campaign.

The relationship between the U.S. delegation and Ubico during this crisis was critical. When Orellano seized power, Ubico immediately sought protection in the American legation, where the U.S. chargé McCafferty demanded a guarantee of protection for him. While U.S. refusal to recognize General Orellano complied with the provisions of the 1923 Peace and Amity Treaty and, according to ambassador Sheldon Whitehouse, was designed to "have a salutory effect in dampening the enthusiasm of ambitious generals in Central America",[42] it fit the needs of Ubico (and the UFCo) wonderfully. On numerous occasions the U.S. administration had shown little real attachment to the terms of the treaty. Yet in this instance the United States virtually imposed Reina Andrade on the Guatemalan congress and insisted on quick elections. This too played into the hands of Ubico. Since his defeat in 1926 Ubico had carefully cultivated his contacts and maintained the organization of his now moderate Liberal Progressive party. There was simply no one who could furnish competition in time for the hasty election, particularly since the strongest opponent, Adrian Recinos, was out of the country on a diplomatic posting. The American delegation was well aware of this. Ambassador Whitehouse informed the State Department, "If elections are held soon [the opposition] have no possibility of beating Ubico as they have no candidate."[43]

This apparently suited the Americans. Reports from members of the mission to the State Department shortly before the elections on Feb. 6-8, 1931, rang with praise for Ubico. The military attaché dubbed Ubico as "practically a military genius". The American chargé d'affaires reported that Ubico was "favourably inclined towards the U.S." The ambassador himself, upon Ubico's inauguration, commented: "It is gratifying to be able to say ... that Guatemala is as friendly with the U.S. as any Latin American republic, and perhaps is the friendliest."[44]

Ubico's presidency would also suit the United Fruit Company. The 1930 contract for its western lands was still meeting stiff opposition in congress and UFCo needed both a friendly and powerful president able to override congressional opposition. In any event, Ubico was the sole candidate in 1931. According to Joseph Pitti in his detailed study of this election: "The backdrop [to the election] was cluttered with copies of the 1923 Treaty of Peace and Amity, the shadow of the United Fruit Company, figures from the American legation and the spector [sic] of the economic depression."[45]

Ubico quickly justified the American expectations. According to one assessment, "Friendship for the U.S. was a hallmark of the Ubico regime, and the Guatemalan president prided himself on his self-assumed role as the staunchest ally in the Isthmus."[46] Trusting no one in his own government, Ubico developed close relations with members of the American legation and U.S. business leaders, who formed a "tennis cabinet" to advise him. He also immediately grasped dictatorial control over the country. The supreme court was forced to resign en masse and was staffed with political allies. Most importantly, opposition to the 1930 contract with UFCo was completely stifled.

According to William Krehm, a *New York Times* Central American correspondent at the time, "The UFCo obtained its concessions and Guatemala a fitting successor to Cabrera."[47]

Ubico in Power: Repression and "Honest" Government

UBICO TOOK OVER the presidency at a difficult time. The depression hit Guatemala, a commodity exporting country, particularly severely. By 1932 Guatemalan exports had fallen to 40 per cent of their 1929 value and especially hard hit were coffee exports, upon which the government relied for most of its revenue.[48] In addition, the Ubico government inherited a debt of over $5 million in loans and unpaid bills, with interest payments that threatened to gobble up nearly all government income. Teetering on the brink of bankruptcy, the economy in shambles, with a government bureaucracy mired in graft and riddled with corruption, the economic future appeared bleak.

Ubico performed near miracles with government and fiscal reform. A determined campaign against corruption at all levels of government and harsh treatment for those suspected of lining their pockets through their government positions created perhaps the most honest administration Guatemala had yet seen. Ubico aggressively pushed for an expanded market for Guatemalan coffee. He implemented new taxes to ease the government's financial shortfalls in the United States and signed a trade agreement that allowed coffee and bananas into the United States free of duty. In the process, however, he was forced to abandon trade agreements with Germany, Italy and Great Britain effectively tightening U.S. trade and capital dominance in Guatemala. Of course, the major benefactors of the duty reduction on coffee and, particularly, on bananas were the United Fruit Company and Great White Fleet. By 1940, 90 per cent of Guatemalan produce was being sold in the United States.

In an attempt to reduce demands on foreign exchange, Ubico fostered agricultural diversification. During the 1930s corn cultivation increased by 500 per cent and the rice harvest went up by 700 per cent. An energetic program of road construction, carried out at little cost with forced labour, linked many previously isolated villages to the national economy. The success of this road building campaign was commented on by the British Overseas Trade Commissioner, who in 1930 had warned potential investors that large areas of the country were left untended by a traversable road. However, in 1937 he reported: "Roads in Guatemala have been vastly improved during the last five years and, with exception of Puerto Barrios and the remote department of the Petén, almost every part of the country can be reached by car in comparative comfort."[49]

This road-building campaign accounted for much of Ubico's renowned popularity in the countryside. It not only aided the economies of many smaller towns but also facilitated Ubico's constant personal tours during which he visited areas of the country that had never before seen ranking government officials.

But throughout this period of fiscal and economic reforms, Ubico remained the steadfast ally of the United States and benefactor for *el pulpo*. He forced the 1930 contract through congress despite opposition. In 1936, he extended the generous terms of the 1924 agreement to last until 1981, and removed the obligation of operating a Pacific port (construction of which still hadn't begun) from the 1930 contract. When Ubico attempted to raise the tax on banana exports by one-half a per cent, he garnered ready acceptance from the company in return for generous extensions of IRCA rail concessions and the promise that IRCA could set its own rates free of government interference.[50] In 1936, he cancelled a claim for compensation demanded by IRCA since the 1920s, a claim denied by all previous Guatemalan governments, by paying the rail company Q400,000. The president, labelled "a master of anti-inflation technique" by *Reader's Digest*, even urged UFCo to lower its already reduced wages from 70 to 30 cents a day, a suggestion readily seized by the company.

This string of attractive concessions granted to UFCo in 1936 was a reward for the company's support for Ubico's machinations to extend his term in office, due to expire that same year. Of particular significance for later events in Guatemala, these events also marked the entry into Guatemalan affairs of John Foster Dulles and his brother Allen, Secretary of State and CIA director respectively during the later Eisenhower administration. Acting as lawyers for the United Fruit Company, they were instrumental in framing the 1930 and 1936 contracts.[51]

In a history that abounds with eccentrics, Ubico stands out. A pathologically secretive man, he trusted no one and was close to no one. He once remarked to a reporter, "I have no friends, only domesticated enemies."[52] Believing himself to be a reincarnation of Napoleon and fascinated by the military, he surrounded himself with portraits of the "little emperor" and multiple replicas of cannons and soldiers. He advised the Guatemalan symphony to dress in military uniforms and selected the music and instruments they were to play. Ubico reformed the Escuela Politécnica, insisted on hiring a former U.S. military attaché to direct the school, and provided him with the rank of Brigadier-General in the Guatemalan military.

Never very attached to the forms of constitutional democracy, Ubico ruled Guatemala with a firm hand. Congress cowed before his will. Seeing conspiracy against him everywhere, he employed a complete system of spies and informants that permeated the whole society. A *New York Times* correspondent was amazed that "retired diplomats, visiting foreigners, people most incredible were spies for the detectives. The walls began to have ears."[53] Ubico lived in a fortress, constantly on guard for conspiracy in one part of the military or another and jealous of any officer who seemed to be attracting a following. The presidential palace, as *Time* magazine saw it, was "steel shuttered at every window, guarded by different uniforms at every corner, surrounded by army barracks and protected by anti-aircraft battery."[54] While Ubico's harsh measures to avoid corruption assisted in creating what was considered a relatively honest administration, the arbitrary justice meted out to subordinates discouraged decision-making and initiative. Thousands of employees lost jobs for minor errors; hundreds lost their lives for more serious mistakes.

Ubico regularly used repression to maintain power. The tyranny became most violent in the periods leading to his two campaigns for re-election. The Guatemalan constitution, like that of most Latin American nations, forbids presidents to seek immediate re-election. Attempts to circumvent this provision of the constitution invariably provoked intense opposition, although the principle was often violated. In 1934, gearing up for the end of his first term in office in 1936, Ubico began manoeuvres meant to insure his continuation in office despite the constitution.

Opposition to his expected attempt at re-election was widespread, engulfing even some members of the Liberal party. In 1934 Ubico "discovered" a purported plot to kill him and unleashed a "wave of arrests [that] encircled the city". According to one report, Ubico killed 300 people in two days.[55] This was followed by a "spontaneous expression of popular will" in the form of letters from all departments of the country urging his re-election. The letters were remarkably similar and carried more than a hint of "pre-arrangement".[56] Ubico also adroitly arranged an official statement of support for his presidency from the U.S. State Department.

Despite this "impressive" display of popular support, Ubico insisted on a referendum to truly gauge the popular will. When he received 834,168 votes in favour of his continuation and only 1,227 opposed, Ubico allowed the "tide of popular sentiment" to carry him back to office.

Safely ensconced in the presidency for another term, Ubico strengthened his grip on the country. In 1937 he registered all printing presses to stem the flow of opposition articles and manifestos. In 1938 he militarized all public schools to ensure that children received the proper instruction in obedience.

But when Ubico once again began measures to extend his presidency he faced more opposition than in 1936. The most serious concern was an American delegation that had turned from ostentatious support to rather lukewarm acceptance of the tyrant. In order to guarantee U.S. favour, Ubico began to take action, under pressure from the U.S. War Board, against German planters in the Alta Verapaz and Cobán.

German coffee planters had long controlled the bulk of coffee production in Guatemala. By 1940 there were 5,000 of them, owning 109 plantations (72,932 hectares) and accounting for the bulk of Guatemala's exports. For half a century these planters had enjoyed an integrated, efficient, commercial empire established through their control of coffee plantations, marketing facilities and banks. They dominated both business and politics in the department of Alta Verapaz and its capital, Cobán, and according to sociologist José Aybar de Soto "formed a tight, cohesive subculture maintaining dual nationality".[57]

As the United States became involved in World War II, it pressured Ubico to act against these planters. Ubico had always demonstrated admiration for the German fascists and resisted this demand until 1941. However, as part of his second campaign for re-election he confiscated all German property and sent German settlers off to internment camps in North Carolina and Texas: a move designed to win U.S. approval and to help him overcome opposition to the extension of his presidency for yet another term. After he began his third term, an obsequious congress voted him a gift of Q200,000 for his contribution to the country. Further "donations" made him the third largest landowner in the country.[58]

Ubico and the Peasantry

NUMEROUS OBSERVERS HAVE commented on Ubico's popularity among the rural masses. Indeed, his occasional trips to isolated villages, his charismatic public meetings and his frequent personal interventions in response to petitions from villages garnered significant support. Ubico cultivated an air of paternalism while extending his control over all areas of the country. He replaced the prevailing system of elected *alcaldes,* or town mayors, with *intendentes,* or managers, appointed by and answerable only to himself. His practice of arbitrarily replacing these *intendentes* in response to complaints from villagers created the impression that he was prepared to respond to popular will. In addition, the decline in export prices that accompanied the depression and the previous extensive spread of coffee cultivation ensured that during his presidency there would be little impulse for further encroachment on village land.

Ubico's measures in office indicate little concern for the lot of peasants, however. Shortly after assuming the presidency Ubico announced that he would offer a substantial amount of free land to anyone who wished to farm and was willing to move to the lowland where land was plentiful. Whether this offer was serious or not, immediate complaints from landowners concerned about the potential loss of labourers prompted Ubico to quickly withdraw the proposal.

In 1934, Ubico abolished the system of debt peonage. While this theoretically allowed peasants to choose between competing employers and increased rural wages for a brief period, it did little to improve the lot of the highland peasant and was not meant to challenge the economic position of the landowner. For a number of years plantation owners had been clamouring for a more efficient system of recruiting labour. Debt bondage was not particularly effective and proved costly in the initial outlay of cash required to entrap the worker. Ubico replaced debt bondage with Decree Law 1996, the Vagrancy Law.

It was the responsibility of citizens to work productively, Ubico argued; freedom lay in choosing for whom you worked. Thus the Vagrancy Law required landless peasants to work for an employer 150 days a year while those with some land were required to work 100 days. The vast majority of the Indian population of the highlands and most of the *ladino* peasants were required to work for over three months of the year, enough time to ensure labourers for the harvest. A record of days worked was to be kept by all peasants, with notations made by landlords and periodically checked by the rural police force. Because it was the responsibility of peasants to ensure they had worked the sufficient number of days, the system was open to abuse. While the Vagrancy Law provided a more efficient system of labour recruitment for the landlords, it also helped extend centralized control over village communities and plantation labour. Peasants who had not worked the proper number of days were often put to work on road construction and other tasks, so the law also provided Ubico with a ready supply of cheap labour for the ambitious public works projects he carried out. While never truly challenging the authority of the wealthy landowners, the new law did begin to reduce their feudal-like domain over rural workers.

The power of the landlords was buttressed by a 1943 law that allowed them extensive privileges in defending their property, granting them the right to shoot poachers or anyone else damaging property. In effect the law gave landlords unrestricted authority over the *finca,*

finca workers and those living in villages on *finca* land. At the same time the law suited Ubico's penchant for "law and order".

Ubico shared many of the distorted images of Indians and peasants common to positivist thought and the ideas of the Liberal Progressive party. He felt the best way to begin integrating Indians into Guatemalan society was through conscription into the military and defended this belief by pointing out that they "come [to the military] rude, brutish, and with primitive origin, but they return learned, polished, with good manners and in condition to face life".[59]

For Ubico, Indians were particularly unsuited to politics. His *intendentes* usually came from Guatemala City and seldom stayed long in the community. They had little appreciation of village concerns but held absolute authority there. Self-government and limited village autonomy were submerged by Ubico's obsession with centralization.

Nor did Ubico believe that peasants had any role to play in national politics, which were best left to the easily controlled Guatemala City elite. When he was greeted in the village of Chinautla by Indians bearing signs declaring the formation of a Liberal Progressive Club of Indians, to be allied with his Liberal Progressive party, he warned: "It is not yet time for the Indians to consciously poison themselves with politics."[60]

It is difficult to determine the extent to which Ubico's reforms penetrated the villages. Anthropologist Kay Warren found that the oral history of the village of San Andrés divided the early 20th century into two epochs, the second of which began with the reforms of Ubico. Warren sees Ubico's measures that lessened the control of local landowners "as the first evidence of a split in social ideology between the government and the local *ladino* landowners". With the national government no longer seen as automatically supporting local oppressors, Indians began to organize locally to confront their demands.[61]

However, Robert Carmack, in detailing the history of a village in the Quiché highlands, argues that there was little difference locally between the Ubico period and that of Cabrera. While some of the links between dominant *ladinos* and subject Indians were broken, new ones were put in their place. Ubico installed new power brokers in positions of authority, people meant to orchestrate local support for Ubico and help him control the village. But generally the national government was no more responsive to peasant needs than those which came before it. As a consequence, during the 1940s local revolts broke out against Ubico's appointees.[62]

The Overthrow of Ubico

UBICO WAS NOT CONCERNED with changing the position of *ladino* and Indian peasants in Guatemalan society. None of his decrees significantly improved their condition. The common refrain throughout Ubico's administration was the extension of central control over all aspects of society. His measures in relation to debt bondage and village politics were designed to foster that end. These measures did, however, weaken the hold of some of the major landowners over peasants and labourers previously kept in a position close to feudal serfdom. But in centralizing control Ubico completely eradicated the surviving elements of *municipio* government and self-rule, leaving village authority under the autocratic control of *intendentes* sometimes informally advised by the remnants of village religious authorities.[63]

Ubico's other measures, mostly inspired as a means of attracting American support for his continued rule, completed the dominance of American monopoly capital over the economy, at the expense of both smaller European interests and indigenous elites not aligned with UFCo, IRCA and the Great White Fleet. That Ubico did not face greater opposition from competing members of the elite can be attributed to the fact that he did little to attack the economic position of the still dominant coffee producers (excluding, of course, the German planters). He also received significant support from those elements of the elite who relied upon the "unholy trinity" for their well-being.

But, like the ailing dictator in Gabriel García Márquez's novel *The Autumn of the Patriarch*, who sold the Caribbean to the Americans to stay in power, Ubico, hidden behind his wall of suspicion and paranoia, became more and more isolated from the winds of change that buffeted Guatemalan society. His personalized style of government became increasingly anachronistic. The level of tyranny grew as whispers of conspiracy against him abounded.

One by one his staunchest allies left him. A new generation of students ferociously opposed his undemocratic rule. A growing middle class of professionals joined them. Congress conspired behind his back. There were rumours of opposition within the once slavish military; he was opposed by young reformist officers, inspired by a world war they viewed as being fought for "freedom". With nothing left of the country to sell or mortgage, even his old allies from the U.S. mission seemed to desert him. In contrast to his close relations with Ambassador Whitehouse in the days of the "tennis cabinet", the new ambassador, Boaz Long, perceived Ubico's unstable position and strove to maintain a distance. It appeared that Ubico had arranged some illusionist's trick; he was suspended in the presidency without visible means of support. Finally, again like García Márquez's patriarch, there were only the rumours of his presence and the memories of his power to keep the vultures from the palace.

In 1944, in the face of violent student demonstrations and widespread opposition among the middle class and professionals, Ubico resigned his post to a military triumvirate and fled the country, condemning the "trickery" of the people he had ruled with terror for almost 14 years.

— 5 —
The Ten Years of Spring: "Spiritual Socialism" and the Capitalist Revolution

We are going to divest ourselves of the guilty fear of generous ideas. We are going to add justice to humanity and order, because order based on injustice and humiliation is good for nothing. We are going to give civic and legal value to all people who live in this Republic.
— Juan José Arévalo, on his presidential inauguration, 1945

THE 1944 OVERTHROW OF Jorge Ubico and, afterwards, the military triumvirate that succeeded him was accomplished by a near-spontaneous eruption of long-repressed political sentiment among students, professionals and young military officers. Inspired by the breezes of democracy and freedom that had wafted into Guatemala during the Second World War, these young political neophytes, with little preparation and no experience, were called upon to establish a government.

The government and society they proposed was to be drastically altered from that which had preceded it. As students, they naturally chose a teacher, Juan José Arévalo, for president. Arévalo and his successor, Jacobo Arbenz, headed governments that followed a course of accelerated reform, governments that faced constant attacks from conservative elements within the society — landowners, the church and parts of the military — and clung tenaciously to power. In the process they affected a wide spectrum of change touching all aspects of life in Guatemala.

The ethos of the Guatemalan "revolution" was decidedly capitalist. Arévalo and Arbenz were determined to create within Guatemala a modern capitalist economy, breaking down what they perceived to be the lingering remnants of feudalism. The character of the revolution was also nationalist and democratic. Despite a tenuous hold on power, the revolutionary governments abetted widespread political activity, encouraged political organization in the villages and were less inclined than previous governments to manipulate the electoral machinery. Arévalo and Arbenz also believed that a capitalist transformation required control over the type and extent of foreign investment in the country. They were determined that foreign enterprises, particularly the United Fruit Company, be subject to the laws of the nation.

The revolutionary government faced many opponents from both within and outside the country. Aware of the dangers this opposition presented, the Arévalo government stepped gingerly around the issues of most controversy. Consequently, little reform was attempted in the countryside, and there was little alteration of the prevailing land-holding system. Arbenz, building on the success of the Arévalo administration, confronted the question more directly by passing the Agrarian Reform Law of 1952: a measure that solidified the opposition and doomed the "ten years of spring" to an untimely death.

The 1944 Revolution

IN THE LAST YEARS of Ubico's regime, ideals of democracy and economic modernization shook Guatemala. The 1930s and early 1940s witnessed the growth of a small middle class of businessmen, professionals and students. Economically constricted, members of this group formed "an insoluble lump" that resented Guatemala's backwardness and their own inability to carve a viable niche out of that society.[1] They were also impressed by American war propaganda, which spread throughout Guatemala in the early 1940s when the Americans established a base there and stressed that the battle was being fought for the basic "four freedoms". To many Guatemalans, the rule of Jorge Ubico too closely resembled the European and Japanese fascist dictatorships they were now joined in struggle against.

Students initially organized the opposition to Ubico. Students' associations had been vigorous during the brief democratic opening that followed the overthrow of Estrada Cabrera early in the 1920s. Attacked relentlessly by Ubico, they revived slowly during the late 1930s. By 1942 law students at the University of San Carlos had formed a society, which in 1943 was joined by an overall organization of students, the Association of University Students.[2] In 1944, university students in El Salvador unsuccessfully attempted to overthrow Ubico's contemporary, General Maximiliano Hernández Martínez. Immediately after the failure of the coup many of these students fled to Guatemala to seek solidarity at the University of San Carlos. When, in the following month, students, teachers and workers successfully forced Hernández from office, Guatemalan students joined in the celebration.

Alarmed at the extent of organization among the students, Ubico attempted to replace the dean and secretary of the university with allies who could be trusted to repress student activism. The students, angered by this attack on cherished university autonomy, organized a series of strikes. Ubico initially answered with violence and recalcitrance. On June 25, the cavalry charged a group of strikers, injuring many of them and killing one young teacher.[3] In response to the increasing opposition Ubico warned: "While I am president, I will not grant liberty of press nor of association, because the people of Guatemala are not prepared for democracy and need a strong hand."[4] The tide of protest continued to grow, however, and student demonstrations shook Guatemala City.

In Guatemala during the 1940s most students attended university part-time over a long period of time while continuing to work at their professions. Because of this they often occupied positions of significant prestige within their professions and formed a potent political force.[5] It is not surprising, then, that the striking students were joined by professional associations.

Finally, on July 1, 1944, faced with an extensive petition from some of Guatemala's most respected professionals and business people in solicarity with the strikers, Ubico resigned, handing over power to a military junta composed of three generals. The junta initially promised elections; But General Federico Ponce Vaídes, quickly dominating the junta, ordered congress to appoint him provisional president and threatened to forestall the elections. Ponce, described as an "old, retired skeleton with a drinking problem",[6] had once been dismissed by Ubico for excessive cruelty. He was widely thought to be manipulated by Ubico, and opposition to this *Ubiquismo* without Ubico soon mounted. Students and professionals organized a broad-based Civic Union and again began a series of demonstrations, planned a general strike and were attempting to obtain arms when their leaders were arrested.

Finally, cadets from the Escuela Politécnica, the Guatemalan military academy, and members of the military Honor Guard based in Guatemala City joined students in a revolt that forced Ponce's capitulation after a bloody battle. During the battle Captain Jacobo Arbenz, until recently commander of the cadet company, and Major Francisco Arana, commander of the Honor Guard, took control of the revolt and subsequently formed a junta with one civilian member.[7]

The reasons for the army revolt against Ponce were complex. The rigid regime of Ubico had relied upon the support of the military, especially the senior officers, and there was little indication that Ubico had lost that support. However, American military propaganda stressing the "four freedoms" and the obvious contrast between the efficient, professional U.S. troops and the muddled, archaic Guatemalan military had inspired a collective sense of inferiority. The obvious wealth of American soldiers in relation to the dismal position of lower-level Guatemalan officers fostered resentment — particularly among talented and bright officers like Arbenz, who faced little prospect of rapid promotion through the deadening ranks of the aging officers clustered around Ubico. A combination of personal resentment coupled with a desire for modernization, which included a democratic tendency, combined to prompt the revolt.[8]

The new junta held power only long enough to have a new constitution written and to oversee the presidential elections, often considered the fairest Guatemala had witnessed to date. Soon after, in 1945, the junta carefully and legally installed a new civilian regime under President Juan José Arévalo.

Arévalo and the Student Congress

THE YOUNG PEOPLE WHO worked feverishly towards elections in late 1944, casting suspicious glances at a military junta they did not trust, were not seasoned politicians. Joined in two loose political parties, the Popular Liberation Front (FPL) and the National Renovation (RN), these students and professionals quickly coalesced around the presidential candidate, Juan José Arévalo. At the age of 40 in 1944, Arévalo had spent the past decade in self-imposed exile in Argentina, where he had received his doctorate in philosophy and taught at the University of Tucumán. With the exception of a vicarious connection through his writings, he was unknown to most Guatemalans. According to one commentator, "Guatemala selected him the way one buys a lottery ticket. Guatemala did not know Arévalo nor Arévalo Guatemala."[9]

Arévalo did, however, fit the bill. He had opposed Ubico and was perceived to be a committed democrat and nationalist. Swept along by the enthusiasm of his student supporters, Arévalo easily won a lopsided victory over Adrian Recinos, a member of one of Guatemala's most prominent families.[10] Arévalo thus became head of a congress of political novices, predominantly students, with an average age of slightly over 35. At his inauguration early in 1945 Arévalo indicated clearly the direction he wanted his administration to take:

There has been in the past a fundamental lack of sympathy for the working man and the faintest cry for justice was avoided and punished as if one were trying to eradicate the beginnings of a frightful epidemic. Now we are going to begin a period of sympathy for the man who works in the fields, in the shops, on the military bases, in small business.[11]

Declaring that his ideas were based on those of Franklin D. Roosevelt, who "taught us that there is no need to cancel the concept of freedom in the democratic system in order to breathe into it a socialist spirit", Arévalo detailed a somewhat confused political philosophy based on the concept of "spiritual socialism". According to Arévalo:

> Like Liberalism, spiritual socialism will restore to the personality all of its civic and moral grandeur; but it will go further than Liberalism in obliging man to leave his isolated position to enter the sphere of social values, to embrace the needs and goals of society understood simultaneously as economic organism and spiritual entity.[12]

Arévalo and his disciples were not "material socialists". They did not believe in the primacy of an individual's worldly nature but, rather, in the importance of dignity. "Our socialism then," Arévalo explained, "does not embrace the ingenious redistribution of material goods based on a foolish economic comparison of man. Our socialism is to liberate man psychologically."[13] While recognizing the rights of the individual, the state was to serve an "aggregate of collective interests" and, henceforth, "Individual liberty must be exercised within the limits of social order."[14]

The first step of the revolutionary government was to devise a new framework for political life in Guatemala. The 1945 constitution, described as a "political manifestation of the repressed nationalist aspirations of the urban ladinos who were not members of the governing class," provided a list of political reforms. The constitution established new voting regulations and gave the vote to illiterate males over 18 and to literate females. It prevented the president from seeking re-election. It called upon the military to play a completely apolitical role and to support the constitution. Finally it granted the right of association and guaranteed autonomy to the University of San Carlos, providing it with funding at the level of 2 per cent of the national budget.[15]

Arévalo next embarked on a series of health and social reforms. His administration established rural health clinics in isolated villages and started a number of projects to provide potable water. In the cities, White Cross clinics were set up and sewers installed in many poor neighbourhoods. These measures, coupled with higher income levels, insured that the mortality rate fell an average of 2.5 per cent per year over the ten years of spring.[26]

In April 1946, Arévalo passed a Social Security Law, establishing the Guatemala Social Security Institute (IGSS) and providing for injury compensation, maternity benefits and health care. In addition, the state was no longer to rely on military conscription as the primary

means of educating peasants. From 1946 to 1950, education expenditures rose 155 per cent. Schools were expanded, literacy campaigns
begun and by 1950 the Arévalo government was spending over $7
million on educational projects.[17]

In 1947, following long and bitter debates, the Arévalo government passed the Labour Code. Under the terms of the 1945 constitution, unions had been made free to organize and operate. The 1947
code, however, was a far-ranging and generous accord. It recognized
the right to strike and to collective bargaining, set minimum wages,
restricted child and female labour and legislated hours. In accord with
Arévalo's somewhat corporate perception of society and his view of
government as the arbiter between collective interests, the new code
established special labour courts to decide labour-management disputes. Significantly, workers were to be reimbursed for lost wages if a
strike was found to be the fault of management.[18]

As Arévalo's minister of labour explained, the government was
directed by the philosophy that: "A capitalist democracy ought to
compensate with the means at its disposal, some of which are legislative, for the economic inequality between those who possess the means
of production and those who sell manual labour."[19] Due to the generally sympathetic attitude of the Arévalo government and the
strengthened position of workers in disputes with owners, urban
wages increased 80 per cent during Arévalo's term in office.

Arévalo's commitment to democracy, evident in the 1945 constitution, was carried into the international sphere. He instructed his foreign minister, Munoz Meany, to propose at the Inter-American Conference in Mexico in 1945 that Latin American nations refrain from
recognizing undemocratic regimes. He recommended that "electoral
farce must be denounced like a veritable coup d'etat", and stressed:
"Democracy is not a private good that is subject to the caprice of each
American government. Democracy is a continental American value
and ought to be the backbone of the Continent."[20]

When the conference refused to support this resolution, Arévalo
broke off diplomatic relations with Spain, Nicaragua and the Dominican Republic. While arguing, "We should not meddle in the internal
affairs of other countries," he asserted his right ot refuse to "maintain
friendship with governments that have thus transformed republican
practices into those of monarchy".[21] The next year he began tacitly to
support the Caribbean league, a small group of primarily Nicaraguan
and Dominican exiles who actively sought to foster democratic revolution in those countries. While the league never amounted to much and
gradually faded from prominence, Arévalo's support and his actions in
the diplomatic sphere won him the undying enmity of dictators Anas-

tasio Somoza in Nicaragua and Rafael Trujillo in the Dominican Republic.

Consistent with his view of society as being composed of corporate elements, Arévalo sponsored a series of discussions among the various sectors of the Guatemalan economy. The first of these, held in the city of Escuintla, was designed as a means of increasing co-operation between government, business and labour through ongoing dialogue. Submissions were accepted from various sources, including the military and IRCA. From this discussion grew the National Institute to Encourage Production (INFOP). Capitalized with Q6.5 million, INFOP was designed to promote indigenous enterprises and to help direct development in a socially productive manner. Although viewed initially with some scepticism, according to the American economists Adler and Schlesenger it was soon "accepted by the business and financial community as a valuable and useful addition to the institutional framework of economic development" and was providing Q7 million annually in loans to private investors.[22]

Arévalo's Uneasy Power

THE ECONOMIC REFORMS INSPIRED by the Arévalo government, as widespread as they were, had yet to touch the bulk of the population. Until the government could force an alteration in the predominant system of land ownership the transition from feudalism to capitalism would remain incomplete. Arévalo's frustrated attempts to effect this alteration best demonstrate his government's tenuous grip on the reins of power.

In the agrarian sector, Arévalo was able to manage only a few minor reforms. In 1947 his government created the Agrarian Studies Commission to look into Guatemalan land ownership and use and to investigate agrarian reform in Switzerland, Italy, Mexico, Rumania and the U.S.S.R. The Commission would make its recommendations following a detailed census to be prepared in 1950. In addition Arévalo introduced a variety of colonization projects aimed at providing land in the sparsely populated areas of the country to peasants from the highlands. He abolished the vagrancy law and other coercive measures affecting rural labour passed by the Ubico government. A Labour Code passed in 1947 regulated rural employment but restricted the legal formation of rural unions to agricultural enterprises employing 500 people or more. By 1948 the restrictions on rural unions were removed. Finally, in 1949, after a hurricane had destroyed much of the corn crop, Arévalo put through the first Law of Forced Rental, which fixed the amount of rent that could be charged from a shareholder at 10 per cent of the yield. In 1951, after the death of the Chief of the Armed Forces, Colonel Francisco Arana, had weakened opposition, a new Law of Forced Rental was passed. This one reduced the rent to 5 per cent and extended the application of the law.[23]

Despite this plethora of decrees, the Arévalo administration scarcely touched land tenure in Guatemala. It did somewhat restrict the coercive power of landowners. The Labour Code and the abolition of the vagrancy law increased rural labour's bargaining position. A series of strikes on government-owned *fincas* starting in 1950 soon spread to large private estates, with the result that at least on many large *fincas* wages went from 5 to 25 cents a day to 80 cents.[24] The Law of Forced Rental strengthened the security of tenure for small farmers, particularly in the eastern districts where it was most frequently applied. Nonetheless, the pattern of minifundia-latifundia* remained intact and the bulk of the population in the highlands was left with too little land to provide for anything but the bare minimum of subsistence.

Arévalo was well aware of the importance of a fundamental agrarian reform in Guatemala. By 1945 there was an apparent need for a redistribution of land both to reduce inequity and foster increased national output. The long line of peasants who denounced both conditions on plantations and their bosses at the Escuintla meeting made the point obvious. It became increasingly so as a result of numerous studies done under the auspices of the Agrarian Studies Commission, particularly after the 1950 census was published.

However, Arévalo was also aware of the tenuous position of the revolution. The overthrow of Ubico had done little to alter the distribution of power, especially in rural Guatemala. Landowners still dominated the economy and while their parties did poorly in elections, they themselves maintained significant economic and political clout. Also, the democratic impulse within the military — which had helped prompt Arbenz to overthrow Ubico and held off a military coup while the government of Arévalo was being installed — was of a fairly ephemeral quality. The church, despite almost a century of Liberal rule, retained considerable influence and steadfastly opposed the "revolution".[25]

Arévalo was convinced that any impetuous attack against the pillars of reaction in Guatemala would bring the revolutionary interlude to an end. It was partly because of this perception that he approached

---

* These terms refer respectively to small farms (i.e. below 25 acres in size) and the larger, more extensive landholdings.

government with a "sufficiently ambiguous political philosophy which defied categorization".[26] As it was Arévalo barely clung ot power.

Of the three forces ranged against him — the landowners, church and military — the most serious challenge came from the military. During his time in office, Arévalo withstood almost 30 attempted coups, most of them emanating from active members of the armed forces. Despite the accord that Arévalo had wrung from 15 senior members of the military at the time of the 1945 constitution, their allegiance remained in doubt throughout the revolutionary period.

Military opposition grew as sectors of the press increasingly accused Arévalo of communist sympathies. Communism had long been used in Guatemala to defame any movement towards social reform. This tactic had gained particularly currency under Ubico, who routinely jailed "communists". Thus, to conservatives in Guatemala much of Arévalo's program smacked of "communism". Arévalo explained these attacks to a Guatemala City audience in 1946 as "an indefatigable campaign of your enemies, my enemies". He added:

> You know that for those traditional politicians, those of the dictatorial ilk, the president of Guatemala is "communist" because he loves his people, because he suffers with his people, because he is with the poor, because he supports the workers, because he refuses to co-operate with the illegitimate interests of the potentates, because he refuses to make deals with those who would corrupt his public function.[27]

Arévalo, of course, was not a communist. He said in one of his most publicized statements:

> Communism is contrary to human nature, for it is contrary to the psychology of man, which is composed of great and small things, of noble and ignoble desires, of high and low instincts, of capabilities and weaknesses, of frivolity and heroism. . . . Here we see the superiority of the doctrine of democracy, which does not seek to destroy anything that man has accomplished, but humbly seeks to straighten out crooked paths.[28]

Despite these sentiments and Arévalo's periodic attempts to suppress communist activities (which remained illegal throughout most of his presidency), those forces that opposed democratic reforms continued to paint him with the communist brush, and military conspiracy against his regime redoubled.

Arévalo probably survived these attacks because of the competition between Colonel Francisco Arana and Colonel Jacobo Arbenz. They were the two military officers most responsible for Ubico's overthrow, and Arévalo had rewarded them with roughly equal posts. Arana was the chief of staff while Arbenz became the minister of defence. In these two positions they carved out separate spheres of influence. Arbenz retained his support among the junior officers of the

Escuela Politécnica and carefully cultivated relations with the labour unions and other "democratic" sectors by supporting nationalist policies. Arana, jealously guarding his control over military promotions, was the more powerful of the two. He reportedly blocked the execution of a number of planned coups against the Arévalo government, but his commitment to the more far-reaching reforms of the revolution was tentative at best. Especially after the passage of the amendments to the Labour Code in 1948, relations between Arévalo and Arana became increasingly strained. In 1949 Arévalo complained: "In Guatemala, there are two presidents and one of them has a machine gun with which he is always threatening the other." Even the U.S. ambassador reported, "It is difficult not to attach significance to rumours that [Arana] is seeking the right opportunity and a reasonable excuse for a military coup d'etat."[29] Finally, in 1949, an embattled congress voted to impeach Arana on conspiracy.

However, on July 18, 1949, Arana was killed before he could be arrested. Opponents of the regime asserted that Arana was killed in a premeditated assassination attempt planned by Arbenz. Arbenz and others close to him maintained that Arana resisted arrest when his motorcade was stopped outside the city; when members of Arana's entourage opened fire on his would-be captors, Arana was killed in the exchange.[30]

Arana's death prompted the most serious challenge to Arévalo's government: a revolt by Arana's supporters in the military. The coup attempt, which left 150 dead and 300 wounded, was defeated only by the prompt action of Arbenz, who distributed arms to students and workers, and the continued support of the airforce. Following the revolt the government began a wholesale purge of the military, replacing close to one-quarter of the officers and promoting those who had proved most loyal. While there were less serious attempts later to overthrow the government, including one in 1950 led by Colonel Carlos Castillo Armas, the Arévalo government was never again seriously challenged by internal forces.[31] In 1950, the "defender of the revolution", Colonel Jacobo Arbenz, was elected president and Arévalo was able to finish his term in relative peace.

"At its lowest point," according to one American observer, the arévalo regime "appeared as a somewhat uneasy coalition of groups competing for the spoils of office while watching apprehensively over their shoulders for a military coup which would put an end to it."[32] Although his government accomplished much, Arévalo was well aware of how much was left undone because of the pressures that had encircled his government. When he left office on March 15, 1951, he was not optimistic about the eventual success of the revolution.

Prophetically, Arévalo's greatest concern was not for the forces of conservatism from within, but for how "perishable, frail and slippery the brilliant international doctrines of democracy and freedom were". He was mindful of the challenge to the revolution from outside of the country. Nonetheless, he recounted how:

> When I ascended to the presidency of the nation, I was possessed by a romantic fire. I was still a believer in the essential nobleness of man, as fervent a believer as the most devout in the sincerity of political doctrines, and inspired by the deep aspiration to help people create their own happiness. I believed that six years of government therefore were sufficient to satisfy the crushed popular aspirations and to create structures of social service denied the people by feudal governments. . . . To achieve this in Guatemala we had to combat the peculiar economic and social system . . . of a country in which the culture, politics and economy were in the hands of 300 families.[33]

Towards the end of his government, Arévalo's statements were imbued with a deep-seeded pessimism brought about by his government's inability to effect structural change in the Guatemalan economy. The fervour for reform that had inspired the student congress in 1945 had crashed headlong into a constant battle with conservative forces. But Arévalo had been able to serve out his term in power; the revolution had survived; and the necessary framework had been laid for more radical reforms. The revolution, however, still faced powerful enemies.

The Arbenz Administration

ARÉVALO'S POLITICAL PHILOSOPHY was well-known. Copious writings and numerous fiery, impassioned speeches detailed his beliefs and ideals. The second president of the "revolution", Colonel Jacobo Arbenz, proved much harder to define. Arbenz seldom put his thoughts to paper and his speeches were most often dry enunciations of specific policies, singularly devoid of the appeal to broad ideals that so often peppered Arévalo's addresses. This, in turn, had led commentators to speculate that Arbenz, lacking a political philosophy of his own, was controlled by other elements of the Guatemalan political landscape. Most often mentioned were his wife, Maria, and the "minions of international communism" which "stood poised" to use Guatemala as their stepping stone to the rest of Latin America.

This perception of Arbenz has also invited speculation that when the invasion occurred, the president gave in too easily, that in submitting to the demands of the military he failed to use the real support he had elsewhere, support that could have prevented the destruction of the revolution and ten years' work.

Yet, closer examination reveals that Arbenz was no one's puppet. Intelligent and strong-willed, Arbenz possessed a clearer understanding of the Guatemalan political situation than many of his advisors. His support for the communists who actively assisted his regime was neither one-sided nor unbalanced. His decision to give in to the demands of the military in 1954 was the only alternative to a bloody civil war. By resigning, Arbenz felt he could save at least some of the reforms instituted in the past decade from the combined onslaught of U.S. business interests, U.S. strategic interests and the agents of conservatism within Guatemala.

Arbenz became for many in Guatemala the "personification of nationalism and agrarianism". Under his direction the revolution, which up to his coming to power had been felt primarily in Guatemala City, was carried to the countryside. During his presidency the latifundia was finally attacked and the monopoly enjoyed by the United Fruit Company, the International Railways of Central America and Electric Bond and Share was most forcefully confronted.

Age 37 at the time of his inauguration in 1951, Colonel Jacobo Arbenz was firmly wedded to the military. He had known little family — his father had killed himself when Arbenz was young — and had been finally shunted off to the Escuela Politécnica. There Arbenz flourished. The Guatemalan military academy was a closed, insulated environment where cadets were encouraged to develop a heightened sense of loyalty to the institution and other cadets. It was during these years in the academy that allegiances were forged and important contacts for career advancement were made.[34]

Jacobo Arbenz was the cadet *par excellence*. One of the brightest, most popular students and a star athlete, Arbenz was well liked and often emulated by the other cadets. Graduating with the highest marks in the history of the academy, he returned there to teach and rose to the position of director before Ubico removed him shortly before the dictator's overthrow. Arbenz, the favoured product of the academy, epitomized the middle-class youth who increasingly sought careers in the army.[35]

While competing at a sports meet in El Salvador he met and later wed Maria Cristina Villenova, the daughter of one of El Salvador's wealthiest coffee families. Villenova's father had been one of General Hernádez's advisors during *La Matanza* — the massacre of peasants in 1932 — but Maria had proved of independent mind and had embraced the ideals of El Salvador's student activists. Her leftist leanings, which became more pronounced while Arbenz was president, appear to have influenced him significantly.[36]

Arbenz followed determinedly in Arévalo's footsteps but concentrated more exclusively on economic reforms. At his inauguration he declared:

> Our government proposes to begin the march toward the economic development of Guatemala, and proposes three fundamental objectives: to convert our country from a dependent nation with a semi-colonial economy to an economically independent country; to convert Guatemala from a backward country with a predominantly feudal economy into a modern capitalist state; and to make this transformation in a way that will raise the standard of living of the great mass of our people to the highest level. . . .
>
> Our economic policy must necessarily be based on strengthening private initiative and developing Guatemalan capital, in whose hands rest the fundamental economic activity of the country.[37]

Arbenz's drive for economic modernization was abetted by the various studies conducted under the Agrarian Studies Commission, the comprehensive census of 1950 and a report carried out by the International Bank for Reconstruction and Development. In fact, much of Arbenz's policy was based on the IBRD Report prepared by the head of the mission in Guatemala, George Britnell, an economist at the University of Saskatchewan.

Britnell's 1951 report called for, among other things, a variety of measures to increase agricultural production. These ranged from the stimulation of alternate crops, such as cotton and essential oils, to the more productive use of land and labour in the highlands, to settlement programs on the Pacific coast. The report stressed, "Any appreciable rise in Guatemala's standard of living can come only through improvements in agriculture." It pointed out:

> Many large landowners have the traditional attitudes of absentee landlords, content with one yearly inspection of their farms and interested only in the total amount of immediate cash income however ruinous the production methods used. . . . In the lower Pacific Coastal region, potentially one of the richest and with fairly adequate railway transportation, some of the best land has been held in complete idleness.[38]

The report detailed how the highlands needed to be oriented into the economic life of the nation to diversify crops and increase output. Moreover, it said that any successful policy of economic development "in the long view" needed to raise the standard of living of the bulk of the population: "The basic poverty of Indian highland agriculture permanently hampers not only any agricultural progress but the whole economic growth of Guatemala; for the Indian population constitutes the bulk of the potential internal market, without which industry cannot develop adequately."[39]

In keeping with Britnell's suggestions, Arbenz vigorously encouraged agricultural diversification. He supported the Controlling Office for Essential Oils established under Arévalo. He fostered sugarcane cultivation by establishing a minimum price for sugar. His most vigorous efforts went to promoting cotton production. A cotton producer himself, he moved to protect the crop from foreign competition by requiring local merchants to buy equal amounts of local to imported fabric and by setting up a marketing and purchasing board within the National Institute to Encourage Production (INFOP). Arbenz also expanded access to agricultural credit, provided INFOP with more resources and allowed the Bank of Guatemala a heightened role in financing indigenous development.

Arbenz was most concerned with increasing the economic autonomy of Guatemala. Consequently, in the early years of his administration the major focus of his government was the construction of the Atlantic highway and a new port at Santo Tómas, both moves designed to attack the IRCA and UFCo monopoly on shipping within the country.[40]

Arbenz also expanded the previous administration's nucleus of village schools, and had them focus more specifically on agricultural education. By 1953, the education budget was $11 million, or 15 per cent of the total national budget.[41]

Along with these aggressive economic measures the commitment to democracy apparently remained intact. Some observers questioned the fairness of the 1950 elections that brought Arbenz to power. But Arbenz's major opponent in the election was the eccentric ex-officer Miguel Ydígoras Fuentes, who enjoyed a considerable reputation for dishonesty and cruelty and was most widely known as Ubico's enforcer of the vagrancy laws. The two most powerful political parties, the National Renovation (RN) and the Revolutionary Action Party (PAR), joined in a coalition to support Arbenz. This Electoral Front received 60 per cent of the vote; Ydígoras and two other candidates divided the rest. Arbenz would have needed no fraud to defeat Ydígoras.[42]

Throughout the Arbenz administration, both congressional and local elections were energetic contests where a variety of parties competed for votes. In a 1953 study, the American political scientist Kalman Silvert reported that congress:

> remains the symbol of popular government and is often the scene of sharp conflicts of opinion, not only among the members, but between the members and the ebullient audience which crowds the galleries when important issues are at stake. . . . The result is often noisy, but clearly indicative that Congress is one of the most sensitive organs of the government.[43]

Local political contests in most localities were lively occasions with an increasing percentage of the population taking part. While in some municipalities the local affiliates of the political parties or the trade unions and peasant leagues determined candidates for the revolutionary parties, those selected were almost always popular local leaders who truly represented the will of the bulk of the population. Candidates in opposition to the government won election at all levels in municipal and national politics.[44] In addition the press was free to criticize the government, and the country's major newspaper, *El Imparcial,* consistently attacked all aspects of the government with impunity. The rare occasions when the police and the military overstepped the legal bounds given them in the constitution and denied legal rights to civilians were widely reported, vehemently criticized and generally quickly investigated and denounced by the government. Despite constant criticism, government and society operated with a measure of freedom and democracy new to Guatemala, and which would not be experienced at any time in the four decades following the overthrow of the Arbenz government.[45]

Organized Labour and the Ten Years of Spring

ORGANIZED LABOUR HAD NOT PLAYED a prominent role in the overthrow of General Jorge Ubico. But, as it quickly organized under the benevolent protection of the Arévalo government, it became an important element in support of the revolution. Nonetheless, labour was seriously divided throughout the decade, which reduced its effectiveness in defending the Arévalo and Arbenz administrations against opponents. Two umbrella organizations, one dominated by the teachers' union and the other by the union of railway workers, each held different views of the proper role for unions in politics. At the heart of the conflict was a dispute over the increasingly powerful position of communists in the union movement. By the end of the ten years of spring, however, labour was a more united force and had evolved as the key defender of the revolution. But this in itself caused problems for the Arbenz government, as its increasing reliance on labour for support led to escalating attacks from critics who complained of the influence these "communist" labour leaders had over the government.

Free of the rigid restraints clamped upon them by Ubico, a variety of labour unions emerged soon after the overthrow of Ponce. One, the union of rail workers employed by IRCA, the Syndicate for Action and Betterment of Railway Workers (SAMF), emerged as a full-fledged union immediately after Ubico's fall. Well organized, with 4,000 workers, it was the largest single union in Guatemala and initially dominated the labour movement. Later, in January 1945, teachers organized into the Syndicate of Workers in Education in Guatemala (STEG), which, with approximately 2,000 members, soon became SAMF's only effective opposition.

Initially organized with other smaller unions into the Confederation of Workers of Guatemala (CTG), the two unions soon came to loggerheads. The first secretary of the CTG, a SAMF member, opposed affiliation with the Confederation of Workers of Latin America (CTAL), which had links to the communist movement. But in 1945 the original SAMF-dominated CTG executive was voted out by a coalition headed by the teachers' union. The CTG now resolved to join with CTAL and organized the Clarity School which promoted adult education in a decidedly leftist and vaguely Marxist fashion.

The teacher-dominated CTG espoused a program of active involvement in politics, stating, "For us to speak about democracy, civil liberties, free civic institutions, is the same as saying better salaries, better houses and better clothing, better health and, in brief, a better life."[46] By necessity, in the perilous early period of the revolution, CTG set itself up as a staunch opponent of conservative reaction. The more radical elements of the CTG helped establish a Democratic Vanguard, which was to operate within the majority revolutionary party (PAR) and guard against co-option of its members by the agents of reaction.

In 1946 SAMF, which had grown increasingly uncomfortable with the activism of CTG, withdrew from the federation, taking nine other unions with it. They formed their own association, the Federation of Syndicates of Guatemala (FSG), which agreed "not to play party politics and to limit activities to the welfare of workers".[47]

The Labour Code of 1947, with its provisions for labour courts, an eight-hour day and (in 1948) the lifting of restrictions on rural unions, aided union organization immensely. By 1951, with the rivalry between SAMF and STEG abated, the General Confederation of Guatemalan Workers (CGTG) was formed, claiming 288 unions and 50,000 members. By the spring of 1952, FSG had been reconciled sufficiently to join CGTG and by 1954, CGTG claimed over 200,000 members.[48]

Throughout the revolutionary period Guatemalan labour organizations involved themselves intimately with politics and included a significant number of communists among their number. Both factors are easy to explain. The American historian Ronald Schneider, in his book *Communism in Guatemala*, suggests that:

> The outstanding characteristic of the Guatemalan Labor movement was its involvement in politics. Born as the product of a drastic political change and surrounded by enemies who refused to recognize its right to

exist, the Guatemalan labor movement could survive only by insuring the success of the revolutionary government and protecting it from continual plotting of the intransigent opposition.[49]

It had long been a common complaint of Guatemalan labour that it was dominated by communists. This was especially the case during the regime of Jorge Ubico. Political scientist José Aybar de Soto suggests that "Ubico's injudicious use of the word 'communist' to label anyone who opposed the government created a new socially accepted definition where being a communist characterized an individual who was anti-Ubico, anti-repression and pro-democracy."[50] This type of alarmist mislabelling continued throughout the revolutionary decade. Ronald Schneider, although openly anti-communist, concluded in his study: "By calling the labour code and agrarian reform Communist inspired, the anti-communists actually enhanced the prestige of the Communists among the workers and facilitated their efforts to identify themselves as the champions of popular demands."[51]

Guatemalan communists were, soon after the revolution, able to attract honest and dedicated adherents to their organizations. Throughout the decade some of these people were to prove themselves the most effective instruments of government policy. One such example, the Secretary of the CGTG, Victor Manuel Gutíerrez, did much to further the fortunes of labour in Guatemala. Scrupulously honest, Gutíerrez inspired innumerable disciples with his example of hard work and obvious dedication. But most importantly, Guatemalan communists achieved recognition and government support because they were, in the opinion of Arbenz, "willing to work with a fair degree of application and relative personal honesty".[52] They were also prepared to stay within the constraints of the constitution — a factor apparent in their tireless work around the Agrarian Reform of 1952.

Political Parties and the Communists

IN THE MUDDLED POLITICAL ATMOSPHERE of post-Ubico Guatemala, the attributes that Victor Manuel Gutíerrez brought to politics were particularly appreciated. Between 1945 and 1954 the revolutionary parties split into 20 different groups. Many of these parties were composed of, or at least dominated by, self-seeking individuals more intent on personal privilege than on producing a sound body of social legislation. For most of the period these parties were able to coalesce only temporarily around particularly significant crises. When the crisis was over, they would quickly splinter again. The political parties, dominated as they were by the middle class, became increasingly ineffective as the Arbenz administration passed legislation attacking the position of rural landowners and as rural unions became more and more powerful. Much of the middle class responded to this perceived radicalization of the regime by withdrawing their support for it.

This situation was aggravated by a conservative opposition, that consistently refused to take a responsible position within the legislature. The little political organization which did develop among the traditional elite was marked by a strident anti-communism and demonstrated a noted unwillingness "to serve, to stay within the rules and to formulate a body of policy".[53] Given this situation Arbenz performed a delicate balancing act, picking administrators and supporters from wherever he could find capable, dedicated men. He found these adherents not only in congress, but also in the labour movement and, most notably, among the only middle-class institution that could provide discipline, the military.

Communists obviously did not dominate the revolutionary regimes. Article 16 of the Constitution of 1945 forbade the participation of any party in Guatemala "which may form part of or act in accord with or in subordination to an international or foreign organization".[54] This provision was periodically applied to communists during the Arévalo administration. As a result, before 1950 the only political expression of the communists in Guatemala was the tiny Democratic Vanguard of the governmental PAR. Its sole representative in congress, José Manuel Fortúny, was temperate and not especially powerful. When belatedly Arévalo and then Arbenz allowed open communist organization, the Communist Party of Guatemala (PCG) was formed and began to publish its own newspaper, Octubre. In 1950, Gutíerrez split from the PCG and formed an independent workers' party. However, by 1952, the differences of the leaders had mended, and their organizations united into the Guatemalan Workers' Party (PTG).

Despite this newly forged unity, their important position within the labour movement, and their exertions in helping enact the agrarian reform, communists remained a minor political force in Guatemala. The PTG never had more than 4,000 members and at its height seated only 5 of the 58 elected deputies in congress.[55] No open communist was appointed to a cabinet post. Their position of leadership in the labour movement was dependent upon maintaining policies that were accepted by the rank and file of labour, most of whom were not communist. Clearly, even if they could wield labour as an effective political tool, the urban labour force was a tiny percentage of the Guatemalan population and any effort to organize rural workers or peasants effectively remained notably unsuccessful until the passage of the Agrarian Reform Law in 1952.

Throughout the Arévalo administration and the first few years of the Arbenz government little had been done to alter the prevailing landholding system in the country. An important body of social legislation had been passed, but the reforms were relatively minor, bourgeois reforms, primarily benefiting the middle class and a tiny percentage of the labour force. Arbenz's determination to extend and deepen the government reforms, by proceeding with an extensive agrarian reform, and the attendant unrest in the countryside provided a focus for escalating attacks both on the government and on the role of communists in the Arbenz administration. These attacks came from all sectors of the traditional, conservative forces in Guatemala, but in the end it was to be the Guatemalan military and the U.S. State Department that proved capable of overwhelming the revolution.

— 6 —
The Arbenz Administration: Agrarian Reform and the Counter-Revolution of 1954

> To recount the errors of the Revolution it would be necessary to write at great length. The chief one is geographical: to be in the zone where North American imperialism exercises its greatest influence. . . . The United States squashed a little butterfly that wished to fly a little more freely within the capitalist system. . . .
> — Luis Cardoza y Aragon, Guatemalan reform politician, NACLA interview, 1974

THE ECONOMIC MEASURES proposed by Juan José Arévalo and Jacobo Arbenz were of an obviously capitalist temper, many of them inspired by a Canadian economist reporting for the International Bank for Reconstruction and Development. At the same the atmosphere in Guatemala City and the functioning of government demonstrated a noticeable, even exaggerated, democratic air. Under the healthy atmosphere of the revolutionary regime, popular organization blossomed. Urban and rural unions abounded; congress pulsated with activity; the press criticized freely; and even in isolated villages, political parties vied for office. Wages increased both in urban areas and in the countryside and eventually agrarian reform began the tough task of redistributing land and rationalizing production.

Guatemala was being pried loose from the grip of coffee and banana export, from the United Fruit Company and latifundia and from dictators and the military. Despite this — or perhaps because of it all — the Arbenz government was continually and increasingly attacked both from within and outside the country. The impetus for opposition to Arbenz came from four basic sources: Arbenz's attempts to foster Guatemala's economic independence; his refusal to repress communist organizations: the military's intense concern over control of the countryside; and the moderate agrarian reform bill passed in 1952, along with the rural unrest that accompanied it.

The Agrarian Reform Law, 1952

IN HIS 1953 ANNUAL REPORT, President Arbenz argued that the "question of the Agrarian Reform Law has drawn the classical line in the sand: those who are definitely with the revolution are on one side; and those definitely opposed to the revolution on the other".[1] In many respects he was correct. The Agrarian Reform Law finally initiated the long delayed "revolution in the countryside" and began to alter significantly the basis of economic power in Guatemala. The law prodded the traditional conservative elements — landowners and church — into fervent opposition. The organization of peasant leagues in connection with the law aroused concern among the military officers. And the reform threatened the holdings of the United Fruit Company.

The key members of the government shared Arbenz's enthusiasm for agrarian reform. In 1951 the secretary-general of the Revolutionary Action Party (PAR), then the major government party, declared:

> The realization of agrarian reform through the abolition of latifundias and the distribution of land to the campesinos who work it . . . is the fundamental prerequisite for all the economic, political and social reforms of the October Revolution. No democratic conquest will be stable or permanent without the previous achievement of agrarian reform. . . . Without the realization of agrarian reform, the sovereignty of the Republic will always be threatened and the people will continue to live in misery.

The Arévalo government did take some initial steps in extending the revolution to rural areas. The effects of the abolition of the vagrancy law used throughout the Ubico administrations were significant. While many inhabitants of the highlands still found it necessary to labour on plantations to subsist, the removal of compulsion allowed them increased bargaining power and took on a special symbolic importance. Shortly after the abolition of the law, one commentator who travelled extensively throughout the highlands noted that he was repeatedly told by peasants: "Now we are free. We are equal to ladinos. . . . No one can force us to work on a coffee plantation far away against our will. We will go only if we want to."[3]

The other decrees of the Arévalo government had more ambiguous consequences. The Law of Forced Rental in 1949 and its revision in 1951 provided increased security of tenure and allowed many peasants to rent land formerly denied them; but the changes were severely restricted in scope and application. A sympathetic attitude towards labour organization had inspired the formation of unions at the two United Fruit Company plantations in 1944 and unions were set up on the government-owned farms (national fincas). But the government requested that the organization of rural unions be postponed until after the promulgation of the Labour Code in 1947. This code then effectively restricted union organization to those few latifundia employing more than 500 workers. Consequently, labour and peasant organization in rural areas was minimal through most of the Arévalo administration.[4]

Rural unions and peasant leagues organized more quickly after the restrictions on rural unions were eased somewhat with the revisions to the labour codes passed in 1948. But it was May 1950 before there were enough peasant unions to form the National Confederation of Peasants of Guatemala (CNCG). They held their first national peasant conference the following year. The CNCG, organized under the former school teacher, Castillo Flores, was initially an important element of the tiny Socialist Party. After Castillo Flores left the Socialist Party to join PAR, the federation adopted a careful non-partisan stance.[5] However, rural unions had little power and little effect until the publication of the Agrarian Reform Law.

The functioning of democratic government, the abolition of Ubico's *intendente* system and the activities of political parties in rural areas had differing effects in villages. One of the cardinal principles of the 1945 revolution had been the "abolition of the highly centralized control exercised by the previous regime". In keeping with this the 1945 constitution called for municipal rule to be directed by "autonomous county councils ... elected in popular and direct form." In some villages it appears the *principales* (the elders who had progressed through the various offices of the *cofradia** system) were able to continue dominating local government. These elders chose candidates for local offices from lists of men who had already performed the traditionally requisite duties in the various *cofradias*. They then presented local parties with slates of candidates that met the requirements of the village tradition. It is doubtful that candidates chosen in this manner, having been processed first by traditional authority, would be prepared to champion the interests of the disadvantaged, support such "radical" new organizations as peasant leagues, or promote substantial alteration in the economic structure of the village.[6]

In other villages, while the *principales* no longer retained sufficient authority to impose candidates for office, political parties either did not reach the local area; or they were forced to restrict their party platform to one side of traditional village disputes in order to win adherents, and could not be used to promote the local extensions of national policy.[7]

However, in other areas as early as 1946, candidates for office were using local affiliates of national political parties to escape tradi-

*See chapter 1.

tional obligations and gain new positions of local authority. In the village of Chinaulta, anthropologist Ruben Reina concluded: "Subjugated young and 'progressive' Indians who were predisposed to change, found a field for new expressions super-imposed on the conservative elements."[9] Three nationally linked parties were active in the village by 1951. Manning Nash, in a study of the village of Cantel, observed that seven elections held there between 1945 and 1954 were "events where real situations of political choice among defined and different organized political entities could be made". Finally, Kalman Silvert observed that by 1948, 22 of 45 Indian communities he studied had succeeded in electing Indian mayors. Silvert suggested that even in the more isolated communities political parties were becoming increasingly significant.[8]

In many villages, especially during the early part of the Ten Years of Spring, revolutionary political parties were often co-opted by the still dominant elite. Thus, a party that worked to implement reforms on the national level and enjoyed the support of the government would actually oppose those reforms on the local level and occasionally use the local civil guard or military commissioner to repress peasants and rural workers. This appeared especially to be the case with local affiliates of the Popular Liberation Front (FPL).[9]

In addition, rivalry between the revolutionary parties and between the General Confederation of Guatemalan Workers (CGTC) and CNCG fostered an obsession with petty squabbles that insured real progress in solving local problems would be difficult. Conflict between various municipalities over land, and between workers who lived on neighbouring *fincas* and village peasants, often broke out in a violence that dampened the reform ardour of the revolutionary organizations.[10]

One of the most serious problems for the revolution was that the urban politicians who organized political parties in most villages carried with them a distorted perception of rural communities, which ensured they did not recognize the predominantly class nature of the conflicts there. Thus, they often reinforced the interests of the traditional local elite, either Indian or *ladino*, because they too often saw the enemy solely as the *finca* owners or rich *ladino* merchants.[11]

Nonetheless, there were indications that real political contests were developing between parties grouped around significant economic interests in many villages. In a number of regions the caste nature (*ladino* vs. Indian) of politics was giving way to a clearer perception of class problems and the need for political co-operation in solving them. This process was aided immensely with the establishment of peasant leagues in most villages, bodies prepared to work with any local political party as long as that party demonstrated it had the interests of the peasants at heart.[12] With the passage of the Agrarian Reform Law in 1952, political activity in the villages intensified, new economic opportunities arose, and the process of political modernization accelerated.

In the partial paralysis inflicted on the Arévalo government by the reactionary elements within Guatemala, little of a positive nature was done to affect land tenure. However, the groundwork had been prepared and by 1952 those people pushing for agrarian reform were armed with a body of statistics and a bundle of studies. The National Indian Institute established by Arévalo in 1945 provided reports detailing land tenure and use, charging that the 32 largest *fincas* controlled some 1.7 million acres, of which over 1.5 million were *not* cultivated. It also pointed out that extensive landholdings classified as latifundia cultivated between 5 to 25 per cent of their land, with the percentage decreasing as the size of the holding increased. Minifundia, on the other hand, cultivated between 80 to 95 per cent of their holdings.[13]

The 1950 census provided additional ammunition. The census showed that 2 per cent of the population controlled slightly over 74 per cent of arable land whereas 76 per cent of the nation's farms had access to only 9 per cent of the land. In a country where three-quarters of the population worked the land, this meant that 88.4 per cent of all farms possessed under 17 acres and fully 21.3 per cent were under 2 acres. At the time 9 acres were considered to be the bare minimum needed to support a family at poverty level. Tenants routinely paid 50 per cent of their yield in rent; in some areas that figure approached 66 per cent.[14]

It was originally intended that the Agrarian Studies Commission, under the direction of Mario Monteforte Toledo, would propose an agrarian reform for Guatemala; but Arbenz and the CNCG and CGTG supporters grew impatient with the seemingly endless rounds of study and evaluation. Consequently Arbenz presented his own scheme to congress, drawn from the recommendations of the IBRD report and the proposals of the CNCG and CGTG.[15]

Like Arbenz's other measures, the prevailing mood of the agrarian reform was capitalist. It was designed to correct some of the faults outlined by the recent studies. It would foster the growth of a class of small, capitalist farmers and be one more step in a progression that Arbenz and Arévalo had perceived as a journey from a feudal, dependent economy to an independent, fully capitalist one. Arbenz declared:

> Agrarian reform entails a process whereby the owners will be induced to work and treat agricultural farms as capitalist enterprises in both production methods and worker relationship. It is not our purpose to break

up all the rural property of the country that could be judged large or fallow and distribute that land to those who work it. This will be done to latifundia but we will not do it to agricultural economic entities of the capitalist type.[16]

As proposed, the agrarian reform was a moderate attempt towards more efficient use of the land, to increase national output by depriving inefficient landlords of their excess land. This land would be given to landless Indian peasants who would cultivate it more intensively (as they had demonstrated a propensity to do). Under the terms of the law the bulk of the land made available for resettlement would be on the Pacific coast, which had been singled out by IBRD researcher George Britness as particularly needing rationalization. The law, Decree 900, called for expropriation with indemnification based on self-declared values for the 1950 tax assessment. *Fincas* under 219 acres in size would not be touched, nor would those between 219 and 488 acres when three-quarters of the property was under cultivation. Landholdings larger than 488 acres would lose a portion of their unused lands. The state would pay for the expropriated land in the form of government bonds bearing interest. These bonds would be amortized over a varying period of time depending on the value of the expropriated land. In order to reduce the economic impact on the smallest of the landholders affected, those landlords with bonds worth Q100 or less would have their bonds amortized at 50 per cent per year; between Q100 and Q1,000 the figure was 25 per cent per year; and so on until the largest landowners would be paid back at the rate of 3 per cent per year.[17]

The agrarian reform quickly began to reshape economic and social relations in the country. By June 1954 over 917,659 acres had been expropriated from slightly over 1,000 of the country's largest *fincas*. Under the program land was distributed to 87,589 individuals, at an average of 10.5 acres each. In addition, of 107 national *fincas*, 61 were divided among 7,822 small farmers while another 46 were turned into full co-operatives. Thus, by the time of the coup in 1954, just one and a half years after the first expropriation, over 100,000 families (or 500,000 individuals) in a population of slightly over three million had benefited from the reform.[18]

Along with the distributed land the Arbenz government provided access to credit through the National Agrarian Bank. By June 1954 the bank had provided $8.5 million to individual farmers at an average of $188 per person.[19]

In a remarkably short period the agrarian reform had altered the prevailing economic structure more profoundly than anything else in the previous century of Guatemalan history. Over 100,000 landless peasants (most of them Indian) had received a valuable farming unit. Just as important, traditional reliance upon the usurious moneylenders who operated in the highland villages, locking peasants into an ever deepening spiral of debt, was broken with access to government controlled credit. By the time of the harvest in late 1953, plantation wages, as the result of the decreased labour supply, were over $1 per day.

While no transformation of this scope could be attained without some serious problems in production, Guatemalan plantation agriculture showed few signs of serious disarray. A Guatemalan economist, José Luis Paredes, calculated that the 1953 harvest of corn increased 11.8 per cent over the 1950 harvest; the harvest of beans increased 14.3 per cent; and the harvest of coffee, the major export crop, had risen in response to the threat to uncultivated land and rising world prices.

In addition, Paredes' analysis of the prices received for *fincas* sold after the Agrarian Reform Law was promulgated indicates little panic selling and relatively stable prices for agricultural land. Whatever the political response of Guatemalan landowners to Decree 900, it is clear that its economic effects produced little panic and that it was well on the way to achieving the desired goals. While the increased social spending occasionally produced shortfalls in government income, a glance at the economic conditions of Guatemala at the beginning and end of the ten-year period indicates substantial improvement.[20]

	1943	1953
Population	2,368,662	3,029,155
Gross National Product	131,613,600	558,281,300
GNP per capita	55.56	180.55
Public investment	2,981,500	29,294,700
Internal private investment	3,931,400	38,669,800
Exports	20,154,242	107,794,300
State receipts	14,671,200	65,266,100

Source: Memoría del Banco de Guatemala 1953, 1954, and Estudio económica para America Latina, 1953).

The Politics of Agrarian Reform

THE IMPLEMENTATION OF THE AGRARIAN REFORMS was designed to function from the grass roots up. Local agrarian committees were formed in almost all localities, and three of the five members in those committees came from either the CGTG or the CNCG. These local committees responded to denunciations (appeals for land to be expropriated and divided up) of *finca* land; these appeals usually originated from the peasant league or the rural union. The committee was then required to inspect the denounced *finca*, and submit its report and recommendations concerning the amount of land and the percentage of land cultivated to the Departmental Agrarian Committee headed by the governor. The National Agrarian Commission and finally the president made the final decisions on expropriation. Appeals were to be directed to the National Commission or, as a last resort, to the president himself.

Article 98 of the law decreed that the regular courts had no power to decide matters pertaining to the reform. Specifically, they could not rule on landlords' appeals. The first serious test for the reform came in 1953 when the Supreme Court narrowly voted in favour of reviewing the case of one landowner whose appeal had been turned down by the Commission and Arbenz. The Supreme Court's decision temporarily threw the reform process into disarray and prompted a storm of protest and letters of support to the president from the peasant leagues, revolutionary political parties and rural unions. Arbenz finally dismissed the four judges who voted for the landowner. This prompted its own storm of protest, mostly from the landowner's association and from the Law Student Society at the University of San Carlos.[21] Complaints soon abated, however, and the reform was able to progress. By late 1953 there were 1,497 local agrarian committees.[22]

The Agrarian Reform Law inevitably caused tremendous political upheaval. Peasant leagues and "revolutionary" political parties had been forming in villages for years before the law was promulgated, but the decree accelerated political organization while polarizing village society. Peasant leagues affiliated to the CNCG increased rapidly in number through 1952 and 1953 until in 1954 the CNCG claimed to have 1,785 local unions.[23]

The Agrarian Reform Law and the peasant leagues were understood only imperfectly in many villages. The professed intention of distributing land to those without it aroused the concern of the relatively more prosperous small farmers. Many of these people saw agrarian reform as a threat to their holdings and as a result shifted their support to more conservative local parties. In addition, the union often supported political parties which paid little attention to the religious and political structure of the community. The party members were often viewed as usurpers rebelling against ancient customs.[24]

The process of dividing up land expropriated from *fincas* caused enormous tension in rural areas. There was resentment from peasants who were judged to have too much land to benefit from the reform. There was conflict between *finca* residents who generally got first crack at expropriated land and nearby villagers. This conflict was heightened often because the *finca* workers were represented by the CGTG while the villagers were generally members of the CNCG. Finally there was conflict as *fincas* and even municipal land from one locality were given out to residents of the nearby *municipios*. Simmering resentment caused by four centuries of competition over land bubbled to the surface as the agrarian reform proceeded.[25]

Concerns about the agrarian reform increased because of the dominant position of radical politicians in its implementation. Organization in the countryside was difficult and, at times, dangerous. It attracted the most radical and the most dedicated of Guatemala's reformers. Many of these were communists or had links to the communist Guatemalan Workers' Party (PGT), the communist-linked CGTG or the radical CNCG. While not all CGTG or CNCG organizers were communists or communist-linked, most journalists and observers, foreign or Guatemalan, saw them that way.

Village organization was the scene of greatest success for the most dedicated of the country's reformers. Keith Monroe, a journalist who travelled through Guatemala in 1954, reported:

> When a poor man's shack burned down the communist rustled up some boards and tin and built him a new one. When an Indian child was sickly, communists rallied around with aspirins and hot water bottles. People who were hungry, or broke, or in trouble had virtually nowhere to turn... but they could always go to communist headquarters for tortillas, pennies, help and friendship.[26]

Prominent members of the CGTG and CNCG were appealed to by the poorest peasants for tiny favours, from medical care for their children to help in stopping a landlord from throwing them off land they rented. These petitions were invariably answered promptly and with sympathy.[27]

Fully cognizant of the activities and success of the communists in organizing for the agrarian reform, Arbenz accepted them as a legitimate political force. They made themselves invaluable to the process of land redistribution simply because they were, according to Arbenz, "precisely the most effective and those who do not sell out to the landlords".[28]

However, allowing the CNCG and CGTG organizers a relatively free hand in the villages had its disadvantages. The intent of the agrarian reform had clearly been to free land from the largest latifundia, primarily on the Pacific coast. But the most radical of the peasant organizers were not content to wait for latifundia land on the coast to be handed over. They inspired their members to a number of illegal land seizures of *fincas* close to their own villages. After pressure by local peasant unions and often from CGTG and CNCG members of the Agrarian Committees, these illegal seizures were occasionally allowed to stand.[29]

Despite the occasional excesses of union organizers and brief periods of heightened conflict in the villages, the agrarian reform never truly got "out of hand". Only 16.3 per cent of the country's total private, arable lands were expropriated, much less than eligible under the terms of the law.[30] Most members in the local peasant leagues were, according to sociologist Richard Adams, "fairly serious, locally rooted countrymen, who found in the *Union* a means for solving local problems as well as exercising a certain amount of political power".[31] The CNCG remained a supporter of the government rather than simply of the communist party, and the Department of National Agriculture (DAN) was in the hands of the moderate and loyal Major Alfonso Martínez. Final decisions over expropriation were made by Arbenz. There was no attempt at — or even suggestion of — socializing the land. The CNCG, CGTG and the government laboured to fulfill Arbenz's inauguration promise: create a more vibrant, more active and more prosperous capitalist country by extending and strengthening the position of small farmers throughout Guatemala.[32]

Yet the agrarian reform prompted escalating opposition to the Arbenz government from landowners, church and military. With the passage of Decree 900 the landowners' General Growers' Association (AGA) issued a strong protest to the government, ran newspaper advertisements criticizing the government's plan, and kept up a constant attack on the government. The AGA refused to join in the proposed National Council of Agrarian Affairs and began to support opposition parties more forcefully. Many of them began to form violent vigilante groups in the countryside, while others conspired to overthrow the government.[33]

The church hierarchy in Guatemala, always powerful, was implacably opposed to the changes. Its foremost spokesman, Archbishop Mariano Rossell Arellano, had been a strong supporter of Franco and the Falangist movement in Spain, and had encouraged Ubico in his support for the fascists.[34] Rossell attacked all aspects of the government's reform. He argued that democracy was not necessarily good for Guatemalans because "Sad experience shows that liberty left to the caprice of each individual only disorganizes [our people] into opposing bands, weakens them and begins to destroy them."[35] Rossell also criticized Arévalo's educational reforms: "Books are too fragile a staircase for our Indians to climb to civilization. One does not need, as a first step, literacy for Indians. What is essential is to redeem them." The official church newspaper, *Acción Social Cristiana,* in opposing the reform, stressed the need for social stability. Rossell's most harsh criticism was aimed at agrarian reform and the role of communists. In 1952 he dubbed Decree 900 as "completely communistic" and declared that the agrarian problem had been "provoked almost artificially ... in order to gain the vote of the illiterate". Finally, in 1954 he called on the people of Guatemala to "rise up as one man against the enemy of God, of the fatherland" against "the worst of the atheistic doctrines of all time, anti-Christian communism". Besides rather ironically declaring that inequality in Guatemala was "divine permission for the wealthy to be masters and fathers of the less fortunate", Rosseell and the church offered no constructive program for economic change in Guatemala.[36]

To help counter church criticism, the government responded by explaining the agrarian reform in religious terms. It reprinted an article by a North American Jesuit who explained that while "It is blasphemy to claim God has not provided man with material goods sufficient to enable him to lead a life of virtue and decency, [agrarian reform] is not a question then of scarcity of material goods causing millions of human beings to live in poverty and destitution. The problem is bad distribution and this problem is man-made." The government also circulated a book by Tulio Benitez entitled *Meditations of a Catholic before the Agrarian Reform*, which justified the changes through the writings of church spokesmen from Pope Leon XIII and Pius XI to the Dominican Friar Bartolomeu de las Casas.[37]

The Revolution and the Military

THE OPPOSITION OF THE CHURCH, although worrisome, did little to affect the progress of the agrarian reform in the villages, and did not pose a substantial threat to the government. Rather, the final defeat for the revolution came as a result of the military's refusal to defend Arbenz against outside aggression.

Elements of the military had been instrumental in the 1944 revolution. During the Arévalo administration many of the officers most opposed to the proposed social and economic reforms had been removed from their posts and had left the country. Under Arbenz the military had been allotted an increasingly influential role in government administration and the revolutionary governments had won military support through a whole list of perquisites, ranging from commissaries to subsidized housing, granted officers. As late as 1954, therefore, it appeared that the military was solidly behind Arbenz.[38]

Yet in many ways the military became the primary internal villain in the overthrow of Arbenz. Revolutionary movements elsewhere in Latin America have pointed to the Guatemalan experience as an example of the danger of not purging the armed forces before enacting reform; Arbenz's foreign minister has argued that the major failure of the revolutionary governments was in not proceeding with enough vigour in re-educating the military.[39]

According to the constitution, the armed forces were never to be "an instrument of arbitrariness nor of oppression". In 1945, 15 of the highest officers swore to "guarantee the reign of democracy on our soil ... and maintain the Army as a professional, worthy and absolutely apolitical institution".[40] Yet the Guatemalan military had accepted the revolutionary government only hesitantly, and Arévalo had to withstand 30 coup attempts during his presidency. Colon Elfego Monzón has argued that it was only Colonel Francisco Arana's loyalty in the early days that protected the revolution from an early demise. But Arana's plotting apparently led to the most serious challenge to the government: a challenge only successfully confronted because of Arbenz's support within the military and the actions of students and workers he was able to arm.[41]

Some analysts of the Arbenz government have pointed to an internal division in the Guatemalan military, one which became apparent during the revolt after Arana's death. Ronald Schneider suggests, "A new force was coming into control of Guatemala, an alliance of the young 'school officers' of the army with the extremist leaders of organized labour." This new force was supposedly opposed by the older, more conservative officers in higher ranks. Many of those officers had not attended the Escuela Politécnica and had attained officer rank during the rabidly anti-communist days of Ubico. Arbenz, the school's prize pupil, was the representative of the young "school officers".[42]

But a survey of officers done by Mario Monteforte Toledo in 1951 seemingly contradicts this hypothesis. Monteforte's results demonstrate little difference between the opinions of officers and cadets. Both groups showed a decided antipathy towards the revolution, the labour movement and a directed economy.[43] Yet, Arbenz obviously enjoyed some support among the military and a number of officers approved of the revolution. And it is clear that Arbenz's main support in the military came from a group of officers who had graduated from the Escuela with him or had gone through the academy when he was a teacher and commander of the cadet company. In general, however, the military remained guardedly jealous of its position in Guatemalan society. After the 1950 revolt, the military insisted on rounding up any arms left in the hands of workers and students, aiming to disarm completely all labour organizations. The military command was especially suspicious of the Agrarian Reform Law, both because the officers retained some of their traditional allegiance with landowners and more importantly because they believed that the peasant leagues would seriously erode their traditional power in the countryside.

Before the revolution the military, through military commissioners and the civil guard, had been one of the few national institutions that had penetrated rural communities. The military commissioners were especially important because they commanded the local militias, organized conscription and acted as the military's rural watchdogs. As the political parties and the peasant leagues began to extend their activities into villages, conflicts often developed. The army first responded by dramatically increasing the number of commissioners in an attempt to maintain its control. But, with the support of the president, the leaders of the CNCG and CGTG were able to have military commissioners and civil guard commanders transferred seemingly at will. The military became increasingly alarmed at its inability to retain its dominance in the countryside and by 1954, citing the "total lack of control and absolute disorganization of the militias", the Superior Council of National Defence began to strenuously appeal for a reassertion of its control over rural areas. Many officers in the military command were also worried that the government's plans to develop worker militias would be used as a force to counteract the military.[44]

By late in the Arbenz administration the military felt increasingly threatened by union strength and pressured Arbenz to restrict the activities of the communists. Arbenz continually refused to do so, one time quoting the Argentinian president Juan Perón: "Communism is like strychnine, beneficial in small doses but highly dangerous in large quantities." Arbenz argued that the communists were assisting the government in its reform program and had done nothing to warrant persecution.[45]

Despite this growing rift, Arbenz remained confident of military support should the revolution face armed aggression. In retrospect it seems relatively easy to explain why, at the final moment, the military refused that support. Arbenz's main military support came from that small group of officers who had graduated from the Escuela with him or had come through the Escuela when he taught there. By the 1950s most of these officers were actively carrying out the government programs in various parts of the country. At the same time the revolutionary governments had done little to ensure that new cadets were educated in a manner that would prompt support for the ideals of the ten years of spring. Instead, they were trained in a traditional manner, replete with anti-communist, anti-democratic sentiment.[46]

The most efficient, best trained and loyal officers had increasingly been used by Arbenz in administrative positions in the government. Arbenz did this partly out of necessity due to the lack of discipline and administrative skills among members of the civilian parties, and partly because these were the men he could trust to carry out government policy (and act as a counterweight to the communists) without being sidetracked by party interests. However, this practice did have its disadvantages. The civilian positions, with their substantial salaries, were highly prized. Arbenz's distribution of jobs to his circle of most trusted officers inspired resentment. At the same time Arbenz's most loyal colleagues became fixed in civilian posts and were thus outside the military command, meaning they could not direct the Superior Council of National Defence and were unable to come decisively to the aid of the revolution. Despite some minor purges, Arbenz was faced with substantially the same military that had plagued Arévalo. Consequently, when faced with the external pressure of a CIA invasion, the military refused to defend Guatemala unless Arbenz either resigned or agreed to act against the communists.

American Business: Pathway to Intervention

THE CIA-BACKED INVASION of Guatemala marked the first U.S. military intervention in Latin America since the inception of Franklin D. Roosevelt's Good Neighbour Policy. When the action occurred, it was because of a conjuncture of pressures and influences upon the U.S. government. The Republican administration of Dwight D. Eisenhower which came to power in 1952 was particularly susceptible to the pleas of U.S. businesses abroad and ready to see the hand of international communism in any foreign restriction of U.S. business. In an America convulsed by McCarthyite paranoia, it took little to convince the Eisenhower government to unleash "Operation Success" against the Arbenz administration.[47]

By 1950 Latin America was an extremely significant field for U.S. capital and, it appeared, would become increasingly so. Between 1947 and 1949 $1.7 billion (U.S.) had been invested in Latin America, bringing the total American investment there to $6 billion. Just as important, in 1950 Latin America purchased $2.7 billion worth of U.S. goods. U.S. exports to all of western Europe in the same year accounted only for $2 million more and Marshall Plan aid money had financed most of that. In addition, by 1950, 35 per cent of U.S. imports came from Latin America, including a disproportionate amount of strategic material (for instance, 80 per cent of crude oil imports). In Guatemala itself, U.S. companies had assets worth approximately $100 million in 1944.[48] Obviously, any attempt to restrict the activities of U.S. firms there would be considered particularly serious.

An important element in both the Arévalo and Arbenz government was an appeal to economic nationalism. Both leaders believed that Guatemala could not progress in the grip of a "semi-colonial" economic empire controlled by large U.S. companies. The predominance of the United Fruit Company, International Railways of America (IRCA) and the Electric Bond and Share subsidiary (EEG) within the Guatemalan economy — and the type of relations they had enjoyed with previous governments — made those companies the special target of nationalist politicians and the unions that supported nationalist goals.

At the heart of the revolution envisaged by Arévalo and carried on by Arbenz were two concepts: that capital had a social component and thus needed to be directed in ways that benefited society as a whole; and, consequently, that all private investment no matter what its source must be answerable to the nation's laws. Both revolutionary governments stressed that economic development would result from properly placed, properly managed private initiative. They thus attempted to encourage investment. However, as Arbenz warned in his inaugural address:

> Foreign capital will always be welcome as long as it adjusts to local conditions, remains always subordinate to Guatemalan Laws, cooperates with the economic development of the country and strictly abstains from intervening in the nation's social and political life.[49]

Given the traditionally arrogant manner of U.S. business operations in Guatemala, these new ideas when translated into policy were bound to create conflict. And tension became quickly apparent.

Even before Arévalo took office, the junta nationalized a local airline affiliated with Pan Am but run by an American, a close friend of Ubico who had fled the country with him. Neither Arévalo nor Arbenz threatened further nationalization but they did promote a string of laws that placed them in conflict with the major U.S. business interests in Guatemala. One of Arévalo's first projects was the construction of a road to Santo Tómas and the creation of a new port there. This move was designed to break the monopoly held by the IRCA and the UFCo port at Puerto Barrios. Arbenz also pushed construction of a new hydroelectric plant to be nationally owned and designed to supply energy at far cheaper rates than the monopolistic EEG. In an attempt to support local, light manufacturers and reduce imports, Arévalo began a campaign to revoke the 1936 trade agreement with the United States, and his government began negotiating with European countries for agreements that would help diversify Guatemalan trade.

In 1947, in response to a "rash of requests for exploration concessions", Arévalo passed a Petroleum Law that restricted mineral development to Guatemalan nationals. He also attempted to foster greater independence by resurrecting the idea of a Central American federation. Arévalo had reached an agreement of economic co-operation with the El Salvadorean president Castenada Castro, shortly before Castro was overthrown in 1948.[50]

The greatest conflict between the Arévalo government and the United Fruit Company came, predictably enough, through the new government's attitude to labour. In 1946 Arévalo stated, "It is imperative of our time to heed the claims of workers who have been reduced to servitude by economic imperialism."[51] Following this philosophy, Arévalo continually, if sometimes hesitantly, supported UFCo and IRCA workers in their struggles with these companies. The unions for their part went on strike repeatedly during this time, not only for better economic benefits but also in protest over company measures considered to be anti-nationalist.[52]

The UFCo complained forcefully that the 1947 labour code, which granted workers on agricultural enterprises employing more than 500 people the same rights as industrial workers, was direct discrimination against the company.[53] The company's running feud with its workers came to a head in the early 1950s when it tried to discharge 7,000 of them in an attempt to stop operations altogether. The Guatemalan labour court ordered the company to reinstate the workers and pay $650,000 in lost wages. When the company refused, the government called its bluff and made preparations to auction off some company land for the back wages. The company, temporarily bested, settled with the workers.[54]

Arbenz treated the UFCo and IRCA no more gently. In 1951, a top U.S. executive of UFCo, Walter Turnbull, visited Arbenz in an attempt to convince him to stifle worker demands and to renegotiate a contract with the company. When Arbenz demanded respect for Guatemalan law, payment of export duties and compensation for the "exhaustion of Guatemalan land", the company tried to pressure the government by cutting off marine transport. Finally, after the government was able to force the first audit ever of the railroad company's books, it impounded IRCA assets for an estimated $10.5 million in back taxes.[55]

Throughout all these disputes the U.S. embassy acted as the most powerful advocate of the company's claims, effectively expanding the conflict to one between the U.S. and Guatemalan governments.

Dulles, the CIA and the State Department

THE REVOLUTIONARY GOVERNMENT'S treatment of U.S. business of course affected the way Guatemala was viewed by the American administrations. Despite some dissenting opinion in the American embassy, union demands against the big U.S. companies were most often seen as deliberate government attacks. The Guatemalan government's attempt to tax the companies was also seen as the prelude to an expected nationalization of the IRCA and the EEG.[56] By the end of Arévalo's term, relations had deteriorated sufficiently that the Guatemalan president was described by the Assistant Secretary of State for Inter-American Affairs as "an enemy of the United States".[57]

While Arbenz was briefly seen as a moderate influence who might temper Guatemalan demands on U.S. business, relations between the two countries deteriorated steadily after his inauguration. They plummeted after the Eisenhower administration came to office in 1952.

The United Fruit Company was well placed to pressure the U.S. government to come to its rescue. The UFCo had a plethora of defenders, former associates, publicists and directors sprinkled throughout all levels of U.S. government. With the election of Eisenhower, however, UFCo's domain penetrated even further. According to one analyst, Victor Perlo, the Eisenhower administration marked a "new height in the level of direct control of power on the part of big business". Perlo cites *Fortune* magazine, which determined that the proportion of wealthy entrepreneurs with control over policy during the Eisenhower adminstration was double that of the previous administation.[58]

By far the most important tentacle of *el pulpo* wound its way directly to the heart of the State Department and the CIA. John Foster Dulles, the Secretary of State who "carried the State Department in his pocket", was the prime architect of U.S. foreign policy under Eisenhower. Described by Winston Churchill as "the only case I know of a bull who carries his china shop with him", Dulles had an obstinate and myopic view of foreign relations. Attempting to run roughshod over allies and enemies alike, he was particularly insensitive in America's backyard, Central America.[59] Dulles's connections with UFCo were longstanding. As a partner in the Sullivan and Cromwell law firm, Dulles had often acted as counsel for UFCo. He and his brother, Allen, then also a lawyer for the firm, had been the driving forces behind the very lucrative 1931 and 1936 contracts between UFCo and Ubico — contracts the Guatemalan government was now intent on revoking.

By the 1950s Allen Dulles was the head of the CIA. Described by an American journalist as being governed by the philosophy that "The countries which have the most power to resist communist subversion are those in which the military are in power", he shared his brother's bi-polar view of the world. He had been awarded substantial UFCo stock from a thankful company after the 1931 contract had been signed.[60]

Throughout the late 1940s and early 1950s, the UFCo's problems with the Guatemalan government became more and more serious. Samuel Zemurray, the president of the fruit company, began a campaign to prompt the company's allies into action and to influence public and congressional opinion against the "revolutionary" government. He hired a battery of high-powered publicists who concocted one of the most successful lobbying campaigns seen on Capitol Hill. Armies of North American reporters were ferried to Guatemala and subjected to lectures from UFCo publicity men who portrayed the company as a "beleaguered progressive institution, uplifting living standards while being unfairly attacked by Communists". The newsmen, wined and dined and briefed by the fruit company, saw little of the country and routinely attacked the government.[61]

The campaign had the desired effect. In the early 1950s virtually every newspaper and periodical in the United States ran articles on Guatemala. Early in 1950, a series of articles in the *New York Herald Tribune* predicted that Arbenz would lose the elections of that year, but would take power by force and attempt to perpetuate his rule. In 1952 *Newsweek* commented that the agrarian reform "recalled methods taken in countries behind the iron curtain and all the forces of communism were mobilized to assist it". In 1953 the National Planning Association published a pamphlet entitled *Communism vs Progress in Guatemala*, which argued that the communists were in danger of taking over power in Guatemala, a matter that should provoke "painful decisions" for the other countries in the western hemisphere.[62]

One incident in particular provided fodder the U.S. press. The Guatemalan government had been denied access to U.S. arms since 1947. Arms deals between the Guatemalan government and Denmark, Mexico, Cuba, Argentina and Switzerland had all been stopped by U.S. pressure or intrigue between 1948 and 1954. The Guatemalan military was desperate for equipment; besieged on all sides by hostile elements, it was critically short of ammunition and parts for vehicles. The air force functioned on pre-World War II American cast-offs with improvised replacement parts. Finally, in 1954 Guatemala arranged a shipment of Czechoslovakian arms to be delivered from a Polish port on a Swedish ship, the Alfhem. Through a web of intrigue the Alfhem was able to elude an American blockade and deliver its cargo. The arms, a motley collection of impractical, obsolete weaponry, did little to improve the effectiveness of the Guatemalan military but it did provide abundant ammunition for a North American press already on the scent of communists in Guatemala. Conveniently forgetting Guatemala's previous attempts to rearm from such subversive countries as Denmark, Sweden and Canada, *Time* magazine declared: "The deal amounted to the Red Bloc's first public display of big-brotherly trust and confidence in Guatemala." Keith Monroe of *Harper's* magazine fancifully warned that most of the guns would be used to "foment revolution" in neighbouring republics. The rest, he observed, would be used by the communists to arm "phalanxes of peons and Indians who [are] already drilling openly on golf courses around Guatemala City."[63]

Perhaps the most prolific journalist was Daniel James, correspondent for the *New York Times*, the *New Leader* and author of *Red Design for the Americas*. Writing in the *Times* in March 1954, he warned:

> There can be no battle more decisive than the Battle for the Western Hemisphere. We can afford to be defeated in China, Indo-China and even perhaps India and Western Europe but the loss to our cause of the Republics next door would be fatal, for then we should be ringed by hostile nations in our own vicinity. In that event . . . we would be compelled in sheer self-defence to withdraw from commitments to other parts of the globe, thus unavoidably sacrificing the rest of the world, or most of it, to communism.[64]

Samuel Guy Inman, one of the few journalists who did not fall into UFCo's orchestrated, anti-communist news frame, attempted to publish an interview he had done with Arévalo in which the president explained his political views. No North American paper was interested. Inman, writing in the early 1950s, concluded that press coverage of Guatemala was "too unanimous to be a mere coincidence". According to Inman the multitude of articles denouncing Guatemala, from hundreds of periodicals large and small, could not have happened without some plan, "especially in dealing with a small Latin American country that generally merits some dozen notices in the press in the course of a year".[65]

As the ten years of spring progressed the publicity campaign took its effect on relations between the two countries. In 1948 the United States replaced ambassador Kyle, who had been in favour of many of Arévalo's economic reforms, with Richard Patterson. Patterson took every opportunity to complain loudly of Guatemalan treatment of the United Fruit Company. Finally in 1950, after Patterson had warned Arévalo, "As far as I am concerned, your government will never get a dime or a pair of shoes from my government until you cease the persecution of American business," Guatemala demanded his recall.[66]

Arévalo invariably refused to bow to U.S. pressure. Rejecting rampant fears of communism, he insisted on his right to direct the affairs of Guatemala in response to local needs, and to use his government to promote the interests of Guatemalans. In his estimation the cold war was only a ruse, "a trick to reconcile Latin Americans to the idea of being fatally minuscule nations subjected to the leaders of the west: the U.S."[67]

With Arbenz's election, U.S. pressure on the Guatemalan government did not abate. In 1951 the World Bank, following U.S. suggestions, refused to grant loans to Guatemala. The Americans similarly refused to provide Arbenz with funding to complete the road to Santo Tómas and withdrew all of its aid missions. Early in 1952, in response to the promise of Nicaragua's Anastasio Somoza — "just give me the guns and I will clean up Guatemala in no time" — the U.S. State Department began to organize a way to send the required arms.[68] As it turned out, President Truman eventually scuttled the operation — leaving Guatemala's fate in other hands.

The Coup: Mercenaries and the CIA

WITH THE AGRARIAN REFORM LAW in 1952, the U.S. administration was even more convinced that it needed to oust the "revolutionary" government. The landowner most affected by the reform was the United Fruit Company, which controlled over 550 million acres of land in Guatemala, and by the most generous estimates cultivated less than 15 per cent of this land.[69] In February 1953, the National Agrarian Commission expropriated 200 thousand acres from the UFCo plantation at Tiquisate on the Pacific and distributed the land to 23 thousand peasants. In February 1954 an additional 172 thousand acres were taken from the company's Atlantic operations.

The UFCo immediately protested, basing its complaints on two factors. First, it argued that given the potential of tropical diseases, huge expanses of land were needed to allow operations to continue while diseased land rested, and thus the company should be exempt from the agrarian reform provisions. Secondly, it claimed that its own self-declared tax valuation was too low a compensation for the property and that payments in bonds to be amortized over 25 years was not prompt payment, but constituted, in reality, expropriation without compensation. The U.S. government immediately became the fruit company's bargaining agent, and demanded $16.5 million rather than the nearly $1.2 million offered. Even at the level of compensation offered by the Guatemalan government, UFCo would receive $2.86 per acre for empty land on the Pacific coast that it had purchased for

$1.48 per acre. It would receive $3.21 per acre for its Atlantic land, which it had obtained free of charge.[70]

While the American administration was forcefully bargaining for the company, UFCo was taking more direct action elsewhere. In 1953, 200 rebels seized the town of Salamá. Quickly defeated by loyal government troops, the rebels later revealed that they had received $64,000 from the United Fruit Company to attempt the coup.[71]

By the summer of 1953, Eisenhower, reacting to political pressure from allies of UFCo, obsessed with communism in Guatemala and advised by Dulles, agreed to a plan for the overthrow of the Arbenz government. The plan, dubbed "Operation Success", proceeded on a variety of fronts. The CIA established a co-ordinating office above a nursery in Florida. Eisenhower assigned John Peurifoy, described at the time as a man with "a loud voice, a swaggering manner, a blatant style and a flair for intrigue", as ambassador to Guatemala.[72] Peurifoy's task was to exploit disillusionment within the military, to help apply psychological pressure on the government and, generally, to heighten the atmosphere of conflict. At the same time the United States worked to isolate Guatemala diplomatically through the machinations of American ambassadors and its client dictators in Central America, as well as through U.S. dominance of the Organization American States. It established a clandestine propaganda radio station to increase tension. Finally, U.S. personnel recruited an invasion force and selected a leader from the flotsam of mercenaries and Guatemalan exiles that floated around Central America.

After an initial battle between the National Security Council (which opposed unilateral action in Guatemala) and the CIA under Allen Dulles, Operation Success was launched. John Foster Dulles initially approached Kermit Roosevelt, fresh from a CIA coup in Iran, to direct the operation. Roosevelt refused, believing the operation would not succeed because the people didn't "want what we want".[73] Consequently, the Americans appointed Colonel Albert Haney, who enjoyed a reputation for bravery and recklessness from his command in South Korea.

The first step was to weaken the loyalty of the Guatemalan military officers. Records were compiled on all top ranking officers, many of whom were approached with bribes. U.S. officials kept up pressure on the Guatemalan government by issuing a number of inflammatory statements, most of them designed to exaggerate the role of communists in the government. After his only meeting with Arbenz, Peurifoy cabled Dulles: "I spent six hours with him one evening, and he talked like a communist, he thought like a communist, he acted like a communist and if he is not one . . . he will do until one comes along."[74]

John Foster Dulles publicly warned of "a network of Soviet Agents in every country [of Latin America]... an aggressive, tough, political force, backed by great resources and serving the most ruthless empire of modern times". On April 26, President Eisenhower alerted congress that Guatemala was "spreading Marxist tentacles" throughout Central America. "The Reds are in control", he stressed, "and they are trying to spread their influence to San Salvador as a first step to breaking out of Guatemala to other South American countries."[75]

The United States next attempted to get the sanction of the Organization of American States (OAS) for intervention at the Tenth Inter-American Conference in Caracas in March 1954. While most Latin American countries had approached the conference hoping to discuss economic development, the United States forced a debate on the "Declaration of Solidarity for the Preservation of Political Integrity of the American States against International Communist Intervention". Dulles rushed into the conference, stayed for the six days of debate on the issue and left before any program of economic development could be discussed. During his stay he proposed a resolution calling for a "common defence" against any American state in which the communists had control.

The resolution was clearly a ploy to further isolate Guatemala and provide some sort of international legitimacy for an intervention already set in motion. Guillermo Toriello Garrido, Guatemala's delegate, declared that his country had attended the conference "with faith and enthusiasm for the democratic doctrines which inspired our revolution". He emphasized that the Guatemalan government was capitalist and welcomed foreign investment so long as it was loyal to the laws of the country and subject to the same conditions as Guatemala's own investors. Guatemala, Toriello said, did reject investment of the "colonial type" that had previously predominated in the country. He warned other Latin American delegates at the conference:

> One speaks repeatedly of the investment of foreign capital as a panacea to cure the ills of those countries whose economic development has fallen behind. But little importance has been given to the modes of this investment and frequently one forgets that some investments are the principal cause of that backwardness one encounters in some countries. Investments of the monopolistic type in many cases have asphyxiated development.

Toriello described the U.S. proposal as an example of the "internationalization of McCarthyism". If the resolution passed, he predicted: "Pan-americanism would become an instrument exclusively in the service of monopolistic interests and a weapon of coercion to strangle any attempt at political and economic liberation."[76]

This argument brought on a new wave of denunciation in the U.S. press. Donald Grant in the *St. Louis Dispatch* wrote: "At Caracas a close study of the words spoken by Toriello certainly leads to the conclusion that he spoke there as the voice of Moscow — the docile instrument of his communist advisors."[77] Toriello's answer to that charge was:

> What is the real and effective reason for describing our government as communist? . . . The answers are simple and evident. The plan of national liberation being carried out with firmness by my government has necessarily affected the privileges of foreign enterprises that are impeding the progress and the economic development of the country.[78]

Despite Toriello's arguments, the resolution passed with a vote of 17 to 1, with Mexico and Argentina abstaining. Most countries tempered their acceptance of the resolution with counsel against intervention and a warning that if intervention was needed it must be decided upon collectively. Even with these provisos many of the delegates voted, as the Uruguayan delegate said, "without enthusiasm, without optimism, without joy". Indeed, one diplomat told Toriello that the Guatemalan had said "many of the things some of the rest of us would like to say if we dared".[79]

In spite of the restriction on intervention placed before the U.S. delegation, the State Department and the CIA continued Operation Success unchecked. The president of Honduras, Mariano Galvéz, a former counsel for UFCo, was pressured into co-operation by ambassador Whiting Wilhauer to supply a training base for a "liberation army". This army was subsequently made up of Guatemalan exiles and mercenaries from other Central American countries, soldiers paid, as one U.S. reporter asserted, "with wads of dollar bills passed out by men who were unmistakenly American".[80] A dummy company set up by the CIA supplied the Liberation Army with U.S. weapons and planes through a false charitable organization, the Medical Institute. U.S. pilots, generally ex-servicemen, were recruited and paid between $5000 and $1,000 a month.[81]

Meanwhile, E. Howard Hunt and representatives of the fruit company searched for a suitable leader for the invasion. Apparently they first approached Miguel Ydígoras Fuentes to front the invasion, but the U.S. demands of preference for UFCo by the subsequent government and repayment of the money spent on Operation Success were too onerous for even Ydígoras. The next candidate, a landowner who had also acted as a representative for UFCo, developed throat cancer at an inopportune time. Finally, the team chose ex-Colonel Castillo Armas, found working as a furniture salesman in Honduras.[82]

With Peurifoy and his agents sowing dissension among military commanders in Guatemala, with a network of ambassadors and dictators in Nicaragua, Costa Rica and Honduras in readiness, with a "Voice of Liberation" radio station, an army of Central American misfits and an air force composed of cast-off American planes and mercenary American pilots waiting, Operation Success was ready.

The Arbenz government was well aware of the CIA plans. In the early months of 1954, Arbenz had seen correspondence that detailed some of the preparations for intervention. Hoping to forestall the invasion, Arbenz published the details in Guatemala's papers. *Time* magazine ridiculed the revealed plot as "completely fanciful". It suggested, "The real plot in the situation was less of a plot than a scenario — a sort of Reichstag fire in reverse, masterminded in Moscow."[83]

With the American public thus assured that its government had no intention of intervening, on June 17, 1954, "rebel" airplanes took to the air and Castillo Armas' motley band of conspirators moved from the Honduras camp into the border areas of Guatemala. The "liberation" army stayed in villages near the border, generally unmolested, whilst the air force violated Guatemalan air space at will, strafed and bombed parts of Guatemala City, Puerto San José and the towns of Chiquimula and Zacapa.

Concerned that engaging the attacking forces would be used as an excuse for more direct intervention, Arbenz and Toriello initially tried to rely on diplomacy. Toriello repeatedly met with Peurifoy, who denied he was connnected to the invasion, and at the same time suggested he could arrange for it to be stopped should Arbenz resign. Guatemala finally took the matter to the Security Council of the United Nations, where the United States used all its powers of influence to have the matter sent to the OAS for discussion — so blatantly that it prompted UN president Dag Hammerskjold to threaten to resign. Eventually, the Security Council agreed on a compromise French resolution calling for no government to lend assistance to any action that would threaten human life.

The State Department ignored the UN resolution and would not of course admit to any involvement in the invasion. It did make its first public statement, claiming it had "no evidence that indicates that this is anything other than a revolt of Guatemalans against the government".[84]

On June 19, in a radio broadcast made almost inaudible through CIA interference, Arbenz announced that the country was being invaded by a "heterogeneous Fruit Company expeditionary force". He declared, "This is an armed invasion carried out by ... adventurers, mercenaries of various stripes and some Guatemalan exiles. Such is the composition of the expeditionary force equipped, supplied and armed on Honduran and Nicaraguan territory." He called for Guatemalans not to forget what they stood to lose if "Mr. Foster Dulles' Guatemalan friends come to power."[85]

Finally, in the dying days of June, Arbenz attempted to rally the military against the invaders. His personal friend, Colonel Anselmo Getella, polled top officers and informed Arbenz that the military would not defend him; but if he resigned they would promise to drive Armas out of Guatemala. Arbenz, unsure of the extent of his support in the countryside and unable to get arms to peasant and worker supporters, agreed to turn over power to a junta headed by Colonel Enrique Díaz, in return for a promise that the new leaders would respect the ideals of the revolution and the rights of all workers without exception.[86]

With the resignation of Arbenz the revolution came to an end: There remained only a few loose ends for Peurifoy to tidy up. The new military junta was composed of Diáz, Colonel Elfegío Monzón and Colonel José Angel Sánchez. When Diáz proved intent on fulfilling at least some of the promises made to Arbenz, Peurifoy along with Monzón arranged to have him forced from the junta and its direction taken over by Monzón. No sooner had that been done than Monzón, under the tutelage of Peurifoy, began a series of discussions with Armas, now in El Salvador.[87]

Guatemala's experiment with economic and social change had ended. The country's only crime, as Arbenz stated in his June 19th radio address, was to have enacted an agrarian reform that affected the interests of an American-owned fruit company. The Guatemalan "revolution" threatened the favoured monopoly position of U.S. capital, presenting a challenge perceived in Washington not solely as a threat to the United Fruit Company but also as a potential menace to U.S. hegemony throughout Latin America. Alongside U.S. intervention, however, went a long-developing sequence of internal factors: the implacable opposition to change of large landowners and the church, a disorganization in the ranks of those supporting the reforms, and a military jealously guarding its own position of power and obsessively raising the spectre of communist influence. When Armas entered Guatemala City accompanied by the U.S. ambassador, the opponents of the revolution were poised to take power.

— 7 —
Politics and the Military, 1954-1970:
The Failure of Electoral Politics

No, don't be alarmed...
Tomorrow will die more trade unionists,
more students, more professionals,
for having the privilege to think,
for having the audacity to defend popular interests;
surely... tomorrow more will die...
for the single sin
of searching for just remuneration
and who knows if upon concluding this
I too will go...
— Luis Sam Colop, "Oiga Senor", *Versos sin refugios*

THE COUP OF 1954 ended Guatemala's popular "revolution". The ten
years of government led by Juan José Arévalo and Jacobo Arbenz
represented Guatemala's last attempt for at least three decades at
either substantial reform or a functioning democracy. The governments that followed the Arbenz adminstration consistently refused to
acknowledge the need for a substantial realignment of the economic
forces at play, and actively sought to prevent the formation of local
autonomous organizations that might foster local economic and social
development.

In the years immediately following the 1954 intervention,
Guatemalan governments attempted to combine a repressive economic policy with a form of electoral democracy. But it became
increasingly apparent that, given the choice, the bulk of the population
would choose popular parties advocating economic reforms similar to
those proposed by the Arévalo and Arbenz governments. The conservative forces that had been elevated to a position of dominance after
the overthrow of Arbenz were not prepared to allow these reform
parties to regain political power. In their attempts to prevent
Guatemala's centre-left political parties from winning elections, the
trappings of democracy were consistently brushed aside. In the process

the military became by far the predominant political force in the country.

Before 1970 the military's involvement in politics took on a variety of forms, but its goal was consistent: to prop up conservative forces and maintain a type of political stability that would prevent reform-minded parties from achieving political power. From 1957 to 1958 this required the military to force the rabid political followers of the "Liberation" to allow another conservative party to "win" elections. From 1958 to 1963, the same impulse required that the military collaborate with an incompetent and corrupt adminstration. In 1963 the military was forced to intervene directly in politics to prevent the return of Juan José Arévalo and, it was presumed, a level of reform the army was unwilling to countenance. From 1963 to 1966 the military attempted to restructure the Guatemalan political scene to ensure that only certain acceptable political parties could participate in elections. And from 1966 to 1970, when this attempt proved impossible, military officers frustrated attempts at reform by perpetrating increasing levels of violence.

As a consequence, the political process lost all legitimacy and significant sectors of the society reacted to continued violence by supporting armed revolution. By 1970 the stage was set for the horrid, brutal nightmare of constantly escalating violence that would torment Guatemala through the 1970s and 1980s.

The New Regime Consolidates Power

FOLLOWING THE RESIGNATION of Jacobo Arbenz, the U.S. ambassador to Guatemala, John Peurifoy, was intent on making certain the "revolution" had truly ended. He used a combination of threats and influence to ensure that the State Department's chosen successor, Castillo Armas, was placed in a position of power from which he could emerge as Guatemala's new president. In the space of three days after Arbenz's resignation a complicated game of musical chairs among top military officers finally created a junta Peurifoy could approve. With moderates such as Colonel Díaz safely out of the way, Armas' way to the presidency was cleared and the attacks by the "Liberation Army" were stopped.[1]

But Armas had further minor hurdles to leap. He needed to create a power base for himself within the Guatemalan army, but the military was steadfastly opposed to the integration of the "liberation" forces and itself. When Armas announced in a speech that he had triumphed because the military had been divided and the "liberation" united, his comments sparked increased anger from a jealous officer corps increasingly concerned about the president's intentions. Finally, cadets at the Escuela Politécnica, those with the most to lose in the way of future promotions if the liberation forces joined the army, attacked Armas' troops housed in the newly constructed Roosevelt Hospital. The conflict between the two forces was only stopped when Armas promised that he would not integrate his followers into the military and that no action would be taken against the cadets.[2]

This was the first in a long string of broken promises by Armas. No sooner had the cadets given up the struggle, when the Escuela was temporarily closed and many of the cadets were expelled. Armas was thus able to plug loyal "liberation" cohorts into positions formerly held by officers close to Arbenz. In addition Armas used the "discovery" of a plot against him among senior officers to oust a number of officers and to fill their positions with his own followers.[3] Assured in this manner of a cadre of loyal "liberation" cohorts in the upper ranks of the military, Armas set about consolidating his regime in other ways.

Wishing "to spare the Guatemalan people the cost of an election", Armas decided upon a simple referendum to legitimize his regime. In a public oral vote, with the military and liberation forces looking on, a reported 95 per cent of the voters approved of Armas' assumption of the presidency.[4] Buoyed by the "obvious support of the people", Armas embarked on his program to reconstruct Guatemala: a reconstruction that included wholesale arrests of those who had collaborated with the previous regimes and the banning of numerous organizations created during the ten years of spring.[5]

To try to win support for his new government, Armas espoused a vision of "New Life" to rival Arévalo's spiritual socialism. Armas argued, "No human being is free . . . while he is a victim of misery, illness or ignorance." His philosophy of New Life was meant to symbolize Guatemala's future path and was to be "a dynamic attitude, not of the people before the government, nor of the government before the people, but of the nation toward the conquest of its own happiness."[6]

But New Life was a political philosophy still-born. The Armas government was trapped in a whirlwind of anti-communist obsession. This obsession undermined the role of the political centre and any elements of political reform that might have seriously challenged the hegemony of the landowning elite and Armas' National Democratic Movement (MDN). In the months following the coup over 1,000 politicians and labour leaders took asylum in foreign embassies; 17,000 people were taken prisoner, and many thousands more fled the country.[7]

In the violent retribution that the political followers of the 1954 coup carried out on those people associated with the revolution, the remnants of even the most moderate of the political parties that supported the Arévalo or Arbenz government sank out of sight. But the MDN did face a political challenger. Miguel Ydígoras Fuentes had been the major focus of conservative opposition to Arbenz in the elections of 1951 and after that had been one of the regime's most vocal opponents from outside of the country. He had been temporarily considered by the State Department for the position of leader of the invasion. Armas had attempted to prevent a challenge from Ydígoras by denying him a visa to return to the country, but Ydígoras' conservative supporters had forced Armas to reconsider.

When Armas was killed by one of his personal guards in 1957 (in what appeared to be an internal power struggle in the MDN), Ydígoras emerged as the major opponent for the MDN. In the campaign for the elections of 1957 Ydígoras promised to end the violence inflicted by the liberation followers and to begin a program of national reconciliation. His party, the National Democratic Renovation party, or Redención, won some support, although apparent electoral fraud prevented it from defeating the MDN candidate.

Losing at the polls but determined to claim victory in any case, the MDN followers proved too clumsy to pull fraud off gracefully. Their attempts at imposing their candidate alienated even more people and when Ydígoras called for street demonstrations to oppose the fraud, large numbers of people responded. The military, which still had testy relations with the MDN, forced the party from power and called new elections for the following year.

In those new elections, Ydígoras continued to attack the MDN, stressing its links with the United States. He received surprising support, much of it attracted by his call for a national reconciliation. He promised the voters: "Before God and the people, that my government will be nationalistic and that the day I assume power all of the memories of the past and present struggle will be erased in a generous spirit of authentic national reconciliation."[8] Ydígoras' promises of peace carried the day with the predominantly middle-class electorate. The old war horse, Ubico's public works minister and (according to Ydígoras himself) the CIA's first choice to lead the coup finally obtained the presidency he felt had rightfully belonged to him for almost a decade.

Ydígoras' five years in office were a farce of incompetence, corruption and patronage. Perhaps the long years of waiting for his chance at power had made him determined to wring every penny he could from his position. His party, Redención, was held together not by any common ideological binding, but solely by the strands of patronage liberally cast about by its leader. One of his first accomplishments in office was to raise the presidential salary to $150,000 annually — making himself the highest-paid head of state in the western hemisphere — and to establish a generous million-dollar pension fund. His patronage extended to his daughter, appointed ambassador to France, and to a cousin who became education minister. He auctioned off the national *fincas* for the biggest bribes and under his touch all levels of government disintegrated in a morass of corruption.[9]

Ydígoras' government was a disaster. His old cronies, men left over from the days of Ubico, had little capacity for administration and less interest. One chronicler described his government as "administrative irrationality degenerated into bureaucratic venality and procedural stagnation."[10]

The corruption and incompetence prompted criticism from all sides. By 1961 *El Imparcial*, Guatemala's most influential newspaper, lamented the "lack of discipline [which] increases from the top to bottom, consuming social energy and discouraging everyone".[11] More active opposition came from public-sector workers and students who organized a series of strikes and demonstrations against Ydígoras. These strikes intensified when Redención used quite blatant fraud to grab 30 of the 33 seats up for election to the national assembly in 1961; the strikers were eventually joined by the powerful railway workers' union and businessmen. By 1962, 21 members of the government coalition in congress had withdrawn their support, leaving Ydígoras isolated and opposed from all sides.[12]

The Military Takes Control

YDÍGORAS ALSO FACED opposition from within the ranks of the military. His tendency to promote older officers, his allies during the Ubico period, upset the normal progression of promotion and advancement and was especially resented by the most competent officers who were beginning to view the military as an important tool for the promotion of government policy. In 1960 Ydígoras faced a widespread officers' revolt that started in Guatemala City. He was probably only saved by the actions of the then minister of agriculture, Colonel Enrique Peralta Azurdía, and the fact that at the last moment many of the officers who were to take part in the uprising failed to participate. The revolt, although quickly defeated, was nonetheless of later importance as two of the leaders, Captain Marco Antonio Yon Sosa and Lt. Luis Turcios Lima, went on to lead a revolutionary movement throughout the 1960s.[13]

After this near escape, Ydígoras began actively to seek military support. The air force, loyal during the attempted coup, was rewarded

with distinctive new uniforms, increased flight pay and, most importantly, extended holidays during crop-dusting time. The holidays
allowed air force pilots to more than double their annual salaries
during only a few months of the year. In addition, a new round of
promotions meant that soon 500 of the 900 officers in the combined
forces were colonels or lieutenant-colonels.[14]

Ydígoras also attempted to divert military opposition by offering
bellicose rhetoric concerning Belize, the site of Guatemala's perpetual
dispute with Britain. Nationalist spirit was kindled by his suggestion
that "Every Guatemalan soldier should go to bed every night and get
up every morning, thinking about Belize."[15]

After the defection of the coalition members in 1962, Ydígoras
virtually surrendered his government to the military. He filled nine of
ten cabinet posts (all except foreign relations) with officers. Even with
this he still continued to face military opposition. In 1962 air force
officers in conjunction with wealthy landowners attempted yet
another coup. When it became apparent that the army was not going
to join in, the leaders of the coup fled to El Salvador. Finally, in 1963
the military formally took over the reins of power when Colonel
Peralta Azurdía, the defence minister, deposed Ydígoras.[16]

The reasons for the final assumption of power by the military in
1963 were diverse. Certainly Ydígoras had lost all support from outside of the military. Rampant corruption and repression had alienated
students, labour and reform politicians, while Ydígoras' creaky
bureaucratic machinery and disastrous economic policies had
prompted opposition from the economic elite. In addition, the small
yet troublesome guerrilla campaign being waged by Yon Sosa and
Turcios Lima in Guatemala's eastern districts heightened traditional
concern about a leftist takeover of the government. As one of the
leaders of the air force revolt explained, the officers had acted against
Ydígoras because the government "was making things easier for the
communists by their incompetence".[17]

But the final spark that prompted the overthrow of Ydígoras was
the prospect of Juan José Arévalo returning to Guatemala to contest
the elections scheduled for 1963. When two centre-left reform parties,
Revolutionary Democratic Unity (URD) and the Authentic Revolutionary Party (PRA), first proposed Arévalo as their candidate for the elections, Ydígoras threatened the former president with arrest should he
return to Guatemala. But after the Supreme Court upheld Arévalo's
right to contest the election, Ydígoras (who had himself come to
power through public demonstrations protesting electoral fraud)
seemed ready to allow the candidacy to stand.

This development created serious problems for both the Guatemalan military and its American advisors. According to Susan Jonas Bodenheimer, author of the most detailed study of American foreign policy in Guatemala following the revolution, Arévalo's threatened return prompted a debate within the John F. Kennedy administration. While some people argued that Arévalo represented the democratic left, which should be allowed to operate within Latin American politics, the hard-line majority disagreed. Arévalo's past contacts with communists and his radical nationalism made him unacceptable. According to Jonas, the Kennedy administration "gave the green light" to Colonel Peralta Azurdía.[18]

Although it is unlikely the military would have proceeded against strong opposition from the U.S. government, Peralta probably needed little prompting. The Ydígoras government had proved disastrous. Of greater import, the other bourgeois parties, the MDN (which was involved in a struggle with the National Liberation Movement), Ydígoras' discredited Redención and to some extent the Revolutionary Party (PR) suffered from severe political splintering and were unable to provide a coherent and organized political challenge to the reform parties. The only parties that seemed capable of both formulating a policy for national development and gaining a popular following — the URD, PRA and Social Democrats — were not acceptable to an obsessively anti-communist military, particularly one with a collective memory of Arbenz's peasant leagues and facing a threat of revolution in the eastern districts. These parties, especially with Arévalo to lead them, threatened reforms the military was not prepared to condone. They also promised to reduce the military's involvement in politics and government administration substantially. To much of the Guatemalan elite, both military and civilian, the only organized force not tainted with radicalism and which could prevent the victory of the reform parties was the military itself.

The Militarization of Guatemalan Politics

BY 1963 MANY GUATEMALAN OFFICERS felt that the military was well prepared to take over the government. In contrast to the tattered political parties, especially of the right, the army had undergone a form of institutional strengthening for over three decades. During the Ubico regime the military was increasingly centralized and officers were called upon to perform functions at all levels of government. This function continued throughout the revolution as the Arbenz administration relied upon military officers to help carry out his ambitious, nationalist development program. As a result, a large group of officers developed a taste for wider responsibilities. In addition, the higher salary levels and increasing array of perquisites awarded officers by the nervous revolutionary government had made military careers more attractive.

This tendency was reinforced in the years immediately following the coup. During the revolution the curriculum of the military academy had been expanded to include instruction in political economy. Following the coup, the curriculum was enlarged further. The school added studies in management, administration and other more civilian-oriented topics. The increased breadth of training helped lead many officers to search for a more active role in civilian administration.[19]

The militarization of Guatemalan society was helped along by two processes in the 1960s: increased levels of military assistance from the United States, much of it allocated to a military civic-action program in the countryside; and the opportunity afforded officers to augment official salaries through civilian posts.

In the wake of the Cuban revolution the U.S. government began more consciously to concern itself with preparing Latin American militaries to combat internal opposition. Guatemala, with its troublesome history and a guerrilla force already operating, was given special attention. Between 1956 and 1963 annual U.S. military assistance to Guatemala multiplied by ten times. Between 1963 and 1969, 29 per cent of all U.S. military-assistance loans went to Guatemala. In 1965 military aid to Guatemala averaged $538 per soldier.[20]

Much of the increased resources handed to the Guatemalan military was employed in a military civic-action program that began in November 1960. An Alliance for Progress cornerstone, military civic-action was designed to improve the public image of the army and eliminate support for insurgent forces in the countryside. As Ydígoras expressed it to the Guatemalan congress, the army was going to promote "a new spirit of cooperation in favour of community development at the site of each military unit".[21]

Infrastructure projects such as wells, roads and irrigation construction co-ordinated by community relations councils were widespread, but probably the keystone of the "new" army was the military literacy program. Begun in 1964, the program had 21,832 pupils by 1966.[22] While these obvious attempts at image-making had a debatable effect on the public impression of the military, they did foster military involvement in a wide range of development projects.

Increased military expenditures, a heightened level of technological competence, a better educated officer corps and growing involvement in non-traditional development projects in villages had a tremendous impact on the Guatemalan military. It solidified itself as the most cohesive and efficient organization in Guatemala.

Officers were also pushed into the political arena as an accepted means of augmenting official salaries. In the early 1960s a graduating second lieutenant from the Escuela received $75 a month basic salary. This minuscule amount was increased by about $25 with each promotion, which generally came in three-year intervals. According to sociologist Richard Adams:

> The problem of income is a serious one for officers. Training in the Escuela Politécnica together with upper sector aspirations and tastes, gives the younger officer graduate a view into the perquisites of good living but almost no means of access to them.[23]

There were only two limited but accepted avenues to increase official salaries and both led to political involvement, inevitably straining the institutional cohesion cherished by the military establishment. Officers could obtain a government position with an additional salary or, using the access to credit, influence and services available through their military position, they could engage in business pursuits. Both of these directions pulled officers into the vortex of Guatemalan politics as active players in the squabbles of the bourgeoisie. By the early 1980s this process had continued long enough to ensure that the military high command had disintegrated into a constantly quarrelling body of competing interests held together, if at all, by a vague sense of military loyalty and the intensity of the brutal civil war being waged against popular forces.

Constitution-Juggling and Party Politics

IN 1963 ALL OF THESE FACTORS had evolved sufficiently to prompt military intervention in the sea of political instability surrounding the Ydígoras regime. The spark that had caused Peralta's intervention was the threatened return of Arévalo. But once the military had blocked Arévalo's return, Peralta was not prepared to turn the political arena back over to the same cabal of disorganized and self-serving politicians who had ruled since the 1954 coup. Peralta and the military technocrats who were aligned with him were intent on revamping a bankrupt political system while effectively precluding all reform political parties from participating in politics.

Peralta Azurdía held power as the head of state in Guatemala for only three years, but in that time he significantly altered the political landscape by creating a new party, the Institutional Democratic Party (PID) and by having his government frame a new constitution. PID was to be a centre-right party that would provide a stable, disciplined alternative to the cabal of splintered parties that had almost allowed the return of Juan José Arévalo. The model for PID was the Institutional Revolutionary Party (PRI) of Mexico, a party created after the Mexican revolution. PID was meant to be a more moderate force than the rightist National Liberation Movement (MLN), and its ideological fluidity was to allow it to co-opt moderate reform ideas. Like the PRI in Mexico, all elements of real reform were to be smothered under the sheer weight of the party-controlled state apparatus.[24]

The other measure devised to prune the political system was the new constitution of 1965. The most important article in the constitution was a new electoral law requiring political parties seeking legal status to submit lists of 50,000 members. This article proved to be an ideal way for the government to determine which political parties could participate in elections. For any number of reasons the government could simply refuse to accept the party list of centre-left reform parties. This strategy became the major tool of electoral fraud for the two decades to follow.[25]

Despite the grandiose plans Peralta and the senior officers had for the PID, it failed to attract much support in its first electoral contest in 1966. The attempt to restrict the political field to centrist or right-wing parties was reasonably successful. Neither the URD nor the PRA was able to submit a list of members acceptable to the electoral commission. Even the centrist Christian Democrats were rejected despite submitting a list of members far in excess of the required number. At the same time the PID was quickly recognized, as was the right-wing MLN.[26]

Even the generally tame Guatemalan press criticized this obvious manipulation of the electoral machinery. The *Diario Grafico* argued:

> In order for fraud to exist you do not have to rob ballots or votes. It is sufficient to prohibit the open participation in the elections so that only a part of the public will can be expressed.[27]

The third party permitted to contest the 1966 elections was the Revolutionary Party (PR). The PR was in many ways very different from both the MLN or the PID. It traced its roots back to the moderate bourgeois parties that supported Arévalo in the early years of the revolution. The leader of the PR, Mario Méndez Montenegro, had been active in the movement to unseat Ubico and had been a founding member of the Popular Liberation Front, one of the parties responsible for the wide range of political reforms associated with the 1945 constitution.

However, since the PR had emerged in 1958 it had not pursued its reform roots consistently. When Peralta had needed to legitimize the constitution he was devising by bringing politicians of other political stripes into the legislature, the PR had joined with the MLN in agreeing to the division of powers the PID had arranged. Mario Méndez had proved to be ready to abandon most of the party's original principles when necessary to obtain political power. His control of the party had caused a number of schisms and helped spawn a handful of smaller reform parties. Approaching the 1966 elections it appeared the PR was going to enter into a coalition with the PID, which still had limited civilian support. Consequently, the PR was permitted to register officially for the elections as well.[28]

But Peralta's plans for an alliance between the centre-right military (PID) and the centrist PR were disrupted. Before the elections could occur Mario Méndez died — a suspicious suicide — and his brother, Julio César Méndez Montenegro took over the leadership of the party. Julio César Méndez had maintained his reformist roots more carefully than his brother. As the dean of the law school at the University of San Carlos, he had kept in touch with many of Guatemala's reform politicians, most of whom were also academics. He also had the support of the powerful University of San Carlos student association. His ascension broke the unofficial alliance with the PID and substantially strengthened the PR by bringing back to the fold many of the reform politicians who had broken with the party when it was led by his brother. Villagrán Kramer's URD and even the guerrilla organization Rebel Armed Forces (FAR) supported his presidential bid.

For the MLN and PID the focus of the 1966 election campaign was the threat of communist subversion. The MLN candidate claimed that his party was the only thing that could save Guatemala from the communist menace represented in the western hemisphere by Fidel Castro. The MLN slogan — "Cuba or Guatemala! Miguel Angel Ponciano or Castro's communism" — was not subtle about the alternatives. The PID, slightly more sophisticated in its approach, also argued that its program of "national unity" was the only means of preventing widespread political unrest that would in the end, it argued, benefit the communists.[29]

But it was the PR's call for cautious reform that won most adherents. In a campaign marked by the arrest and execution of 30 left-wing leaders on the eve of the election, the PR won a substantial victory. While the PID appeared to be poised to use government machinery to commit electoral fraud and thus preserve its position, it was taken by surprise by the extent of the PR victory and seemingly not prepared to alter figures sufficiently to wipe out the winning margin.[30]

But the military was not prepared, without some assurances, to hand power over to a reform politician with suspicious connections to left-wing organizations. According to the constitution, because the PR had not won a majority in the elections, it had to be given a mandate by the outgoing PID-dominated congress. The congress and the military delayed its decision for over a week while Méndez bargained desperately, sprinkling promises to the military with occasional veiled threats. On one occasion Méndez warned that if he were denied the presidency, 60,000 of his followers would take to to the streets. "It would be a peaceful demonstration at first," he suggested, "but there is no telling how it would turn out." [31] He also appealed for support from officers who had been left out of the ruling circle of PID. The PID, Méndez argued, was not a "government of the army. It is rather a government of a group that is abusing the name of the army."[32] Finally, in return for a promise that the president would not interfere with the internal mechanisms of the military, the military high command allowed Méndez to assume the presidency.

The Third Government of the Revolution

IT PROVED TO BE a costly promise. From 1966 to 1970 the military dominated the government. Méndez's inability to carry out urgent economic reforms against the implacable opposition of the bulk of the military and the anti-communist warriors of the MLN was the most visible aspect of his government. In the end, his unwillingness to confront the conservative forces that threatened his government lost the PR the support of many of Guatemala's most committed politicians, and weakened the party. As it felt power slipping from its fingers, according to Guatemalan sociologist Mario Monteforte Toledo, the party's strategy "centred on one objective: gaining power at whatever cost, including leaving aside their rhetorical principles, collaborating with the right and pledging itself to North American interests and the conditions of the army".[33]

The Méndez government was constantly beset by violence or threatened violence from the right and rumours of a coup from a military that took advantage of the guerrilla operations in the eastern departments of the country to increase its funding and political strength. The sporadic operations of the two guerrilla forces, the FAR and the Revolutionary Movement of November 13 (MR-13) provided an ideological justification for the right-wing terror of so-called death squads — a violence that far exceeded the activity of the guerrilla forces and was most often aimed at moderate reformers. (For more on the guerrilla opposition during this period, see chapter 11).

Méndez assumed the presidency under a state of siege called by the defence minister after the kidnappings of a justice of the supreme court and the head of the government information offfice. Thereafter Méndez constantly exerted most of his efforts at placating the military and getting control of the government. The PID was given control over three powerful congressional committees and one of the Méndez's first official acts was a tour of military bases. At his first stop, the strategically important Zacapa base, site of most of the counter-insurgency activity and commanded by the powerful colonel, Carlos Arana Osorío, Méndez promised support for the army. He addressed the troops stating, "I hope that you will interpret my conduct as a friend of the army, a friend who recognizes and esteems the true worth of the armed forces."[34]

But Méndez's appeal for the military's trust had little effect. The counter-insurgency program carried out under the command of Colonel Arana and U.S. military advisors was to become a dominant characteristic of the Méndez administration. It has been argued that the program helped the Méndez government to "maintain its precarious political position . . . by providing the military institution with a professional task".[35] But the military's involvement in the counter-insurgency also helped the army expand its resources and increase its autonomy. In addition, it helped reinforce a MLN/military coalition that lasted well into the 1970s.

In the hands of Colonel Arana the campaign against a couple of hundred guerrillas became a brutal "scorched earth" drive that claimed the lives of thousands of peasants; only a small number of the dead had any links to the guerrillas.[36] Using tactics developed during Operation Phoenix in Vietnam, the Guatemalan military was determined to wipe out potential sources of guerrilla support by forcing whole villages to be abandoned, denying the guerrilla forces a sphere in which to operate.

The counter-insurgency was assisted by large amounts of U.S. military assistance and by U.S. tactical advisors. Approximately 22 per cent of the close to $20 million in assistance during this period was ear-marked for an expanded military civic-action program concentrated in the northeast "combat zone". The military's attempt to improve its image in rural areas through involvement in small construction projects as part of the program cemented a relationship with local MLN bosses who controlled the municipal government in most of the area. This relationship had a direct effect on the political alignment leading to the 1970 elections, and helped forge a decade-long coalition between the MLN and PID.[37]

Along with the campaign against the guerrillas the army attempted to augment its control over rural areas by increasing the number of military commissioners in the villages. By 1966 there were over 9,000 of these commissioners, and as Méndez himself explained, their job was "to provide for the function of trying to exercise complete control and surveillance in towns and villages of each miltary zone". But the commissioners often worked hand in hand with local landowners, most often allied with the MLN, to form armed vigilante groups that increasingly attacked all proponents of local autonomy or organization among the poor.[38]

During the latter part of the Méndez administration these vigilante organizations expanded their operations to the urban areas. The most active and brutal of these was the Mano Blanca (White Hand). Justifying its actions on the premise that "gangrene demands the amputation of affected limbs: cancer must be cut out at its roots," Mano Blanca embarked on a spree of brutal killings against elements of reform. It was soon joined by other such groups, the most active of them Ojo por Ojo (Eye for an Eye).

While the military continually asserted that it had nothing to do with these death squads, the division between the gangs, military and police became increasingly blurred. As Henry Ginger, a correspondent in Guatemala for the *New York Times*, reported: "No amount of army denial has been able to stem the conviction, widely held among informed persons here, that most of the rightist, anti-communist groups are in fact a creation of the army and that many of their members are junior officers."[39] On the other hand, the MLN was not shy in claiming credit for its role in the violence. MLN leader Sandoval Alarcón continually boasted of the party's involvement in the creation of the death squads and constantly described their operations as a necessary part of the global struggle against communist subversion.[40]

The violence directed by the death squads was aimed primarily against traditional areas of popular organization — students and trade unionists — and members of the PR. The University of San Carlos, as the most active centre of political reformism, was the hardest hit. A seemingly endless list of student leaders, academics and lawyers active in defending trade unionists was threatened and many fell vicitim to the deadly gangs. The level of violence reached epidemic proportions by mid-term of the Méndez administration. At the funeral of academic and labour lawyer Julio Camey Herrera, the rector of the University of San Carlos expressed the frustration of those trying to reform the political system:

> The black banner that preaches the death of intelligence has been raised many times.... It seems that the blood of the university is being demanded as the solution to the problems of Guatemala. It seems that giving bands of killers a licence to operate is seen as the solution to our problems.[41]

The Méndez government was completely unable to deal with the increasing violence. Holding power at the behest of the military, Méndez could not oppose a military institution that had, since 1966, aligned itself more firmly with the MLN and had itself encouraged the spread of violence. Méndez continually stressed that he was being as conciliatory as possible to those "defending their own interests". Yet he was inundated, like Arévalo before him, with plots to remove him from office. In his first year alone, two extensive conspiracies involving conservative officers were barely uncovered in time. Méndez complained that members of the MLN were bribing officers to win support for a coup and that the party had even approached leaders in El Salvador and Honduras to intervene to remove him.[42]

The defence minister was allowed to declare a state of siege at will, effectively taking power out of the hands of the president and putting it in the hands of the top military commanders. But violence had been so pervasive that the restriction of constitutional guarantees which went along with the declaration of a state of siege was described by one businessman as resembling "athlete's foot in a leper's colony: it is hardly noticeable".[43] With the exception of forcing the resignation of an occasional officer, Méndez could do little. For the most part he acquiesced in the brutal campaign against the left and allowed the perpetrators of the violence to roam untouched.

In 1968, however, an extensive group of prominent MLN activists, businessman, military officers and security personnel embarked on a bizarre, ill-advised plan that temporarily strengthened Méndez's hand. On March 27, 1968, an armed band kidnapped the archbishop of Guatemala, Cardinal Mario Casariego. They apparently hoped that FAR would be blamed and in the resulting outrage the PR government would tumble. But, faced with the continued support for the government of the church hierarchy and some military officers, the kidnappers panicked, leaving Casariego behind in an abandoned farmhouse in the department of Quezaltenango. While Casariego refused to testify against his kidnappers, a "who's who" of the right was implicated. Conservative landowner Roberto Alejos Arzu, the defence minister, the Zacapa commander, Colonel Arana, and the national police chief — and reputedly director of the Mano Blanca — were among the most prominent. The defence minister was replaced by a more moderate officer, the police chief was dismissed and Colonel Arana was sent to Nicaragua where he became a protegé of Anastasio Somoza. The Mano Blanca was discredited and the most conservative members of the military temporarily cowed.[44]

Méndez's relative strength raised new hope for significant reform. But these hopes faded rapidly. The government failed to take advantage of its opportunity, and by 1969 right-wing officers in the military had removed the moderate defence minister. To further placate the military Méndez was forced to promote five colonels to generals: the first such promotions since the 1944 revolution. By the time of the 1970 elections, the most conservative officers had regained control of the military, partly in response to a series of FAR kidnappings in Guatemala City. The military again called a state of siege and a new right-wing terrorist organization rose from the ashes of the Mano Blanca. The brief respite from terror had ended.

With the victory of the "jackal of Zacapa", Colonel Arana, in the 1970 elections, the one post-1954 attempt at political moderation ended. Pumped up by infusions of military aid from the United States and increasingly aligned with the most reactionary elements in the MLN, the military had constantly stymied the PR's attempts at reform. The PR was left in 1970 a weakened shell, its members discouraged by its ineffectual efforts in office and the party dominated by opportunistic politicians who differed little from the views of the middle ground of PID and the military. Those politicians increasingly sought personal advantage by tying themselves to the coat-tails of the military and by 1978 would be prepared to align themselves in a corrupt coalition with the PID. As the Guatemalan political scientist Edelberto Torres-Rivas explains, Méndez's administration, which called itself the third government of the revolution, was not "a victory for electoral democracy, only a clear sorry lesson of how military power is superior [to that] based upon civil authority".[45] As the military tightened its hold on Guatemalan society in following years, the lesson became even clearer.

— 8 —
Politics and the Military in the 1970s: The Violence Escalates

Each new government is chosen by the military hierarchy and the oligarchy which negotiate on a presidential candidate. It is very comfortable
to have a disposable president who can be traded in every four years for
another democratically "elected" one. . . . The army is the number one
political party in the country.
—Manuel Colom Argueta's final interview, March 1979

BY THE 1970s the escalating involvement of the army's top command in
both politics and a multitude of business ventures had divided the
military hierarchy into competing cliques linked to civilian political
parties. In this the military, despite its inherent institutional cohesion,
reflected the strains of the rest of the country's political-economic
elite. The lack of legitimacy in a political process intent on ignoring the
will of the populace had heightened the internal contradictions within
the bourgeoisie. That class no longer believed in the ability of the
political system or the military to arbitrate its conflicting interests.
Tied to different economic enclaves, the political parties and the military increasingly used the apparatus of state violence not only to confront popular movements but also to solve their own continual, internecine squabbles.

But these petty battles for personal advantage were fought against
a backdrop of opposition to popular movements. As the revolutionary
struggle broadened and the capacity of the dominant elite to effectively combat the insurgence diminished, the true nature of the political divisions in Guatemalan society became readily apparent. Finally,
internal contradictions that threatened to paralyze the military were
brushed aside in March 1982, when a group of junior officers, those
most involved in fighting the guerrilla forces, took power from their
corrupt generals in a desperate bid to defeat popular forces in the
escalating civil war. Just as important, the coup was meant to

safeguard the institutional cohesion of the military and to paper over the increasingly dangerous cracks scarring the face of the dominant Guatemalan bourgeoisie.

The 1970 Elections: Campaign of Terror

THE POLITICAL SPECTRUM in Guatemala had fleshed itself out between 1966 and 1970. The reform parties to the left of the Revolutionary Party (PR) had regrouped from the purges that accompanied the 1954 coup, and had successfully withstood right-wing terror during the last four years. The Revolutionary Democratic Unity (URD) and the centrist Christian Democrats had developed widespread followings and strong party organization, athough only the Christian Democrats were able to obtain official recognition for the 1970 elections.

The Christian Democratic party, formed in 1955 by wealthy, primarily rural businessmen and landowners, had followed a steady course to the left. Increasingly influenced by the shifting position of the church, which had begun to support social justice for the poor, the party had developed into a solid centre party that was well organized despite a number of internal divisions. In 1970 it entered into a loose coalition with the unrecognized URD and other parties to form the National Front. But the alliance was shaky and before the elections the more radical parties in the coalition were forced out.[1]

The death in the late 1960s of Emilio Arenales, who had best represented the "developmentalist" tradition in the PR, weakened an already anemic party. Arenales had been able to attract to the party many of the reformers from the Christian and Social Democrats. But with his death the party chose a weak candidate who was a compromise between the right and left wings of the party. The campaign lacked energy and the party lost adherents in the crucial months leading to the elections.[2]

While the moderate parties emerged divided, the right presented a solid alliance for the election. The most powerful candidate was the National Liberation Movement's Colonel Carlos Arana Osorío, fresh from Nicaragua where he had been impressed with Anastasio Somoza's blend of political dominance and a business empire held in place through the might of the National Guard. Arana was reportedly aided considerably by election contributions from Somoza.[3] With extensive contacts among landowners in the MLN-dominated and violent eastern districts, he was a natural candidate for the party.

Arana also enjoyed substantial support within the military. As commander of the counter-insurgency campaign in the department of Zacapa, he had been a powerful figure in the military command. His strength was enhanced by loyalties developed during his stint as head of the Escuela Politécnica and widespread contacts with U.S. military advisors.

Arana's support within the military pushed the MLN into an alliance with the Institutional Democratic Party (PID), for the most part the party of the military. Arana ran a campaign appealing for "law and order", vowing, "If it is necessary to turn the country into a cemetery in order to pacify it, I will not hesitate to do so." He campaigned surrounded by military bodyguards armed with machine guns.[4]

The military used a variety of tricks to help Arana's cause in the election. According to Norman Gall, a *New York Times* correspondent, military commissioners in the countryside threatened to burn down whole villages that did not vote for the MLN. Military control over the electoral commission also insured that only 13 polling booths were open in Guatemala City where the MLN was expected to do poorly; none of these booths were in working-class districts.[5]

The election was complicated by a series of actions — many directed against Arana — co-ordinated by the Rebel Armed Forces (FAR). The head of the electoral commission barely escaped an assassination attempt and two national policemen were shot in the weeks preceding the election. The most devastating blow was the kidnapping of Alberto Fuentes Mohr — now Julio César Méndez Montenegro's foreign minister — during the final week of the campaign. The kidnapping of Fuentes Mohr, it was argued, lent currency to Arana's law and order platform and led much of the middle class to desert the PR.[6]

Arana was also helped by a growing perception that as long as the military stifled reform, elections in Guatemala were meaningless. FAR (which had briefly supported Méndez Montenegro in 1966) and reformist parties to the left of the PR called for a boycott of the elections. The most powerful student publication, *El Derecho,* the law school journal, argued before the elections:

> The vote will not give power to the people. Definitely the road to revolution will not pass through the ballot box. . . . With the vote, the people will not advance, they will move backwards. Thus the people should find the true road to their liberation through direct and organized action and never by means of electoral farce.[7]

Reflecting this growing disillusionment, few people bothered to vote. Out of close to six million people in the country, a total of 546,000 votes were cast, less than 50 per cent of the registered voters and under 10 per cent of the population. Arana was elected with 43 per cent of the vote, approximately 4 per cent of the population.[8]

Arana wasted little time in living up to his campaign promise. Declaring that "there will be no halfway measures against subversion in my government", Arana and the death squads his government controlled littered Guatemala with corpses. By June 1970, 30 reformist politicians had been placed on a death-list published by Ojo por Ojo and warned to leave the country. In November of the same year Arana declared a state of siege and troops invaded three university campuses to begin a campaign against academics and lawyers. Lawyer, politician and nationalist Alfonso Bauer Paíz was one of the first shot. By late December a drive against trade unionists started with the murder of Jaime Mongé Donis. Between November 1970, when the state of siege was called, and March 1971, there were over 700 political killings in Guatemala.[9]

Government control of the right-wing death squads was widely assumed and only half-heartedly denied by Arana and his advisors. Indeed, Arana justified the killings to congress. "You elected me," he reminded them, "and you gave me this mandate to pacify the country and put an end to the crime wave. You did not place any conditions on me and you did not tell me how to do it. [My government] is going to keep that promise, no matter what the cost."[10]

In March 1971 Joseph Goulden, writing in The Nation, argued that the violence was directed by a four-person committee consisting of three cabinet ministers and Mario Sandoval Alarcón, the head of the MLN. One of those cabinet ministers was reportedly chief of staff General Kjell Eugenio Laugerud García. Finally, even a U.S. Senate staff memorandum admitted, "Rightist terrorists are certainly influenced but perhaps not totally controlled by the government."[11]

The campaign of terror and the state of siege left the opposition in complete disarray for both the municipal elections of 1971 and the later mid-term congressional vote. This was especially true for the PR. Alberto Fuentes Mohr had been expected to become the new secretary-general of the party after its 1970 defeat and to lead the PR in an unbeatable alliance with the Christian Democrats and the URD. Fuentes Mohr, however, was forced from the country when the state of siege was called, allowing the more conservative candidate Carlos Sagastrume to take over the PR leadership. The already weakened PR was hurt badly by the ensuing internal struggles when Fuentes Mohr returned.[12]

The policy of disrupting the activity of all opposition parties was part of an MLN plan to help it more completely dominate politics. A Guatemalan congressman told journalist Joseph Goulden, "Members of the ruling MLN had stated repeatedly that they should get rid of political opposition by the next elections. . . . To achieve this it seems that they have decided upon the physical disappearance of the leaders of the opposition rather than their exile."[13] With their hold over the military seemingly assured through Colonel Arana, the fascist MLN hoped for a complete monopoly over political power.[14]

By 1972, however, it had become apparent that the balance of power within the ruling coalition was shifting from the MLN faction to the PID. Arana had surprised many in the MLN shortly after coming to power by defining his economic policy in nationalist terms allowing for substantial government involvement in the economy. After 1970 Arana and the military began slowly to draw away from the MLN. One indication of this swing was the virtual disappearance of the Mano Blanca, with its long-established connections to the MLN. The death squad was replaced by a number of others clearly controlled by the military. The periodical *Latin America* pointed to the killing of the MLN president of congress, considered to be one of the directors of the Mano Blanca, as a sign of the final break between the military and the MLN.[15]

While the formal alliance between the PID and the MLN would survive one more election campaign, it had become clear that there were many officers who had come to resent the archaic image of the MLN. The MLN's open boasting of its ties to violence, its fascist image, its ultra-conservative economic and monetary policy, and the party's dominance by incompetent "country" politicians linked to the 1954 coup all alienated many of the officers who had come to see the military as a technically proficient, highly organized political tool. One top military officer expressed what seems to have been the prevailing opinion among the army hierarchy in 1973: "In the present conditions of chaos and violence the Army is the only force which is capable, morally and materially, of governing."[16] Of course, much of that very chaos and violence had been purposefully fostered by the military.

The 1974 Elections: An Electoral System Discredited

THE CAMPAIGN for the 1974 presidential elections reflected both the instability in Guatemalan politics and the military's dominance. In the months leading up to the election, the four legally recognized parties scrambled to entice suitable military figureheads, leading to strange alliances.

The PR continued its political decline, and its hesitant but consistent slide to the right. Despite some final attempts by Fuentes Mohr to reinforce the party's reformist tradition, the increasingly conservative hierarchy within the PR decided upon an uninspiring military candidate, who did little to revive the party's fortunes.

The ruling PID/MLN coalition was preserved, largely through the efforts of Arana. He and the military technocrats who had determined government policy under his administration rejected the MLN leader, Sandoval Alarcón, described by the Guatemala City mayor Manuel Colom Argueta as a "buffoon straight out of the middle ages".[17] Instead they chose Arana's chief of staff, General Kjell Laugerud, as their presidential candidate. Arana was able to temporarily patch things with the MLN by offering Sandoval Alarcón the position of vice-president.[18]

The Christian Democrats emerged with perhaps the most surprising candidate, General Efraín Ríos Montt. The Christian Democrats also benefited from the fact that the more reform-minded parties could not get legal recognition for the elections. The most powerful of these other parties were the URD, led by Villagrán Kramer, and a new party, the social democratic United Revolutionary Front (FUR), led by the popular mayor Manuel Colom Argueta. Early in 1973 the government refused to accept the registration of FUR despite its submission of a list of 90,000 members, almost double the legal requirement. Consequently, the Christian Democrats, the left of the PR, FUR and the URD organized into the National Opposition Front (FND) and eventually decided upon Ríos Montt as presidential candidate with Alberto Fuentes Mohr as vice-president.

Ríos Montt was a military careerist who fit the army mode perfectly. Like most officers, he came from the provinces, in his case the department of Huehuetenango, one of the most "Indian" of regions. He joined the military in 1943 and like Arbenz, Armas, Arana and Laugerud, distinguished himself at the Escuela Politécnica. Graduating at the top of his class, he — again like the other four — returned to teach at the academy. After serving as commander of the elite Mariscal Zavala brigade in Guatemala City, he was promoted to Arana's chief of staff in 1970. He clashed with Arana however, and was removed from his position in favour of Laugerud in 1973 and sent to direct the Inter-American Centre of Military Studies in Washington.[19]

According to the secretary-general of the Christian Democrats, the coalition chose Ríos Montt not because he shared their views but because he was one of the few "honest" officers they felt could be trusted "to keep his word" on implementing Christian Democrat policy if he were elected. They also expected that given Ríos Montt's support among junior officers and his wide contacts within the military hierarchy it would be difficult for the military to deny the Christian Democrats the presidency through fraud.[20]

The options presented in the campaign were not encouraging. As the editors of *Latin America* commented:

The election, whatever its outcome, implies a choice only of political emphasis, not of any fundamental changes. The poor will stay poor in any event, but a Ríos Montt victory could bring a move towards a more modern form of capitalism.[21]

In the end Christian Democrat preparations to forestall fraud had little effect. When the early returns from Guatemala City were announced, the FNO appeared to be on its way to a lopsided victory, with more than double the votes of the ruling coalition. But at that point the government began to delay the counts and the announcing of results. When the official results were finally announced, it turned out that Kjell Laugerud had beaten Ríos Montt, although just barely.[22]

The FNO immediately charged fraud, claiming the true figures would show that the FNO had achieved between 45 and 49 per cent of the vote, with Laugerud getting no more than 34 per cent. The FNO charge was followed by three days of haggling within the closed circles of the military, a discussion the *New York Times* described as being between those who wanted to impose Laugerud and those who wished to respond to "the will of the people". Arana had earlier declared that he would employ "all the might that goes with holding power" to ensure Laugerud's election, and his demand that Laugerud be imposed reportedly carried the day.[23]

The imposition created quite a stir. Ríos Montt announced to supporters: "My historic responsibility and my honor as a soldier oblige me to reject emphatically in the name of the people the fraud that is being attempted." Two days later students urged him to provide them with guns to combat the military. MLN leader Sandoval Alarcón brought 3,000 armed supporters in from rural areas and challenged the FNO to a street fight. "We will be waiting to meet them," he boasted, "and show them that we will not tolerate blackmail and threats."[24]

The days were tense. Speculation was rife that reform-minded members of the military would compel the government to hand power over to the FNO. But Arana carried the day. After a private talk with him, Ríos Montt backed off from his demands and was later quietly shipped off to a diplomatic post in Spain. With the capitulation of Ríos Montt the protests over the election slowly died down.[25]

The fraud completed the country's long-growing disillusionment with the electoral process. In an open letter to the defence minister, Christian Democrat secretary general Danilio Barillas calculated that the military had altered 180,000 votes. He later argued that the election prompted the regeneration of a militant left that was willing to use arms to achieve victory. Barillas then called for the army "as an institution or by means of a group of daring, capable and modern officers to assume the national government of Guatemala. They should call to collaborate with them politicians disposed to participate in the task of governing, the task of reconstruction, the task of implanting new political ideologies for the country."[26]

Barillas' call for a coup of reforming officers was indicative of the political strength of the military. The military hierarchy had shown that it would allow no change to come about through the electoral process. The only way even minor reforms could be initiated, the Christian Democrats reasoned, was by appealing to a faction of the military that would be more willing to accept some of these reforms, and to try to prompt them to action. Barillas' plea marked the beginning of the Christian Democrats' attempt to obtain power through building a coalition with the military, a process that lasted into the 1980s.

The Kjell Laugerud Government: Minor Reforms

GENERAL Kjell Eugenio Laugerud García proved a surprising president. His earlier image as a hard-line, cold-war warrior was tempered and he incorporated Christian Democrat ideas and politicians into his administration. The level of military-controlled violence decreased and the government even tolerated a minimal level of trade union activity. But his administration accentuated two trends underway since 1954: The military stretched its tentacles further into all levels of government administration; and officers became more and more intimately connected with PID landowners and businessmen, especially in the Northern Development Strip (the Franja Transversal del Norte).

Laugerud was one of the military's top technocrats and according to one chronicler represented "efficient and management conscious professionalism".[27] Under his direction the PID and the military completed its split with MLN politicians, who were increasingly left off congressional committees and refused administrative posts. Early in his administration Laugerud also began to try to divorce himself from his former patron, Colonel Arana. To do so, he needed support in congress from other areas, and so engineered an alliance between the PID and the Christian Democrats, with the PR occasionally joining in, to oppose the interests of the MLN and the deputies personally aligned with Arana.

This alliance was reflected in government policy. Christian Democrats were given control of a number of congressional committees and the government gave its support to a co-operative program in the highlands coordinated primarily by Christian Democrats and by Manuel Colom Argueta of FUR.

The biggest struggle in congress occurred with the earthquake of February 1976. The MLN, Arana and Laugerud fought for control of the National Reconstruction Committee (CRN). The prospect of directing the allocation of vast sums of foreign aid and government financing was particularly tempting for Arana, who controlled a large construction company and had been impressed by the example of Nicaragua's Anastasio Somoza. Somoza had augmented his personal resources and consolidated his control over Nicaragua after the earthquake there in 1972. Laugerud, with the help of the Christian Democrats and PR members in congress, was able to appoint a moderate committee of deputies headed by Colonel Peralta Méndez who was linked to the Christian Democrats.

This seems to have been the start of an escalation in the battle between Laugerud and Arana. Two men, Rolando Andrede Pena and Manuel Colom Argueta, both active after the earthquake in helping homeless slum dwellers settle on unoccupied land, much of it owned by Arana, were shot — Andrede Pena died — and a number of attacks occurred against businessmen who were assisting the reconstruction committee. Finally, in what some considered to be a warning against Arana, Laugerud orchestrated a raid on the home of one of Arana's associates, who was arrested when a cache of arms was found along with military uniforms believed to have been used for death-squad activity.[28]

Violence directed against rival business interests with links to the various political parties became particularly widespread in the latter half of the 1970s. This violence was the result of increasing centralization of economic control and the tendency for economic opportunity to be closely tied to political and military influence. Christian Democrat Danilio Barillas believed that Anastasio Somoza served as political model and through the Central American Defence Council had helped strengthen the Guatemalan military's resistance to social change. According to Barillas, Somoza had also helped inspire the movement towards increasing monopolization of political and economic power in the hands of a "tiny and closed national group". The violence was a battle for predominance among the few players in this tiny circle.[29]

While Laugerud had been able to force many of Arana's cohorts from office by early June 1976, his success was short-lived. Reconstruction after the earthquake had prompted new, dynamic centres of local influence to arise in rural communities. Local organizations for reconstruction and the co-operative movement Laugerud had supported reinvigorated autonomous peasant organizations which, in turn, challenged local patron-dominated politics and the control of military commissioners. A revived trade-union movement protested the escalating inflation that followed the quake. Out of the debris of the earthquake arose a new guerrilla organization, the Guerrilla Army of the Poor (EGP). All of this alarmed the military commanders, who pulled Laugerud back towards the familiar ground of repression of local and reform organizations. Amidst rumours that he had been threatened with a coup, the president ended his flirtation with the Christian Democrats in congress.

Laugerud made little effort to control the violence in rural areas. While no concerted wave of terror swept Guatemala during his presidency, unlike during the regimes of Méndez and Arana, death squads operated sporadically and the military was increasingly brutal in the countryside, especially in the Franja Transversal. In 1977 the Carter administration in the United States was able to push through a bill denying military aid and credit sales to Guatemala, Argentina, El Salvador and Brazil because of the frequent violation of human rights in those countries. While this caused some concern in Guatemala, where Carter became known as Jimmy Castro, the slack was quickly filled by Israel and South Africa.[30] The bill had little effect on the Guatemalan military, which continued to increase the level of brutality of its operations in the Franja Transversal.

The Government of General Romeo Lucas García: A New Stage in Repression

BY THE TIME of new elections for president in 1978, the trends started in 1963 when the military overthrew Ydígoras had reached some sort of fruition. The military was no longer identified with the increasingly anachronistic MLN. The military's new position was solidified with a PID/PR coalition that more accurately reflected the diversified business interests of senior officers. After four years of the Laugerud government, the military extended itself into all aspects of government. Officers were in charge of most government departments and were active supporters of government and military involvement in the economy. This involvement allowed top officers to siphon off huge sums of money from government accounts in a level of official corruption that exceeded that of the Ydígoras government. The military continued to demand total control of rural Guatemala. Its attempt to dismantle local, autonomous organizations, bodies that had developed with great difficulty in the three decades following the overthrow of Arbenz, led to a highlands military campaign more brutal than even that pursued by Arana in the 1970s.

For the 1978 elections the dominant political coalition was the new alliance between the PID, the PR and the personalistic following of

Arana, the Central Aranista Organization (CAO). This Broad Front ran as its candidate Laugerud's former defence minister, General Romeo Lucas García. Lucas excited no one, but was powerfully placed within the military establishment, had connections with the leading figures in the PR, and was not vehemently opposed by either Arana or Laugerud.

The MLN had so completely lost favour within the military, despite some last-minute attempts by Arana to once again patch things up between the PID and MLN, that it could find no active military officer who would run for office under its banner. It finally enticed the retired General Peralta Azurdía from his retirement in Florida to run for the party.[31]

The biggest concern for the PID/PR coalition was the strength of the centrist-reform coalition that was expected to align with the Christian Democrats once again. The decisive success of the FNO in 1974 frightened the Broad Front. Consequently, Lucas embarked on a campaign to cut the Christian Democrats off from the support of the FUR and the Social Democrats, led by Alberto Fuentes Mohr. Both of these parties had again been unable to obtain official recognition. Lucas attempted to prompt them to abandon their support for the Christian Democrats by offering a "democratic opening" should he be elected, promising to allow the legal registration of the two parties. In addition, he tried to cultivate a moderate image publicly by offering the vice-presidency to Manuel Colom Argueta, and probably Alberto Fuentes Mohr, both of whom turned him down. Finally, he convinced the old leader of the URD, Villagrán Kramer, to return to the country to take the position. Lucas promised "gradual reform to combat the causes of violence" and said his government would be open to "dialogue and negotiation".[32]

It is doubtful that these ploys convinced many people in the reform parties to swing their votes to the Broad Front, but the Christian Democrats failed to win their votes either. The Christian Democrats ran a cautious campaign devoid of many of the more reformist stands they had supported in 1974. And in an attempt to win military support, the party nominated Colonel Peralta Méndez as its candidate. In the end the reform leaders, anticipating legal recognition following the elections and dismayed at the choice presented them, called on their followers to boycott the elections.

The elections meant little. Electoral politics had been tried repeatedly and had failed to make any difference in the way Guatemala was governed. General interest in the elections was less than overwhelming. The Guatemala correspondent for the *New York Times* suggested: "One may wonder whether it matters who wins. Indeed one senses a growing anti-electoral feeling or at least an indifference. One American firm, hired to do a study of voter attitudes, found that fewer than half the people polled had any preference at all."[33]

Despite laws making it compulsory to vote, 69 per cent of the registered voters abstained and 20 per cent spoiled their ballots — as FUR had called for them to do. Only 15 per cent of eligible voters went to the polls, less than 7 per cent of the population.[34]

Surprising no one, Lucas was given the most votes by the electoral commission, 262,960 to 221,223 for Peralta Azurdía. Although most observers believed Peralta had actually won and he briefly contested the results, once again with a warning about likely violence, Lucas' appointment was confirmed by congress after eight days of debate.[35]

The 1978 elections had been held in the aftermath of one of the most bitter protests in Guatemalan history. The government had proposed a 100 per cent increase in the cost of public transit in Guatemala City — a serious concern for poor workers in the city. The proposal prompted a widespread demonstration beginning on Sept. 28, 1978, and was joined by the National Committee of Labour Unity (CNUS) and organized shanty town dwellers. In the initial five days 12 people died, 200 were wounded and 500 arrested. The demonstrators responded by erecting barricades and forming strike committees. The protest spread outside the capital to other cities before, after 12 hours of pitched fighting, the authorities tore down the barricades and squashed the strike. Nonetheless, the increase was rolled back, and the strike was seen as an important victory.

The protest had tremendous impact on Guatemala. It was obviously not just a response to a rise in transit rates but a vigorous expression of anger at the whole economic and political system. The extent of that anger and the capacity for organization among popular forces shocked the ruling PID and the military. The government's response was increased repression. Lucas, soon to be president, vowed in the wake of the strike: "[The workers] are trying to screw me, but I'll screw them."[36] It was an ominous harbinger of things to come.

Despite his carefully cultivated image of moderation during the election campaign, Lucas García quickly revealed his true stripes. Rather than fronting a government open to dialogue and negotiation he initiated an escalation of terror and murder, a campaign far surpassing even Arana's gory days in Zacapa. All elements of reform in Guatemala were ruthlessly attacked. Trade unionists, students, teachers, lawyers, journalists and opposition politicians were killed at the rate of five or more a day. For peasants, especially those in the Franja Transversal, the four years of the Lucas government were a nightmare of brutality and anguish. While the guerrilla organizations and opposition politicians in exile were augmented daily by the relatives, friends and colleagues of the dead, the contradictions and rivalries within the military and bourgeoisie deepened.

The Lucas government had promised to promote "a social pact . . . to conciliate the interests of the workers and the private sector".[37] But it had barely taken office when a new death squad emerged from the shadowy confines of the national palace. The Anti-Communist Secret Army (ESA) immediately placed the names of 38 people on a death-list and quickly consolidated its operations in successive waves of terror aimed at popular sectors. Trade unionists, universities and politicians were all targets.

The reorganization of the CNUS in 1976 and its demonstrated strength in the transit demonstration of September 1978 frightened the military. Lucas wasted no time in fulfilling his promise to "screw" the workers. Individual unions newly forming were met with determined resistance. Guatemalan security forces, most notably the Mobile Military Police, were continually employed as private policing agencies for manufacturing firms and plantations. Most often their duties were directed at the repression of nascent unions. The best known case was the action taken against the workers at the Guatemala Bottling Plant, an American-owned company which bottled Coca-Cola and other soft drink products under the management of U.S. lawyer John Trotter (later an advisor to the private but influential American Security Council). From 1978 to 1981, every executive member and most of the organizers of the fledgling union at the plant were either killed or forced to flee the country after failed attempts on their lives. On a number of occasions the army attacked and beat up striking workers at the plant. The spate of violence appeared to abate when, responding to pressure from a boycott called by the International Union of Food and Allied Workers, Coca-Cola arranged for new owners to purchase the plant. Still, four years later the confrontation — and violence — dragged on as the new owners prepared to close the plant in what workers called a deliberate attempt to destroy the union.[38]

The government also embarked on a generalized campaign against trade unions. In June and August 1980, army and death-squad forces combined to kidnap 44 trade union leaders, members of the National Workers Central (CNT). The detained members disappeared. The government campaign against unionists continued throughout the Lucas administration.[39]

The most significant triumph for labour during the Lucas regime was a strike at cotton and sugar-cane plantations in spring 1980. Organized by the Peasant Unity Committee (CUC) with the assistance of the CNUS and CNT, the workers displayed remarkable solidarity. The common front presented by the workers along with international attention paid to the strike prevented the government from attacking the workers openly. Instead, in at least one village, peasants who were suspected by the military of being involved in the strike were rounded up after they had returned home, and killed.[40]

Students and academics were specifically marked for attack by government forces. Lucas publicly accused the University of San Carlos of being the "centre of subversion" and from the beginning his administration attacked both professors and students. The first ESA death-list contained a number of academics and its first acknowledged victim was the 23-year-old president of the University Students' Association, who was killed in full view of police and security forces. After his death, the student associations declared that the operations of the ESA marked a new stage in repression in Guatemala. They argued, "The violence has ceased to be blind and vengeful, but it is now systematic and inexorable, carried to the fullest extremes of dehumanization and hatred."

In March 1980 a new campaign against the university intensified the violence and from March to September of that year 27 teachers and administrators and over 50 students were killed. At the height of the violence, in July 1980, 25 armed men in a convoy of cars without licence plates drove through the campus randomly machine-gunning groups of students, killing eight and wounding 40. Afterwards, university representatives asserted: "Everything points to a government policy to totally destroy the University of San Carlos of Guatemala as a centre of democratic and scientific thought."[41]

But the people who suffered most under the Lucas government were peasants and rural workers. As the guerrilla forces that had begun to operate in the highlands after the 1976 earthquake began to grow in strength, and as the military became even more determined to extend its control over all forms of rural organization, the army embarked on a heightened version of the counter-insurgency program initiated by Colonel Arana in the 1960s. The government's "scorched earth" campaign against isolated peasant villages believed to support the opposition carried a deadly toll, with a massacre at Panzós in May 1978 being perhaps the best known military operation of this type (see also chapters 10 and 11).

In urban areas Lucas extended his repressive apparatus to opposition politicians. Immediately following the 1978 elections Lucas began what he called a "national dialogue", ostensibly designed to reconcile differences between political parties and to lend a more democratic air to the badly tarnished electoral process. Part of this process, and a key campaign promise, was to allow formerly excluded reform parties to register for elections. The two most important were the Social Democrats, now led by Alberto Fuentes Mohr, and Manuel Colom Argueta's FUR.

Fuentes Mohr and Colom Argueta were expected to lead an unbeatable combined ticket in 1982, with Fuentes Mohr as president and Colom Argueta his vice-president. But they paid for their party's recognition with their lives. On the 25th of January 1979, the very day his party was to be registered, Alberto Fuentes Mohr was brutally murdered. Amidst world-wide condemnation of the killing, the Social Democrat party was forced to meet in secret to avoid further assassinations. Eventually many of its members were driven into exile where they joined the Democratic Front Against Repression (FDCR). Similarly, violent action against members of Colom Argueta's FUR led to international concern for the safety of its leader. But on March 22, 1979, Colom Argueta was also murdered on the day he registered his party for the upcoming elections. His family would allow no government officials to attend his funeral, which attracted 200,000 people.

Colom Argueta had little doubt about his life being in danger. In his last interview before his death he predicted: "The government is attempting to give itself a democratic veneer, which is why they are recognizing my party. But, in exchange, they may want my head." In the same interview he discussed the new wave of killings. "If you look back," he noted, "you'll see that every single murder is of a key person — people in each sector or movement who have the ability to organize the population around a cause." He pointed to Minister of the Interior Donaldo Alvárez Ruiz and General David Cancinos Barrios as the major architects of government repression.[42]

In the months that followed an ever growing list of Social Democrat and FUR leaders were assassinated. At the very time President Lucas was promoting a dialogue for a new social pact, his government was directing the murder of all politicians who offered any democratic alternative to his government and any hope of significant political reform through elections.

By 1980, with the Social Democrats in exile and the FUR in disarray, government attention swung to the Christian Democrats. In the summer of 1981, Vinicio Cerezo, secretary general of the party, stated that 76 members had been killed between September 1980 and May 1981. By August the number had grown to 120, Vinício Cerezo was in semi-hiding to avoid a similar fate and the party had withdrawn its deputies from congress. Cerezo declared: "My government would have you believe that communism is the enemy of democracy in Guatemala, when in reality it itself is freedom's foe."[43]

For his part, President Lucas responded to growing international condemnation of his government by suggesting that in Guatemala violence was "an allergy people simply must get used to". At the same time his vice-president condemned the government he reportedly was too frightened to leave, saying: "Death or exile is the fate of those who fight for justice in Guatemala."[44]

Not all political violence was directed at opposition politicians. The rivalry between various enclaves of power inspired irregular expressions of violence. One example was a continuing battle between Tachito Arana and Kjell Laugerud's son, Kjellito. Both reportedly controlled "underworld" gangs and were involved in a variety of questionable business operations. Buttressed by their fathers' money and connections, competition between the two occasionally erupted in gangland-style warfare until the death of Kjellito in 1979. In addition to these personal conflicts, rival gangs of detectives protecting influence and power embarked on bouts of internecine warfare. One particularly blatant episode between a former and current chief of detectives was described by a Guatemalan journalist as a "struggle for control of the forms of plunder".[45]

Throughout his presidency Lucas continually asserted that his government was not responsible for the repression. Relying on traditional party rhetoric, Lucas argued that the PID reflected a moderate political view caught between the violent right and left: a patently ridiculous claim, derided by most people in Guatemala. Uniformed military personnel routinely and openly collaborated with death squads. Assassins captured in the University of San Carlos carried military security identification. On Sept. 3, 1980, a press secretary for the minister of the interior resigned his post and fled the country. In exile he reported that blank letterhead of the two most prominent death squads was stored in the desk of the minister. The death lists, he said, were prepared in an office of military transmissions on the fourth floor of the presidential annex and later approved in meetings between the minister of interior and minister of defence and the chief of staff. Finally, in 1981, Amnesty International published a report including an interview with a military conscript who had been promoted to the special intelligence unit, describing the operations of these assassination squads as a "government program of political murder".[46]

Other independent organizations that investigated the situation concluded that the Lucas government was responsible for over 10,000 deaths, not including combatants in the war with guerrilla forces. The Washington Committee on Hemispheric Affairs reported in January 1982 that the government had initiated over 9,000 deaths in 1981 alone in an attempt to "wipe out political opposition". In late 1981 even the Organization of American States admitted that the government was the director of the "great majority [of] thousands of illegal executions".[47]

The government became increasingly dominated by the military during the Lucas administration. While civilian members of the alliance, particularly the most conservative members of the PR, retained significant influence, a cabal of top military officers made all important political decisions. Administrative positions at all levels of the civil service were increasingly going to officers. Partly as a result of the increased demand for officers to fill these positions, the Escuela Politécnica tripled the number of students admitted annually between 1970 and 1979.[48]

Gabriel Aguilera Peralta, one of Guatemala's most knowledgeable military analysts, describes the army's increasing control:

> The most important decisions concerning the political process of the country are discussed and decided within the army. Several of the legal political parties (PID, PR, CAO) in some ways represent the interests of the monopoly sector and they do decide minor matters such as the distribution of seats in congress, appointments of mayors and so on. However, the most important decisions — such as the struggles within the political parties, the selection of official candidates and alternate candidates for general elections and, finally, the turning over of power once the electoral process has been defined — were generally discussed and decided at the level of the high command and officers.[49]

Lucas Loses Control of the Military

THROUGHOUT THE LUCAS administration the military was divided into a number of competing cliques, supporters of Arana, Laugerud, General Fausto David Coronado, Romeo Lucas García and his brother, General Benedicto Lucas. The president, although in a position of power, did not control all military appointments and was therefore unable to ensure that his supporters would occupy positions of authority. In the first few years of his presidency Lucas lost support within the military for what some saw as his indecisive waging of war against the guerrilla forces. This criticism was reduced somewhat when his brother took command of the counter-insurgency and followed a more vigorous and effective policy.[50]

Nonetheless, the military was experiencing continued difficulties in fighting the popular guerrilla forces. The Guatemalan military relied on conscription, primarily in highland villages, for its soldiers. As military casualties reached 250 a month the demand for more conscripts was more than the villages could bear. The conscription drives were resented, pushing more villagers to support the guerrillas and causing an increased desertion rate. It was feared that many of the deserters were going over to the guerrillas and that the army was thus training and arming the very people it was fighting.[51]

One of the military's most serious concerns was its increasing difficulty in obtaining the necessary equipment to continue in the war. In the first couple of years of the Lucas government the restrictions on U.S. military assistance had little effect as the government held substantial reserves with which to purchase equipment. By 1980, as government foreign reserves declined, it became a serious problem and much of the army was fighting with severely limited supplies. Junior commanders involved in fighting the war at the garrison level viewed with dismay the corruption among top commanders, who were increasingly skimming huge amounts off the already restricted military budget. In addition, they were concerned with other illegal operations which they felt were hurting unity and purpose within the army. Some even called for reduced levels of brutality in the highlands as a means of improving the military's image.

In 1981, a number of garrison commanders publicized their complaints in a Mexican newspaper. They complained of the murder of five junior officers who had wanted to expose illegal operations by officers. But, most seriously, they complained of poor and inadequate equipment, charging that eight top generals had pocketed $250 million of the total $425 million arms acquisition budget for that year. They called for a campaign to improve the army's image in the highlands, and warned that U.S. military aid was essential to win the war. They implicitly threatened a coup if conditions didn't improve.[52]

But the Lucas administration failed to respond effectively to these demands. Benedicto Lucas' improvements in the operation of the counter-insurgency answered some of them. But the military hierarchy clustered around Lucas chose Lucas' former defence minister General Aníbal Guevara as the official candidate for the 1982 elections. Aníbal Guevara had been in charge of military operations when most of the problems had surfaced within the army and he was linked to corruption among the top generals.

When Aníbal Guevara was imposed by the PID/PR ruling coalition over the moderate candidate, Alejandro Maldonado, in another patent example of electoral fraud, all opposition political parties once again joined in condemnation of the Lucas government. When armed supporters of these parties met in a Guatemala City hotel to plan demonstrations they were surrounded by police and a shootout was narrowly averted. Throughout the week after the elections riot police repeatedly broke up demonstrations and opposition party leaders were routinely placed in "protective" custody.[53]

In the midst of this seething resentment, junior officers led a successful revolt to overthrow the government on March 23, 1982. There was much speculation following the revolt that it had been caused by the government's continued electoral fraud. This conviction was fuelled by the statement of the leader of the junta that was eventually formed, General Efraín Ríos Montt. He explained the military's actions by saying: "We could not endure any longer; eight years ago they rigged the elections; four years ago they did it again; and, the final straw, there was fraud again a few days ago."[54] All of the opposition political parties supported the coup.

But at its heart the coup had little to do with the fraudulent elections in 1982. It had been planned by junior officers well before the elections. American State Department officials later admitted knowledge of the preparations a month before the coup occurred, and before the elections.[55] The junior officers revolted because they had become increasingly upset at the corrupt and incompetent activities of the top military command linked to the PID and the Lucas administration. These activities, the junior commanders believed, led the military' hierarchy to make decisions that were not based on the welfare of the institution but rather were made for personal gain or for the benefit of the restricted section of the Guatemalan elite linked to the PID. This corruption had hurt the military at a crucial time, when it was locked in bloody battle with guerrilla forces that had already secured control of much of the country. The coup that forced Lucas García from power was a bid by garrison commanders to improve military efficiency in a bloody war they feared they might be losing.

— 9 —
The Post-1954 Economy: "Showcase of Capitalist Development"

The intention of Castillo Armas to 'do more for the people in two years, than the communists were able to do in ten' is very important. This is the first case in history that a communist government has been replaced by a free government. All the world is watching to see which will do a better job. If [it is] Castillo Armas, communism will suffer a blow from which it will never be able to recover in the Americas.
— U.S. Vice-President Richard Nixon, after the 1954 overthrow

WITH THE COLLAPSE OF THE ARBENZ government, Guatemalan politics again fell under the control of politicians allied to the landowning elite and military. But Guatemala had changed too drastically, expectations had been lifted too high, for it to slip easily into the patron-dominated politics of pre-Arévalo days. The Castillo Armas government and to a lesser extent those that followed needed to front their repressive economic policies with a veneer of development and reform. Abetted by substantial doses of aid from an American government determined to make Guatemala a "showcase of capitalist development", the subsequent governments rhetorically supported reform while dismantling the popular organizations fostered by the previous revolutionary governments of Arévalo and Arbenz. The new regimes continued to dispossess peasants, repress workers and encourage the growth of large agro-export enterprises.

In the three decades after the overthrow of Arbenz, the Guatemala economy diversified and expanded, and in some ways the economic growth appeared to be positive. Building on the development of the reform period, agricultural exports diversified, previously unexploited parts of the territory were opened for development and the beginnings of a manufacturing base were laid. Economic growth measured by

Gross National Product was substantial, averaging over 5 per cent per year through the 1960s and 1970s.

New pockets of economic influence developed. The traditional coffee oligarchy was challenged by a more aggressive, landed elite exploiting cotton, sugar and cattle and linked to processing plants tapping new markets. This new elite, allied with foreign partners and, to some extent, a small indigenous manufacturing sector (responding to opportunities presented by the Central American Common Market) prompted significant political jockeying which occasionally took the shape of electoral contests between parties representing various sectors of the bourgeoisie and their military allies.

But this was also an extremely unbalanced economic growth. The strengthened conservative elite that grasped power after the "liberation" successfully resisted any economic policy designed to distribute income more equitably. Consequently, economic growth was tied to commodity export with a tiny internal market and truncated manufacturing sector. The economy was unstable, dependent upon foreign markets, with little internal capital generation, a high level of imports and consequent current account deficits and severe restrictions on government income and expenditures.

This underlying instability combined with the collapse of commodity prices in the late 1970s and the effects of political unrest and a brutal civil war to stop even this inequitable, unbalanced growth. While Guatemalan landowners and businessmen invested impressive profits in American enterprises, Florida condominiums or Cayman Island bank accounts, the Guatemalan government was forced to plead with the International Monetary Fund for loans to pay debts, and the government of Romeo Lucas García was increasingly unable to foster growth or to pay the costs of the brutal genocide it waged in the highlands.

Consolidating the "Liberation": Undoing Reforms

Once in power, buoyed by the "obvious support of the people", Armas embarked on his program to reconstruct Guatemala politically and economically. Despite his protestations that "to eradicate communism does not signify to persecute the worker and the honest peasant who in every case merits the protection of the government", peasants and workers were rounded up and imprisoned in droves.[1] Armas surrounded himself with long-time Ubico supporters who again controlled the secret police. By July 13, 1954, over 4,000 "communists" were in jail in Guatemala. Armas abolished the General Confederation of Guatemalan Workers (CGTG), and the National Confederation of

Peasants of Guatemala (CNCG) and cancelled the legal registration of over 553 unions. He placed impossible restrictions on further union organization. Important sections of the 1947 Labour Code were annulled and by late 1955 labour union membership had declined from 100,000 in 1954 to 27,000.[2]

The Preventive Penal Law against Communism was promulgated, prescribing the death penalty for an extensive list of crimes. With the help of the CIA, the Armas government created the Committee for National Defence Against Communism, later replaced by the General Office of Security to ferret out communist activity. An untold number of labour leaders, peasants and students lost their lives in the early days of the "liberation".

Most important of the measures to undo the reforms of Arévalo and Arbenz was Armas' wholesale return of land expropriated under the 1952 agrarian reform. Declaring that Decree 900 had produced "discontent in our labour relations and sharp struggle between classes in the rural sector", Armas established the General Office of Agrarian Affairs (DGAA) to allow landlords to appeal earlier expropriations. In a remarkably quick time, over 99 per cent of the land affected by the agrarian reform was returned to previous owners, including the United Fruit Company, and many of the institutions established by the reform governments to meet the needs of highland peasants were disbanded or deprived of funds. One result of this attack on newly distributed land was a rapidly declining corn harvest, which plummeted in value from Q940,000 in 1953 to just slightly over Q800,000 in 1955 and 1956. This shortfall was only relieved by a donation of 30,000 tons of corn from the United States in 1955.[3]

The Armas government, however, was not able simply to ignore the reforms of the previous decade. The experiences of the ten years of spring had increased expectations and developed a political consciousness among a certain part of the population who would not simply allow all that was won to be pulled from their grasp. Armas faced student demonstrations throughout 1956 and during the early years of his government much of the countryside was engulfed in unrest.

Just as importantly, Armas had to deal with his backers in the invasion, the American government. As William O'Dwyer, a former ambassador to Guatemala, expressed it after the overthrow: "The foreign policy of the United States is ... on trial in Guatemala. Each nation of Latin America is watching to see [how] the United States is going to aid Guatemala."[4]

With these goals in mind a campaign was begun to wring from a pre-Alliance for Progress congress large sums of aid for Guatemala. In 1955 Richard Nixon visited Guatemala; shortly thereafter Castillo

Armas spoke to the General Assembly of the United Nations and made the rounds of government offices soliciting increased levels of aid and encouraging investment. Many of the journalists who had most ardently attacked the Arbenz government fervently pushed for aid in a new press campaign. The Armas government hired the John Clements public relations firm to polish the Guatemalan image in the United States. The agency promptly commissioned numerous articles in U.S. publications. Even American academics who were somewhat critical of the Armas government and the 1954 overthrow, such as Kalman Silvert and John Gillin, cautioned that the United States "cannot afford to lose interest". They warned:

> If our first "Liberation" is to degenerate into a tawdry poorhouse of quarrelling inmates, or another experiment in communist infiltration, or a revision to traditional banana republic, many people are going to think we would do better to remain out of the liberation business. People of the underdeveloped areas outside of the Iron Curtain ... are going to judge the results of the liberation in terms of their ideal of a better life.[5]

The Armas government, in addition to returning land and powers to the traditional elite, embarked on a policy to impress the business-dominated Eisenhower administration and to promote investment. Armas' Plan for Economic Development 1955-1960 emphasized that the "objective of the program is to stimulate private enterprise, sure that private initiative and enterprise are the principal forces of progress".[6] Armas encouraged traditional agricultural exports by removing export taxes and supported new industrial investments through a variety of "tax holidays". He reassured the Eisenhower administration by turning over the operation and construction of the hydroelectric plant begun by Arévalo to an Electric Bond and Share subsidiary. Arévalo had developed the plant to challenge the Electric Bond and Share monopoly.

A variety of road construction projects, traditionally directed in Guatemala by the government, were tendered out to U.S. construction firms. In addition, the "ultra-laissez faire" development consultants Klein and Sak were hired to direct the economic program. According to Susanne Jonas Bodenheimer, the foremost analyst of the links between the Guatemalan and U.S. economies, Klein and Sak had a "prescription of private enterprise for sick national economies designated to make real friends for the North American mode of free enterprise". They employed this prescription freely in Guatemala.[7]

The arguments of those who saw reconstruction in Guatemala as both a strategic and economic necessity were sufficient to prompt a rain of development and aid funds. From the first grant to the Armas government of $6.5 million in October 1954 to the end of 1957, direct aid to the Armas government amounted to close to $100 million. This was during a period when total U.S. aid to all of Latin America was under $60 million annually.[8] In addition the United States used its influence in the United Nations and World Bank to force increasing amounts of international aid and soft loans for Guatemala, including a loan of $18.2 million from the World Bank to finish the highway to the Atlantic. The World Bank had refused to support that loan during the Arbenz presidency.

In a drive to mould Guatemala into a "showcase of capitalist development", American aid agencies came to control all major aspects of government and economic policy in Guatemala. In effect they created a parallel government of aid offices ostensibly designed to assist Guatemalan planners. While this parallel government was most powerful during the presidency of Castillo Armas, it continued to have a decisive voice in Guatemalan economic planning until the 1970s.

U.S. AID (Agency for International Development), World Bank officials and representatives of Klein and Sak virtually assumed the operation of such crucial government departments as agriculture, finance and public works and developed policy in many others, including the military. According to one economic planner for Klein and Sak, "The U.S. dictated policies, Castillo Armas obeyed orders well."[9] The 1955-60 development plan written by Donald Gordon, the World Bank representative in Guatemala, was accepted by the Guatemalan National Council of Economic Planning as the official government plan. It predictably stressed the creation of a favourable investment climate and the growth of export crops as well as demonstrating a preoccupation with the development of infrastructure. According to Susanne Jonas Bodenheimer, these aid programs were important for American economic interests. They were "utilized to subordinate the Guatemalan functionaries and make them adopt policies favourable for American investments".[10]

Given these interests, the Guatemalan economy and the aid funds channelled through it were almost exclusively directed to plantations producing crops for export, particularly the new export crops of cattle and cotton located on the Pacific littoral. While the Guatemalan population in general, especially the highland peasantry, saw their standard of living decline and the new opportunities for economic advancement that had opened for them during the Arbenz presidency closed off, the economic and political power of the privileged landowning elite was strengthened.

With the death of Armas in 1957, the old Ubico General, Miguel Ydígoras Fuentes, was finally able to obtain the presidency he had long coveted. Ydígoras began to revise plans for state control of

electrical generation, initiating construction of a state-owned hydroelectric plant and creating INDE (National Institute of Electrification).
He also passed an Industrial Incentives Law (1959) and a bill further
guaranteeing foreign investment against expropriation (1961). In
1962, Ydígoras created the National Institute for Agrarian Transformation (INTA) to take charge of the hesitant, intermittent agrarian
reform program and to promote agricultural efficiency. But Ydígoras
was not planning to disrupt the traditional economic and social structure. According to an Inter-American Committee of Agricultural
Development (CIDA) report, the 1962 laws "represented the most conservative expression that has ever been known on the subject in
Guatemala".[11] Most of the national *fincas,* which had accounted for
10 to 15 per cent of government revenue under Armas, were sold off
to private investors or returned to former owners, in one of the most
corrupt land giveaways in Guatemalan history. Under the direction of
his Minister of Agriculture, Colonel Enrique Peralta Azurdía, distribution of land, which had carried on sporadically under Armas, came to
a standstill. By 1960, Crisostomo Castillos, Ydígoras's head of the
DGAA, argued that "native peasants lack sufficient preparation, labori-
ousness and a spirit of initiative" for valuable resources to be wasted
settling them on new land.[12]

The Ydígoras government was most noted for a paralysis of will
brought about by unrelieved bungling and unparalleled corruption.
Huge amounts of aid money were siphoned off by the president and
his advisors; foreign investors could purchase seemingly unlimited
advantages by channelling the proper money to the right people; the
best national *fincas* were purchased for tiny sums, while vast expanses
of colonization land were handed over to favourites. Faced with government ineptitude and declining international prices for Guatemala's
exports, the economy, which had been experiencing real growth rates
until 1959, stagnated. The corrupt Ydígoras government, plagued by
student and worker demonstrations, was confronted with a number of
challenges to its authority by the military until, in 1963, the seemingly
loyal Colonel Peralta Azurdía, now defence minister, overthrew
Ydígoras in a widely supported coup.

While many of the worst excesses of the Ydígoras government
were eliminated by Peralta's caretaker administration, no real reforms
were planned. Peralta, founding his unconstitutional regime on the
necessity of bringing "honesty" back to government, reduced government salaries and ferreted out many areas of corruption. He also
attempted, unsuccessfully, to regain some of the property given away
by Ydígoras.

Demands for New Agrarian Reform

PERALTA AZURDÍA AS HEAD of government did little to respond to increasing demands from some sectors of the political spectrum for a resumption of agrarian reform. Alliance for Progress representatives, who during this period began to push for mild agrarian reform as the only sure bulwark against communist infiltration in the Americas, added their voices to Christian Democratic congressmen and the most moderate of the remnants of the "revolutionary" parties from the Arévalo/Arbenz governments.

The opposition to change was steadfast, however. In response to pressure, the conservatives rallied, demanding instead a stimulus for increasing production. Sandoval Alarcón, one of Armas' principal advisers during the 1954 coup and a perennial power in congress, argued: "The real agrarian problem of Guatemala is not the scarcity of land but rather that the lands be made to produce more."[13] In addition, Guatemala's most influential newspaper, El Imparcial, counselled, "We are not against social justice, but rather against the demagogic way this term is used. Private enterprise might collapse if we augment the burdens of the owners."[14]

In response to these arguments the Peralta government reinvigorated the colonization program in the Petén, creating the National Council for Agriculture which declared, "The colonization of the Petén is of national urgency and public necessity in order to increase the production of basic foods, to relieve the congestion of overpopulation in certain regions, to combat crime and decrease unemployment, to maintain the sovereignty of our territory in the North, to stop the invasions of National Lands and guarantee the respect and inviolability of private property."[15] While the rate of colonization did not increase during the Peralta regime, it did gain some momentum in the succeeding government of Méndez Montenegro.

Colonization, designed as a way to prevent a challenge to large plantations in the highlands and Pacific littoral, had already proven under Arévalo and Arbenz to be an ineffective substitute for a distribution of land held in latifundia. Costly and limited, the colonization program came to be simply another means through which the landowning elite could extend its monopoly control over land and wealth.

Hope for Reform: The PR Government

THERE WAS SOME EXPECTATION that long-delayed economic reform would be initiated by the government of Julio César Méndez Montenegro when it came to power in 1966. Méndez Montenegro's Revolutionary Party (PR) saw itself as an heir to the Revolutionary Action

Party (PAR) and called itself the third government of the revolution. Méndez himself was a respected law professor at the University of San Carlos and had much support among students and reformers. The PR's finance minister, the well-known economist Alberto Fuentes Mohr, was similarly perceived as a reformer.

But the Méndez government was paralyzed by a lack of political will. Voted into power by the growing urban middle class and members of the new domestic manufacturing bourgeoisie stimulated by the Central American Common Market (CACM), it had not divorced itself completely from the interests that opposed change. Of more immediate concern, Méndez was forced to bargain extensively with the military. He had to promise the military autonomy before it would allow the PR candidate to assume the presidency. Confronted by guerrilla forces in the east of the country, the military opposed any concessions to popular movements. The traditional coffee oligarchy — represented by the National Liberation Movement (MLN) and its spokesman, Sandoval Alarcón — had retained powerful connections within the military. It controlled violent paramilitary organizations and continually talked of plots to bring down the government. Faced with these pressures, any reform measures anticipated by the PR government were stymied.

After the coup in 1954 the Guatemalan coffee oligarchy had used its unchallenged political dominance to ensure not only that government kept expenditures down, but also that the burden of government services did not fall heavily on landowners. The consequent perpetual lack of funds had continuously undermined both government planning agencies and the remnants of the Guatemalan Social Security Institute (IGSS) left from the Arbenz era.

While Guatemala had experienced substantial growth since the 1950s (averaging an increase in Gross Domestic Product of 4.4 per cent between 1950-52 and 1964-66), this growth had been unbalanced. Export earnings had increased by 7.8 per cent annually, while the GDP of the highland departments where the bulk of the population lived had fallen.[16] The Méndez government attempted to tax some of this increased export income, and there was significant pressure to do so. A team of American economists reported that economic growth, despite the substantial increase in export earnings, was retarded in Guatemala because of the lack of indigenous investment. While the export oligarchy in a country such as Peru was reinvesting 23 per cent of GDP, the Guatemalan elite averaged less than one-half of that. The Americans recommended increased taxation to reduce the consumption expenditures of the wealthy.[17] In addition, in 1968, the finance ministers of the five Central American republics agreed at a CACM meeting to push for higher sales and luxury taxes to help prompt more indigenous capital for investment and to increase government revenues needed for economic planning.

Ydígoras had taken some tentative steps towards increasing the load of taxation on the bourgeoisie. After a long struggle, he had implemented an income tax in 1963. (Guatemala was the last Latin American country to do so.) It was partly the virulent opposition to this measure by the General Growers Association (AGA) and other agents for landlords that prompted his overthrow. While less than 1 per cent of the population had been affected by this tax, Peralta was forced to reduce the measure even further. Consequently, by the mid-1960s, in an International Monetary Fund (IMF) study of 72 countries, Guatemala's tax system ranked 71st in effectiveness and equality.[18]

With some AID officials pushing for tax measures, and the Méndez government perpetually short of money, the new administration perceived tax reform as its major priority. According to a *New York Times* reporter in 1966:

> The tax bill has... become a question of fundamental principle for many people here. If it cannot be passed or if it is emasculated, then it will mean that nothing really basic can be done in Guatemala — that those who have wealth will not yield something to those who have nothing. If it loses its fight, it is felt, the Government will be doomed to ineffectuality.[19]

Throughout the Méndez administration the MLN and most of the military effectively opposed taxation measures. Perched uneasily between the talons of the landowning oligarchy and the military, the Méndez government repeatedly initiated and then withdrew tax legislation. In 1966, Méndez first presented a property tax bill, which was almost immediately revoked when MLN ministers protested. In 1967, the PR proposed a sliding sales tax which would be applied to luxury goods. Passed in congress, the tax was repealed one month later amidst rumours of a coup. Alberto Fuentes Mohr was forced to resign from the cabinet and, according to one government official, "The forces of stagnation had won."[20] The rescinded tax cost the government between $15 million and $20 million annually, prompting it to cancel a number of infrastructure projects, reduce state workers' salaries and severely cut the budget of the National Institute for Agrarian Transformation (INTA). In this atmosphere of intense opposition to even the most minor reform measures, and constant threats of military and violent opposition to the PR government, Fuentes Mohr explained the dilemma of the government.

> We are confronted by a situation in which political conditions impede the adoption of policies that we recognize as necessary to create political

stability. One could conclude that we are trapped by a form of the vicious circle: it is impossible to promulgate policies that assure political stability, because there is no political stability; and by not making these policies we cannot hope to achieve political stability.[21]

The Méndez government's zeal for reform was soon lost, however, and the party devoted all of its rapidly wasting energy to clinging to power, finishing its term in office and attempting nothing that might prompt conservative reaction.[22] Near the end of the Méndez regime one economic analysis team reported:

> The fiscal system is outmoded; economic planning is still in its infancy, public investment [is] quite inadequate and agrarian reform non-existent, with the result that the growth of agricultural production [is] at a standstill.... While the armed forces continue to monopolize the government's time and energy, the country's real problems are unlikely to receive the attention they need.[23]

Due to its inability to enforce effective fiscal reform, the PR government was both limited in any social welfare programs it could implement and reliant upon U.S. and international aid agencies. The government suffered chronic deficits and, despite the increase in exports and manufacturing, severe balance of payment problems. In its first three months, the Méndez administration signed $16 million in long-term loan agreements, with some $48 million worth pending. In 1968 the IMF provided Guatemala with stand-by credit of $10 million and by 1970, Guatemala's foreign debt stood at $84,712,000.[24]

Reliant as it was on aid money and the international banking organizations dominated by the United States, the "third government of the revolution" could not afford to follow any of the nationalist, development policies implemented by the first two under Arévalo and Arbenz. Nor did it give any indication of a desire to do so. The PR government had come to power with the support of a growing urban middle class and new elements of the bourgeoisie tied to manufacturing and commercial growth and the U.S. -dominated Central American Common Market. Much of the foreign borrowing of the government had been used to purchase increasing amounts of capital goods from the United States. In 1965 alone, Guatemala imported $96 million worth of U.S. goods. Rather than working towards economic independence, the PR government pulled the Guatemalan economy more securely into the arms of the United States.

The Rise and Fall of the Central American Common Market

GUATEMALA'S PURCHASES OF U.S. goods and the substantial U.S. investment in Guatemala were associated with the growth of import substitution manufacturing, attendant with the development of the Central American Common Market. Since the days of the first Central American federation under Morazán, the ideal of a united isthmus had never been completely abandoned. Arévalo espoused economic federation with the other Central American republics as a way of wresting control of their economies from U.S. concerns. In the late 1950s concrete steps were again being taken to encourage co-operation among the five republics. In 1960, prompted by the United Nations Economic Commission for Latin America (ECLA) and U.S. AID officials, four of the five nations signed a general treaty on economic co-operation.

However, ECLA and U.S. officials each pushed for a different type of economic organization, and after an aggressive campaign the U.S. plan for a free-trade association triumphed. The abandonment of the more ambitious and appropriate ECLA plan helped lead to the virtual dismantling of the CACM less than a decade after its inception. In the process the Central American economies became even more dominated by North American private enterprise and the prospects for significant reform became in turn increasingly dismal.

ECLA planners had contemplated a kind of controlled industrialization aided by significant state planning. Industrialization was to benefit the whole region through a series of designated industries "appropriate to and supplying the needs of the region".[25] Extensive planning was to insure both balanced growth within the region and at least a small attempt at redistribution of wealth to increase the size of the internal market.

In the U.S. view, the proposal for planned economic growth, necessitating some level of governmental control and the encouragement of certain key industries, unduly restricted the field for private enterprise and U.S. firms. The United States instead promoted a plan for economic integration that relied primarily on the creation of a free market with very limited state planning. Through a variety of inducements, including the offer of $100 million in assistance funds in 1958, Central American officials were slowly won over to the U.S. viewpoint.[26]

With the CACM in the end favouring foreign, private enterprise and consciously discouraging state interference, American investment in Central America redoubled. The Central American Bank for Economic Integration (BCIE), established in 1960, acted primarily to attract U.S. capital rather than stimulating indigenous investment. By 1970 the BCIE was loaning over 32 per cent of its funds to foreign-controlled firms rather than to Central American producers. However, Central American intra-regional trade under the stimulus of the common market increased from $37 million in 1961 to $257 million in 1968.[27]

Guatemala, with over 35 per cent of the region's population, and El Salvador benefited the most from this common market strategy. The first regional manufacturing plant was a tire factory established in Guatemala in 1958. This was followed by a steel plant, a petrochemicals complex and a Kellogg's plant, all designed to tap the Central American market. Throughout the 1960s, industrial production in Guatemala increased by 10 per cent annually. By 1971, 81 per cent of all U.S. investment in Central America was located in Guatemala and manufacturing employed 11.5 per cent of the economically active population.[28]

By the late 1960s the common market was in disarray. While new industries had in some ways benefited Guatemala and El Salvador, without allocative planning the other republics had experienced little manufacturing investment. In addition, with the increase in intraregional trade and the agreement on tariffs and free trade, Costa Rica and Nicaragua were experiencing budget difficulties due to severely reduced tariff revenue. Nicaragua, Honduras and Costa Rica consistently complained that they were receiving little benefit from the common market and demanded that the Permanent Secretariat for Central American Economic Integration (SIECA) direct regional manufacturing to their countries. Finally, simmering resentment exploded in the 1969 Soccer War between Honduras and El Salvador. The common market all but collapsed. Honduras formally withdrew from the CACM in 1971 and Costa Rica followed temporarily in 1972. Although the Common Market lived on, and in 1980 Guatemala exported $440 million worth of goods to the other CACM countries, the CACM no longer played a dominant role in the economies of the region.

Although part of the problem with the CACM was a growing regional disparity, the major fault in using it as a tool for industrial expansion went much deeper. The common market became a substitute for restructuring national economies rather than an impetus to effect that restructuring as originally planned. Designed to provide an increased market for locally manufactured goods without first distributing wealth to facilitate the growth of an international market, it was doomed to failure. One U.N. development programs administrator, in analyzing the failure of the common market, suggested, "It was illusory to think that a country could be industrialized by building factories; the reality [is] that industrialization [means] building markets."[29] One analyst, surveying the prospects for the CACM in the early 1970s, put it more clearly. "Regional integration, whatever its theoretical economic advantages," he warned, "will have a very limited value if it is regarded by those who participate in it as an alternative to or substitute for social, political and economic reforms at the national level."[30]

New Agro-Export Industries Fuel Economic Growth

AS A CONSEQUENCE OF THE REFUSAL of the Guatemalan bourgeoisie to countenance any type of even minor redistributive policy (a refusal most apparent during the Méndez years), an internal market never developed. By the early 1970s import-substitution manufacturing growth had stagnated and intra-regional trade dwindled. Guatemalan manufacturers were using only 38 per cent of installed capacity. The most dynamic sector of the economy was still agriculture, with activity increasingly concentrating on new products that could be processed in the country and exported.

In 1970, with the assumption of the presidency by Colonel Carlos Arana Osorío as the National Liberation Movement candidate — in uneasy coalition with the military-associated Institutional Democratic Party (PID) — it was apparent that there would be no further attempt at reforming Guatemala's economic structure. AID money continued to flow into Guatemala ($92 million between 1970 and 1974) but it was increasingly directed to the growth of new agro-export industries rather than the import-substitution manufacturing or colonization projects of the 1960s. As early as 1967, the Central American Bank for Economic Integration announced the formation of a finance company with $5 million in AID funds primarily oriented to expanding agricultural exports.

Despite an urbanization rate of 3 per cent annually from 1950 to 1964 and a fall in agriculture's share of the Gross Domestic Product from 28.2 per cent in 1960 to 25.4 per cent in 1971, in the late 1960s agriculture still comprised 81 per cent of total exports and employed 65 per cent of the labour force.[31]

Coffee cultivation, in spite of an erratic and declining world price, increased substantially. Between 1950 and 1964, coffee acreage grew by 85 per cent and output by 157 per cent. Coffee exports were worth $158 million in 1975.[32] Nonetheless, as other agricultural products increased more rapidly, coffee as a percentage of total exports declined. In 1956, coffee made up 73.9 per cent of Guatemala's exports. By 1966 this had fallen to 44.3 per cent and by 1973 to 31.7 per cent.

Bananas, the other traditional agricultural export, also declined. Making up close to 30 per cent of Guatemala's exports at their peak, bananas had fallen to 12.1 per cent in 1956. By 1966, with the United Fruit Company plagued by anti-combines decisions in the U.S. courts, banana exports were only 2 per cent of total exports. By 1973, after

Del Monte had acquired UFCo's operations in Guatemala, exports had risen to 6.8 per cent.

In 1958, anti-combines legislation in the U.S. District Court in Louisiana ordered UFCo to "divest itself of banana lands and purchasing, shipping, marketing capacity to allow the recipient of the divested lands to import approximately 9 million stems annually". All plans for this divestiture were to be presented to the court by 1966.[33] This court ruling presented a problem for United Fruit. With substantial cash reserves and no significant debt, it was prevented by the anti-combines law from using its reserves to expand its banana production.

Consequently, UFCo began to diversify into food processing operations and eventually prepared to attempt a takeover of Del Monte. In an effort to forestall this acquisition, Del Monte involved itself in banana production, the one area where UFCo was prevented from expanding. Discovering that, as Del Monte chairman Alfred Eames expressed it, "Banana trees are like money trees," Del Monte was soon second to United Fruit in banana production and by 1972 purchased UFCo's Guatemalan holdings.[34]

Del Monte operated in Guatemala in much the same fashion as the old UFCo did, although with a carefully reduced profile. Initially, the Arana government refused to allow Del Monte's purchase of UFCo's holdings, because local entrepreneurs were also bargaining for purchase. Nonetheless, after a costly lobby directed by Cuban-born Domingo Moreira (which reportedly included a substantial bribe to Arana) the purchase was permitted. Despite substantially reduced holdings, by the end of the 1970s Del Monte had become the country's largest single private employer, with a work force of 4,500 and controlling 55,000 acres, of which 9,000 were under cultivation. The other 46,000 acres were used to graze 7,000 head of cattle to discourage squatters and forestall the unlikely prospect of expropriation.[35]

When banana producing countries began to co-operate to curtail the power of United Brands (United Fruit), Del Monte and Standard Fruit by creating the Union of Banana Exporting Countries (UPEB) in the early 1970s, these companies resorted to a variety of tactics to break the power of the cartel, tactics that would have made Minor Keith proud. When UPEB members agreed to impose a one dollar per box export tax, Standard Fruit — operating in Honduras — arranged for the Banana Handler's Council of the Longshoremen's Union in the U.S. to threaten to strike against imports of bananas from those countries.[36] In Guatemala the tax was blocked by MLN members in congress and when it appeared that President Kjell Laugerud was prepared to force the law through, Del Monte publicly threatened to pull out of Guatemala altogether. Finally, a compromise tax of 40 cents per box was arranged. However, a number of reports from international agencies stated that Del Monte was consistently under-declaring its total exports by as much as two million boxes annually.[37]

Del Monte devised a number of ways to protect its $20 million investment (reportedly recouped in the first three years) and its $30 million annual trade from Guatemala. It reduced labour agitation through company support of an American Institute for Free Labour Development Union, supported by AID and the AFL-CIO. It restricted access to the plantation on its privately-owned railway. In addition, the heart of the plantation came to be occupied by a Guatemalan army base.

The declining percentage of coffee and banana exports was the result of substantial increases in cotton, cattle and sugarcane production. Throughout the 1960s huge amounts of aid funds earmarked for agricultural "development" went into the promotion of large agro-export enterprises. In 1971 the periodical *Latin America* reported, "Since 1961 the large landowners of Central America — particularly in Nicaragua and Guatemala — have shown considerable ingenuity in abusing international assistance, channelling large sums of money into their own pockets." The report specifically pointed to $100 million which went to cattle ranching during the decade "providing cheaper credit to enterprises which would have anyway been eligible for commercial credit".[38] Despite this type of criticism, the World Bank lent a further $4 million to Guatemala producers to encourage cattle production in 1970. As well as taking up extensive grazing lands in the Pacific littoral, cattle ranches expanded in other areas of the country. After the mid-1970s this was most notable in the Petén and Alta Verapaz regions, where ranches dispossessed both long-resident farmers, Indian cultivators and new migrants.

Cattle grazing became particularly attractive for Guatemalan producers. It allowed for retention of immense amounts of land, demanded little direction from absentee landlords and, using domestic cattle breeds, required little capital investment. In addition, cattle production had the dubious advantage of requiring relatively few labourers, which became increasingly important as the brutal counter-insurgency program started to disrupt traditional labour migration patterns.

By 1964, chilled beef exports from Central America comprised 6.6 per cent of U.S. beef imports.[39] Under the Nixon administration this amount increased when restrictions on imports were relaxed. By 1973 meat exports were 6 per cent of Guatemalan agricultural exports (up from .1 per cent in 1960) and by 1975 exports of beef were worth $19 million. During this period internal beef consumption declined in Guatemala.

Guatemala's two other major export crops also increased their market share. Sugar, with a large internal market, increased its exports to 4.1 per cent of the total by 1973 (also up from .1 per cent in 1960). Cotton, however, showed the most dramatic increase and received the most governmental assistance. Cotton increased from .5 per cent of the total agricultural production in 1950-52 to 13.7 per cent by 1964-66 and from Q5 million worth of exports to Q45 million. It accounted for 19 per cent of agricultural exports in 1966. Throughout the 1960s, coffee and cotton between them received 75 per cent of private bank credit and 44 per cent of public bank credit available to agriculture, whereas basic food crop production was allocated only 19 per cent of public and 2 per cent of private credit.[40] As a further encouragement, cotton was taxed extremely lightly, at 1 per cent of total value.

Guatemalan cotton producers also came to enjoy the highest yields for non-irrigated land in the world. They achieved those high yields through the use of large and frequent doses of commercial fertilizer and chemical pesticides. They began to spray their fields as often as 50 times a year (the norm in the United States is four), using the most deadly pesticides long banned in the United States, and with little regard for environmental damage or the safety of workers. They even experimented with spraying chemical defoliants to reduce vegetative growth and increase fibre content.

Despite the growth of these huge agro-export enterprises, Guatemalan landowners continued to demonstrate the same type of productive relationships outlined by George Britnell in the 1950 IBRD study. A 1970 report by a group of American economists found that the 365,000 minifundia (below 25 acres), which comprised 90 per cent of all farm units in Guatemala and owned 20 per cent of the land, used between 80 and 90 per cent of the land available on their holdings. The percentage of farmland in use declined drastically as farm size increased, however, until well less than one-half of available cropland was under cultivation on large holdings — the owners of which farmed "neither intensely nor efficiently" according to one U.S.-authored report on agriculture in Guatemala.[41] A 1965 study by the Inter-American Committee of Agricultural Development described these large holdings as being "characterized by absentee owners, dedicated to other activities". These landlords were said to enjoy a "high and luxurious" lifestyle, maintaining "an aristocratic colonial lifestyle, while they also try to idealize and imitate North American standards". Most importantly, the CIDA team observed "that like investors in any

Latin American country, the wealthiest of them invest in land as a form of speculation".[42] Jorge Casteñada, director of the National Indian Institute, pointed out what this means to the Indian. "The rural wealthy are not modern capitalists," he suggested. "They still have a colonial mentality. They pay the lowest possible wages and risk nothing. Then they say that the Indians are the obstacle to progress."[43]

While there was a tendency in the 1970s for the percentage of the large landholdings in active production to increase, particularly in the Pacific piedmont, most *finca* owners continued to hold a substantial portion of their land idle. Nonetheless, Guatemalan planters made impressive profits. One study in 1975 estimated the net profit at 30 per cent of sales and substantially over $100 per hectare, or $247 an acre.[44] A substantial sector of the agro-export elite turned export-crop wealth into diversified mini-empires with investments in processing, tourism, real estate and banking operations. These businessmen continually pressured for increased government subsidies, dominated institutional credit and technical services and asserted that their profits were essential for Guatemala's economic well-being. As one planter cum businessman told a *New York Times* reporter: "This country has grown a lot in the past twenty years. We've turned the south coast into the richest farmland in the Americas. We've created thousands of jobs. Just look how Guatemala City has expanded. Look at the middle class that has emerged."[45]

The growth of this agro-export sector, the expansion of processing plants that went along with it, the establishment of import-substitution manufacturing and the growth of the tourist industry indeed sparked a substantial increase in the size of the middle class, almost exclusively located in Guatemala City. By 1980, the population of Guatemala City was 1,180,000, while the second largest city had a population of less than one-tenth of that. One commentator noted that the combination of economic, political and social distortions that has predominated in Central America fostered the growth of "city-states": "nations in which almost all social, political, economic and cultural activities were concentrated in a single primate city".[46]

Dependent on agro-export industries or on the growing public sector, the middle class had little economic power but provided the bulk of the civil service and military officer corps and in some ways dominated congress. Nonetheless, with the exception of the four years of the Méndez government, the civilian middle class was unable to affect government policy significantly. Richard Millet, a U.S. historian, has suggested that by the late 1970s falling commodity prices and negative growth created despair among the middle class, who lost faith in the democratic system and in some ways came to resemble the middle class in Germany in the 1930s, supporting such violent, far right figures as Roberto D'Abuisson in El Salvador and Sandoval Alarcón in Guatemala.[47] While this is true to some extent, the continued success at the polls of the Christian Democrats and the lack of same by the MLN — particularly in the 1982 elections when the MLN was formally led by Sandoval Alarcón — indicates that it was more the corrupt nature of Guatemalan politics than middle-class loss of faith in the electoral process which led to their exclusion from effective policy making.

By 1980 the Guatemalan economy was showing signs of instability prompted by inequitable growth, an unreformed fiscal system and reliance upon foreign capital and foreign markets. The expansion of exports and export revenue and a conservative fiscal policy ensured that the government had more than sufficient revenue through the 1970s. By late 1979 its foreign reserves hovered around $800 million and its repayment of foreign debt was only 3 per cent of export income. Overall growth rates remained relatively high, at greater than 5 per cent throughout the decade, while inflation was relatively low for Latin America at approximately 10 per cent per year.[48] However, the collapse of commodity markets, the reliance upon an increasingly tight supply of international capital, the unparalleled corruption in the upper ranks of the Lucas García government and the strains of a deepening civil war — with popular forces continually gaining strength — precipitated a collapse of Guatemala's economy beginning in 1981.

The increasing political violence also sparked a constant decline in tourist earnings (the second biggest foreign currency earner) from 1979 on. Tourist revenue fell by 15 per cent in 1980, 35 per cent in 1981 and, after the U.S. State Department finally warned Americans against travelling to Guatemala in August 1981, tourist earnings plummeted in the last part of 1981 and the early months of 1982.[49] The Lucas García government was forced to declare a moratorium on debt payments in that sector.

Government income from foreign trade overall fell 26.5 per cent in 1981. In the midst of a serious financial crisis, the coffee oligarchy pushed through a reduction in export taxes on coffee, which precipitated the resignation of the finance minister in protest. Overall growth rates fell to 1 per cent in 1981. More importantly, foreign capital invested in Guatemala declined by over 900 per cent between late 1976 and 1981. During one week in September 1981 alone, $114 million of capital fled the country. The 1980 budget deficit was $362 million and $249 million of that had to be funded by foreign borrowing. The 1981 deficit was even higher. Foreign reserves, at $800 million in 1978 through to 1981, had by October 1981 fallen to $81 million and by the end of the year had disappeared. Foreign credit lines collapsed and most state infrastructure projects were abandoned.[50]

By 1982 the government of Lucas García was unable to cope. The well of corruption had run dry. The economic plums which his government distributed to friends, disciples and protectors sapped capital from an economy that couldn't support it. No longer able to fund the costly civil war, and challenged by those elements of the bourgeoisie not privy to government favours, the PID/military government had virtually ceased to function when it fell to a coup of tough garrison commanders in March 1982.

— 10 —
The Economy and the Highland Peasantry: Land, Profits and Poverty

It is a sad, sad people.
The Indian cries and the land dies of thirst,
The Indian cries and the land dies of hunger,
A people saddened by torment.
—Luis Sam Colop, "Elegía India", *Versos sin refugio*

GUATEMALA'S ECONOMIC GROWTH FROM the 1950s on had little positive benefit for the majority of its population: the highland peasantry. It was economic growth benefiting a tiny minority. The political coalition of landed elite and an intervening, corrupt military ensured that no substantial reforms would occur. The bulk of the population remained in the grips of a rapacious landowning elite determined to maintain control over the principal source of labour, the peasantry. Agricultural diversification only multiplied the demand for migrant labour to work the harvest on lowland plantations.

The extremely inequitable land-ownership pattern recorded in the 1950 census changed little in the succeeding three decades. In absolute terms, the highland peasantry was worse off in 1982 than in 1950. With even less land for subsistence, plantation wages increased hardly at all while prices rose rapidly. Many highland villages sank even farther into collective destitution; illiteracy was widespread, malnutrition universal, hunger frequent, disease rampant, living rudimentary and life short.

Traditional Agriculture: Diminishing Land and Migrant Labour

MUCH OF GUATEMALA'S AGRO-EXPORT growth came at the expense of traditional food crop production. While the share of agriculture in total output between 1950-66 fell only slightly (from 32.5 per cent to 30.1 per cent) the percentage of Gross Domestic Product from traditional highland agriculture declined significantly. The share of GDP generated in the well-populated highland departments of Chimaltenango, El Quiché, Sololá, Totonicapán, San Marcos,

Huehuetenango, Alta Verapaz and Jalapa fell from 16 per cent to 6.4 per cent, while per capita output in those provinces declined absolutely from Q97 to Q51. In the four predominantly corn-growing departments of Sololá, Totonicapán, Huehuetenango and El Quiché, corn production fell from 102,856 metric tons in 1960 to 88,826 in 1966.[1]

The tremendous increase in coffee, cotton and sugarcane production in the 1960s and 1970s augmented the demand for migrant workers from the highlands. Driven by poverty in their home villages, every year hundreds of thousands of migrant workers crowded onto trucks hired by labour contractors and journeyed to the Pacific coast for a few months' work. Estimates of the number of migrant workers involved in the annual harvest vary from a count of 275,000 in the mid-1960s by Humberto Flores Alvarado, to another around the same time of close to one million including women and children.[2] At the plantations the workers endured 14-hour days, back-breaking work, miserable rations and unsanitary living conditions for miserly wages. They returned to their villages wracked with malaria and dysentery or debilitated by pesticide poisoning.

During the Arbenz regime the agrarian reform and the abolition of coercive measures like Ubico's vagrancy law combined to increase rural labour's bargaining power. By 1952, plantation wages had risen to 80 cents a day. After the 1954 coup, dispossession of the hundreds of thousands of peasants who received land through the previous agrarian reform ensured there would be no shortage of migrant labourers in the late 1950s and early 1960s. However, when the expansion of newer plantation crops created fears of a shortage, extra-monetary coercive measures again began to be used. Some of the largest *finca* owners, with land on the Pacific littoral, maintained "extra land" in the highlands, which they rented to labourers who were perpetually tied to the harvest as part of their rental agreement.[3]

Cotton *fincas,* particularly throughout the early 1960s, had problems recruiting labourers. While they traditionally paid a marginally higher wage, the work was much harder and of shorter duration, the living conditions generally worse. Consequently, for the 1963-64 harvest, the National Cotton Council prompted the military to round up peasants to augment migratory labour. In the same year, Colonel Peralta Azurdía reportedly considered reinstatement of the vagrancy law.[4]

These were exceptional instances, however. Generally, the increasing poverty of highland peasants and the activity of labour contractors in highland villages provided an adequate work force. Labour contractors, long a tradition in Guatemala, acted as landlords' agents in hooking highland peasants into a labour contract through meagre loans made to them earlier in the year.

Wages on lowland *fincas* were generally no more than 60 cents a day in 1965, and the highest daily rate for agricultural work in the highlands was 50 cents a day.[5] In an extensive 1967 study, Lester Schmid found that the value of wages paid on a piece-work basis, along with other benefits including rations, averaged between $1.05 and $1.15 a day. Wages were kept low through a variety of measures including inaccurate weighing scales and illegal discounting for foreign material in each worker's harvest. In 1976, the government of Kjell Laugerud fixed a minimum daily wage of $1.12 on cotton and sugar plantations and $1.04 on coffee *fincas*. But this regulation was routinely ignored by owners. Finally, in the spring of 1980, in an unprecedented show of solidarity, 110,000 migrant workers on cotton and sugar plantations withstood intimidation and struck the harvest for almost a month. While the cane rotted in the fields, workers and owners battled until the government set piece-work rates at levels providing wages of about $3.00 a day. Plantation owners only agreed to this increase when they were assured privately that the minimum wage would not be enforced.[6]

Conditions on the plantations had improved little for migrant workers in a century. In the mid-1960s Lester Schmid reported how labourers and their families were frequently housed in open shelters composed of dirt floors and a tin roof supported by poles. For months on end, as many as 500 people were crowded into these quarters. Only 30 per cent of the *fincas* had sanitary facilities of any kind, and not many had electricity or any food supply other than that brought by the workers. Few health precautions were taken and as a result 7 per cent of coffee workers and 30 per cent of sugarcane and cotton workers came down with malaria, dysentry or diarrhea.

By the late 1970s little had changed. Alan Riding of the *New York Times* followed migrant workers to a number of plantations on the coast. At a typical sugar plantation, he found that the 1,500 cutters and their families slept "shoulder to shoulder on concrete floors sharing discomfort and disease. They use a stream as wash basin and toilet." The only recent improvement on most plantations was a military security guard-post. Alan Riding also noted the widespread, reckless use of pesticides, especially on cotton plantations. Cotton planters routinely ignored what few regulations there were, spraying while whole families still worked in the fields. As a result, thousands of cases of pesticide poisoning were being reported to government clinics every year, and many times more that number never got reported. Although few deaths were acknowledged, observers believed those who died of pesticide poisoning were simply buried on the plantations. A study by the Central American Nutritional Institute found Guatemalan mothers' milk to have the highest DDT levels in the western world: 18 times higher than the medically safe limit.[7]

Because of the meagre pay, the inhumane conditions and the danger involved in working the harvest, it was avoided by those who could subsist in any other manner. According to anthropological studies over the years, in most villages only the poorest travelled to the coast. Nonetheless, land dispossession so eroded the highland landbase that in some villages almost the entire economically active population made the yearly journey. The rewards were meagre but, for the migrant worker who "lives the agrarian reality with [an] almost constantly empty stomach" those months of back-breaking labour for miserly pay became a necessity.[8]

Peasant Landholding and Income

THIRTY YEARS AFTER AN EFFECTIVE agrarian reform had temporarily distributed land to 100,000 peasant families, land distribution in Guatemala remained as unequal and unjust as it was before the reform. Over half the population and fully 80 per cent of the Indians subsisted on plots of land "the size of a grave", to use Eduardo Galeano's famous phrase.[9] The 1950 census reported that 2 per cent of the population controlled approximately 70 per cent of the agricultural land. Every study in the intervening three decades indicated that monopoly control over productive land had grown tighter and the amount of land available to the peasant farmer had decreased. Even more apparent was the growing impoverishment of the highland peasants through the loss of fertility on overused land, an increased population base, exclusion from institutional assistance such as credit and marketing facilities and a continued, systematic dispossession of the most valuable and productive lands. Caught in the grip of constant or declining incomes and dramatically rising prices, Guatemalan peasants sank into greater depths of poverty.

The 1964 census, despite government attempts to alter embarrassing figures, adequately indicated this. A full decade after Armas declared he would "do more for the people in two years than the communists did in ten", 2.1 per cent of landholders controlled 62.5 per cent of the land, while 87.4 per cent of farming units had access to only 18.6 per cent of the land. A 1965 study by the Inter-American Committee of Agricultural Development (CIDA) suggested that these figures underestimated land-ownership inequity. CIDA suggested rather that 2.1 per cent of farm units controlled 72.2 per cent of all land, and that 88.4 per cent of the total farms subsisted on 14.3 per cent of the available land. By 1979, official figures reported that 89.7 per cent of farming units had access to only 16 per cent of the land, while the top 2.2 per cent of farm units controlled almost 65 per cent of all arable land.[10]

The actual situation was in fact even more dismal. The population in the eight highland departments increased between 1950 and 1964 by 41.3 per cent, but the amount of land available to peasant farmers in these departments decreased. At the same time as the size and number of large *fincas* constantly grew, the number of people dependent on agriculture for a living also steadily increased. In 1950, 67.3 per cent of Guatemala's 2.8 million people depended on agriculture. This amounted to about 1.9 million people. By 1980 57.3 per cent of the country's 7.3 million people — or about 4 million in all — still relied on agriculture for a living. The majority of the 2 million extra people were forced to remain in the highlands, where the percentage of land held in minifundia declined somewhere between 1 and 14 per cent depending on the department. The number of landless or "almost landless" highland dwellers was still increasing yearly in the 1980s.[11]

The consequences of the lack of agrarian reform were readily apparent. During the mid-1960s the Guatemalan National Planning Council estimated that 90 per cent of all rural families were either landless or possessed insufficient land for subsistence. The number of landless increased by 140,000 between 1950 and 1962. Because of this dispossession, along with the large expanses of uncultivated land held by latifundia and the restrictions placed in the way of peasants attempting to acquire new land outside of the highlands, by the 1970s Guatemala had the highest population density per hectare of cultivated land in Central America.[12] While 90 per cent of the country's farming units grew corn, the tiny size of the farms meant that Guatemala had to import approximately 80,000 metric tons of corn a year to meet internal demand.

Quite clearly the income levels of the highland peasantry must also have declined since 1950. While the per capita Gross Domestic Product increased substantially since the 1950s and in 1981 hovered around the $700 mark, according to all reports the poorest people in Guatemala received an increasingly tiny percentage of national income. The income of most highland peasants remained under Q100 per year. Three studies of income levels were carried out in the early 1970s, by the United Nations Economic Commission for Latin America (ECLA), the Guatemalan press and the Guatemalan Social Security Institute (IGSS). All were predominantly urban-oriented and consequently overstated the income levels of the lowest percentiles. However, the most generous of these, the IGSS study, reported that the poorest 60 per cent of the population received 17.3 per cent of the total national income. The poorest 20 per cent earned only 1.8 per cent of that national income in 1971, as compared to 2.9 per cent in 1958. In contrast, the ECLA study reported that the bottom 50 per cent received 13 per cent of the national income, while in the press study the bottom 50 per cent received 9.7 per cent.[12]

Inequity in the highlands was even worse than these national averages indicated. The average farm in the highlands required only 40 days of work a year. A 1973 AID study consequently estimated that the owners of small farms in the highlands were only gainfully employed on their farms or in outside work 43 per cent of the available work days. If only the smallest farms were considered, the average would be under 21 per cent. While other studies questioned whether small farmers did not find more outside employment than this indicates, all suggested that highland peasants were constantly underemployed or engaged in pursuits with minimal returns.[14] In 1971, well over 660,000 people were unemployed while over one million more of the economically active population were chronically underemployed. According to one study the gross value of farm output per person in minifundia in the highlands was Q42 per year. With all outside sources of income considered (including plantation work) the average family income (for a family of five) was Q250.[15] This estimate, and that of other studies that agree with it, included the value of farm produce consumed, not marketed.

In some areas of the highlands the vicious spiral of diminishing land and declining yields was halted (or slowed) in the mid-1970s by the increasing use of chemical fertilizers: a practice that became more widespread after the 1976 earthquake. Higher yields and concentration in new cash crops (such as garlic) substantially increased the income of the more prosperous peasants in a few communities. However, poorer peasants, with little or no funds available in the form of aid or farm credit, were unable to take advantage of these opportunities. Generally speaking, the changes that occurred in some communities during the late 1970s exaggerated income differences among peasants but did little to increase income levels for the bulk of the peasantry.

Peasants and Economic Opportunity

GUATEMALAN ECONOMIC PLANNERS have long asserted, as the Guatemalan elite has done since the conquest, that Guatemalan peasants lack economic initiative and are inefficient producers. Locked in rhythms and traditions centuries old, the argument goes, they are unable to take advantage of economic opportunities afforded them. Like the worst of the "positivists" in the 19th century, economists argued that the apparent "dualism" in the Guatemalan agricultural sector is the peasantry's own doing.

Numerous studies of Guatemalan minifundia, however, have rejected this hypothesis. Anthropologists resident in highland villages from the early 1940s on, including Robert Redfield, Charles Wagley, E.M. Mendelson, B. Spencer, B. Hinshaw and Ruben Reina have all described the Guatemalan peasant's "deep and intimate connection with the market". According to Sol Tax, the Indian is "above all else an entrepreneur, a business man".[16] Others have seen peasants as quick to grasp the few economic opportunities presented and efficient users of the scarce resources available to assist in production. According to an AID study, relative to their income peasants invest a surprising amount in their farms and receive "significantly higher. . . value of production" for every dollar of capital invested than farmers in the United States or Canada.[17]

Guatemalan peasants not only produced a higher yield per dollar invested and cultivated a substantially greater proportion of their holdings than owners of larger *fincas,* but they also achieved yields up to 20 times more per hectare than the largest farm size, despite inferior land and limited use of chemical fertilizer and pesticides. Guatemalan peasants also used institutional inputs more efficiently. An AID study published in 1973 showed that minifundia receiving government credit increased their production 147 per cent more than those without access to credit.[18] Despite this propensity for efficient agricultural production, by the 1970s only 4.3 per cent of the Guatemalan national budget went to agriculture; agricultural credit per hectare in Guatemala was one-half that in Mexico and one-fifth that available in Costa Rica.[19]

As CIDA reported in 1965, Guatemalan peasants were poor because they had been defrauded of their land and suffered from "indifference and outright exclusion . . . from governmental credit, extension and technical aid programs". As the 1973 AID study felt compelled to reassert throughout its text: "The principal explanation for the abject poverty level of the Guatemalan small farmer is the absolute size of his operations and not the efficiency of his processes."[20]

Health and Nutrition

THE POVERTY OF GUATEMALAN PEASANTS had the expected results in life style and health. In the late 1970s, Guatemala's mortality rate was the highest in Central America, and life expectancy was the lowest. Average Guatemalans died before they reached 53 years of age (compared to 57.8 in El Salvador and 68.2 in Costa Rica), and the mortality rate was 30 per 1,000 (it was 14.5 in El Salvador and 4.0 in Costa Rica during the same period).[21]

Of 68,000 deaths recorded in 1960, 49 per cent were children under the age of five, and over 10 per cent died in the first 28 days of life. Most infant deaths, however, went unreported. One study done in the highlands in the 1960s found that in over half of the rural families interviewed two or more children had died.[22] The averages covering the whole country are deceiving; if the population of the highlands were considered separately, the mortality rate and the number of infant deaths would increase dramatically.

High mortality rates were the result of constant malnutrition, unhealthy and unsanitary living conditions, a lack of medical care and constant, wearying work. The Guatemalan National Planning Council estimated in 1966 that on the average the population was consuming one-third of the basic dietary requirements.[23] By the early 1970s, 75 per cent of Guatemala's children was seriously undernourished, while the diet of the Guatemalan adult lacked between 60 and 85 per cent of the necessary dietary intake of all food types except corn and beans.[24] In the same period, investment in health care per capita was one-quarter that of Costa Rica, one-fifth that of Cuba and less than one-tenth that of the United States. What care existed was disproportionately clustered in Guatemala City.

Before the 1976 earthquake Guatemala lacked more than one million housing units. Those in existence were mostly rudimentary. In the mid-1960s less than 1 per cent of rural homes had water and 97 per cent had dirt floors (47 per cent of urban homes also had dirt floors). Over 90 per cent of rural homes had no sanitary facilities.[25]

The 1976 earthquake caused further deterioration in the living conditions of the highland peasantry and urban poor. The earthquake brought little disruption in the industrial and export agricultural sector and only slight damage in the more affluent suburbs of Guatemala City. The value of the agricultural export and industrial sector capital was only reduced by 1 per cent. But among the poor the quake was devastating: 22,800 people were killed, 75,000 injured and one million people left homeless.[26] The most seriously affected areas were the poor Guatemalan City *barrios* of squatters' shacks built on ravines and on other unstable vacant land, along with highland communities in the departments of Chimaltenango and Sacatepéquez.

Land Reform after 1954

THE PRINCIPAL REASON FOR THE CONTINUAL and accelerating impoverishment of the bulk of the Guatemalan population was the consistent refusal by the Guatemalan bougeoisie to enact any meaningful agrarian reform. In 1956 President Castillo Armas declared: "Every Guatemalan has a right that land, necessary to insure his economic subsistence and that of his family, be given to him and fully guaranteed as his private property."[27] Despite Armas' promise, his government dispossessed hundreds of thousands of families who had benefited under the 1952 agrarian reform and distributed land to only 15,494 families. Most of these people were settled on United Fruit Company land "donated" to the Guatemalan government after the coup.

However, despite this slow rate of distribution, Armas was more vigorous than any of his successors in distributing land to peasant cultivators. From 1957 to 1963, despite the formation of the National Institute for Agrarian Transformation (INTA) in 1962, 2,451 families received land under the agrarian reform. During the Peralta government (1963-66), the slow trickle of land relocations stopped; less than 600 families received land titles.[28] There was an attempt under the PR government of Méndez Montenegro (1966-70) to increase this miserly rate, spurred on by Alliance for Progress rhetoric. However, prevented from altering the size of latifundia by its tenuous political position and the political power of the large landowners, the PR government was unable to accomplish any significant redistribution.

With the state deprived of necessary funding by a landowning bourgeoisie that refused to tax itself, plans for agricultural colonization were never more than partially realized. With the assistance of AID funding, INTA under the administration of Manuel Colom Argueta was able to organize some 14,000 families into producing and marketing co-operatives. INTA also made plans to divide the remaining national *fincas* among peasants. Colom Argueta also initiated the Indian Economic Development Service to provide institutional services to highland communities. However, faced with increasingly virulent opposition and a growing government deficit, the agrarian program, declared a "national emergency" in the early 1960s, ground to a halt.

By the 1970 presidential elections, agrarian reform was one of the major campaign topics. The PR candidate declared that his party if re-elected would "give land to everyone who wants land, even if it means that we have to buy land, so that every peasant can be a landowner". The Christian Democrats, competing in their first presidential election, ran a more vigorous campaign. Rejecting gradual reform of the PR type, which "won't guarantee our peasants land until the year 2100, when other men will be cultivating the moon and Mars", their candidate, Major Jorgé Lucas Caballeros, promised "a complete and rapid agrarian reform with the object of increasing the productivity of the peasant".[29]

However, the eventual winner of the election, the candidate of the traditional landed oligarchy and the mainstream of the military, Colonel Carlos Arana Osorío, opposed any agrarian reform. Labelling the Christian Democrats as communists, Arana promised "stability" and declared that the idea of a significant agrarian reform was "incompatible with the existence of a constitutional state".[30] Using MLN control of the rural political apparatus, intimidation by the MLN-controlled paramilitary organizations and dissatisfaction with the PR government, Arana, as the MLN/PID candidate, won the election. With the return of the coffee oligarchy and military parties to dominance, even the rhetoric of agrarian reform was abandoned.

During the mid-1960s the most dynamic economic force in the country had been the growing manufacturing sector tied to the Central American Common Market (CACM). The PR was an expression of the relatively more progressive political ideas of this sector of the bourgeoisie and their middle-class professional allies. These people had been hamstrung by the military while in power but by 1970, with the collapse of the CACM, politics were again controlled by elements of the bourgeoisie associated with agriculture. No sector of the MLN, PID and PR would seriously contemplate agrarian reform.

The political climate of Guatemala after the 1954 coup and the exclusion from power of any of the reformers involved in the Arévalo and Arbenz governments ensured a continual rejection of the Arbenz-style land reform. Expropriation, which had "intensified class conflict in the countryside", was specifically ruled out. The most energetic measure to encourage increased productivity was a moderate, easily circumvented tax on idle land. With expropriation politically impossible, the only alternative that would provide land for the highland peasantry was colonization of untitled national lands on the frontier or the distribution of the producing national *fincas*.

With between 68 and 80 per cent of the national territory still in the hands of the state in the late 1950s, an aggressive relocation with vast inputs of money might have been able to relieve congestion slightly in the highlands. A lack of political will on the part of reformers, the steadfast opposition of the dominant elite worried about a labour force, the lack of funding for agricultural colonization, and a development program (provided by AID officials) that unrealistically concentrated on establishing commercial, middle-sized farms, ensured that colonization would accomplish little of lasting benefit.

The least costly lands available for relocation were the national *fincas* left in state hands after the expropriations of the Second World War. The *fincas*, relatively fertile land already in production, had been divided among peasants or turned into co-operatives by the 1952 Agrarian Reform. After the coup they were returned to the state and between 1954 and 1963, 41 *fincas* were either sold or returned to their previous owners. Many of these transfers occurred in the midst of the worst days of corruption during the Ydígoras government. By 1967, then, 26 national *fincas* were still held by the PR government. These were the smallest, least fertile *fincas* and amounted to only 45,140 hectares of semi-marginal land. The Méndez government succeeded in turning some of these remaining *fincas* into co-operatives benefiting some 949 families.[31]

The only other alternative for providing land to peasants was land colonization on untitled land in national development zones on both the Pacific and Atlantic piedmont. The major area of settlement was the largely unpopulated Petén. Frontier colonization had been attempted by the Arévalo government in 1945. Over the next three years, several million dollars were spent on the project at Poptún in the Petén before being abandoned for more practical agrarian measures.

With the takeover in 1954, colonization was again contemplated. AID provided approximately $14 million for agricultural colonization between 1954 and 1959. The country began 19 projects, 17 on the Pacific and 2 on the Atlantic slope, mostly on UFCo land or on land purchased from a European lumber company. The AID plan demanded, "Settlers... be selected that have interest and capability for development into successful middle class commercial farmers."[32] Funds were only made available to projects establishing "economic concerns" of 50 acres or more.

Because of the high cost of settlement and the government's inability to provide backup services, these projects were quickly abandoned. AID planners continued to argue into the 1960s that Armas' reforms contained "substantial improvements" over the "former haphazard method" of Arbenz and pushed for impractical and inappropriately large landholdings in their agrarian colonization schemes throughout the decade.[33]

Colonization schemes eventually centred around the Petén and Alta Verapaz. An early colonization project was begun along the Sebol River in Alta Verapaz in the early 1960s. An in-depth study of this project by the American anthropologist George Fisher details the particular problems of that scheme. While the land was legally vacant at the inception of the project, a number of Ketchi Indians had migrated to the area years previously; they were simply pushed off their land when the settlers came. After much of the colonized land was settled and cleared, a group of "efficient" *ladinos*, brandishing titles dating from the Ubico era, demanded repossession and started to "dominate the landscape along the main trails and rivers". These *finca* owners later turned to cattle ranching and while a few of the more aggressive colonists were able to retain their land and attempted cattle grazing on a small scale, many of them became resident labourers on the new *fincas*, employed in clearing bush on cattle-grazing land. Fisher notes that some of the owners took to mechanized clearing, allowing them to increase the size of their operations and putting more pressure on local small farmers.[34]

Colonization projects began in the Petén with the creation of the National Enterprise for the Promotion and Economic Development of the Petén (FYDEP) in 1959. Few concrete plans were made until the late 1960s, however, when FYDEP was pressured by congress to begin colonization along the banks of the Usamacínta and Pasíon rivers to forestall a projected Mexican hydroelectric dam on the Usamacínta. The dam would have flooded a substantial section of Guatemala. Consequently, between 1969 and 1973, 600 peasant colonists were settled along the two rivers. However, most of the settlers were simply dumped on isolated plots, given little or no technical assistance and little security of tenure.[35] One priest who visited the settlement reported that the "600 families are in an anguished and dramatic situation, since they lack the tools to work the lands. They have neither food, medical attention nor medicine and it is difficult for them to take care of their basic needs."[36]

FYDEP showed little enthusiasm for colonization with highland peasants. The agency wished to attract a limited number of capitalized *ladinos* to develop the area, and despite the rhetoric of national politicians and INTA throughout the 1960s and early 1970s, FYDEP did not see the Petén as a solution to the lack of land in the highlands. The head of the General Office of Agrarian Affairs explained this attitude:

> Let us speak clearly. It is not a question of settling the Petén at any price and thus contaminating from its birth a organism that must remain imperatively healthy in order to communicate its health to the whole country.... We would also clarify that of the 2,849 immigrants to the Petén, 1,908 were Indians and 941 non-Indians: coefficient of regression, since no matter how much sympathy we may have for the Indian problem, they are not the human contingent that the Petén needs to progress.[37]

In order to promote the kind of colonization it desired in the Petén, FYDEP provided an extremely low estimate of the number of colonists it felt could be supported in the department. In the early 1970s it reported to the congress that due to a poor grade of soil, the Petén could only be expected to support 150,000 people. However, independent reports suggested that as many as 500,000 people could be supported through agricultural production in the region.[38] The low FYDEP estimate was designed to avoid criticism of a settlement program intended to foster the growth of latifundia style development. FYDEP's rival, INTA, continued to use the prospect of colonizing land as a means of quelling pressure to expropriate latifundia in other parts of the country. *Latin America* reported in June of 1971:

> Land colonization schemes have been favourite instruments of agrarian oppression. In Guatemala the colonization program seems specifically designed to drain the population pressures existing in the highlands, down into the Atlantic zone so that the *latifundias* on the Pacific Coast shall remain unaffected by demands for agrarian reforms.[39]

The feud between INTA and FYDEP continued through the 1970s. In 1966, some Maryknoll fathers began to settle highland peasants from Huehuetenango in co-operatives in the Ixcán region of the Transversal del Norte development zone. By 1976, these 1,800 families were to be joined by 5,000 more, resettled by INTA with $5.6 million in AID money.[40] These settlers, however, were placed on marginal land with little capital assistance. The co-operative organization established under the Maryknolls was attacked by government forces as a part of a nation-wide campaign against indigenous organizations. These new settlers appear destined to be forced into labour on neighbouring, newly formed latifundia.

The prevailing land tenure system in the rest of the country was to be reproduced in the Petén. In 1970 Christian Democrat Rene de Leon Schlotter warned:

> In the zones which have been opened to exploitation by means of infrastructural works, such as El Petén, the lands have been distributed by the government of President Méndez Montenegro among private businesses which will use the land for cattle production. These vast lands are destined to form new *latifundias*. Meanwhile, the poorest lands of the same region have been distributed among co-operatives of landless campesinos, originating from the South Coast who within very few years will serve as cheap labour to the new class of landlords which are [sic] being created.[41]

After 1970 this trend accelerated. Under cultivation the soils of the Petén lost their fertility at a rapid rate. Colonists who experienced relatively high corn harvests in the first years of cultivation were quickly discouraged by subsequent crops. Consequently, FYDEP suggested that after clearing and two years of maize crops, land should be planted with cattle-grazing grasses.[42] It also introduced a production quota stipulation demanding that colonists continue to increase their yields through the first years of production, or else lose their land; this meant that highland peasants were consistently deprived of their land after they had done the costly work of clearing and breaking the soil. This land was then often turned over to cattle latifundia. As a consequence, grain harvests from the Petén declined precipitously. The 1976 harvest of 1,500,000 *quintales* of maize fell to slightly over 500,000 in 1978.

The Northern Development Zone

FROM THE 1970S ON, much of the Petén as well as parts of Alta Verapaz, El Quiché and Huehuetenango became coveted land. Along with profits from cattle grazing, the prospects of new resource discoveries and the development of state infrastructures in this frontier zone prompted considerable excitement. Sparked by oil discoveries, a largely Inco-owned nickel plant and road and hydroelectric projects, the value of land in the Petén and a broad strip running through the other departments in a northeasterly direction from Huehuetenango, known as the Franja Transversal del Norte, increased astronomically. Also called the "Land of the Generals", the region was systematically parcelled off in huge expanses to top military commanders, their associates in the ruling PID/PR coalition and others of the traditional landowning bourgeoisie. Much of the "development" in this region, including many of the cattle ranches, was capitalized through partnerships with North American resource companies and U.S. "sun belt" agro-industry concerns.

It was in this region that the most violent confrontations between peasants and a military bent on dispossessing them occurred in the late 1970s and early 1980s. While foreign firms continued to drill for oil and vast cattle ranches gained profits on the international market, peasant villages in the region were converted into desolate graveyards or armed camps.

The resources of the Franja Transversal del Norte were expected to help Guatemala diversify its economy and exports. Developments in the area were also viewed by many of the economic and political elite as a perfect opportunity to accumulate large profits and substantial holdings of soon-to-be valuable land. While by early 1982 the bloom had gone off much of the projected windfall of profits, at least temporarily, the area's potential was still enticing. It was attractive enough to prompt wholesale dispossession of the Ixil, Ketchi and Quiché Indians who populated the area, as well as newer *ladino* and highland Indian colonizers enticed to the area by earlier settlement plans.

The once largely unpopulated region of the Petén and the less densely populated departments of El Quiché and Alta Verapaz had always been the projected site of grand schemes. During the early liberal experiments, much of the Alta Verapaz and the Petén were included in "wilderness empires" consigned to lumber barons-cum-colonizers. Parts of El Quiché and Alta Verapaz hosted the first German coffee *fincas* when the later liberal regimes laid the basis for a newly defined Guatemalan economy.

During the 1970s and 1980s, the area again became the focus of both those interested in Guatemalan economic growth and those determined to wring huge fortunes from peasant land and labour. Earlier, in the 1950s shortly after the overthrow of Arbenz, the Hanna Mining Company of Cleveland had purchased a mining concession from the accommodating Armas government on the shores of Lake Izabal. The Hanna company did not act on its concession of nickel bearing land, but in 1960 it handed control over to Inco and the two companies established the jointly-owned Mineral Explorations and Exploitations (Exmibal). In the midst of high world prices for nickel, Exmibal began to prepare seriously for production when an Exmibal-hired mining engineer drafted a new mining code accepted by the Peralta Azurdía administration in April 1965. Inco required a few other concessions from the Guatemalan government before it would commit itself to investment, however. It pushed for classification as a "transition industry", thus winning significant tax concessions, and demanded that the Guatemalan government guarantee political stability in the region. The company won agreement on all demands from the Méndez government. The area, a scene of operations for the Armed Rebel Forces (FAR) in the mid-1960s, was subsequently the focus of a brutal counter-insurgency operation directed by Colonel Carlos Arana and U.S. military advisors.

In response to widespread protest fostered by the University of San Carlos in 1969, the tax concessions to Exmibal were tightened somewhat. Nonetheless, shortly after Arana's election in 1970, Exmibal — spurred on by a lengthy strike at Inco's Sudbury, Ont., operations in 1969 — signed the first agreement with the Guatemalan government. The Exmibal plant cost over $220 million and could produce 28 million pounds of nickel annually. Exmibal, 20 per cent owned by Hanna and 80 per cent by Inco, was to pay taxes to the Guatemalan government in the form of stocks in the company, which eventually provided the government with 30 per cent ownership. The Guatemalan government was never to have a member on the board of directors, however.

At the inauguration of the plant in 1977, President Kjell Laugerud warned that Exmibal must recognize that "what stays here is the sweat of the Guatemalans, who are men like whoever else and, that while they aren't blond like the North Americans, they are still human beings."[43] While the Exmibal plant could potentially provide substantial benefits for Guatemala, the various concessions gained by the company and the way the project was conceived by Inco ensured that those benefits would be minimal. A capital-intensive, high-energy-use operation, the Exmibal plant employed fewer than 500 Guatemalans at between $2.50 and $7.50 a day in all its operations, while its strip mining and tailings irreversibly damaged the fragile environment around Lake Izabal. In addition, a powerful economic and political force that lent its support to continued military government was created. One Inco executive stated the company's view of Guatemalan politics quite clearly: "The military will continue to rule in Guatemala for the foreseeable future. . . . It is the only base of stability, really. It will rule even with a civilian government in power." He concluded that the political prospects in Guatemala were among "the best . . . in terms of realism and pragmatism regarding foreign investment".[44]

Exmibal shipped its first load of nickel ore out in February 1978. But the plant did not prove to be very profitable. Conceived before the 1974 oil price hikes, the operation was an uncommonly high energy consumer, with energy accounting for more than 50 per cent of its total operating costs. Exmibal faced escalating energy costs and declining world prices for nickel and mothballed the plant in 1981, before it really got rolling. The company placed its hope for future profitability on cheap energy from the huge Chixoy River hydroelectric plant under construction in Alta Verapaz.

One of the original plans for development in the Transversal was construction of a number of hydroelectric projects tapping the various rivers that flow from the Sierra de Chama and Sierra de Santa Cruz ranges. The most important of these was to be a huge hydroelectric dam at Chixoy. Projected at a cost of $165 million in 1974 (revised to $414 million in 1978), it was to produce 70 per cent of Guatemala's energy requirements. But the Guatemalan government found it increasingly difficult to fund these projects. In 1978 the World Bank required a 27 per cent increase in electrical rates before it would continue to loan money for construction. By 1982, as Guatemala's financial situation became increasingly precarious, all of the other hydroelectric projects were shelved, while funding for further construction of the Chixoy plant was rapidly drying up.[45]

In addition, one of the major economic hopes for the Franja was the possibility of large-scale oil production. Oil companies and the Guatemalan government had known of oil pockets in the area, an extension of Mexico's oil bearing Chiápas rain forest, since the 1950s. Except for a slight flurry of activity at that time, little was done to explore for commercially viable deposits until increasing world prices and the Mexican oil finds made the area more enticing. Between 1971 and 1975, 42 oil companies applied for exploration contracts. The first commercial strike at Rubelsanto in 1974 was originally widely exaggerated, prompting a wholesale rush by the Guatemalan bourgeoisie to gather up grants to land in the region. While the original estimates were later scaled down drastically, other commercial wells were brought into production in 1977. By the end of 1982, the total flow was expected to be 10,000 barrels per day. Although Guatemala still imported oil and needed a flow of 30,000 barrels per day to be self-sufficient, this production and plans for a pipeline from a well-head at Chinaja to Santo Tómas on the Caribbean and a possible pipeline along the zone to transport U.S. west-coast oil to the eastern seaboard, were primarily responsible for the increase in the value of the land in this frontier region.[46]

The oil exploration program not only promised windfall profits to landowners who could gain control of newly valuable land near well-sites, but also provided significant foreign revenues for the Guatemalan government. Until the overthrow of the Lucas García government in March of 1982, oil exploration contracts cost a million-dollar signing fee and 50 per cent of profits were to accrue to the government. Consequently, all possible measures were taken to ensure access to sites being explored by foreign oil companies.

Although these new resource explorations seemed to foretell of new economic opportunities for Guatemala, they only prompted dispossession and deepening misery for the peasant inhabitants of the area. As early as 1972, 2,000 small landholders in the region were forced off land on which they had been squatters for 50 years.[47] In 1977 the army forcibly evicted Ketchi Indians from homes near the oil discovery at Chinaja and in the same year a 120-family community near Sebol in the Franja was forcibly removed and the land transferred to then defence minister Romeo Lucas García. According to Lucas' former secretary, Lucas by 1979 owned more than 81,000 acres of land in the Transversal and was worth more than $10 million in land alone, most of it recently acquired.[48]

Many of these expulsions of peasants precipitated violent confrontation between peasants and the marauding military. In 1976, Guatemalan bishops, still conservative but slowly becoming aware of a sense of responsibility to their parishioners, felt compelled to denounce a situation "becoming more and more critical every day".

As proof of this is the tensions that have arisen in the so-called Development Zones where continuous turmoil prevails. And this is because large landowners want to possess ever greater amounts and take over lands which have been acquired legitimately by those who worked them for many years. Perhaps the expectation of discovering oil in the region has awakened immoderate ambitions and has sparked off an unjustified violence that we cannot refrain from denouncing. Chixec, Moran, Nebaj and others are names of places where peasants have died for the "crime" of defending the land they have possessed for a long time.[49]

Perhaps the best known "conflict" over land in this region was the massacre of over 100 Ketchi men, women and children in the quiet town of Panzós, Alta Verapaz on May 29, 1978. Peasants in the region traditionally enjoyed insecure title to their land. By the 1970s however, dispossession of Indian cultivators had escalated as part of the general process of peasant expropriation in the whole Franja. Agitation and organization on the part of the Ketchi against arbitrary removal had been fomenting for over a year. In most cases this type of opposition was met by the "disappearance" or brutal torture and murder of opposition leaders. In this instance, however, between 500 and 700 Ketchi of the region gathered in Panzós on May 29th to protest their expulsions before the mayor and an official of INTA and to demand secure title to their land. Once the peasants had collected inside the central square, however, the military, which had ringed the square, opened fire, killing over 100 of the protesters. The bodies of the slain were dumped into mass graves, which according to some local observers had been dug beforehand. While the government denied the deaths at first, and only later admitted to 38 killings, it asserted that the Indians had started the violence. However, independent church and press reports argued that the massacre was completely unprovoked.[50]

Throughout the 1970s and increasingly so and in the early years of the 1980s, peasant villages in the "land of the Generals" were occupied and terrorized by the military. The bourgeoisie and top commanders of the military were determined that the rights (and lives) of peasant cultivators — the majority of the population — would not interfere with economic growth, the development of new exports from the region and the escalation of profits.

"A Smouldering Element":
The Rebirth of Popular Organization

My country, Let us walk together, you and I;
I will descend into the abyss where you send me,
I will drink your bitter cup,
I will be blind so you may have eyes,
I will be voiceless so you may sing,
I have to die so you may live.
— Otto René Castillo, Guatemalan poet and FAR guerrilla, killed by
the military in 1967

WITH THE COLLAPSE of the Arbenz reform government in 1954, the popular organizations that had thrived under the benevolent conditions of the "ten years of spring" withered and died beneath the heavy weight of government repression. Destroyed by new labour laws or beheaded by the arrest or forced exile of their leaders, the peasant leagues, labour unions and reform political parties soon crumbled. In the years following, in the face of three decades of repression, the resurgence of popular, peasant and political organizations was a painful process.

But the resurgence occurred. Student organizations, primarily at the University of San Carlos, maintained their traditional role as organizers of opposition to government's arbitrary measures. Labour unions fought off restrictive labour laws, government-controlled and pro-business union federations and, finally, terror and torture to emerge by the late 1970s as a powerful force in the defence of workers' rights. The corrupt and dictatorial governments that followed the overthrow of Arbenz prompted the flowering of armed revolution in the early 1960s, which by the end of the decade was completely routed by a U.S.-backed counter-insurgency.

During the early 1970s, however, remnants of these guerrilla forces emerged at the head of a new and infinitely more powerful revolutionary movement. Indian peasants in the highlands had largely failed to join the call to revolution in the 1960s. But by the early part of the next decade conditions in Indian villages had changed and the trickle of Indian converts to the revolution became a torrent: a torrent the Romeo Lucas García government proved unable to quell.

Confronted by fraudulent, undemocratic government and escalating violence, reform politicians abandoned the electoral process in droves. Along with the leaders of other popular organizations, these politicians established a political front — a government in exile — which played an important role in focusing international opposition on the Lucas government. As some of the best known and most respected of Guatemala's public figures, these exiles gave added legitimacy to the revolutionary struggle.

As various factions of the Guatemalan bourgeoisie struggled for political advantage and split apart in a myriad of competing cliques, opponents of the government who fought for significant, structural change were able to forge an effective coalition: a coalition that hid serious divisions but which was nonetheless solid and represented the majority of the Guatemalan populace. By the beginning of the 1980s, these popular organizations seemed prepared to overthrow the government and end the three decades of conservative, repressive government that had followed the "ten years of spring".

The Early Years: Students as the Focus of Popular Resistance

ONE OF THE FEW ARENAS of viable resistance that survived the chaotic post-1954 coup era was the University of San Carlos. Enjoying both a measure of inherent organization and a certain degree of constitutionally guaranteed autonomy, the university made its opposition felt in a number of ways. Students actively protested attempted electoral fraud in 1957. In a series of bitter strikes they continually fought Ydígoras' corruption and incompetence. It was in large measure student support that helped propel Julio César Méndez Montenegro to power in 1966. And during the 1960s many of the more radical students worked with guerrilla organizations.

In the 1960s the university sponsored a dialogue that protested the initial contract drawn up between the government and Exmibal. The harsh criticism levelled at the contract forced the government to renegotiate a slightly more rigorous agreement with the Inco-controlled company and prompted a wave of terror against the organizers of the conference. During the 1970s university faculty and students helped organize co-operatives, unions and reform political parties. An equally important student initiative was the establishment of "street" legal offices administered by students and faculty of the law school at the University of San Carlos. Advisors at these offices assisted in union organization and helped people from *barrios* in Guatemala City use the courts to pursue redress for violation of human rights.

All of these activities served to bring government repression into the university itself. The Arana-controlled death squad Ojo por Ojo especially attacked student organizations during the worst wave of violence in the 1970s. The university was consequently in the forefront of organizations protesting violence. In 1970, to meet the threat of Ojo por Ojo, students formed a Front Against Violence. On Oct. 8, 1971, 12,000 university students struck to protest the escalating violence and to demand an immediate end to the government-declared state of siege that had suspended constitutional guarantees.[1]

Students and faculty at the University of San Carlos were instrumental in ensuring that the National Reconstruction Committee after the 1976 earthquake did not fall into the hands of Arana and his National Liberation Movement (MLN) cohorts, and helped set up local organizations for reconstruction. In following years these local organizations were the focus of government repression in rural areas and helped prompt peasant support for the revolution.[2]

In 1976 the University Students' Association again formed a committee against violence and published an open letter to then President Kjell Laugerud. The letter stated:

> The Guatemalan people appear to be condemned to . . . the daily worry of hundreds of mothers, wives, sisters etc. who see how their husbands disappear into the hands of armed bands of men acting with impunity in broad daylight, or are captured by security forces. With luck the relatives of the kidnapped worker, peasant or student may find the corpse of their loved one beside some local road. Those who do not have this "luck" have to spend entire years waiting for some news of the missing person. The terror in which we Guatemalans have lived for ten years is unbearable. At the turn of any corner, at any moment, may appear that treacherous gunfire that ends courageous lives.[3]

The students called for a full-scale investigation into the violence and accused the government of complicity in it.

During the latter part of the decade and into the 1980s, activists at the university kept up their opposition to the increasing spiral of violence, violence consistently directed at themselves. University students also lent their support to other popular organizations. They were an important element in the widespread busfare protest shortly before General Lucas came to power in 1978.

The importance of the university as a centre of opposition to the government was demonstrated by the barrage of repression unleashed against its members, most notably in the spring of 1980 and the early months of 1982. By 1982, the University of San Carlos, reeling under brutal attacks, was only a shell of its former self. The most active and concerned faculty had fled or been murdered. Students were unable to meet freely; and administrators were imposed by the government. Nevertheless, one of the first measures of the Ríos Montt administration after coming to power in an 1982 coup was an attack on the university's autonomy in the form of the Fundamental Charter, promulgated to replace the 1964 constitution.

Despite these measures the University of San Carlos remained an important source of opposition to the government. In December 1982, the former rector of the university, Raul Molina, led a delegation of Guatemalans to lobby successfully for United Nations' condemnation of the Ríos Montt government: a condemnation jointly sponsored by the Canadian representatives.

Labour Reorganizes

LABOUR, ORGANIZED INTO the powerful umbrella organization CGTG (General Confederation of Guatemalan Workers), had been a key supporter of the Arbenz government and responsible for pushing the government to enact much of its reform legislation. In fact, with the exception of a brief period in the 1920s, the "ten years of spring" had been the first era in Guatemalan history in which labour was free to organize. Taking full advantage of government encouragement and the euphoria produced by the pace of reform, labour federations had close to 90 per cent of the urban labour force organized by 1953.[4]

Given the power of this widespread influence and the perceived radicalism of labour leaders during the period, unions were among the first remnants of the Arbenz administration attacked by Armas and the "liberation". Within three months of the coup, unions recognized under the Arévalo and Arbenz administrations were required to file a new list of officers with the authorities. One of the requirements for new officers was that they could not have held any position in the union before the coup, so most unions were unable to maintain their official status. In any case, violence directed by right-wing vigilante groups made many people reluctant to link themselves closely to unions. Consequently, from 655 registered unions in 1954 the ranks had been pared to 23 unions by April 1955. Only two of these were rural unions.

After attacking labour the new regime began a campaign to replace the former "radical" and independent unions with ones linked to the government and certain to restrict their demands to isolated economic issues. Between 1954 and the late 1960s, a variety of internationally affiliated union organizations began to operate in Guatemala with the blessing of the various Guatemalan governments and the U.S. administrations. However, labour in Guatemala demonstrated a decided propensity for independent action and, at least from 1970 on, for couching demands in the form of a call for a return to democracy and an end to repression.

After the coup, Armas and the MDN started the Autonomous Federation of Trade Unions (FASGUA), intending that it would be dominated by the government. Initially FASGUA presented no challenge, but by early 1957 the federation was showing signs of independence and government patronage soon turned to repression.[5]

The Trade Union Confederation of Guatemala (CONSIGUA), an American Federation of Free Labour Organization product, received better treatment from the post "liberation" governments, as did the Confederation of Guatemalan Workers (CONTRAGUA). Both of them scrupulously restricted the demands of their members to "business" matters. A number of other anti-communist labour organizations began to operate in Guatemala, all marked by ineffectiveness and a lack of support among Guatemalan workers.[6]

The government of Ydígoras Fuentes, with its rhetoric of national reconciliation, was more tolerant of the growth of independent trade unions. The union at the United Fruit Company's Atlantic operations was revived and the Christian Democrats, with some support from the Revolutionary Party (PR), began a Christian labour federation, the most important product of which was the Guatemalan Federation of Peasants, the beginnings of a resurgence in peasant organization.

After Ydígoras was overthrown in a coup by Colonel Peralta Azurdía in 1963, the government controlled labour more rigidly. FASGUA was declared illegal for its "communist" tendencies and was forced to join with CONSIGUA to create the Central Federation of Workers.

Although labour was slightly more free to organize legally under the Méndez Montenegro government from 1966-1970, repression meted out by both the military and death squads kept labour disorganized. The worst blow was the murder of 28 union leaders and outlawed Guatemalan Workers' Party (PGT) members by security forces in the weeks preceding the 1966 election. Among those killed were Victor Manuel Gutíerrez and Leonardo Castillo Flores, both prominent labour figures from 1945 to 1954.

By 1970 the Guatemalan labour movement showed few signs of vitality. Although there were 12 labour federations, the largest, the Trade Union Council of Guatemala, had less than 16,000 members. With less than one-quarter the number of unions that had been evident in 1954 and a minuscule percentage of the labour force represented, labour had neither an active nor powerful voice in Guatemala.[7]

Labour had no chance to resume the process of reorganization in the face of the brutal wave of repression unleashed by Carlos Arana in the first two years (1970-1972) of his administration. However, with the lifting of the state of siege in 1972, partly as a result of public protest, labour organizations became more active. In 1973, union resentment became apparent in strikes that began after the passing of a new public employees law that excluded teachers. The teachers were soon joined by doctors, railway workers and university students, who all joined into a broad National Front of Popular Unity to protect strikers from repression and to extend the organization. Many observers saw this as the spark that would lift popular organizations out of a long period of somnolence into a revival of political awareness.[8]

Indeed, the succeeding four years of the Kjell administration was a period of dramatic labour activity. There had been attempts by the National Workers Central (CNT) and FASGUA to form a national labour federation throughout the late 1960s and early 1970s. These efforts had met with partial success with formation of the National Council of Labour Consultation (CNCS) in 1973. But, after 1974, with many people angered by the electoral fraud that brought Kjell Laugerud to the presidency, labour organization accelerated. When Coca-Cola Bottling Company workers became embroiled in a longstanding dispute with the company's American management (see chapter 8), a national assembly of labour organizations was called. This led to the formation of the National Committee of Labour Unity (CNUS) in early 1976. With 65 large labour federations participating, the CNUS threatened a national strike if fired workers at the bottling plant were not reinstated. When the government capitulated by forcing the plant to rehire fired workers, it was a dramatic signal of the new strength of labour. In 1975 only 1.6 per cent of the Guatemalan labour force was organized. But according to a director of the CNUS, by late 1976 this figure had increased to 8 per cent.[9]

Because of the demonstrated strength of the labour movement, now solidified in the CNUS, government repression intensified. In May 1977, the man most responsible for the formation of the CNUS, its lawyer Mario López Larrave, was killed. This murder prompted the first in a long string of angry demonstrations co-ordinated by the CNUS to condemn government repression. Approximately 15,000 people joined the protest over López Larrave's murder. In November 1977, workers at the Ixtuahuacán mines, in a strike over unsafe working conditions, marched to the capital. Their trek caught national attention and they were joined along the way by workers and shantytown dwellers. The mine owners were forced to give in to a number of demands, marking yet another very public victory for labour protest.

Also in November of 1977, coastal sugar workers staged their own march to the capital and were eventually joined by 100,000 people. Public sector workers went on strike in February 1978. Co-ordinated by the increasingly powerful public employees union, 85,000 workers held a nine-day strike. In June 1978, at a combined demonstration to commemorate the anniversary of the death of López Larrave and to protest the Panzós massacre, over 100,000 people again joined in an angry denunciation of the government.

The largest, most successful labour action during the Laugerud government was the protest over bus fare increases in October 1978, just as Lucas was assuming the presidency. The proposed doubling of bus fares met with immediate protest. Bus drivers charged that the Guatemala City mayor, Colonel Abundio Maldonado, had been bribed by the transit companies to accept the increase. The CNUS and the University Students Association co-ordinated the protest, which was joined by the National Movement of Slum Dwellers and the Committee in Defence of the Consumer. Eventually 60 per cent of the industrial and public sector workers were off the job across the country. On October 9 the government reversed the increase, replacing it with a $38 million subsidy to the bus companies.[10]

After assuming the presidency in 1978, General Romeo Lucas García took an increasingly hard line towards labour. Forty union members were arrested after the October bus strike and an ever growing list of labour organizations became the target of government repression. This campaign culminated in the arrest and murder of 45 CNT organizers on two occasions in June and July of 1980. Escalating repression did not stop union activity, however. In spring 1980, the CNUS in collaboration with the Peasant Unity Committee (CUC) fostered a strike on the sugar and cotton harvests. From a base of 200 people the striking workers soon numbered 75,000. When the CNUS warned that it would call a sympathy strike of urban workers, who would then demand an increase in the urban minimum wage, the government again capitulated and forced plantation owners to accept a minimum wage of $3.20 a day (but only after privately advising the planters that there would be no attempt to enforce the wage).[15]

In the climate of terror and repression that accompanied the Lucas government, union organization became increasingly difficult. When the electoral frauds of 1974 and 1978 made it apparent that electoral politics would never provide a government sympathetic to or tolerant of workers' demands, the labour organizations began to investigate alternate possibilities. In February 1979, the CNUS initiated discussions that led to the formation of the Democratic Front Against Repression (FDCR). Comprised of over 170 popular organizations, including the

Social Democratic Party, the United Revolutionary Front (FUR), the CNUS and the Association of University Students, the FDCR soon became the major focus of international opposition to the Lucas government.

By the early 1980s the majority of people and organizations in opposition to the government and advocating significant structural change were in exile. They represented a broad cross-section of the Guatemalan population and had begun to link together into a consolidated front opposing the government. Along with the FDCR, there was the Popular Front of January 31, (FP-31), composed of the Peasant Unity Committee, the Revolutionary Workers Nucleus, the Christian Revolutionaries, the Settlers Co-ordinating Committee (an organization of slum dwellers from the capital) and the Revolutionary Student Front, Robin García.

In addition there were a number of church organizations in exile that had a long history. In 1977 the Committee for Justice and Peace was formed by a number of church members. It quickly became a major critic of government repression and linked itself to other popular movements, including the Peasant Unity Committee. In 1980, more than 50 priests and church workers who had been forced to leave Guatemala by government violence formed the Guatemalan Church in Exile. These church organizations integrated with the other popular organizations in exile and became an important force in publicizing the worst abuses of the Guatemalan government. By 1982, these organizations represented a powerful voice of condemnation, and were generally agreed to contain within their ranks many of the most respected of Guatemala's public figures.

Revolution in the Eastern Mountains

AS THE YDÍGORAS GOVERNMENT SANK into a quagmire of corruption, a revolutionary movement sprang up in the eastern mountains of Guatemala. Although torn by internal dissent and remaining relatively small, the guerrilla forces proved surprisingly tenacious throughout the 1960s. Barraged by U.S. aided and trained counter-insurgency forces, the guerrillas eventually abandoned rural revolt for an urban campaign and, for the most part, had faded from sight by the late 1960s. But the revolutionary movement did provide both a precedent and a series of examples for the stronger, more durable revolution that emerged in the mid-1970s and rose to full life from the rubble of the 1976 earthquake.

The revolutionary movement of the 1960s grew from the unsuccessful army coup of November 1960 (see also chapter 7). While that attempted coup was quickly defeated, a number of the officers involved refused to surrender and struggled to win support for their goals in rural eastern Guatemala. Among the officers were Colonel Alejandro de Leon, Marco Antonio Yon Sosa, and Luis Turcios Lima. The coup attempt had been inspired by traditional military grievances: complaints over army command, political tampering with promotions, frustration with Ydígoras' incompetence and corruption, along with a feeling of resentment over U.S. use of Guatemalan territory to train mercenaries for the Bay of Pigs invasion. It had little about it of a revolutionary character. As Yon Sosa put it: "If we had succeeded, it would have been one more military coup."[12]

But the coup didn't succeed. The fleeing commanders survived a number of experiences that radicalized them, drawing them inexorably to lead a movement aimed at overthrowing the government through the support of the populace. According to journalist Adolfo Gilly, the first experience of this kind occurred when 800 peasants presented themselves to the army commanders before the initial coup had been defeated. The peasants demanded arms from the rebel soldiers to help combat the government and demonstrated to the soldiers the depth of popular disenchantment with the government.[13]

The rebel officers had no clear idea of how to go about overthrowing the government and no clear political philosophy. Both Yon Sosa and Turcios Lima had been trained through stints at U.S. military academies and had undergone indoctrination meant to heighten soldiers' loyalty to command and to the military as an institution. This training had done little to provide them with a political ideology to support revolutionary struggle. According to Yon Sosa, the leaders floundered in the waters of political indecision and "talked with people on the right and left — anyone who was in agreement with toppling the Ydígoras government."[14]

In their discussions with Guatemala's opposition political parties, the guerrilla organizations found that the Guatemalan Workers' Party (PGT) offered the most positive assistance. Turcios Lima argued that the PGT was "different from all the others. They really care about the people."[15] This alliance with the PGT and, according to Yon Sosa "the very process of fighting, living with the peasants and encountering many, many frustrations" prompted the guerrilla forces to identify more closely with Guatemala's rural poor and gradually to adopt a socialist political bent.[16]

The armed struggle went through a number of phases in the early 1960s. In 1962 the Rebel Armed Forces (FAR) was established with three distinct fronts. The two most important were headed by Yon Sosa in the department of Izábal and Turcios Lima in Zacapa. But the two commanders differed on political and military strategy. Turcios Lima was more closely aligned with the PGT which, following the example of the Cuban revolution, continued to believe in the revolutionary potential of the Guatemalan middle class. The PGT gave halting support to the armed struggle, seeing it primarily as a means of forcing the government to call free elections and to permit the PGT to participate in them. In 1962, during the time of widespread street demonstrations against Ydígoras, the PGT temporarily abandoned this cautious approach and supported its own front led by Colonel Paz Tejada. This front was almost immediately wiped out, and from then on the PGT only hesitantly supported the guerrilla movement.

Yon Sosa, on the other hand, had been influenced by the Mexican Trotskyist Amada Granados, and began to pressure for an immediate socialist revolution. He differed from Turcios Lima's policy in his aim to establish "free zones" of liberated areas where the guerrillas would establish a nascent government. He refused to accept the political direction of the PGT's United Revolutionary Front.

In March 1965 the two forces split, with Yon Sosa heading the MR-13 and Turcios Lima commanding FAR. FAR became more closely tied to the PGT after the young law student César Montes became Turcios' lieutenant. A member of the PGT youth wing, César Montes was able to perpetuate the links between FAR and the PGT, as well as push the PGT to support the armed struggle more fully.[17]

Despite these links, both MR-13 and FAR were adamant about their independence. The guerrilla movements of the 1960s, like their counterparts in the 1970s, were never dominated by Guatemalan political parties or any outside influence. Turcios Lima assured New York Times correspondent Alan Howard: "One thing I guarantee you. We depend on nobody — not for arms, not for anything. We have done it all ourselves." Of the guerrillas' arms, 80 per cent were obtained from the Guatemalan military through raids and corruption; the rest came from purchases on the black market and were financed by bank robberies and kidnapping. César Montes totally refuted the idea that a revolution can come from outside. "A revolution cannot be exported," he argued, "not a true revolution. It grows out of the needs of the people. Our movement cannot be destroyed until those needs are satisfied." Even the U.S. State Department, always quick to see a supposed Soviet hand in all unrest, admitted that Yon Sosa's MR-13 had no international links.[18]

The success of the Revolutionary Party at the polls and the assumption of the presidency by Julio César Méndez Montenegro in 1966 presented a problem for the revolutionary forces. The PGT, taking advantage of a temporary absence by Turcios Lima, was able to issue a declaration that FAR supported the presidency. Turcios Lima was unwilling to reverse that stance when he returned to the country. This fit well into the PGT desire for the opening of a democratic alternative that would allow it to compete in electoral contests like other political parties. But FAR did not trust Méndez Montenegro's ability to force the military to broaden the scope of democracy in Guatemala. After the election, FAR refused the offered amnesty, but it did temporarily suspend military activity while it saw to what extent the president could control the military.

César Montes explained FAR's attitude towards the government: "I have a great deal of respect for Méndez. He was my professor in law school and I believe he is an honest and intelligent man. But the army will never allow him to carry out the profound reforms our country needs."[19] The official FAR position on the PR victory was expressed in a communiqué in July 1966. "Despite the popular extraction of the new regime", the statement said, "The army retains most of the effective power. The Guatemalan army is still the same reactionary tool of the native plutocracy and foreign companies and therefore must be fought to the bitter end."[20] Nevertheless, the election of the PR proved difficult for the guerrilla forces. Many people who had supported the revolutionary movement because of a severe disenchantment with the potential for democracy in Guatemala took new heart in the military's decision to allow Méndez Montenegro to assume the presidency. By the time the military's behind the scenes violence had confirmed FAR's assessment of the situation, the revolutionary movement had been seriously weakened.

The elections of 1966 marked the beginning of the end for the guerrilla forces of that era. Taking advantage of the guerrillas' unofficial truce, the army unleashed a brutal counter-insurgency under the command of Colonel Carlos Arana Osorío: a campaign that included the use of U.S. advisers and, it was asserted by then-vice-president Clemente Marroquin Rojas, American pilots flying napalm attacks on suspected guerrilla strongholds from the U.S. base in Panama. Local political *caudillos* and landowners in the eastern districts were encouraged by the military and the MLN to form vigilante groups, which along with the military attacked peasant villages and killed between 6,000 and 10,000 people in the indiscriminate slaughter. While most of those killed had no connection to the guerrillas, the concerted attack seriously weakened the guerrilla forces. Turcios Lima had been killed in a car accident in 1966, and the guerrilla forces, never numbering more than 300 fighting men, were simply unable to withstand the prolonged attack.

By 1968 FAR had abandoned the rural struggle for urban warfare, which was never very intensive or effective. While scattered forces struggled on into 1970-1971 (and a small nucleus survived to form the more powerful Guerrilla Army of the Poor in the early 1970s), they were not a significant political or military consideration after 1968. In 1970 and 1971, a number of setbacks served to weaken the movement even further. In 1970 Yon Sosa was killed by Mexican soldiers on the border and in 1971 three top rebel leaders were killed, effectively decapitating what was left of the rebel forces.

While the revolutionary movement was beaten militarily by the late 1960s, it provided important lessons for guerrillas in the next decade. With few exceptions, the leaders of the four guerrilla organizations that developed in the 1970s had fought for FAR or MR-13. They had learned lessons about the lack of security, and about the too heavy reliance on propaganda played out in North American and European media by journalists who flocked to their rural hideouts. They had learned about over-confidence and about the need to develop a solid base of support among the peasants. Most importantly they realized that a strong revolutionary movement must work slowly at winning the widespread support of the Indian population of the highlands.

Peasant Villages and the Revolution

ONE OF THE problems the guerrilla movement struggled with in the 1960s was the inappropriateness of prevailing revolutionary theory. During the early years of the revolution the guerrillas adopted a strategy called *foco guerrillero*. This strategy, as described by its best known proponent, Ernesto 'Che' Guevara, worked on the assumption: "It isn't necessary to wait until all the conditions propitious for rebellion mature. . . . It is enough that a 'permanent' focus [exists] that serves as a catalyst for the elements discontented with the current system and that will destroy the constituted government little by little."[21] Pursuing this strategy, the Guatemalan guerrillas concentrated on maintaining small cadres of dedicated revolutionaries, rather than proselytizing their message throughout the society. Consequently the guerrilla movement remained small.

The problem of building a large and active resistance movement was most obvious in the absence of Indian participation. Given the accumulated Indian grievances towards the national government, the guerrillas initially believed that Indian peasants would support the revolution *en masse,* inspired by the continued existence of the revolutionary "focus", with little need for direct guerrilla appeals to the Indian population. By the latter part of the decade, the guerrilla forces had come to appreciate the importance of Indian involvement in the struggle and had adapted policies to win their support. But by that time valuable years had been lost.

When the guerrillas did begin to concentrate on winning native support, they encountered many problems. In an interview with Eduardo Galeano, César Montes of FAR explained: "Half the people of Guatemala are Indians, and you can be sure they will play a decisive role in our revolution. But it is a slow and difficult job. We are faced with four centuries of distrust which the Indians have had for the whites and mestizos."[22] Yon Sosa of MR-13 attempted to establish governments in liberated areas with significant peasant control. Both guerrilla organizations stressed village autonomy and land reform as goals of post-revolutionary governments. When the rebels entered a village, they sought the support of village leaders, held open discussions with peasants, and, according to César Montes, pointed to the latest position of the church to encourage peasant participation.

Nonetheless, except for a short-lived Cakchiquel front headed by Emilio Roldán Lopez, Indian participation in the campaigns of the 1960s was minimal and the guerrillas were unable to tap that wellspring of peasant resentment against national authorities that had touched off periodic revolts in the 18th and 19th centuries. The Indian reluctance was, in retrospect, not surprising. Despite the appointment of *intendentes* during Ubico's period of power and the operation of political parties and peasant leagues in numerous villages during the Arévalo and Arbenz administrations, village traditions had been kept surprisingly intact throughout the century. This tradition included control by an established order of elders, most of whom were significantly better off than the bulk of the village residents. This imbued village politics with a decidedly conservative bent. The failure of the "ten years of spring" and the return of land expropriated during that period placed many peasant villages again under the economic and political dominance of local landowning and merchant elites. Challenging their position was a dangerous proposition. In addition, the church, throughout the early 1960s at least, remained primarily conservative and did little to foster autonomous organization within villages.

Added to this was the underlying ethnic separation between *ladinos* and Indians. Indians often saw *ladinos* as using Indians for their own political ends, with little concern for Indian demands. In the long collective memory of Indian villages, this applied especially to *ladino*-inspired revolts.[23] The experience of the "ten years of spring" was hardly encouraging for peasants; significant reforms had been promised and begun, but they had barely taken shape when a change in government in the city shattered the promises. Many peasant

236   GIFT OF THE DEVIL

organizations had expressed their willingness at that time to fight for the government against the conservative reaction, but the national popular organizations apparently lost their will.[24] Those most involved in promoting change in the villages were persecuted by the succeeding governments.

After the collapse of the Arbenz government, local politics and society in most highland villages regressed to a state approximating that of earlier eras. In the village of Chinautla, for example, local politics lost the "vibrancy" of the reform era. The national ruling party was "only hesitantly opposed" in the village. When lists of Catholic books arrived for the church committee, the president of the committee "secretly" checked with the representatives of the national government to ensure that the books were not political and thus subversive. According to anthropologist Ruben Reina, who spent many years studying the community, "It was the general feeling that due to post 1954 revolutionary experiences, they had better refrain from any political activity."[25]

Economically, the situation in the community also regressed. During the reform era, the Law of Forced Rental had allowed over 100 Indians to rent land on the coast at economically feasible rates. After the 1954 coup owners raised the rent by 12 times, and Indians were forced to abandon their new fields. According to Reina: "That group of Chinautlecos which sought economic improvement by political means returned to work within the framework of the local economic range of possibilities."[26] Observations from numerous other villages during the post-reform period describe a similar process (see also chapter 10).

Thus, the revolutionary movement of the 1960s was a *ladino* revolt. As the guerrilla organizations clarified their political ideology, it became increasingly apparent that their program — which included village self-government and land reform — would be beneficial to Indian peasants. But the process of winning Indian support for the revolution was a long and complicated one. To a great extent class awareness had been effectively distorted by centuries of racial conflict. The guerrilla movement in the 1960s was unable to overcome this ingrained reluctance in time for it to make any difference in the immediate struggle. Thus, despite many strengths, and widespread contempt for the national government and the military, the movement was reduced to one small pocket of revolutionaries buried deep in the jungle of the Northern Quiché by the early 1970s.

Change in Highland Villages

BY THE MID-1970s the situation in Guatemala had changed dramatically. Electoral politics as a means of social and economic change had been fully explored and exhausted (see chapter 8). All attempts at reform were stymied by military control over the ballot box and violence directed at all proponents of reform. By the late 1970s all political parties that advocated significant, structural reform in the society had been forced to abandon electoral politics and, at least rhetorically, supported the revolution through their participation in the Democratic Front Against Repression and, later, the Guatemalan Patriotic Unity Committee.

However, the most significant change occurred in highland villages. Throughout the 1960s and 1970s a new movement had begun to liberate local communities from the dominance of the past. Reform political parties, the church and a new type of village leader emerged to foster local autonomy, independent political action and demand change. A national peasant organization — the Peasant Unity Committee (CUC) — controlled largely by Indians emerged to crystallize opposition.

As these measures were met by a new wave of repression, and as village land was subject to renewed attack in the latter half of the 1970s, Indians joined a new revolutionary movement in increasing numbers. In the words of one Indian leader, Guatemala's Indians were "a smouldering element and they will determine absolutely, how it comes out in the end."[27] By the time of the military coup of 1982, Indians in the highlands had demonstrated that the majority of them were, by necessity, supporting the revolution. Indeed, in many areas the war took on a decidedly racial characteristic, with local *ladinos* tied to the military wreaking havoc in Indian villages.

Despite the set-backs that occurred after the collapse of the Arbenz regime, Indian communities refused to sink back forever into the morass of traditional, patron-dominanted politics. Through the 1960s and 1970s new organizations had developed in the highland villages and in the late 1970s new movements helped promote local autonomy and indirectly contributed support to the guerrilla forces. The roots of these movements stretch back to the reform decade.

Catholic Action

RELIGIOUS CONVICTIONS IN Guatemala took on a very distinct shape in highland villages. The lack of priests had left the villages to develop Christian teachings free from direct control of the Catholic hierarchy. This resulted in a peculiar blend of native/Catholic syncretism and a native religious hierarchy that dominated village politics and mediated between the village and local *ladinos*. This structure was heightened during the Liberal administrations as attacks on village land and

238   GIFT OF THE DEVIL

forced labour prompted highland villages to become more defensive and withdrawn: to become what anthropologist Eric Wolf has called "closed, corporate communities".

The defensive posture of the villages was only slightly disturbed by appointed *intendentes* during Ubico's presidency. However, during the "ten years of spring" the church hierarchy began to search for a means of consolidating its position in villages in the face of government-supported peasant leagues and political parties. The process chosen by Archibishop Mariano Rossell Arellano was a form of religious purification known as Catholic Action. Started in 1946, Catholic Action was meant to augment the position of priests in the villages with a concerted attack on local native religious "impurities".

There was nothing reformist in economic and social terms in Catholic Action. On the contrary, it was designed primarily as a means of combating government reform. For Rossell, "Our small Catholic Action was one of the greatest comforts in those hours of enormous distress in the presence of Marxist advance that invaded everything."[28] But the process, once begun, had unforeseen consequences. At the initiatioin of Catholic Action Rossell had warned: "Today [the Indian population] is a tame and long suffering lamb, but it is very easy to turn it into a cruel wolf, or a ravenous lion, or a poisonous snake."[29]

To avoid this Rossell proposed to forestall Indian protest by encouraging the feeling of "Christian resignation" among the poor. At the same time he talked of the need "to awaken the feeling of charity" among the rich. As the peasant leagues and reform political parties gained more and more support, however, he slowly heightened his calls for some minor reforms by suggesting that the government should provide land for peasants through colonization. The church, and more specifically Catholic Action, were important in heightening unrest in village communities and strengthening opposition to the Arbenz government in the years leading up to its overthrow in 1954.[30]

After the coup, the church hierarchy no longer felt compelled to combat the strength of government-inspired reform. However, in many villages the promotion of Catholic Action had initiated a reform movement that could not be easily stopped. One aspect of Catholic Action had been an attack on native religious organizations. In a number of villages this action prompted a splintering into a variety of opposing groups, fostering increased instability in village communities already shaken by the success of Protestant missionaries and the activities of reform parties and peasant leagues. In some instances, the conflict between the "traditionalists" and Catholic Action adherents approached violent confrontation.[31] While the initial effect of Catholic

Action varied from village to village, it most often resulted in a marked weakening of the power and control of the traditional Indian religious hierarchy, which was generally seen as a conservative influence.

The activity of Catholic Action committees in the villages had other consequences. The number of priests active in Guatemala had grown significantly during the reform decade, from 114 in 1944 to 195 in 1954. After the coup, with the church's position strengthened, the number of priests shot up to 242 in 1955 and 415 by the later 1960s.[32] This accelerated appointment of new priests led to a significant decentralization in the operation of the church in Guatemala. The archbishop of Guatemala, his position of eminence held primarily by respect, enjoyed no formal control over Guatemalan bishops appointed by Rome. This inherent trend to decentralization was accentuated in Guatemala in the years immediately following the 1954 coup by the fact that many of the new priests appointed to districts in Guatemala were foreigners. As a result, by the late 1960s only slightly over 15 per cent of the Guatemalan clergy were native born. The most important foreign sources of priests were Spanish Jesuits and American Maryknoll fathers.[33]

Many foreign priests approached their position differently than Guatemalan ministers. With fewer ties to local and national elites, many promoted, along with Catholic Action, local autonomous organizations. Changes of this type in the perception priests held of their role in the villages were inspired additionally by the need to compete with Protestant missionaries increasingly active in highland communities, and the new direction given the international Catholic church after the Second Vatican Council in the early 1960s, which declared a preference for the poor and argued that along with the church's religious mission "comes a function, a light and an energy which can serve to structure and consolidate the human community according to divine law".[34] Many priests throughout the world interpreted this as an affirmation of the correctness of the church to respond to the deprivation of its charges through both economic and political action: the beginnings of the "theology of liberation".

Ministers in Guatemala saw this statement as encouragement for reformist activity in their parishes and became increasingly involved in social action. The most prominent activities were the organization of co-operatives and the extension of a dialogue on social and economic concerns through church-sponsored Cursillos de Capitación Social. These courses began in Latin America in 1962, spread to Central America in 1965 and were quickly extended to rural areas. For some priests at least, a discussion of the social and economic problems that confronted peasants led to more active opposition to the government.

According to Blase Bonpane, a Maryknoll missionary in Guatemala in the mid-1960s, when the Cursillos began to be opposed by the government, the leaders met with FAR organizers with the intention of forming a Christian Revolutionary Front, which "would be a revolutionary call to the Christian Indian community".[35]

In 1968, the most active of the Maryknolls, including Thomas and Arthur Melville, Blase Bonpane and Sister Marian Peters, were suspended by their superiors for "personally interfering" in the internal affairs of the country. They were later expelled from the country and accused of plotting to smuggle arms into Guatemala. Bonpane explained, "No one wants violence, but when you have American power thrown behind the 2 per cent of the people who own 80 per cent of the land, and supporting a right-wing army that shoots reformers on the spot as 'communists', violence is already institutionalized."[36]

This restricted group of priests who supported revolutionary action among their charges was indicative of the gnawing frustration of those who worked in the village communities. However, of more import was the less radical activity of an increasingly socially conscious Catholic Action, which promoted literacy through courses, scholarships and an extensive network of radio schools, encouraged local political parties that reflected peasant concerns, and, perhaps most importantly, organized an impressive series of native co-operatives.

The Co-operative Movement:
A Search for Local Autonomy

AT ITS HEART THE co-operative movement was anything but revolutionary. It was designed to provide an avenue for limited economic betterment without challenging the national economic structure or the distribution of income in any fundamental fashion. Nonetheless, co-operatives grew rapidly through the late 1960s and early 1970s. From savings and credit co-operatives they expanded to producer and marketing organizations. During the early years of the Laugerud administration, when the government gave limited encouragement to the concept, the movement blossomed. By September 1975, 20 per cent of highland Indians were involved in some form of co-operative.[37] This percentage increased immediately following the earthquake of 1976 as local reconstruction committees flourished.

By the mid-1970s, the combination of Catholic Action activities, an increased level of literacy among Indian youth, the economic independence offered by peasant-controlled co-operatives, and the activity of new political parties, most notably the centrist Christian Democrats, had sparked significant changes in Indian communities and Indian attitudes. In many locales the traditional religious hierarchy still functioned and the system of dual government (that is, a local Indian governmental structure that paralleled but was always subordinate to a local *ladino* one) still predominated. Nonetheless, in all but a very few communities there existed groups of natives who opposed the traditional hierarchy or who had forced it to join them in a struggle for political and economic independence through co-operatives and native-controlled political parties. For these peasants, often but not always young men or women, the usual obsequious attitude to local *ladino* authority and, ultimately, to the national government was abandoned. In many instances this attitude was expressed in personal relations with *ladinos*. One long-time Guatemalan resident remarked to a *New York Times* reporter on the change that had occurred during the 1970s. "I am astounded at the way the Indians talk now," he reported. "When I arrived they used to bow before a white man. Now they want to discuss their 'oppression'."[38]

Two studies of highland villages documenting the changes of the late 1950s and the 1960s focus on the role of Catholic Action. Anthropologist Kay Warren, in a study of San Andrés in the Sololá highlands points out that Catholic Action, which started there in 1956-1958, was the "first Indian group that was not directly under their [local *ladino*] jurisdiction and that did not express its subordination to local ladinos." She found that Catholic Action not only "began to forge a more active Indian population" but also inspired an increased sense of connection with other neighbouring villages and their common problems. By stressing education that often entailed leaving the village temporarily, Catholic Action fostered a group of young people who not only rejected *ladino* dominance and felt restricted by the lack of opportunity in the village, but also eventually gained the support of many village elders. Elders reacted positively to Indian youth who "do not permit ladinos to bother them, now they speak out and give opinions, now that they have ideas and have studied. They know some of the laws and they will not allow ladinos to do something bad in the municipal government."[39]

In San Andrés during the period Warren studied it, local *ladinos* supported the traditional Indian hierarchy and *cofradías* (see chapter 1), both because they helped reinforce *ladino* dominance and because some *ladinos* made money through the selling of the materials needed for local fiestas. In the highland community of Aguacatán, studied by Douglas Brintnall in the 1970s, the coming of Catholic Action in 1955 prompted a bitter battle for predominance between traditionalists and Catholic Action proponents. The traditionalists were supported by local *ladinos,* and Brintnall comments on how one Indian youth responded to a *ladino*'s question of whether the passing of local customs wasn't sad with "Yes it is sad . . . for you."[40]

In Aguacatán, Indians involved in Catholic Action were active in wresting control of local political parties from *ladinos,* beginning with the Christian Democratic party in 1970: a development that greatly increased local political involvement. When an Indian Christian Democrat candidate was elected mayor in 1970, his period in office was almost immediately disrupted by Arana's declaration of a national state of siege, which placed local authority in the hands of the *ladino* military commissioner. When a minor dispute developed, the commissioner rushed to the departmental capital of Huehuetenango, claiming he had been attacked by 1,500 Indians. The army immediately moved into the village and according to one resident, "took pleasure in punishing our people".

After this period, Indians were more cautious of involvement in party politics. But many shifted their focus to the formation of two peasant leagues in the community, which were "the first organizations dominated by the poor". They began to see local political problems not in isolation but as a product of the national political and economic structure.[41]

Despite the Catholic church's intention that the co-operative movement and Catholic Action improve local social and economic conditions without challenging the status quo, the forging of some degree of local independence inexorably drew these initiatives into conflict with the national government. A good example of the way these connections were made was a large co-operative started by a Spanish priest in the Quiché during the early 1960s. When the co-operative impinged upon local *ladino* profits, the local merchants complained to then head of government Peralta Azurdía, who pressured the papal nuncio to have the priest removed from his post.

While in this instance the priest was allowed to return to Guatemala after Méndez Montenegro came to power, in subsequent years both Catholic Action and co-operatives were increasingly opposed by the national government. During the early years of the Lucas regime, the government cancelled the registration of over 250 co-ops, claiming they were Marxist inspired. While the National Co-operative Institute continued to exist throughout the Lucas administration, it was slowly strangled by lack of funds and government opposition.

Repression of Local Organizations

MORE DIRECT ACTION to discourage local autonomy was taken by death squads and the military, which throughout the 1970s and early 1980s consistently focused much of their attention on co-operative leaders and the priests most active in fostering local organizations. Beginning with the death in a mysterious plane crash of Father Willie Woods, who had helped organize a large co-operative in Huehuetenango, these attacks became so frequent that by 1980 the Jesuits were forced to withdraw all their priests from the department of El Quiché, citing "a climate of insecurity which prevents any kind of evangelical or pastoral work".[42]

It quickly became apparent that the very process of gaining a measure of local independence from the machinery of local dominance by landowners and merchants was exactly what the Guatemalan government feared. The villages that were most severely and brutally attacked by military forces were those that had demonstrated a capacity for local organization. The repression in these villages usually started with the murder of local organizers and in many cases never reached the level of wholesale violence, and never received the attention of the media.

The case of Kai Yutah Clouds is an informative example and a ready demonstration of this phase of government repression. Kai, a U.S. citizen, had spent most of his adult life working with North American Indians. A trained agronomist with a degree from Cornell University, he first visited Guatemala with the White Roots of Peace organization after the 1976 earthquake. In this visit he became concerned over the effects of pesticides on native health and about ways to use more effectively the diminishing land base the villagers enjoyed.

Funded by the Canadian Quakers, Kai returned to Guatemala in 1978. Working in a small Cakchiquel village in the highlands of Chimaltenango, he began to help organize a co-operative and to experiment with bee-keeping and aqua-culture as a way of diversifying the Indian economy. Kai realized that the work in the village would bring opposition from the government. Writing to friends in Canada he observed, "Native people prove a very real potential threat to the dominant culture by their very existence." He requested "typewritten letters of support" which prominently displayed might "offer a certain degree of protection".[43]

Realizing fully the danger he personally faced, Kai was reluctant to leave until two young natives who could take over the management of the co-operative returned from courses they were taking. He delayed too long; according to local reports, Kai was kidnapped by security forces, tortured and murdered, his mutilated body flung onto the streets of Antigua. Pressure on the village continued after Kai's death until the new co-operative was destroyed.

Similar violence was wrought against other attempts at local organization in other villages. In the department of El Quiché alone, 168 co-operative or village leaders were killed from 1976 to 1978. Respondents to an Oxfam study conducted in 1982 routinely described attacks on peasant organizations in villages. One respondent concluded:

> It is apparent that the army and secret paramilitary organizations are systematically killing not only the Indian leadership, but the potential Indian leadership as well. People who fall into the second category are any Indians with secondary school education, catechists, cooperative leaders, etc. Increased guerrilla activity and Indian membership in the guerrilla movement are almost entirely a direct result of such severe government repression that people see no other alternative.[44]

As government repression clearly began to attack any organization established to try to alter the status quo, peasant communities began to see more clearly the links between local repression and the national government. Thus, when the remnants of the guerrilla movements of the 1960s re-emerged in the mid-1970s with bases in the Indian highlands, peasant support was forthcoming in a way it had not been in the previous decade.

The Revolution Reborn

IN JANUARY 1972, the Guerrilla Army of the Poor (EGP) made its first appearance in the western highlands. It began slowly to develop contacts in peasant villages and win the support of the inhabitants. A small nucleus of combatants, survivors of the guerrilla battles in the 1960s, crossed the Ixcán river into the jungles of the northern Quiché. From that point they began the slow process of tapping the accumulated grievances of the Indian peasants of the area and winning their trust as the first step towards revolution. According to one of them, Mario Payeres, they had learned sorry lessons from the impatience and over-confidence of the 1960s. They saw themselves as "planters of the slow-growing tree of revolution".[45]

Working out of two fronts in the east and west of the department of El Quiché, they slowly made their way out of the jungle and into the inhabited highlands. They forswore publicity and, in the first few years, any military contact. Instead, they provided small favours for peasants, engaged in endless political discussion with Indian groups, and worked assiduously at building the strong Indian base that the revolution had lacked in the previous decade. Again, according to Payeres: "We always kept in mind Che's defeat in Bolivia — that lone guerrilla unit in the jungle, without a peasant base of support and in constant flight."

They found in the highlands a well-spring of discontent. A number of peasants they ran across remembered the Arbenz period and the beginnings of reforms that would have bettered their lives. One old peasant who had received land under the Agrarian Reform Law of 1952 still kept pictures of Arbenz and posters from the CNCG, the peasant league of the 1950s. This fellow had lost his land with the coup of 1954, but still remembered Arbenz fondly. As he told Payeres, "Too bad he let himself be thrown out just when things were beginning to get better for us."

The most common source of discontent encountered was anger at the greedy conduct of local landowners who had gradually monopolized land in the district and took advantage of this monopoly to pay miserly wages. According to Payeres, one of these landlords, Luis Arenas Barrera, was particularly notorious. He had received his land in an isolated region on the edge of the Ixcán jungle and the Cuchamatán mountains immediately after the overthrow of Arbenz. He kept his workers in a form of debt bondage on debts developed through advances he provided at exorbitant rates and his home was a fortress perched on a hill.

Consequently, the first military action of the EGP was an attack on the landlord designed to win the sympathy of local peasants. After the killing, which had been carried out on pay day in full view of many peasants, Payeres said that the guerrillas immediately began to win more support. "From that moment on, the word spread throughout the region that ... they had surely come to do justice, since they had punished a man who had grown rich from the blood and sweat of the poor."

The military's response to this killing also prompted increasing support for the guerrillas. Following the killing, the army began a counter-insurgency campaign in the Ixil area of El Quiché. But rather than hunting guerrillas, they began to attack local organizations in the district. In 1975 the military killed 37 co-operative members in the Ixcán. By 1976 the government had announced it was waging a war against the guerrilla forces in the highlands, occupying the towns of Chajúl, Nebáj, and San Juan Cotzúl. By early 1977 over 100 village leaders had been killed, and later that same year, peasants from the district publicly denounced the actions of the military in the area.[46] From this point Indian support for the guerrilla organizations grew steadily, especially after the Lucas García administration began to direct increasing repression at all peaceful attempts at change in the villages.

However, there are four incidents generally considered as key in ensuring Indian support for the revolution. The first was the Panzós

massacre in April 1978 (see chapter 10). Until the army responded to
Indian protests over land seizures with this obvious example of premeditated brutality, there appeared to be reason to believe that peasant land could be protected through appeals to such government agencies as the National Institute for Agrarian Transformation (INTA).
With the Panzós massacre it became apparent, at least to Ketchi and
Ixil Indians in the Franja Transversal, that there existed no official
recourse to protect their villages against the military. How quickly the
massacre became part of the popular consciousness was demonstrated
by the gathering of over 100,000 people to commemorate the massacre one year later. Much of the active support the EGP found in Alta
Verapaz and parts of El Quiché dated from this slaughter.

This painful lesson was further accentuated with the killing of 39
peasants and their supporters in the Spanish embassy in Guatemala
City in 1980. In late 1979 and early 1980, Quiché and Ixil peasants
journeyed to Guatemala City to protest military repression in their
villages in the department of El Quiché. The first group of 100 peasants from San Miguel Uspantán came to the city to demand the release
of seven village leaders kidnapped by the military.

In an interview with representatives of Amnesty International, a
group of these Indians described their grievances.[47] Four wealthy
families controlled the area but the peasants there had refused to work
for them because the wages offered were too low (50 to 60 cents a
day). One peasant explained: "Because of this, the soldiers have the
wrong idea about us. . . . The landowners are the kind of people who,
the more they have, the more they want. But we haven't let them get
away with it and they are mad at us now." Because of this defiance the
landlords had encouraged army vigilance in the area. As one of the
villagers pointed out: "Two years ago we used to live here quite hap-
pily, without any trouble at all. . . . Really, nobody bothered us. . . .
But now it's bad because all the northern part is crawling with soldiers . . . as they can't find guerrillas they pounce on the peasants."

After unsuccessfully appealing for attention from the unresponsive
Lucas government throughout a long stay in the capital, many of the
peasants from San Miguel Uspantán returned to their community.
However, a second group of peasants from neighbouring areas in the
Quiché joined the protest in Guatemala City, demanding that the
army be removed from their villages and that a special commission be
established to investigate the activities of the military in the region.
While this group was in Guatemala City, the original seven leaders
from San Miguel Uspantán were found dead in Chajúl.

Other popular sectors in Guatemala City attempted to help the
peasants, but after a member of the reformist FUR party was killed

shortly after a meeting with the peasants, 22 peasants with student and worker supporters decided on a peaceful occupation of the Spanish embassy to publicize the violations of human rights in the region. The choice of the Spanish embassy was not made at random. Most of the priests active in the Quiché since the early 1950s had been Spanish. Because of the increasing number of priests threatened or deported from the region the Spanish ambassador had earlier spent one and a half days discussing the problem of repression with peasants in the district. The ambassador gave the appearance of sympathetic support.[48]

Consequently, when the peasants entered the Spanish embassy on Jan. 31, 1980, they presented a letter to the ambassador:

> We peasants representing the Ixil communities of San Juan Cotzúl, Chajúl and Nebáj and the peasant communities of San Miguel Uspantán, direct ourselves to you because we know you are honourable people who will tell the truth about the criminal repression suffered by the peasants of Guatemala. . . . To a long history of kidnappings, torture, assassinations, theft, rapes and burning of buildings and crops, the National Army has added the massacre at Chajúl. . . . We have come to the capital to denounce this injustice, this evil, this cowardice of the National Army, but we also come because we are persecuted and threatened by forces of repression.[49]

Despite demands by the Spanish ambassador that the peasants inside the building not be attacked, the police stormed the building and 39 people were killed including a former vice-president and a foreign minister of Guatemala, who were both in the building to talk with the peasants. Only the ambassador and one peasant survived. The peasant was later kidnapped from the hospital where he was recuperating from his injuries. After the attack the Spanish government broke off all diplomatic relations with Guatemala and withdrew its ambassador.

The Spanish embassy attack was a pivotal point in Guatemalan history. As in the Panzós massacre, peasants protesting repression and theft of their land had exhausted all peaceful means of seeking redress. Their attempts at reaching a solution proved both ineffective and costly in peasant lives. According to one director of the National Committee of Labour Unity: "The massacre has passed into the political history of our people as a hard experience, that points at the same time to a qualitative leap in the revolutionary struggle."[50]

If the Spanish embassy incident was an important leap, its repercussions provided even more incentive for Indian involvement. Some of the peasants occupying the embassy had come from the town of Nebáj. After the death of the peasants in the embassy this Ixil community was occupied by the military. According to one priest who witnessed the occupation, the army invaded on market day and encircled the town. The 3,000 to 4,000 peasants inside were all detained until they could be given a military identification card. At the end of the first day only 30 cards had been given out, while the peasants were kept in the market in a cold rain. A number of the villagers were separated from the rest and presumably slated for routine military treatment of suspect peasants. On the second day of the occupation women from neighbouring communities, concerned over the fate of their men, went to Nebáj. The soldiers fired on the women, killing at least 11. Months later Padre José Maria Grandes, who had been in Nebáj and had publicized the killings, was in turn killed by the army. According to Father Sean McKenna, a Catholic priest who joined the EGP as their pastor, the occupation of Nebáj was another turning point. Whole Ixil communities which until that time had tried to appeal to the national government for defence against the military decided to join the revolutionary forces.[51]

If any final goad was needed to ensure that peasant organizations would abandon peaceful attempts at change and be forced to support the guerrillas, it came in July of 1981. In 1978, the Peasant Unity Committee (CUC) was established with the support of the National Committee of Labour Unity. Of particular importance was the fact that the CUC was an effective coalition of Indian and *ladino* peasants. Ethnic separation had been overcome by the need for common defence against the military.

Directed by peasants and addressing peasant concerns, the CUC steadily attracted support. Just as steadily it became a focus of government repression. In 1981 the leader of the CUC, Emeterio Toj Medrano was kidnapped by the military. Toj Medrano was tortured and pressured — villages were threatened with napalm — to denounce the CUC and the Democratic Front Against Repression to which the CUC was linked. Finally, in a daring raid the EGP released him from the army barracks where he was held prisoner. From that point on, the implicit link between the CUC and EGP became explicit.

With these incidents spurring them on, Indian peasants in the highlands joined the guerrilla forces in unprecedented numbers. Benefiting most from their support was the EGP, which opened seven different fronts and at times virtually controlled much of the countryside. Learning from the mistakes of the earlier revolutionary groups, the EGP refused to become embroiled in ideological disputes; instead it concentrated on immediate and pressing demands. This strategy and obvious commitment to peasant concerns proved successful. As more and more of its members and commanders were drawn from native communities, the guerrillas were even more easily able to win peasant support. Throughout the early 1980s, the guerrillas entered villages in the highlands at will, held political discussions, and almost always left with new recruits.

In the late 1970s the EGP was joined by three more guerrilla groups. Two of them, the Rebel Armed Forces (FAR) and the Guatemalan Workers' Party (PGT), had direct links to the guerilla forces of the 1960s. The most important new group, after the EGP, was the Organization of People in Arms (ORPA). ORPA developed through a similar process as the EGP but concentrated its forces in the heavily populated Indian highlands of Chimaltenango and Sololá. After beginning activities on the Pacific coast in 1971, ORPA decided to move inland to the highlands. The shift in locale was the result of a decision to address the concerns of the Indian peasants in the area and quickly appeared to bear fruit. According to the official history of the organization, its tiny meetings held at night to discuss peasant concerns grew into large gatherings with close to 100 people attending. By 1973, over 90 per cent of the rebels in ORPA were Indians.[52]

In the following years ORPA opened an urban front in Guatemala City, but the focus of its operations remained the central highlands. There its recruitment of peasants was helped by an army campaign similar to that in northern El Quiché. Perhaps the village hardest hit by the army was San Juan Comolapa, which had developed a number of local organizations following the earthquake in 1976 as well as a reputation for being the home of a number of excellent "primitive" painters. In March 1980 a clandestine grave with 39 bodies was found in a ravine close to the village, and the military had begun to enter the village and neighbouring hamlets periodically and kidnap peasants. In early 1981, 168 people were killed in neighbouring villages and by March of that year many of the residents of the village were trying desperately to flee the area.[53] By 1982, peasant support for the guerrillas in the area was such that ORPA could operate freely throughout much of the Chimaltenango and Sololá highlands, and controlled much of the major resort area around Lake Atitlán.

Both the EGP and ORPA, but especially the EGP, rejected the somewhat ostentatious propensity of the guerrilla leaders in the 1960s to continually grant interviews to explain their position and their progress. They did this partly for security reasons and partly because they saw their primary objective as winning the hearts of the highland peasantry. This would require a long gestation period which could only be jeopardized by publicity that would bring military reaction upon them. Consequently, until 1981 there was little on public record concerning the goals and ultimate objectives of either group. In 1981 one of the directors of the EGP for the first time publicly described its goals and strategy for victory. In this statement he forcefully rejected the old strategy of *foci guerrillero,* saying, "Never did we forget the participation of the masses, not only as help in the war, but as the decisive factor, as participants and protagonists of the popular revolutionary war." His statement went on to point out that although the EGP was by necessity a political and military instrument, EGP saw itself primarily as the basis of a "popular army which will support whatever government is substituted for the tyrannical one" now ruling Guatemala.[54]

By the early 1980s it was apparent that substantial numbers of Indian peasants throughout most of the highlands were supporting the guerrillas, although this was not true in all areas of the highlands. In some regions, where peasants had developed viable alternative economic pursuits and where local village structures had followed a different course of development since the 1950s, (for example, Totonicapán,) active support for the guerrilla organizations remained minimal. In the areas where the revolutionary groups received substantial backing, some observers have pointed to decisions by whole communities to join the guerrillas, but it is clear that in many instances the decision was a very personal one. The whole range of changes that had occurred in highland villages in the preceding two decades — the weakening of the power of the traditional hierarchy, the more "populist" position of the church, the increasing number of educated native youth, and an experience with autonomous organizations such as co-operatives — all assisted in breaking the longstanding bonds of silence.

Brutal Counter-insurgency

THE ACTIONS OF THE MILITARY in the highlands were probably the most important element in prompting peasants to join the guerrilla forces. The army's brutal campaign provoked a dramatic generalization of the conflict. The violence was in some ways an inherent part of counter-insurgency, as Egbert Ahmed pointed out in 1972 in *The Nation* on the "Theory and Fallacies of Counter-Insurgency":

> In theory, pacification demands that the friendly or neutral population be treated with kindness and consideration. In practice it is impossible to distinguish between friendly and hostile villages. . . . Soldiers in an alien environment can do nothing else than perceive the civilians as hostile and meet their ordered or understood quota of body counts.[55]

In Guatemala, the generalization of the violence in the countryside took on the added dimension of race conflict. The *ladino* military commanders, the inheritors of centuries of prejudice, often tended to see all Indian villagers as potential enemies. Consequently, they followed a policy of genocide that drastically escalated the violence, a policy that proved self-fulfilling. By attacking the native population, the military drove whole Indian communities and increasing numbers in others to join the guerrilla forces. By 1982, as it became obvious that some village authorities were swinging to the guerrillas, and thus that village organization was assisting the revolution, the military embarked on a deliberate policy of creating internal refugees by destroying whole villages altogether.

The survivors of these villages were then accumulated in central "safe" towns which the military could more easily control. It is only this combination of racial tension, a paranoid fear of communist subversion, the determination of the local and national landowning elite to retain its advantages, and the military's determination to retain control over highland villages, which explains the barbaric cruelty of the army in the highlands.

The list of Indian villages decimated by the Guatemalan military after the late 1970s is virtually endless. From a policy that throughout the 1970s tended to be selective, focusing repression on "members of grass roots organizations outside of official control", government repression exploded into a Dantesque nightmare of brutality. Often this was associated with the barest evidence of support for the guerrillas. In November 1980, when ORPA entered Santiago Atitlán and spraypainted "the lake is ours, not the foreigners' " on village walls, the military responded to reports that the villagers had not opposed the guerrillas by promptly establishing a base on the outskirts of the village. Two days later the army killed the director of the local radio station, and within one month had slain more than ten other people as well as conscripting many more. More than 300 Indians slept in the church each night to avoid the rampaging military.[56]

In the Mam village of Todos Santos in the department of Huehuetenango the EGP held a similar political meeting. The EGP flag remained flying from the village courthouse for over a week. Later the military slit the throats of 15 villagers for not resisting the EGP when they entered the village.[56] Numerous reports described how the military descended on other Guatemalan villages and wreaked similar havoc. San Juan Comalapa, San Juan Ixcóy, Santiago Atitlán, San Mateo Ixtátan and Coya are only some of the villages from which relatively well documented reports of massacres emanated during the Lucas administration.[58]

The elections of March 1982 altered little in the army campaign. Immediately following the elections, survivors alleged that 200 peasants were killed in the town of Zacualpa in the department of El Quiché. The coup that brought Ríos Montt to power in March 1982 only marked an intensification of the military campaign in the highlands. The litany of massacres continued unabated (see chapter 12).

Guatemala was in a state of war. Throughout the late 1970s and the first few years of the 1980s, government troops and guerrillas regularly engaged in skirmishes that produced numerous casualties. In addition, not all the murders in the villages could be laid at the feet of the military. Guerrillas carried out an intensive campaign aimed at government informants (*orejas*) in the villages. Military commissioners and large landowners were also regular targets of the revolutionary forces. The guerrillas' urban front, which included bombing attacks on government offices, also periodically claimed the lives of innocent bystanders or lower-level government employees.

Nonetheless, all observers not directly linked to the government reported that the vast majority of the killings were the work of the military or right-wing death squads acting in conjunction with the government. In addition, the bulk of the killings was not the result of government encounters with guerrillas, but were rather the fruit of military raids on peasant villages during which peasants with no connection to the revolutionary forces were killed. The thousands of deaths in the Guatemalan highlands during the 1970s and 1980s were not the result of a civil war between guerrillas and the military. They were instead the outcome of a government counter-insurgency program that attacked the very basis of Guatemalan peasant life: the village and its social and political structures.[59]

With much of the Guatemalan highlands a deserted cemetery, the Guatemalan government continued to try to sell the myth of a responsible democracy and assert that it was caught in a civil war between violent right- and left-wing factions. Like the train of bodies that vanished as if in a dream in Gabriel García Marquez's *One Hundred Years of Solitude*, the government simply seemed to hope that nobody would notice the dead. Few in Guatemala were fooled, however, least of all the peasants who bore the full weight of government repression.

Popular Opposition Forces Unite

BY EARLY 1982 the organizations opposing the government represented a broad cross-section of Guatemalan society. They included directors of trade unions, most notably the CNUS, leaders of the CUC, organizers of *barrios* committees, settlers' committees, many academics and student organizers, and many of the left-of-centre reform politicians. Most of the leaders of these movements had been forced to flee Guatemala. Consequently, an extensive organization of leaders of popular movements was created in exile. This force unquestionably represented the majority of the Guatemalan people and served to focus international opposition on the Guatemalan government. Its members' roots and affiliations were diverse, but most were united by a shared concept of the underlying goals of their struggle. As one director of the CNUS suggested:

> For us, the workers, peasants and agricultural labourers, *Peace* is a product of Social Justice. In a society where there exists exploitation, misery and oppression you cannot have peace ... and when, far from Solving the problems of the majority, they are repressed and massacred, [then] is created the conditions for the popular struggle.[60]

In order to carry out this struggle, and because of these shared underlying goals, the popular forces in 1982 effected a unity unparalleled in Guatemalan history. The four rebel forces, the EGP, ORPA, FAR and PGT, joined into the Guatemala National Revolutionary Union in March 1982 to facilitate a more cohesive armed struggle. Pointing to the similar campaigns carried out in various regions of the country, the revolutionary forces announced that the increased strength of their actions and the prospect of victory in the future required that they co-ordinate their commands and decide on a common statement of goals. Consequently, in January 1982 they published a declaration of unity and detailed the principal points that would characterize a revolutionary government.

They promised the Guatemalan people that a revolutionary government would: put an end to repression and guarantee peace, life and human rights to the citizens; put an end to the domination by the rich, both national and foreign, who ruled Guatemala, as a first step in providing the necessities of life for the majority of the population; guarantee equality between Indians and *ladinos* and put an end to the cultural oppression and discrimination Indians had faced; guarantee a government made up of representatives of all the patriotic, democratic and popular sectors; and guarantee a policy of non-alignment and international co-operation for development in international affairs.[61]

The guerrilla forces had clearly shown that they had learned valuable lessons from the divisions that hampered the movement in the 1960s. They also demonstrated that despite some differing opinions concerning the shape and strategy of revolution, they were united in a broad dream of the type of Guatemala they wanted to see created.

Following this call for unity on the part of the guerrilla forces, in February 1982 the Democratic Front Against Repression, itself a coalition of over 170 organizations, joined with the Popular Front of January 31 (a group composed of the CUC, settlers' committees, and labour unions) to form the Guatemalan Committee of Patriotic Unity (GCUP). They agreed with the points expressed by the guerrilla organizations in their earlier call, recognizing them as "the fundamental base

254   GIFT OF THE DEVIL

for the development and consolidation of the New Society", and called on people around the world to condemn the genocide of the Guatemalan government. The GCUP was headed by the respected 80-year-old reformer Luis Cardozo y Aragon and formed a true government in exile.

The revolutionary groups and the GCUP decided on common goals: the complete isolation of the Guatemalan government and military in the international community, and the imposition of negotiations as a first step towards a settlement that would bring democracy and economic reform to Guatemala. Their first major success along these lines was the condemnation of the Ríos Montt government by a majority in the United Nations' General Assembly in December 1982.

In the years after the overthrow of Jacobo Arbenz the development of a mass opposition to the government proved to be a difficult struggle. Nonetheless, in the face of ferocious repression, students, workers, politicians and peasants learned bitter lessons that helped them forge viable and powerful movements. A series of changes in Indian peasant villages during these years paved the way for peasant involvement in the struggle and their integration into the popular movement. By 1982 the Guatemalan bourgeoisie and the government had disintegrated into a myriad of competing cliques, frantically tearing apart the fabric of Guatemalan society as they desperately attempted to cling to power. They were tenuously held together by the national military which itself was rife with factions. Meanwhile, the popular forces that opposed the government forged strong and dynamic organizations that sought common goals through effective co-operation.

— 12 —
Conclusion: Peasants, Politics and Repression in the 1980s

Not even the lives of old people, pregnant women or innocent
children were respected. Never in our history has it come to such
grave extremes.
— Guatemalan Conference of Bishops, May 1982

IN AUGUST 1983 THE RULE of General Efraín Ríos Montt ended much as
it had begun, with a military coup forcing him from office. After his
overthrow the Guatemalan archbishop referred to him as "just
another accident in the history of Guatemala".[1] Yet in a number of
ways the 18 months of Ríos Montt's administration were of particular
importance for Guatemala.

Throughout 1982 and 1983 the military was able to complete a
process that began in 1542: the acquisition of control over the countryside and the total breakdown of village autonomy. In addition, the
military brought to fruition a trend that had been followed, more or
less systematically, since the beginning of counter-insurgency activities
in the early 1960s. By August 1983, when Ríos Montt was overthrown, the military had successfully ensured its national political
dominance and controlled much of the national economy.

But at the same time the Guatemalan military had never been able
to maintain itself as a homogeneous entity. Factions within the military
revolved around political parties, personal advantage and differences
over the scope and brutality of military operations in rural areas. In
1982 and 1983 the army was even more torn apart than usual. The
coup in March 1982, which had occurred largely to help heal the
wounds that divisions within the military had caused, only served to
deepen the rifts between older, more conservative officers, and young
officers who, rhetorically at any rate, advocated a type of rural development, but one that would be closely monitored and controlled by
the military. Guatemala's political parties clustered around the edges
of the various military factions.

The Campaign in the Highlands

THE MAJOR REASON for the coup in March of 1982 that brought Ríos Montt to power was the fear that another four years of government by the Institutional Democratic Party (PID) and Revolutionary Party (PR), in combination with corrupt, inefficient military command would increase guerrilla support in the highlands. At the time of the coup four powerful guerrilla forces were operating with effective control of a number of regions in the country. The most powerful, the Guerrilla Army of the Poor (EGP), was laying plans for establishing "liberated" areas where the revolutionary forces would establish nascent governments. Throughout all of the western highlands and much of the Franja Transversal del Norte government control was nominal at best. Travel to Huehuetenango, one of Guatemala's major cities, was dangerous and erratic and even Quezaltenango, Guatemala's second largest city, was difficult to reach at times. The area around Lake Atitlán, one of Guatemala's major tourist spots, was often firmly in the hands of the Revolutionary Organization of People in Arms (ORPA), which blocked roads, questioned travellers and burned cars seemingly at will. Foreign capital fled the country at unprecedented rates. The tourist industry was in shambles. Wealthy Guatemalans sent their families to live in Miami and long-time American residents sold their homes and left for "safer" paradises.

The military seemed unable to do anything to stem the tide of guerrilla success. Army patrols were slow to respond to guerrilla advances and major highland towns were in the hands of revolutionary forces for days at a time before the military appeared. Most often, in fact, the guerrillas had left these towns long before the military arrived. The army frequently retaliated against the peasant inhabitants of the village. The violence of the military under the regime of Romeo Lucas García, in a program directed by defence minister Aníbal Guevara, only served to propel more Indian peasants to support the guerrilla forces.

Military strategy changed somewhat when Benedicto Lucas García, the president's brother, was named defence minister to replace Aníbal Guevara, who was running for president in the electoral sham scheduled for 1982. Benedicto implemented a counter-insurgency policy that combined brutal attacks on peasant villages suspected of sympathy for the revolutionary forces with a civic-action program in which the military assisted villages in local construction projects. The program was inspired by Benedicto's training in the French military academy and from French experience in Vietnam and Algeria. Central to the program was a scheme for forcing highland peasants to abandon their scattered communities and to relocate in concentrated villages the military could more easily control, again a policy followed in Vietnam and Algeria. This aspect of the army's campaign involved constant pressure and continual attacks on scattered villages to force relocation. The program had only just started when Aníbal Guevara, the official candidate in the 1982 elections, was declared president-elect by the ruling PID/PR. The selection of Aníbal Guevara seemed to promise continued military incompetence, similar to that demonstrated while he was defence minister, a portent unsatisfactory to the junior garrison commanders, who overthrew Lucas García and helped set up a military junta headed by General Ríos Montt.

Following the coup, the counter-insurgency campaign implemented by Benedicto Lucas was pursued with a vengeance. After an initial period during which the government offered amnesty to guerrillas and their supporters, Ríos Montt declared on national television: "Today we are going to begin a merciless struggle... to annihilate the subversives that have not understood the good intentions of the government."[2] This phase of the government campaign was called "Victory 82". Villages throughout the highlands were occupied; all peasants suspected of subversive tendencies were killed, or were forced to flee to the rapidly growing refugee camps in the Mexican state of Chiápas. As always the military definition of subversive was wide ranging. As Ríos Montt explained: "The problem of war is not just a question of who is shooting. For each one who is shooting there are ten working behind him." According to that logic, with guerrilla forces estimated at between 3,000 and 6,000, that left the military with up to 60,000 "subversives" in the highlands to "deal" with.[3] One soldier described to a reporter how this campaign was instituted. He explained that the army captured, tortured and killed those who tried to run away when the military entered the villages. This was justified because "The people who are doing things outside the law run away. But the people who aren't doing anything, they stay." After a little prompting he admitted, "In the villages around here... they all go running."[4]

Mam villages in the department of Huehuetenango, villages in the Ixil triangle around Nebáj and in the Quiché were particularly hard hit. Many virtually ceased to exist as peasants fled to refugee camps in Mexico or wandered in the hills. During the summer and fall of 1982, villages throughout the highlands sat deserted, burned out shells of huts punctuated the silence, and lone, frightened survivors clung to their plots of land, most flying government flags from their roofs in an attempt to avoid attack by the military. By the end of that year up to 200,000 refugees had fled to Mexico and somewhere between

300,000 and one million peasants had fled their villages and were surviving in the mountains or in the ghettos of Guatemala City.[5]

Monitoring newspaper accounts only, Amnesty International reported that the Ríos Montt government had been responsible for at least 2,000 civilian deaths between March and September 1982.[6] According to the descriptions of survivors these killings were often unimaginably brutal. New York lawyer Stephen Kass and Professor Robert L. Goldham, in a series of interviews with people in refugee camps in Mexico, were told horrible tales of massacres, of children being put to terrible deaths. They described these incidents as a "level of [brutality] that seems unimaginable but is true. . . . We were told this kind of thing over and over along the border. We were told it by men, we were told it by women, we were told it by children — at different places by people who could not have known each other." Survivors of a seemingly endless number of massacres described to relief workers and reporters brutal encounters that left little doubt that the attacks were part of a deliberate government policy to destroy the guerillas' base of support by destroying those villages suspected of providing assistance to those forces. Any village which had strong, autonomous institutions, that is, a co-operative or peasant union, was suspect.[7]

According to the testimony of survivors, army attacks on villages were horrific in their total disregard for the lives of innocent people who could have had nothing to do with guerrillas. Reports included accounts of children being beaten to death on rocks and peasants being sliced open on the points of bayonets, although the more usual assaults involved the military burning crops and houses and shooting all villagers they encountered. A typical story was told to a reporter from *Uno más Uno* by a peasant from Huehuetenango. He described how the military "burned our homes, crops, violated our women, tortured the men and massacred entire populations. Everyday could be heard shots in the hamlets; these made us think that the soldiers were fighting guerrillas, but when we went down to look, there they were shooting our poor people."[8] The reports were enough to prompt the bishop of San Cristóbal de las Casas, in Chiápas, Mexico (near the site of most of the refugee camps) to confirm publicly: "Yes, there is genocide. I collected the testimony of various refugees giving proof of it. Neither children, women nor old people were respected." The bishop went on to give the details of a massacre on July 17, 1982 in the village of San Francisco, Huehuetenango, in which only 12 of the village's population of 350 were thought to have survived.[9]

In the heightened level of violence that followed the March coup the highlands were virtually sealed off from the rest of the country and the world. In this atmosphere it became increasingly difficult to verify attacks on villages and to pinpoint responsibility effectively. Much of the information had to come from refugees in camps in Mexico and thus accessible to reporters. In the resulting confusion reports of massacres that never occurred were accepted by reporters and human rights organizations. There is even some indication that occasionally reports were consciously exaggerated.[10] The Guatemalan government steadfastly denied that it was responsible for the majority of the attacks, declaring: "The fact that they are refugees in Mexico shows that they are rebel supporters and their false accusations reveal the subversives' capacity to spread lies about the government."[11]

In response to continued denunciations the Guatemalan regime repeatedly complained of "a campaign to defame the government". In January 1983, Guatemala helped sponsor a resolution submitted to the United Nations which attempted to restrict press coverage of third world countries. The Guatemalan delegate to the U.N. complained of "political groups interested in deteriorating [Guatemala's] image, using the communication media."[12] In April 1983, Ríos Montt publicly disputed the reported massacres by commenting on a national radio broadcast about how the world had become such a small place due to the media. "Imagine," he went on, "Guatemala is better known in Europe than in our Central America. We are being pointed at by all the press . . . saying that we, here, shoot children and after, we stab them with bayonets."[13]

Yet reporters from the *Miami Herald* claimed that in over one hundred interviews with refugees in August of 1982, the refugees "overwhelmingly blamed soldiers" for attacks on their villages. And in the spring of 1983 peasants who had recently returned to their village in Huehuetenango from a period of seven months hiding in the hills clearly stated that it was the military which had driven them from their homes.[14]

The government's protestations of innocence were not widely believed. In December 1982, the Ríos Montt administration was roundly condemned in the United Nations by a motion co-sponsored by the Canadian delegation for "violence against non-combatants". The motion demanded that the government "refrain both from forcefully displacing people belonging to rural and indigenous populations, and from the practice of coercive participation in civilian patrols" — both key elements of the government's campaign in the highlands.[15] In addition the Ríos Montt regime was denounced by a long list of international church organizations for its brutality. In May 1982 the Guatemalan Conference of Bishops recounted the tales of massacres and blamed the government. In August the president of the Catholic Bishops of the United States declared that the "massacre of numerous campesinos and Indian families has reached the level of genocide". The same month the organization Pax Christi declared that the level of human rights violations in Guatemala had reached "horrible proportions" since Ríos Montt had come to power. And in September the Dutch Catholic Congress reported on the violence, saying:

> The massacres were also destroying in a systematic manner all that sustains the life of the community; houses, woods, harvests; to the point that the water in the rivers is polluted to drive the people to desperation. The current wave of terror appears to have as a principal object to disarticulate the social life and the cultural inheritance of the Indian people and the peasant, to end the resistance of those that now won't support the weight of centuries of robbery, of maltreatment and of persecution.[16]

As these denunciations made clear, there *was* a planned campaign by the military which left much of Guatemala a deserted graveyard with burned out caskets of adobe huts as silent testimony. The basic ingredients of the campaign in the highlands were made clear in a presentation submitted to the ministers of the Ríos Montt government by the army Special General Staff in early April 1982. The plan, entitled the National Plan for Security and Development, was meant to work in conjunction with the Fundamental Statute which Ríos Montt had issued to replace the 1964 constitution. The plan and the statute gave greater powers to the executive, in this case Ríos Montt, and the military. The military's anti-subversive campaign was to be directed by the Institutional Co-ordinating Group of the General Staff, which was not only to oversee all military operations in rural areas but to co-ordinate all government institutions and agencies. Along with greater military control the plan proposed:

> to structure and regulate nationalism to promote and encourage it in all organs of State and to propagate it in rural areas; to ensure that it is included in the education and training given to the people as a doctrine opposed to International Communism; to ensure that programmes to reduce the level of illiteracy be carried out in order to make the population more receptive to new ideas and to increase the effectiveness of actions taken to create nationalism and maintain it.[17]

According to the Guatemalan Committee for Justice and Peace, this program was aimed primarily at Indian children in the areas of conflict — in 1982, 455,000 native children were taught Spanish as part of the campaign. "Alongside this, through assassination of the elders of the native communities, who are the repositories and guardians of their culture, an attempt is being made to stop it being preserved and handed on to the younger generations."[18]

The desire to destroy the strength and vitality of the native culture in the highlands and thus more easily extend military control over the area was the key to the second stage of the government program, entitled "Firmness 83". Shortly after coming to power Ríos Montt destroyed the legal basis of municipal government by dismissing 324 village mayors and replacing them with his own appointees. In addition, a few months later, the strength of the military in rural areas was increased by establishing a military zone in each one of the country's 22 departments to replace the former nine military zones.[19]

But the military campaign hinged on two elements: the creation of model villages and strategic hamlets, and the formation of civil guards to be commanded by the army. The model village scheme was first espoused by Ríos Montt early in the spring of 1982, when he declared that the villages would be funded by huge donations to Guatemala from the American fundamentalist churches, especially the Christian Broadcasting Network. While the treasure of donations he envisaged was never forthcoming, the military embarked on its own program of model villages. Information concerning these villages was quite scarce, even their number was unknown. However, many church and human rights organizations denounced the government's efforts to coerce the Indian population into settling in the villages. Organizations in opposition to the government branded them virtual concentration camps where the peasants were kept against their will with little provision for their well-being. While some members of the diplomatic corps in Guatemala, who were taken on army tours of one of the villages, complained that there appeared to be little foundation for the most horrendous reports, the camps clearly were part of the government campaign to destroy the foundation of village life and to reform it with substantial military control.[20]

The military's decision to create a system of strategic hamlets was inspired by a similar desire. In these instances, an existing village, usually a municipal capital, was reinforced with an army garrison, and peasants from the surrounding countryside were forced to relocate there. The military hoped in this manner to stop the guerrillas from recruiting among the population or from receiving provisions from the outlying hamlets. The peasants relocated in these villages and forced from their land were often in dire straits. Even the military officer in charge of the National Reconstruction Committee, while arguing that these people had grouped around the bases for their own security, admitted that there were about 250,000 peasants, "among them children who are forced to eat dirt", who were in need of assistance.[21] Much of the worst violence perpetrated by the military in the highlands was associated with the government program to force relocation in the model villages or the strategic hamlets.

The second aspect of the military's program to extend its control over rural areas, and probably the most ambitious, was the creation of civil patrols. All male residents between certain ages in highland villages were forced into civil patrols under the authority of the local army commander. These patrols blossomed in the highlands. In September 1982 an army spokeperson claimed that 40,000 men were organized into patrols. By the summer of 1984 they were estimated to be 700,000 strong. The army spokesperson argued that the patrols "are not just fighting the guerrillas, but are also organized to develop their villages, distributing food, building materials, setting up schools and health centres".[22]

While the patrols did perform these tasks in a number of villages, their main purpose was to increase army control over highland villages. All men in villages were required to participate in the patrols. The military kept lists of the men in the patrols, and was able in this manner to keep close tabs on the activity of most men in highland villages. In many ways the civil patrols fulfilled the long-held military dream of virtually complete control of rural Guatemala by replacing existing village government with a military instrument.

As well as providing an element of control, the civil patrols were the army's first line of defence against the revolutionary groups. A common saying in the western highlands in the spring of 1983 was that the "civil patrols protect the army". In many ways this was true. They were required to carry out extensive campaigns along highland trails in search of guerrilla enclaves, as well as to report any suspicious activity in their village. The army kept these patrols on a short leash and, reportedly, meted out quite drastic punishment if there was any indication of a lack of zeal in performing duties.[23]

On occasion the civil patrols fostered heightened violence in the highlands. Most Guatemalan municipios traditionally carried on a more or less running feud with neighbouring communities, the result of hundreds of years' competition for limited land. In many areas this took the form of racial conflict as ladino communities, most of them established during the 19th century, deprived the older Indian municipios of much of their land. After the civil patrols were established, ladino patrols, generally better armed than those from Indian communities, at least on a number of occasions took advantage of the opportunity afforded them to attack neighbouring communities.[24]

There were also a number of reports that the military in fact forced these patrols to attack neighbouring villages. A commission of Canadian church representatives that visited Guatemala in August and September 1983 stated that it had received testimony from two "trustworthy people" which confirmed that members of a civil patrol from a neighbouring area had been compelled by the military to kill a number of people in a small hamlet, people who had refused to join the civil patrols.[25]

The fiercest violence associated with the government's campaign had begun to wane by September 1982. In most districts the military was prepared to move to the second stage of its campaign against the guerrillas. A significant portion of the junior officers who had led the coup against the Lucas government had publicly complained about the generalization of counter-insurgency violence under that government, warning that the indiscriminate violence was pushing peasants to support the revolution. They called for a program to win the hearts of the peasants, particularly in areas with a high percentage of Indians. By the summer of 1982 they were threatening the Ríos Montt administration if military strategy didn't shift in that direction. Colonel Roberto Mata, who had taught at the Escuela Politécnica until July 1982 and then was placed in command of the Quiché district, was representative of this "new breed" of Guatemalan soldier. He argued that the civil struggle in Guatemala "is not just a war against subversion. It is a war against hunger, a war against the lack of education."[26]

The shift away from the focus on imported communist aggression as the root cause of unrest indicated a new emphasis for the military. One result of this new emphasis was seen in the increased stress placed on the *"frijoles"* part of the *"frijoles* and *fusiles"* (beans and bullets), as the government had labelled its counter-insurgency campaign. The stress on *frijoles* was designed as a means of improving the image of the military and national government in rural areas and of attacking some of the most immediate causes of peasant unrest. It was a continuation of the campaign barely begun by Benedicto Lucas, but also borrowed heavily from the United States' inspired civic-action programs employed in the 1960s in Zacapa.

In its 1982 incarnation, the army in the initial stages offered food, assistance in reconstruction, worked to provide water, and, on occasion, offered temporary medical clinics for peasants in villages recently repopulated.[27] The next step of the program was more ambitious. Headed by Colonel Eduardo Wohlers, the Program of Aid to Areas in Conflict (PAAC) required permanent army occupation of strategic villages. Through the military the government offered increased credit to small farmers, and prepared a program to encourage co-operatives and to stimulate the adoption of new labour intensive, vegetable crops. Small-farm experts from Taiwan began to advise the program's co-ordinator in early 1983.

This "social side" of the counter-insurgency was a mix of civic-action ideas and the "developmentalist" policies followed briefly during the Kjell Laugerud administration. Much of the funding for the program came from international aid agencies, especially U.S. AID and CARE, but all of it was directed by the military-controlled National Reconstruction Committee, the only agency the government allowed to operate in the highlands. At its heart, however, was military determination to maintain control of highland villages. Colonel Wohlers explained, "Under the previous governments the problem was that we pulled out, leaving the subversives to take advantage of our absence to win back villages."[28] With this new strategy the military was to maintain a permanent presence, a presence that alternated brutal repression with carefully measured benevolence.

In its early stages the emphasis on the *frijoles* aspect of the program seemed to take dramatic effect. Reporters from *Newsweek* in December 1982 cited the example of one Quiché woman who described a massacre in her village in which many people were killed and her children burned. She first assumed they were soldiers "because they wore uniforms and acted as soldiers have always acted". But as the military civic-action began to be implemented in her village she had doubts. She finally decided, "It must have been the subversives because now the soldiers are feeding and protecting us and why would they do that if they wanted to kill us."[29] By carefully nurturing this image the military hoped to dry up guerrilla support in rural areas.

The Ríos Montt administration also aggressively pushed an amnesty offer to rebels and their supporters. In publicizing his offer of amnesty, Ríos Montt tried to make a distinction between his government and previous ones. In a national broadcast announcing yet another of his periodic amnesty offers in March of 1983 he asserted:

> I wish to emphasize that the fight between brothers is no longer justified.... The government has already demonstrated its ability, recognized its errors and regained its dignity; but part of the force of governing is to promise you that we are determined to change. If you are a subversive accept our hand and make peace with us.... [W]e will pardon each other mutually because mutually we have done damage.[30]

The government claimed that 1,936 "subversives" took advantage of the amnesty offered in 1982. In the spring of 1983 the government aggressively pushed a new amnesty. Advertisements proclaiming it were published in all the newspapers, broadcast over radio and television, and notices were posted in villages and spread along mountain trails in areas where the guerrillas still operated. The government played up reports of new groups of subversives turning themselves in and captured guerrillas were "persuaded" to broadcast appeals to comrades to accept the amnesty.[31]

But serious questions surrounded the amnesty offer and government claims for its success. Most of those who accepted the offer were peasants branded as subversive by military informers in villages and thus forced in the preceding months to flee their villages. Few active guerrilla fighters seem to have accepted the government's offer. Part of the reason for the lack of enthusiasm for the government's offer was persistent rumours, given substance by statements from the new regime that took over after the August 1983 coup, that the military under Ríos Montt did not always live up to its promise not to punish those who accepted the amnesty.[32]

The Ríos Montt administration did all it could to foster the impression that the military had gained control of disputed areas and that villages had accepted military assistance and protection. Despite army successes it was a hard image to maintain while tens of thousands of refugees lived across the Mexican border and, even though the torrent of fleeing peasants had been reduced, more continued to arrive at Chiápas refugee camps weekly.[33] Consequently, the government worked diligently to encourage the return of these refugees. When 34 families returned to their village in February 1983, their re-entry into the country was widely publicized, as was military assistance in their resettlement. Less widely known were the government's unsuccessful attempts to convince other refugees to return to their villages. On one occasion a military convoy of PAAC trucks waited just across the border while negotiators tried to entice peasants from a particularly pretty, relatively well off village with promises of assistance to return to Guatemala. The peasants steadfastly refused despite the horrific conditions they endured in the refugee camps.[34] The refugees who remained in Mexico were by their very existence a constant indictment of the government's brutal policy in the highlands.

Political Conflict and Opposition

WHILE THE GOVERNMENT'S campaign in the highlands was the aspect of the Ríos Montt administration that was felt most painfully by the bulk of the Guatemalan population, a number of other issues created conflicts within the government and the military. The most serious of these were disputes over a "return to democracy", the government's economic policies and — intermingled with these two — an increasingly bitter conflict between two powerful factions in the military. It was the last of these which most directly led to Ríos Montt's overthrow and in the process clearly showed the severely restricted possibilities for reform in Guatemala.

Much of the rhetoric surrounding the March 1982 coup was couched in terms of "reinvigorating the democratic principle" after a decade of electoral fraud. While the more important impulse for the coup was military concern over a poorly waged civil war, there were still expectations that new elections would soon follow. These expectations were quickly dashed by the attitude of Ríos Montt and the Advisory Council of Officers. Ríos Montt's declaration immediately following the coup that the military junta was capable of ruling without "cheap politicians" seemed to have received much support among younger officers. While one political party tacitly supported the Ríos Montt administration, most of Guatemala's right-wing politicians opposed what they saw as an attempt to more firmly entrench the military's dominance over the political process.

Throughout the Ríos Montt regime there had been a careful distinction drawn between rural and urban Guatemala. Ríos Montt counted on the urban middle class for much of whatever support he enjoyed. Consequently, the fiction of being a responsible, moral government — a fiction made even more preposterous by the military campaign in the highlands — was pursued vigorously in urban areas.

Ríos Montt's campaign against the right-wing death squads won him support among the middle class, particularly from people aligned with the Christian Democrats, and muted some of the demands for elections and constitutional government. Shortly after taking power Ríos Montt called on the right to "take your machine guns off the roofs of your houses, put your pistols away and place your trust in the professionalism of the country's armed forces."[35] He led a vigorous attack on the interior ministry, which during the Lucas administration had been especially corrupt and responsible for much of the government-orchestrated urban violence. Close to 300 people in the ministry were fired in the months immediately following the coup. Many members of the previous regime who were believed to be responsible for the death squads were placed under house arrest, and some were consigned to be tried by special military courts established by the new administration. The MLN, always the most violent of the right-wing parties, was weakened by Ríos Montt's attacks on it, especially after Sisniega Otero, one of its most rabid spokesmen, was implicated in a coup attempt.[36]

There were still numerous reports of "disappearances" and appeals from relatives for information concerning their fate, but violent incidents in Guatemala City during the early months of the new administration fell by over 90 per cent. The city, which had been silent and dark after nightfall for almost two years, slowly came back to life. A similar process occurred in other urban areas; Antigua revived and tourists returned; marimba bands again played in the park on weekend evenings in Huehuetenango; and peo-ple clustered in cafes around the central park in Quezaltenango.

Ríos Montt also won support from the urban middle class for his campaign against government corruption. In the first months after the coup over 50 people were arrested for corrupt practices under the previous administration.[37] Plans were laid for expropriating some of the land fraudulently obtained by officials in the Franja. The most visible feature of the anti-corruption campaign — indeed perhaps the most visible feature of the administration — was a well-publicized program against dishonest public officials. The campaign rested heav-ily on religion and moral responsibility. With a barrage of publicity aimed at government employees the president called on the country to change its corrupt ways. Government employees were required to wear badges sporting the latest government slogan: "I don't steal, don't lie, don't abuse." Citizens were urged to report dishonest gov-ernment employees and the president made regular trips to accept the pledges of civil servants to abide by this promise. All these matters were dutifully reported by the press. It was a popular campaign, espe-cially among the urban middle class, even though there was some complaint that the "big fish" behind the corruption in the Lucas regime had escaped unscathed.

The administration fared less well with the economic policies it initiated. These policies quickly alienated large landowners, leaders of the business community and eventually much of the middle class. Ríos Montt took over the government with the Guatemalan economy seri-ously depressed. During the early 1980s the worldwide recession had reduced the demand for and price of Guatemala's exports. The increased interest rates that accompanied the recession seriously affected Guatemala and forced the government to abandon a number of large infrastructure projects.

The Guatemalan economy was particularly hard hit because of an archaic tax structure that was completely inadequate to meet the needs of the government, an elite that invested large amounts of wealth outside of the country and so deprived Guatemala of much-needed investment capital, and political unrest that had virtually destroyed the important tourist industry and damaged many other productive sectors. Most importantly, the international recession hit Guatemala especially hard because the poverty of the majority of the populace meant that there was very little internal market, and Guatemala had remained entirely dependent on sales of its agricultural products on the world market. The Ríos Montt government did little to improve the economy.

Shortly after taking power the new administration prompted opposition from the business elite by implementing new taxes and rationing foreign exchange. During the last three years of the Lucas García government, Guatemala had suffered a disastrous increase in its debt and a severe decline in its foreign reserves. A constant outflow of capital, increased government expenditure to wage the civil war and enormous amounts of government funds siphoned off to bank accounts of corrupt government officials all contributed to the government's financial difficulties. The problem was aggravated by a reduction in the export tax on coffee, a measure forced on the Lucas government by the coffee oligarchy.

Consequently, the coup in March 1982 was meant partly to prompt support for renewed aid for Guatemala, both economic and military, through the installation of a more acceptable government than the widely condemned Lucas regime. The influential *Economist Intelligence Unit* emphasized this aspect of the Ríos Montt administration in its 1982 third-quarter report:

> As a former presidential candidate for the Christian Democrats, General Ríos Montt is well placed to lead Guatemala out of its isolation from the rest of the Western World. . . . The most tangible proof of better relations will be provided by the resumption of military aid from the United States.[38]

While U.S. military aid was consistently denied the new government despite the attempts of the Reagan administration to have congress approve such aid, Ríos Montt was remarkably successful in grabbing sizeable loans from international agencies. A sum of $11 million was granted Guatemala as part of the Caribbean Basin Initiative and the State Department agreed to support Guatemala's request for $170 million more from the World Bank. In 1982 the bank gave Guatemala $46 million while the International Monetary Fund provided $240 million in 1983 and slated a further $166 million for 1984. In return the IMF demanded that the government reduce its deficit, remodel the tax system and reduce the miserly level of government services it provided.[39]

Despite these loans the Ríos Montt administration was forced to ration foreign exchange. This was particularly onerous for small shopkeepers and business people who lacked access to funds outside of the country and could no longer import the goods they needed to operate. Ríos Montt also began a campaign to restrict capital flows out of the country. He attacked the business sector, which he said "has impoverished itself and the nation by its tax dodging and its illegal export of dollars, which has made us all poor, not only in money but also in morals".[40]

The government's austerity program did little. By the end of 1982 the country's external debt approached Q765 million and the battle between Ríos Montt and the business elite escalated. A backlog of $400 million in dollar requests confronted the central bank. The MLN was especially virulent in its attack on the government, warning that the new value-added tax would lead to "galloping inflation" and seizing every opportunity to criticize the government. While the administration refused to devalue the currency, a lively black market thrived with the *quetzal* discounted by as much as 30 per cent.[41]

The most serious opposition to Ríos Montt's economic policies occurred because of a continual fear that the new administration was considering implementing some form of land reform. Immediately following the March 1982 coup, relations between large landowners and the Ríos Montt administration were good. During the later years of the Laugerud administration and that of Lucas García, many civilian landowners, who were not linked to the PID officers, had become increasingly bitter towards a military hierarchy which was greedily using its positions to accumulate huge expanses of land, and then monopolizing government contracts and export licences. With the change in government this promised to stop. Ríos Montt's first agricultural minister, Otto Martínez, was a former head of the General Growers' Association (AGA) — the organization of landowners — and a respected member of the landowning elite. He also had important connections with right-wing political parties.

But tensions soon developed. Otto Martínez was killed in an airplane crash and replaced by Leopoldo Sandoval Villeda in August 1982. Sandoval Villeda was a somewhat frightening prospect for Guatemala's landowning elite, having worked on agrarian reform for an international agency in Costa Rica. This apprehension heightened when, shortly after Leopoldo Sandoval's appointment, Ríos Montt declared: "We are planning changes in agricultural policy . . . in line with national reality."[42]

The Ríos Montt administration seems to have been pulled into contemplating agrarian reform initially because it had inherited a number of *fincas* confiscated from members of the Lucas administration. In January 1983, the government announced it had 2,000 *caballerias* of such land in the Franja, which it would distribute to peasants.[43] The apprehension reached hysteric proportions when a report was leaked indicating that the U.S. State Department was drawing up a tentative agrarian reform for Guatemala. Although the government announced that it would accept no such reforms, the statement was somewhat ambiguous and did not rule out a home-grown scheme. One of Guatemala's most influential newspapers followed this with a denunciation of agrarian reform. Citing the anarchy that purportedly accompanied the 1952 agrarian reform, the paper called for "no more agrarian reform projects". And in March, the finance minister promised, "No system of agrarian reform will be implemented in Guatemala."[44] But the distribution of land from a confiscated *finca* to 500 peasants near Santa Cruz del Quiché by the National Institute for Agrarian Transformation later that month prompted a renewed flurry of rumours. It was generally believed that the government was actively working on some reform plan.[45]

One of the most publicized sources of conflict was Guatemala's so-called "religious war". Ríos Montt was a member and elder in an evangelical, fundamentalist, Protestant church, El Verbo. The church was affiliated with the Gospel Outreach Church of Eureka, California and Ríos Montt received support — some monetary, some political, some spiritual — from fundamentalist associations in the United States, especially the Christian Broadcasting Network of Virginia. Ríos Montt was a passionately, many would say fanatically, religious man. Converted to the El Verbo church in 1978, he had become deeply involved in the growth of the church in Guatemala. After taking over the government, he named two elders of the church as important advisors and there were constant rumours that Protestant evangelists were being unfairly appointed to powerful government positions. Membership in Ríos Montt's church exploded from 800 before the coup to 3,500 in July 1982.[46]

Under Ríos Montt the government encouraged Protestant missionaries to spread throughout the country. These missionaries were particularly conservative and joined the most conservative of the Catholic clergy in supporting the government's policy in the highlands, denouncing those who opposed authorities as "resisting the will of God".[47] Most, however, were particularly unsuited for missionary work in Guatemala. It became commonplace to run across young missionaries newly arrived in the country attempting to harangue peasants with a set speech that represented all they knew of Spanish. The Spanish was usually so badly pronounced that the attentive listeners were left completely bewildered. Despite this general ineptitude, this aggressive new campaign in a traditionally Catholic country — yet with an estimated 30 per cent of the highland population converted to Protestantism in the last two decades — worried the Catholic Church.

Catholic priests in Guatemala had more serious complaints concerning the spread of fundamentalist missionaries. The Catholic Church especially after the death of the Conservative Cardinal Mario Casariego, had been one of the few internal critics of the government's atrocities in the highlands. Many of its ministers viewed with some apprehension the fundamentalists' rabid anti-communism and their message of compliance with the government. The Bishop of the Verapaces, Gerardo Flores, called the penetration of these sects "the North American State Department's answer to the options taken by the Catholic Church". So, as the Catholic Church began to more steadfastly condemn the government, it also attacked the activities of the fundamentalist missionaries.[48]

Ríos Montt also distressed many others with his many religious appeals to the nation. Every Sunday the general gave a nationally broadcast speech. While often addressing real problems, the talks were not only peppered with evangelical phrases but were also occasionally embarrassingly incoherent. At one point defence minister Oscar Humberto Mejía Víctores complained that Guatemala didn't need more prayers, it needed more executions.

During the 18 months of his administration Ríos Montt was increasingly opposed by Guatemala's right-wing political parties, but retained throughout it the tacit support of the Christian Democrats. With the PID/PR coalition effectively discredited by the overthrow of Lucas, the most powerful of the right-wing parties was the MLN. Given the policies proposed by the Ríos Montt administration, particularly the tax measures and the rumours of agrarian reform, this party's attacks on the government were not surprising and, hoping to take advantage of the PID/PR collapse, the MLN continued to push for quick elections following the coup. Party members were increasingly disturbed by what they perceived as indications that Ríos Montt was attempting to hang on to power beyond the time needed to stabilize the government.

Other political parties also distrusted Ríos Montt's intentions. Alejandro Maldonado, once a member of the MLN but the presidential candidate of the Christian Democrat coalition in the 1982 elections, warned in September 1982: "A new alliance is needed to confront the military and their habits of power; so that sovereign powers are returned to the people."[49] Nevertheless, the Christian Democrats tacitly supported Ríos Montt. While they were circumspect about how vocal their support would be, they most often refused to join in the chorus of warnings about Ríos Montt's propensity to accumulate power in his own hands. Christian Democrats also collaborated with government programs. The reasons for this support, as cautious as it might have been, is not hard to trace. The coup that brought Ríos Montt to power in 1982 was in many ways not unlike the very revolt a substantial sector of the party had called for following the 1974 electoral fraud that grabbed the presidency away from Ríos Montt.

By early 1983 plans were being made for new electoral laws. The most important of these was a provision that lowered the number of required party members for registration of a party to 4,000 from the 50,000 figure established by the 1964 constitution. This provision would make it increasingly difficult for the government to reject the lists of left-wing parties as it had done for the last two decades. Not surprisingly, the plan was met with fulsome opposition from the established right-wing parties, especially the MLN. Nonetheless, the measure was instituted and formed the basis for organization of parties contesting the elections held in July 1984 for members to a constituent assembly.

As the Ríos Montt administration took rather halting steps towards those new elections, the political landscape in Guatemala fragmented. Established political parties split into numerous factions, and new parties were formed daily. Political activity was intense. Even Juan José Arévalo and Francisco Villagrán Kramer briefly returned to the country in a move that prompted speculation that they were testing the political waters.[50] Nonetheless, there remained widespread scepticism concerning the general's promise of elections.

Factions in the Military: The Conservative Hierarchy Reasserts Itself

THE DIFFERENCE IN THE way political parties viewed Ríos Montt reflected a more serious division in the military. Ríos Montt's firmest support came from a group of junior officers, most of them key participants in the coup of March 1982 and many represented in the Council of Junior Officers that advised the president. While much of Ríos Montt's support within the military came from these junior officers, he continually sought to lessen his reliance on them and to develop his own base of support within the military. The junior officers themselves supported Ríos Montt as a compromise with the traditional conservative hierarchy, and only as long as he followed policies they approved of. In the end he lost the support of many of the junior officers and was overthrown by the traditional military hierarchy reacting both against the continued influence of the junior officers and his economic policies, especially the rumours of agrarian reform.

The coup that had brought Ríos Montt to power had seriously divided the military. Since the overthrow of Jacobo Arbenz in 1954 a variety of factions had solidified within the outwardly cohesive army. The two most powerful factions in the 1950s, 1960s and early 1970s were the military technocrats who had been instrumental in forming the PID, and who by the late 1970s clustered around Lucas; and the more conservative and traditional officers linked to the MLN who had in common an obsessively paranoid anti-communism. During the 1970s a third group had arisen which was more prepared to countenance some limited reform and had links to the Christian Democrats. This group had supported Ríos Montt in 1974 (although, it is clear, not very vigorously) and were briefly in a position of predominance within the Laugerud administration.

During the 1970s the MLN, with its "organized violence" and open pronouncements of its fascist tendencies, had lost support among the military until by 1978 there were few officers who would openly support it. Nonetheless, there remained a core of officers who held political and economic views closely akin to those of the MLN. With the PID officers completely discredited after the overthrow of the Lucas administration, the two opposing factions within the military — the junior officers and the conservative hierarchy — confronted each other. Following the coup in 1982, the younger officers linked to the Christian Democrats seemed to hold the most powerful position within the military. But Ríos Montt was constantly beset by the pressures placed on him by a divided military.

This division was most clearly represented by the Advisory Council of Junior Officers on the one hand and the defence minister Oscar Humberto Mejía Víctores and chief of staff Héctor Mario López Fuentes on the other. Some of the contradictory aspects of the military's operations in the highlands can be traced to the conflict between these two elements. In particular, many of the junior officers opposed the more brutal aspects of the counter-insurgency campaign. It is no coincidence that the shift in emphasis in the *frijoles* and *fusiles* program occurred shortly after Ríos Montt was presented with a petition from 50 field commanders calling for less brutality.[51]

To a considerable extent, Ríos Montt's position depended on how well he could respond to the junior officers' demands without completely antagonizing the more senior officers. It was clear that he would be unable to do both. The influence of the Advisory Council of Officers was particularly resented by the military hierarchy, who complained that, as one officer put it, "The army is now being run by captains and little lieutenants."[51]

Two incidents in the spring and summer of 1983 brought this conflict to a head. The first was the result of pressure from the U.S. administration for the Guatemalan government to find and convict the killer of a Guatemalan working for U.S. AID. The Guatemalan government had never given up hope of receiving military aid from the U.S. To do so it had to overcome the opposition of congress by appearing to improve its record on human rights violations. When the Guatemalan AID worker was killed there was considerable pressure to find a murderer despite the U.S. administration's attempts publicly to play down the incident. Finally, a lieutenant was charged with the murder and committed to stand trial. Junior officers saw the action taken against him as an attempt to pin the blame on a handy scapegoat while senior officers who ordered the killing were left untouched. It also presented a dangerous precedent should there be calls for investigation into other killings. It was primarily Mejía Víctores who ensured that the soldier would be acquitted after touring military zones denouncing the attempt to try him. The incident seriously weakened Ríos Montt's support among the zone commanders and added to Mejía Víctores' prestige.[53]

The second incident occurred in June 1983, when the garrison commander in Quezaltenango refused to carry out an order from military command to bombard a village that had fallen under guerrilla control. This "strike" was quickly supported by commanders in Huehuetenango, San Marcos and Santa Cruz del Quiché. Angered by this demonstration of insubordination, a group of senior officers led by General Guillermo Echeverria Vielman attempted to unseat Ríos Montt. While he was able to withstand this challenge, Ríos Montt was forced by the senior command to disband the advisory council of officers. It was the harbinger of his final defeat. On August 8th, 1983 General Mejía Víctores and General Héctor Mario Lopez Suentes, supported by the bulk of the military command, forced Ríos Montt from office.[54]

None of Mejía Víctores' movements upon taking power were unexpected. In many areas the level of brutality again increased. One Indian leader in the highlands told reporters a month after the coup: "Our people are once again being forced to flee their villages into the mountains to save their lives."[54] The most far-reaching civic-action activities in highland villages were curtailed, and the emphasis of government rhetoric shifted from combating social causes of revolt to striving to "eradicate the marxist-leninist subversion threatening our liberty and sovereignty".[56] Death squads began once again to operate more or less openly in urban areas and attacked what elements of internal opposition still remained in urban Guatemala; university faculty and students, members of the church and trade unionists were gunned down in Guatemala City with distressing frequency.[57] In contrast to Ríos Montt's attempts to keep U.S. policy in the rest of Central America at arms length, Mejía Víctores encouraged an expanded U.S. presence in the region, and publicly declared: "The U.S. is the only country which can help combat guerrillas in the region."[58]

Perhaps the most vigorous measures following the coup were directed at internal military discipline. Immediately after taking power, Mejía Víctores warned junior officers: "We are aware of the need to preserve and strengthen the unity of the army, upholding the principle of hierarchy and subordination to frustrate the attempts of some elements to fracture and confuse the armed institution."[59] In December 1983 the military command passed a new army code which placed greater stress on discipline and adherence to the hierarchical levels of command. It also demanded the retirement of all officers who held employment outside of the military two years from the passage of the code (an attempt to reduce tension within the military from officer involvement in business deals), and of all generals who were not actively performing duties in the high command.[60]

Mejía Víctores also promised quick elections. The first step along that path was voting for a constituent assembly to draft a new constitution. These elections were held without serious mishap, and apparently with little fraud, in July 1984, giving a small plurality to the Christian Democrats in the assembly. The influence that this strength gave them was severely limited, however. Mejía sharply warned that he would react decisively if the Christian Democrats tried to do anything more than draw up a new constitution, advising against any meddling in his administration.

A Painful Legacy in the Highlands

THE 18 MONTHS of the Ríos Montt administration was a tragic period in Guatemala. The military had embarked on a program meant to fulfill its dream of unquestioned dominance in rural Guatemala.

Within the military a number of different tendencies battled for position. The coup in March 1982 had brought a younger group of garrison commanders to a position of influence. Some of these officers were interested in using their newly won influence to effect a change in the manner in which the military exercised its control over highland villages. The "social side" of the military's counter-insurgency campaign blended military-civic action similar to that employed in the 1960s and a development plan for villages borrowed from the early years of the Kjell Laugerud government. At the same time there was support both from junior officers and the military hierarchy for the army to return to the barracks and to leave the government to civilians.

But both of these tendencies represented a minority of the Guatemalan officers. The Guatemalan military was still, by and large, a closed insular institution with an implicit belief in the danger of the communist plot and the military's duty to defend the nation against it. The military hierarchy that reasserted itself after the August 1983 coup was predominantly composed of conservative, senior officers with links to the MLN and the traditional rural elite, the most violent and rabidly anti-communist of Guatemala's officers. Thus there could be little consolation in the new regime's promise of quick elections. There was little chance that the military would for long leave government to civilians, or that it would allow a civilian government with reform intentions to implement policy. Free elections meant little if the elected government had no power. The August 1983 coup snuffed out any hope — dim as it was — that there would be substantial change within the ruling regime of Guatemala.

At the same time the counter-insurgency campaign embarked on by the military under Ríos Montt had seriously weakened the guerrilla forces in Guatemala. Military action had done little to reduce the fighting forces of the revolutionary organizations, but the violent attack on peasant villages and the subsequent civic-action campaign did deprive the guerrillas of important support networks in the highlands.

The civil patrols were a major, if temporary, set-back for the guerrilla organizations. The most serious concern for the revolutionary organizations was not the military activity of the civil patrols, but the way in which the patrols increased army control over rural areas and, through this control, dried up guerrilla support among peasants. In addition, the guerrillas' inability to defend villages after over-confident assurances by the revolutionary forces in the last couple of years of the Lucas administration prompted some bitterness. Keeping in mind Mao's dictum that the rebel must be supported by the rural populace and comfortable among the people, moving through peasant areas like the fish through the sea, the military was intent on using the civil patrols and the military civic-action to drain the sea.

Through civil patrols, military commissioners and terror the army had a stranglehold on village organizations. Autonomous development and village institutions that could not be controlled by the military were decapitated. The military, always obsessed with control over rural areas, had achieved a level of supervision that surpassed the control it enjoyed under the government of General Ubico in the 1930s. A rural development process that had been haltingly growing since the mid-1970s was effectively destroyed.

But the military also exaggerated its claims to have damaged the guerrilla organizations. Recovering from their most serious setbacks in 1982, the guerrilla armies continued to engage the military regularly in

1983. In January 1983, ORPA opened a new front in the highlands close to Guatemala City. After the overthrow of Ríos Montt the guerrilla forces seemed to regain some more of the lost momentum. The EGP declared that in the months of April and May 1984 it had accounted for more than 200 military casualties. While there was little talk of an imminent overthrow of the government, as there had been in the early 1980s, the opposition was clearly strengthening its position vis-à-vis the military once again.[61] With the inequities, injustice and repression that had led to revolution still rampant in the highlands, the popular forces only awaited a renaissance of peasant support to emerge once again as a powerful challenge to the government and the military.

The Ríos Montt regime left a painful legacy in the highlands. Just how painful can perhaps best be illustrated by citing an informal survey done in the department of Chimaltenango for a private aid organization in the summer of 1983. The area had suffered badly during the violence of 1982, but no more than much of Guatemala, and probably not as much as areas of El Quiché and Huehuetenango. In the region surveyed, 7 of 27 small villages had less than three-quarters of the number of families resident in the village one year earlier. In 11 communities over 20 per cent of the family units were headed by widows. A total of 15 communities had been abandoned for close to a year; and all but five were expected to receive either no or a severely limited harvest in 1983. Some communities were virtually wiped out. Chuabaj Grande had only 25 of 240 families remaining, 15 of them headed by widows. Paquixio had 100 of 200 families, Panicuy, 15 of 40. These rather cold statistics represent families shattered, lives lost and years of suffering as the communities, always sunk deep in poverty, struggled to rebuild.[62]

Another clear indication of the bitter legacy of the military's campaign in the highlands survived in refugee camps in Mexico. Perhaps as many as 200,000 peasants fled to Mexico to escape the violence. Despite government assurances and the outward appearance of improvement in conditions in the highlands, the majority of them steadfastly refused to return. In the camps they endured horrific conditions: hunger, disease and poor shelter. They also were threatened by incursions of Guatemalan soldiers on forays into the camps and, according to some reports, even brutal treatment from the Mexican military. In the summer of 1984, pessimism concerning future conditions in the Guatemalan highlands was indicated by the Mexican government's decision to move the refugees away from the border, and to settle them in more or less permanent settlements in the Yucatan.[63]

…overty, neglect and injustice, Guatemalan peas-
…e early years of the 1980s a level of violence that far
experienced since the first days of the conquest. In those
…an survivors described the coming of the Spanish as a "gift
…devil". For many in the highlands in the 1980s, it must have
…ned the devil had once again come among them bestowing gifts.

A History of Injustice and Revolt

IT IS TEMPTING to explain Guatemala as a Conradesque nightmare: a
horror, irrational and inexplicable. But to the contrary, in many ways
Guatemalan society is a logical expression of the country's history. Its
modern history was founded in the bitter injustice of colonial conquest; followed by protracted years of dispossession and racial and
class oppression in the name of capitalist expansion controlled by an
elite based both at home and abroad; and finally buttressed by the
self-protecting tyranny of military interests and U.S. imperialism. It is
this history which has created a deeply polarized, essentially unjust
and violent society.

Highland villages as a result remained isolated, at least until very
recent times, from the national culture and, in some ways, from the
national economy. Despite almost a century of government rhetoric
concerning its intent to "develop" rural Guatemala, highland peasants
remain impoverished and powerless. All serious attempts to alter the
economic framework that perpetuates this poverty and powerlessness
have been confronted by powerful opposition: a traditional landowning oligarchy, an expanding agro-export elite, a frightened rural
middle class that turns easily to fascism, a U.S. foreign policy concerned with protecting the interests of American capital and
hegemony, and a paranoid, brutal military with links to all of these
others.

There have been, however, many forces within Guatemala that
have consistently fought this injustice and opposed the violence that
has kept it in place. On occasion it has even appeared that those forces
would be successful in fostering important change. In the colonial
period church and court officials occasionally fought the most blatant
exploitation of Indians, restricting their use as slaves and their employ
in the most dangerous of occupations. Time after time Indian peasants
took their own direct action through open rebellion. In the 1830s a
"peasant" leader led a successful revolt against a "modernizing"
movement that promised to attack the position of the rural peasantry
in the name of economic growth and "liberalism". While often acting
solely in his own interests and supported by a mercantile alliance that

marketed peasant crops, Rafael Carrera successfully delayed much of the worst effects of "liberal capitalism" on the rural peasantry. The most important attempt at social and economic reform occurred during the "ten years of spring" from 1945 to 1954. In those years moderate bourgeois reforms gave way to more radical, populist government policies and an aggressive agrarian reform that appeared finally to be attacking the root of economic and social inequity.

Nonetheless, these attempts have been consistently thwarted. Colonial legislation designed to protect the Indian was seldom enforced. The spread of coffee cultivation following the Carrera period was pursued relentlessly at the expense of peasant agriculture. The "revolution" of 1945 to 1954 was overthrown by a combination of powerful forces in Guatemala and the interests of U.S. business, along with the Eisenhower administration's fear of communism and its propensity to see communist talons in all popular reform. The military's experience during the "revolution" caused a majority of officers to continue in later years to link reformism in Guatemala with communism and to oppose reforms as their "national duty".

The ultimate failure of these attempts at reform proved that change cannot come piecemeal to Guatemala, altering this aspect of the economy or society while leaving others untouched. The Guatemalan economy, politics, the type of social institutions that have evolved and the country's place in the western sphere of interests are intimately connected. They are all interwoven into a disarticulated capitalist economy which not only takes the resources of many — specifically, land, labour and talent — and returns the benefits to a few; but also, in which labour is seen solely as a cost of production and not an eventual market for the goods that industry produces; in which peasant agriculture is seen as having little importance for the national economy; and in which the surviving Indian villages are seen as an inhibiting feature preventing the economy from growing and society from advancing.

Any reform, to be sustainable, must attack the very basis of that construction: the predominant landholding system. No attempt to significantly improve the living standards of the bulk of Guatemala's population will succeed without it. There can be no workable democracy until the coercive power of the local landowning elite, supported by the military, is destroyed through a substantial, broadly encompassing agrarian reform. Throughout three and a half centuries, landownership has been the central question in Guatemalan history, around which all else has revolved.

Like all societies, Guatemala views its history through the filter of myths, myths that distort the lesson to be learned but which, as always, bear within them a kernel of truth. Prominent in Guatemala are the myths of Barrios the reformer, of the "communist terror" unleashed by the Arbenz government, of the economic inefficiency of peasant agriculture and of the "communist plot" endangering the governments of the region.

In the national histories of Guatemala there exists another myth, hovering around the edges of the portentous events that occur in Guatemala City or infiltrating the halls of the military academy. This is the myth of the stoic, long suffering, peaceful but tradition-bound, ignorant and superstitious Guatemalan peasant. Viewed in this fashion, peasants can never be considered a viable and valuable part of the nation. Viewed in this fashion, peasant revolt against the government can only be explained through the means of a revolution exported from the "Marxist" nations in the region, a poor but peaceful peasantry inspired to revolt by leaders of guerrilla organizations actually working to spread the horrors of Communism.

This perception of the peasantry is the result of a near-sighted view of Guatemalan history. In many ways the history of Guatemala from 1524 to the present has been a history of revolt as much as repression. At times this protest has been isolated, restricted to one village or one district. At other times, such as the late 1970s and early 1980s, it has been generalized, threatening to overthrow the national government. On occasion the spark has been specific and local: a government official striking an elected mayor in the late 18th century, or the killing of a co-operative leader in a highland village in the 1970s. But at heart, peasant revolt has been the result of an economic and social system that has marginalized peasants, deprived them of their land, forced from them their labour with little or no compensation, and refused them protection from economic and physical attack.

With amazing consistency, protest has always first taken a non-violent, "legal" form. Only with repeated demonstration of the inability or unwillingness of government to respond effectively to these protests have peasants turned violent. In the 1770s and the 1780s peasant communities rebelled only after legal defence of their land was rebuffed. In the 1970s and 1980s only after non-violent protest was met with repeated violent response did highland peasants support guerrilla organizations in large numbers.

The perception of current unrest in Guatemala as a result of communist agitation is at heart a justification for the continued use of terror to stem unrest. But true violence in Guatemala lies in the relentless poverty of everyday life. That poverty condemns to death up to 100 infants per 1,000 live births; it causes some 25,000 people to die every year from a host of nutrition-related diseases; and provides

Indian peasants with an average life-expectancy of only 49 years. All of this poverty exists in a country that has proven abilities in food production and abundant agricultural resources.[64] Unless and until revolt is seen as a response to economic and social oppression and responded to with policies designed to end that oppression, it will continue to be endemic in Guatemala, snuffed out in one corner, only to flare up in another.

Putting an end to both the obsessive violence and the poverty of underdevelopment demands radical change. By the mid-1980s, however, there was no indication that the political process could respond in such a manner. Rather, the Guatemalan military and Guatemalan elite were determined to maintain their advantages through constantly escalating levels of repression. But government attempts to drum "subversive" ideas out of the highland population were doomed to failure. A whole array of popular revolutionary forces had forged an effective alliance of urban reform elements in opposition to the government. More importantly for future Guatemalan history, a long process of organization and activity in the highlands by peasant organizers, Catholic Action adherents and, ultimately, guerrillas linked to the EGP or ORPA had succeeded, in many ways, in breaking down the barriers that had divided Indian peasants from *ladino* ones.

Highland peasant villages were no longer the isolated, suspicious places they were in the three decades previous to the introduction of Catholic Action, peasant organizations and the guerrilla forces. Guatemalan Indians no longer saw their identity totally in relation to their village, ignoring the economic ties that bind them to the needs of other villages and indeed, to *ladino* peasants and urban workers. They no longer believed that local repression was the result of greedy local landowners, with no connection to the national government. As one church leader told the Canadian Inter-church Fact Finding Mission in 1983: "Never again will we hear the people say, " 'This suffering is the will of God.' "

Guatemalan Political Parties and Elections Post-1954

Year	Candidate	Party	% of vote	Comments
1957	Miguel Ortiz Pasarelli	MDN	62	Ydígoras claims victory
	Miguel Ydígoras Fuentes	Redencíon	38	
1958	Ydígoras	Redencíon	38.8	
	Jose Luis Salazar	MDN	28.1	
	Mario Méndez Montenegro	PR	27	Slightly over 50% of registered voters vote
1966	Julio C. Méndez Montenegro	PR	44.4	
	Juan de Dios Aquilar	PID	31.7	
	Miguel Angel Ponciano	MLN	23.9	
1970	Colonel Carlos Arana Osorío	MLN/PID	42.9	49% of registered voters vote
	Mario Fuentes Peruccini	PR	35.7	— or 10% of population
	Maj. Jorge Lucas Caballeros	CD	21.4	
1974	Gen. Kjell Laugerud García	PID/MLN	41	Ríos Montt claims victory
	Gen. Ríos Montt	FNO	36	
	Col. Píaz Novales	PR	23	
1978	Gen. Romeo Lucas García	Broad Front	41	Peralta Azurdia claims victory
	Gen. Peralta Azurdia	MLN	33	— 40% of registered voters vote — or 15%
	Gen. Peralta Méndez	CD	26	of those eligible — less than 7% of the population
1982	Gen. Anibal Guevara	FDP		Alejandro Maldonado claims victory
	Alejandro Maldonado	UNO		— 40% of registered voters vote
	Sandoval Alarcón	MLN		
	Anzueto Vielman	CAN		

KEY — To Political Parties

MDN	— National Democratic Movement
Redención	— National Democratic Renovation
PR	— Revolutionary Party
PID	— Institutional Democratic Party
MLN	— National Liberation Movement
CD	— Christian Democrats
FNO	— National Opposition Front: includes CD, United Revolutionary Front (FUR), the left-wing of the PR, and Revolutionary Democratic Unity (URD)
Broad Front	— includes PID, PR and Central Aranista Organization (CAO)
FDP	— Popular Democratic Front: includes PID, PR and National Unity Front (FUN)
CAN	— Authentic National Central
UNO	— United National Opposition: includes CD and MLN moderates

Notes

Notes to chapter 1

[1] Severo Martínez Paláez, *La Patria del Criollo* (Costa Rica, 1979), p. 535.

[2] This brief discussion on the geography of Guatemala relies heavily on: E. Higbee, "The Agricultural Regions of Guatemala", *Geographical Review* (1947), pp. 177-201; N. Whetten, *Guatemala* (Yale, 1961); and F.W. McBryde, *Geografía cultural e historica del suroeste de Guatemala* (Guatemala, 1969).

[3] Arturo Valdez Oliva, *Lenguas Indígenas de Guatemala* (Guatemala, 1965).

[4] Sol Tax, "World View and Social Relations in Guatemala", *American Anthropoligist* (Jan.-March, 1941), p. 21.

[5] Robert Carmack, *Quichean Civilization* (Berkeley, 1973); John Fox, *Quiché Conquest* (Albequerque, 1978); Robert Carmack, *The Quiché Mayas of Utalán* (Norman, 1981), pp. 134-143.

[6] Robert Carmack, *Historia Social de los Quiché* (Guatemala, 1979), pp. 27-28; also see articles by T. Veblen, G. Lovell and C. Lutz in *The Historical Demography of Highland Guatemala* (Albany, 1982).

[7] Murdo MacLeod, *Spanish Central America* (Berkeley, 1973), pp. 18-19.

[8] *Ibid.*, p. 15; Veblen, "Native Population Decline in Totonicapan", in *Historical Demography*, pp. 89-96.

[9] Adrian Recinos and D. Goetz, trans., *Annals of the Cakchiquels* (Norman, 1953), pp. 115-116.

[10] Veblen, "Native Population Decline", p. 89.

[11] Channu, *Conquête et Exploitation*, pp. 83-83, cited in MacLeod, *Spanish C.A.*, p. 20; also see Carmack, *Historia*, p. 59; Veblen, "Native Population Decline", pp. 95-96; Lovell, "Collapse and Recovery" in *Historical Demography*, p. 109.

[12] Veblen, "Native Population Decline", p. 90.

[13] *Titulos de la casa Ixquin-Hebaib*, cited in V. Brickner, *The Indian Christ, the Indian King* (Austin, 1981), p. 40.

[14] D. Brinton, trans., *Annals of the Cakchiquels* (New York, 1969), p. 183.

[15] W. Sherman, *Forced Native Labor in Sixteenth Century Central America* (Lincoln, 1979); also see Martínez P., *Patria*, pp. 65-67.

[16] Eric Wolf, *Sons of the Shaking Earth* (Chicago, 1959), p. 190.

[17] C. Gibson, *Spain in America* (New York, 1966), p. 149-151.

[18] Martínez P., *Patria*, p. 94.

19 *Ibid.*, p. 90.
20 MacLeod, *Spanish C.A.*, p. 132-133.
21 Martínez, P., *Patria* p. 453.
22 P.V. McDowell, "Political and Religious Change in a Guatemala Community" (Ph.D. diss., University of British Columbia, 1974).
23 C.L. Jones, *Guatemala* (Minnesota, 1940), pp. 137, 169; Jose Milla, *Historia de la América Central* (Guatemala, 1937), pp. 118-121.
24 Cited in MacLeod, *Spanish C.A.*, pp. 69-95.
25 R. Smith, "Indigo Production and Trade in Colonial Guatemala", *Hispanic American Historical Review* (1959), pp. 181-211.
26 *Ibid.*, p. 190.
27 *Ibid.*, p. 197; H. Dunn, *Guatimala, o las Provincias Unidas de Centroamericana durante 1827 a 1828* (Guatemala, 1960), p. 230.
28 Veblen, "Native Population Decline"; Lovell, "Collapse and Recovery".
29 MacLeod, *Spanish C.A.*, pp. 292-293.
30 Martínez, P., *Patria*, pp. 165-166; see also S. Zavala, *Contribución al estudio de las instituciones coloniales en Guatemala* (Guatemala, 1953).
31 MacLeod, *Spanish C.A.*, p. 153.
32 C. Gibson, *The Aztecs under Spanish Rule* (Stanford, 1964), p. 155.
33 T. Gage, *Travels in the New World* (London, 1958), p. 227.
34 Cited in J. Kitchen, "Municipal Government in Guatemala", (Ph.D. diss., University of California at Los Angeles, 1955), p. 16.
35 C.H. Haring, *The Spanish Empire in America* (New York, 1947), p. 133.
36 Martínez, P., *Patria*, p. 92.
37 Carmack, *Historia*, pp. 222-223; see also R. Wasserstrom, *Class and Society in Central Chiápas* (Berkeley, 1983).
38 See D. Contreras, *Una rebelión indígena en el partido de Totonicapán* (Guatemala, 1968).
39 Carmack, *Historia*, pp. 209-212.
40 *Ibid.*, p. 219.
41 Jonathan L. Fried, Marvin E. Gettleman, Deborah T. Levenson and Nancy Peckenham (eds.), *Guatemala in Rebellion: Unfinished History* (New York, 1983), p. 24. See pp. 24-25 for a list of Indian rebellions compiled by the editors.

Notes to chapter 2

1 Cited in M. Ingersoll, "The War of the Mountains" (Ph.D. diss., University of Washington, 1971), p. 137.
2 James D. Kitchen, "Municipal Government in Guatemala" (Ph.D. diss., University of California, 1955), p. 38.
3 Ingersoll, "War", pp. V-VI.
4 Cited in R.L. Woodward Jr., *Central America: A Nation Divided* (New York, 1976), p. 94.
5 José Cecilio del Valle, *El Amigo de la Patria* (Nov. 30, 1821), cited in C. Meléndez, *Textos fundamentales de la independer.-ia Centroamericana* (Guatemala, 1971), p. 30.
6 Guatemala's governor, Marino Galvéz, declared before a soldier's court martial in the 1830s: "So long as I remain in office I will not consent that only the lowly suffer the full rigour of the law." Cited in Ingersoll, "War", p. 31.
7 del Valle, cited in Meléndez, *Textos*, p. 31.

[8] C.L. Jones, *Guatemala* (Minneapolis, 1940), p. 201.

[9] Dr. A. Larrazábal, "Apuntamientos sobre la agricultura y comercio del reyno de Guatemala", presented to the Cortes of Cadiz, Oct. 20, 1810, cited in Meléndez, *Textos,* p. 74.

[10] Robert Smith, "Indigo Production and Trade in Colonial Guatemala", *Hispanic American Historical Review* (1959), p. 186.

[11] For perhaps the longest and most famous such complaint see: Francisco Antonio de Fuentes y Guzmán, *Recordación Florida: Discurso historical y demonstración material, militar y política del Reyno de Guatemala* (Guatemala City, 1932).

[12] L. Bumgartner, *José Cecilio del Valle of Central America* (North Carolina, 1968), pp. 147-166.

[13] From *El Amigo de la Patria* (Nov. 30, 1821), cited in Meléndez, *Textos,* p. 23.

[14] Bumgartner, *Cecilio del Valle,* p. 147.

[15] *Ibid.,* p. 106.

[16] Chatfield to Palmerston, Feb. 5, 1838; cited in T.L. Karnes, *The Failure of Union* (North Carolina, 1961), p. 84.

[17] Cited in Ingersoll, "War", p. 40.

[18] Cited in *ibid.,* p. 41.

[19] *Ibid.,* p. 43.

[20] *Ibid.,* pp. 44-74.

[21] Larrazábal, "Apuntamientos", p. 74.

[22] R. Facio, *Trayectoria y crisis de la federación centroamericana* (Costa Rica, 1949), p. 67.

[23] Cited in Bumgartner, *Cecilio del Valle,* p. 133.

[24] Larrazábal, "Apuntamientos", pp. 74-75.

[25] Bumgartner, *Cecilio del Valle,* p. 147.

[26] Ingersoll, "War", p. 86.

[27] G. Thompson, *Narrative of an Official Visit to Guatemala* (London, 1829), pp. 145-148.

[28] Cited in Ingersoll, "War", p. 95.

[29] Cited in *ibid.,* p. 99.

[30] Cited in *ibid.,* p. 100.

[31] M. Rodríguez, *The Cádiz Experiment in Central America* (Berkeley, 1978).

[32] H. Dunn, *Guatimala, o las Provincias unidas de centroamerica durante 1827 a 1828* (Guatemala, 1960), pp. 123-124.

[33] J. Skinner-Klee, *Legislación Indígena de Guatemala* (Mexico, 1954), p. 20.

[34] Woodward, *C.A.,* p. 76.

[35] For a fuller discussion, see Kitchen, "Municipal".

[36] R. Naylor, "Guatemala: Indian Attitudes to the Land", *Journal of Inter-American Studies,* p. 634.

[37] Ingersoll, "War", pp. 43-49.

[38] Cited in Ingersoll, "War".

[39] Cited in D. Contreras, *Una rebelión indígena en el partido de Totonicapán* (Guatemala, 1968), p. 31.

[40] There has not yet been much work done on peasant revolt in Guatemala during this period. The two most important sources are *ibid.,* and Robert Carmack, *Historia Social de los Quiché* (Guatemala, 1981).

[42] W.J. Griffith, *Empires in the Wilderness* (North Carolina, 1965), p. 32.

[42] Cited in Ingersoll, p. 62.

[43] Skinner-Klee, *Legislación*, p. 20; Julio César Méndez Montenegro, *Sumaria . . . Legislación agraria* (Guatemala), p. 89.
[44] Ingersoll, "War", p. 74.
[45] *Ibid.*, p. 70.
[46] *Ibid.*
[47] Cited in *ibid.*, p. 119.
[48] *Ibid.*, pp. 109-110.
[49] Dunn, *Guatimala*, p. 94.
[50] Cited in Ingersoll, "War", p. 163.
[51] J.L. Stephens, *Incidents of Travel in Central America, Chiapas, and the Yucatan*, Vol. 1 (London, 1842), p. 249.
[52] Ingersoll, "War", p. 189.
[53] Cited in Woodward, *C.A.*, p. 115.
[54] Naylor, "Indian Attitudes", p. 627.

Notes to chapter 3

[1] Justo Rufino Barrios, *Acta de Patzícia* (June 3, 1871), cited in Capitan Gregorio Contreras and Subteniente Joaquin Díaz Duran, *Cronica de la Campaña revolucionaria de 1871* (Guatemala City, 1871), p. 37.
[2] G. Laguardia, *El pensamiento liberal de Guatemala* (Costa Rica, 1977), p. 19.
[3] T.R. Herrick, *Desarrollo económico y político de Guatemala: 1871-1885* (Costa Rica, 1974), pp. 25-26; V. Solórzano, *Evolución económica de Guatemala* (Guatemala City, 1977), p. 288.
[4] Solórzano, *Evolución*, p. 286.
[5] Enrique Palacios, cited in *ibid.*, p. 289.
[6] Laguardia, *Pensamiento*, p. 19.
[7] R.L. Woodward, *Central America: A Nation Divided* (New York, 1976), p. 131.
[8] Herrick, *Desarrollo*, p. 42.
[9] M. Aurelio Soto, *Proyecto de una institución de credito nacional de hipotecario* (Guatemala, 1870), p. 3, cited in *ibid.*, p. 116.
[10] Barrios, *Actá de Patzícia*, cited in *Cronica*, p. 37.
[11] Cited in R.L. Woodward Jr. (ed.), *Positivism in Latin America* (Mass., 1971), p. IX.
[12] Cited in J. Fred Rippy, "Justo Rufino Barrios", in A.G. Wilgus (ed.), *Hispanic American Essays* (Chapel Hill, 1942), p. 294, footnote 25.
[13] Laguardia, *Pensamiento*, p. 42.
[14] Jesús Carranza, *Algunos datos o referencias para la biografia del benemerito General Justo Rufino Barrios, reformador de Guatemala y caudillo de la union de Centroamerica* (Guatemala City, 1930); cited in *ibid.*, pp. 64-65. A good modern biography of Barrios doesn't exist. The most complete one, although very dated now, is Paul Burgess, *Justo Rufino Barrios* (Philadelphia, 1926); Spanish version (Costa Rica, 1972).
[15] Laguardia, *Pensamiento*, p. 36.
[16] Justo Rufino Barrios, "Mensaje y memoria dirije a la Asamblea Nacional Consituyente" (Sept. 11, 1876); reprinted in *ibid.*, pp. 68-71.
[17] Cited in H.J. Miller, "Positivism and Education in Guatemala", in Woodward, *Positivism*, p. 109.
[18] Rippy, "Barrios", pp. 293-294.

[19] *Ibid.*
[20] *Ibid.*, pp. 280-284.
[21] D. McCreery, "Financiado el desarrollo en la America Latina del siglo XIX: el caso de Guatemala: 1871-1885", *Revista del Pensamiento Centroamericano* (abril-junio, 1975), p. 2.
[22] Cited in Solórzano, *Evolucion,* p. 323.
[23] D. McCreery, "Coffee and Class: The Structure of Development in Liberal Guatemala", *Hispanic American Historical Review* (August, 1976), p. 445.
[24] McCreery, "Coffee", p. 450.
[25] Cited in *ibid.,* p. 451.
[26] Cited in *ibid.,* p. 453.
[27] Woodward, *C.A.,* p. 165; José Aybar de Soto, *Dependency and Intervention* (Colorado, 1978), p. 84; see also Guillermo Nuñez Falcón, "Paul Dieseldorff, German Entrepreneur in the Alta Verapaz: 1871-1937", (Ph.D. diss., Tulane, 1970); and S. Mosk, "The Coffee Economy of Guatemala, 1859-1918", *Inter-American Economic Affairs* (Winter, 1955), p. 13.
[28] Woodward, *C.A.,* p. 165.
[29] McCreery, "Coffee", p. 456.
[30] *Ibid.*
[31] Cited in Solórzano, *Evolución,* p. 297.
[32] Justo Rufino Barrios, in *El Guatemalteco* (May 7, 1877), cited in Laguardia, *Pensamiento,* pp. 204-205.
[33] As told to Kay Warren and cited in her *Symbolism of Subordination* (Austin, 1978), p. 147.
[34] For example, the anthropologist Douglas Madigan found that in the village of Santiago Atitlan, only 20 per cent of the Atitecos were free of debt to a plantation owner in 1928. D.G. Madigan, "Santiago Atitlan", (Ph.D. diss., Univ. of Pittsburgh, 1976), p. 247.
[35] Cited in Solórzano, *Evolución,* p. 347.
[36] Barrios, "Circular a Jéfe Politicos" (July 9, 1881), cited in Laguardia, *Pensamiento,* p. 223.
[37] C.L. Jones, "Indian Labour in Guatemala", in A.G. Wilgus (ed.), *Hispanic,* p. 316; Solórzano, *Evolución,* p. 350.
[38] McCreery, "Coffee", p. 457.
[39] R. Carmack, *Historia Social de los Quiché* (Guatemala City, 1979), p. 248.
[40] *Ibid.*
[41] Solórzano, *Evolución,* pp. 320-322.
[42] Herrick, *Desarrollo,* pp. 232-233; R. Falla, *Quiché rebelde* (Guatemala City, 1978), p. 227.
[43] Falla, *Quiché,* p. 237; Carmack, *Historia,* p. 248.
[44] Falla, *Quiché,* pp. 280-284.
[45] Carmack, *Historia,* pp. 271-286.
[46] Falla, *Quiché,* p. 278.
[47] M. Valládores Rubio, *Estudios Historias* (Guatemala City, 1962), p. 439.
[48] McCreery, "Coffee".
[49] Warren, *Symbolism,* pp. 148-149.
[50] Solórzano, *Evolución,* p. 349.
[51] Mosk, "Coffee Economy", p. 19.
[52] Woodward, *C.A.,* p. 174.
[53] McCreery, "Coffee", p. 152.
[54] Cited in Woodward, *Positivism,* p. XVII.

Notes to chapter 4

[1] Charles David Kepner and Jay Soothill, *The Banana Empire* (New York, 1935), p. 47.

[2] Cited in G. Toriello Garrido, *Tras la cortina banano* (Mexico, 1976), p. 41.

[3] M. Angel Asturias, *Viento fuerte* (Argentina, 1976), p. 112.

[4] Kepner, *Social Aspects of the Banana Industry* (New York, 1936), p. 41, pp. 19-23; Kepner and Soothill, *Empire*, p. 183; A. Bauer Paiz, *Cómo opera el capital yanqui en Centroamericana: el caso de Guatemala* (Mexico, 1956), p. 155, p. 192.

[5] Cited in S. May and G. Plaza, *The United Fruit Company in Latin America* (New York, 1958), p. 88.

[6] Bauer Paiz, *Cómo*, p. 155.

[7] *Ibid.*, pp. 112-189; *International Railways of Central America: Concessions, Contracts and Decrees: 1877-1912* (Guatemala, no date).

[8] Luis Cardoza y Aragon, "Guatemala y el Imperio Bananero", *Cuadernos Americanos* (March, 1954), p. 19.

[9] May and Plaza, *United Fruit*, p. 22.

[10] K. Grieb, *Guatemalan Caudillo* (Athens, Ohio, 1979), p. 84.

[11] Cardoza y Aragon, "Imperio", p. 24.

[12] Cited in Kepner and Soothill, *Empire*, p. 213.

[13] Department of Overseas Trade, Great Britain, *Report on Economic and Commercial Conditions in the Republic of Guatemala* (1937), p. 11.

[14] Kepner, *Social*, p. 86.

[15] *Ibid.*, p. 85.

[16] *Ibid.*, p. 86, pp. 114-116, p. 129, p. 136.

[17] Bauer Paiz, *Cómo*, p. 220.

[18] *Ibid.*, p. 144, p. 148.

[19] Kepner and Soothill, *Empire*, p. 187.

[20] *Ibid.*

[21] Cited in Kepner and Soothill, *Empire*, p. 159.

[22] Kepner, *Social*, pp. 21-22.

[23] *Ibid.*, p. 25.

[24] Cardoza y Aragon, "Imperio", p. 19.

[25] Cited in Toriello Garrido, *Tras*, p. 40.

[26] *Ibid.*

[27] L. Langley, *The United States and the Caribbean in the Twentieth Century* (Athens, Ohio, 1980), pp. 77-110; W. Perkins, *Constraints of Empire* (Connecticut, 1981); also see a series of speeches by General Darlington Butler cited in the *New York Times* through 1931. Butler, who had angrily resigned from the marines in 1931 because of an official reprimand he received over statements he made concerning Mussolini, and because he was passed over for the position of commander-in-chief of the marines, made a series of speeches describing his career as well as publishing an article about it in *Liberty* (Spring, 1931).

[28] T. Anderson, *Matanza* (Lincoln, Nebraska, 1971).

[29] Bauer Paiz, *Cómo*, pp. 62-65; also see R. Immerman, "Guatemala and the United States, 1954: A Cold War Strategy for the Americas" (Ph.D. diss., Boston, 1978), p. 155.

[30] R.L. Woodward Jr., *Central America* (New York, 1976), p. 201.

[31] W. Krehm, *Democracia y tiranías en el caribe* (Mexico, 1949), p. 73.

[32] *Ibid.*, p. 74; Bauer Paiz, *Cómo*, p. 70.

[33] Grieb, *Caudillo*, p. 3.
[34] J. Pitti, "General Jorge Ubico and Guatemalan Politics in the 1920's", (Ph.D. diss., Univ. of New Mexico, 1975), p. 206.
[35] Ubico, cited in *ibid.*, p. 198.
[37] *Ibid.*, p. 206.
[37] *Ibid.*, p. 70.
[38] Cited in *ibid.*, p. 226.
[39] M. Angel Asturias, *El problema social del indio* (Paris, 1971), first printed in Guatemala, 1923.
[40] Pitti, "Ubico", p. 227.
[41] *Ibid.*, p. 237.
[42] Cited in K. Grieb, "American Involvement in the Rise of Jorge Ubico", *Caribbean Studies* (April, 1970), p. 9.
[43] Cited in *ibid.*, p. 12.
[44] Cited in *ibid.*, p. 19.
[45] Pitti, "Ubico", p. 418.
[46] Grieb, "Involvement", p. 17.
[47] Krehm, *Democracia*, p. 75.
[48] Overseas Trade, *Report*, p. 1.
[49] *Ibid.*, p. vi.
[50] Bauer Paiz, *Cómo*, pp. 222-226.
[51] L. Mosley, *Dulles* (New York, 1979), p. 92.
[52] Cited in Grieb, *Caudillo*, p. 21.
[53] Cited in Krehm, *Democracia*, p. 77.
[54] "Guatemala: Heat on a Tyrant", *Time* (June 26, 1944).
[55] Krehm, *Democracia*, p. 77.
[56] K. Grieb, "The U.S. and General Jorge Ubico's Retention of Power", *Revista de Historia de America* (enero-junio, 1971), p. 127.
[57] José Aybar de Soto, *Dependency and Intervention* (Boulder, 1978), p. 84.
[58] Cited in R. Reina, "Chinautla: A Guatemalan Indian Community" (Ph.D. diss., University of North Carolina, 1957), p. 1.
[59] Cited in *ibid.*, p. 60.
[60] Kay Warren, *Symbolism of Subordination* (Austin, 1978), pp. 144-145.
[61] R. Carmack, *Historia social de los Quiché* (Guatemala City, 1979), pp. 271-300.
[62] There were many studies of Guatemalan Indian communities in the late 1930s and early 1940s, which briefly discuss village politics, although few of them discuss it at any length. Most of these works have been collected by the University of Chicago and placed in their Microfilm Collection of Manuscripts on Middle American Cultural Anthropology. Some of the most informative in the series are: Jackson Lincoln Steward, "An Ethnological Study of Ixil Indians of the Guatemalan Highlands", no. 1, 1945; Melvin Tumin, "San Luis Jilotepeque: A Guatemalan Pueblo", 2, 1945; Sol Tax, "Panajachel, Field Notes", 29, 1950; Juan de Rios Rosales, "Notes on San Pedro la Laguna", 25, 1949 and his "Notes on Santiago Chimaltenango", 30, 1940; and "Notes on Aguacatán", 22, 1949; and Antonio Goubaud Carrera, "Notes on the Indians of Finca Nueva Granada", 21, 1949, and his "Notes on San Juan Chamelco", 23, 1949; and his, Juan de Rios Rosales and Sol Tax, "Reçonnaissance of Northern Guatemala: 1944", 17, 1947. Also see Ruth Bunzel, *Chichicastenango* (Guatemala City, 1981); and Charles Wagley, *Los Chortis de*

Guatemala (Guatemala City, 1961), both of which describe Guatemala village communities before the revolution of 1944.
[63] Reina, "Chinaulat", p. 185

Notes to chapter 5

[1] Edwin Bishop, "The Guatemalan Labor Movement: 1944-1959" (Ph.D. diss., Univ. of Wisconsin, 1959), p. 4.
[2] M. Galich, *Del panique al ataque* (Guatemala City, 1949), p. 71, pp. 75-99.
[3] J. Petersen, "The Political Role of University Students in Guatemala: 1944-1968" (Ph.D. diss., Univ. of Pittsburgh, 1969), pp. 62-74.
[4] Cited in R. Schneider, *Communism in Guatemala: 1944-1954* (New York, 1958), p. 9.
[5] Petersen, "Students", p. 22.
[6] R. Immerman, "The United States and Guatemala, 1954: A Cold War Strategy for the Americas" (Ph.D. diss., Boston College, 1978), p. 72.
[7] For a description of the revolt see Carlos Paz Tejada, "Un militar honesto" in C. Cáceres (ed.), *Aproximación a Guatemala* (Mexico, 1980), pp. 36-51.
[8] The rebellious cadets themselves pointed to incompetence within the Escuela Politécnica and the archaic system of instruction as reasons for the revolt. See "por que actuó el ejército", *Revista Militar* (Guatemala City), Feb. 1945. See also K. Grieb, "The Guatemalan Military and the Revolution of 1944", *Americas*, 32 (April, 1976), pp. 524-543.
[9] Immerman, "U.S. and Guatemala", p. 76.
[10] *El Imparcial*, March 16, 1945. A thorough review of four Guatemala City newspapers and the reports of a number of anthropologists who were in villages at the time of the elections confirms that the elections were relatively fair and just. Certainly Arévalo had the support of the majority of those who voted. See J. Handy, "Civil Rights and Central American Revolutions: The Guardia Civil and Elections in Guatemala, 1945-1954", paper presented to the Canadian Association of Latin American Studies meeting, October 6, 1984, University of Toronto.
[11] Reprinted in Juan José Arévalo, *Escritos Políticos* (Guatemala City, 1945), p. 179.
[12] *Ibid.*, p. 146.
[13] Cited in Immerman, "U.S. and Guatemala", p. 79.
[14] Cited in José Aybar de Soto, *Dependency and Intervention* (Colorado, 1978), p. 113.
[15] The Guatemalan constitution of 1945 is reprinted in K. Silvert, *A Study in Government* (New Orleans, 1954); see also *Diario de la assamblea constituyente, 1944-1945* (Guatemala City, 1945).
[16] Mario Monteforte Toledo, *Guatemala: Monografia sociológica* (Mexico City, 1959), pp. 47-50.
[17] E.B. Jiménez, *La educación rural en Guatemala* (Guatemala City, 1967). See also *Informaciones nacional* (Guatemala City), April 1, 1947, p. 3; and August 1, 1946; pp. 24-25.
[18] Bishop, "Guatemalan Labor", p. 39. Fierce debate accompanied the passage of the Labour Code both in congress and through the press. Many of the congressional debates concerning the code were reprinted in *El Imparcial* throughout the first few months of 1947. The most bitter complaint over the

Labour Code came from the United Fruit Company, which argued that the provision for legalizing rural unions only in those farms which employed more than 500 people discriminated against them. This argument was refuted both by the Guatemalan government and some members of the American mission in Guatemala. Nonetheless, the American embassy supported UFCo arguments and opposed the Labour Code. See Memorandum of the Department of State to Embassy in Guatemala, May 28, 1947; Report by Labor officer of the Office of Regional American Affairs, W. Fishburn to Asst. Sec. for Interamerican Affairs, April 19, 1950; Edward Clark, Office of Middle American Affairs to Chargé at Guatemalan Embassy, June 6, 1950; and memorandum of conversation between Ambassador Kyle and Arévalo, August 8, 1947; all in State Department Archives, Washington, D.C.: Guatemalan Records, (hereinafter SDA).

[19] E. Pons Alcantara, "Hacia una programación del desarrollo económico de Guatemala" (Tesis, Universidad de San Carlos, Guatemala, 1954); see also "Principios de la acción económica del estado de económia y trabajo", *Revista de Económia.* (Guatemala City) enero-marzo, 1950, pp. 7-10; *El més Económico,* March 31, 1947.

[20] Cited in Anita Frankel, "Political Development in Guatemala, 1944-1954", (Ph.D. diss., Univ. of Connecticut, 1969), p. 27.

[21] Cited in L. Cardoza y Aragon, *La revolución guatemalteca* (Mexico City, 1955), pp. 63-64.

[22] J.H. Adler, *et al., Public Finance and Economic Development in Guatemala* (Los Angeles, 1952), p. 266.

[23] *Imparcial,* April 26, 1946; and Long to State Department, April 30, 1946; and Graham to State Department, May 7, 1946, SDA.

[24] See *Imparcial,* Sept. 1, 1951; and *Octubre,* July 24, Dec. 13, 1951 and Jan. 17, 1952.

[25] The Catholic hierarchy in Guatemala, especially the archbishop, Mariano Rossell Arellano, continually spoke out against most of the government reforms, ranging from education to land reform. For examples see *Acción Social Cristiana,* July 19, Aug. 19, 1945; pastoral letter of May 25, 1950 reprinted in *El Imparcial,* May 26, 1950; and pastoral letter of April 14, 1954 enclosed in W. Kreig, first secretary of the Guatemalan embassy to State, April 14, 1954, SDA.

[26] Aybar de Soto, *Dependency,* p. 115.

[27] *El Imparcial,* May 2, 1946.

[28] Cited in Samuel Guy Inman, *A New Day in Guatemala* (Wilton, Conn., 1951), p. 38.

[29] Wells to Secretary of State, Nov. 12, 1948; Arévalo cited by R. Schneider, *Communism,* p. 24; Tómas Sierra Roldán, *Dialógos con el coronel Monzón: História viva de la revolucíon guatemalteca* (Guatemala City, 1958), p. 23; Paz Tejada, "Un militar honesto", pp. 41-43. For a discussion of earlier coup attempts against Arévalo see *El Imparcial,* April 26-28, Aug. 9-10, 1948.

[30] "Un militar honesto"; see also *El Imparcial,* July 11, 1951. Arbenz describes the attempted arrest and the killing of Arana in Marta Cehelsky, "Habla Arbenz, su juicio histórico retrospectivo: entrevista a Jacobo Arbenz Guzmán", *Aléro* (Guatemala City, 3a época, 8 (1975), pp. 120-121.

[31] Juan José Arévalo, *Informé al congreso,* 1950, pp. 30-32. Wells to State, Aug. 1, 1949, SDA.

[32] R. Schneider, *Communism,* p. 22.

[33] Cited in *El Imparcial*, March 16, 1951.

[34] F. Samayoa C., *La Escuela Politécnica a traves de su história* (Guatemala City, 1964); *Anales de la Escuela Politécnica* (1941-1947); see also R. Adams, *Crucifixion by Power* (Austin, 1970), pp. 246-258.

[35] "Curriculum del Coronel Jacobo Arbenz" (Guatemala City, 1952), in Guatemalan Documents, Manuscript Division, Library of Congress, Washington D.C. (hereinafter GD); *Anales de la Escuela*.

[36] The last American ambassador, and one who was deeply involved in the overthrow of Arbenz, commented after his only meeting with Arbenz that Maria was the more formidable of the two: a sentiment echoed by E. Howard Hunt in his description of the American involvement in the overthrow. Maria occupied the attention of the U.S. State Department both before and after the overthrow. State Department officials were especially concerned over her interest in Marxist writings, Freud and her correspondence with such diverse figures in Latin America as Pablo Neruda and Eva Peron. Interview with W. Krieg, first secretary of the American embassy from 1951 to 1954, held in Antigua, Guatemala, Feb. 1983. The comments written in the margins of papers relating to Maria Arbenz and her international contacts located in the Guatemalan Documents are also indicative of this interest. On numerous occasions figures of importance in Guatemalan politics wrote to Maria attempting to convince her of the correctness of a certain policy and to have her sway the opinion of her husband. Maria was also very involved in her own right with the Alianza Feminina de Guatemala, which proposed among other things a credit co-operative for peasant women and promoted better housing and health care. Peurifoy to State, Nov. 6, 1953, SDA; Hunt, *Undercover: Memoirs of an American Secret Agent* (Berkeley, 1974), p. 83; Maria Arbenz to Ismael Gonzalez Arévalo, Guatemalan ambassador in Argentina, March 11, 1952, GD; "Reglamento interno del primer congreso nacional de Alienza Feminina Guatemalteca", Nov. 26-28, 1953, GD; draft articles of the formation of new society Alianza Feminina Guatemalteca y compania sociedad en comandita, undated, GD.

[37] El Imparcial, March 16, 1951.

[38] IBRD, *The Economic Development of Guatemala* (Washington, 1951), pp. 26-35. The U.S. State Department had to somehow explain why this respected economist was agreeing with so many of the policies proposed by the "communist" government of Arbenz. They dismissed Britnell's report by saying that it appeared he was easily swayed by the attention he received from the members of the Guatemalan ministry of economy. Memorandum of meeting between Britnell and Asst. Sec. of State Miller, Aug. 28, 1950. SDA.

[39] *Ibid.*

[40] *Exposición del presidente de la republica, ciudadano Jacobo Arbenz ante la opinión nacional de económia sobre su program de gobierno* (Guatemala City, 1951); *Discurso del doctor Juan José Arévalo y del teniente coronel Jacobo Arbenz Guzmán en el acto de transmissión de la presidencia de la Republica, 15 de marzo de 1951* (Guatemala City, 1951); on government plan to assist cotton, see *El Imparcial*, April 1, 1952; "Cuatro Pasos Historicos Hacia la independencia Nacional", *Octubre*, May 1, 1951.

[41] "Informe del Presidente de la Republica, Coronel Jacobo Arbenz Guzmán al congreso nacional en su primer periodo de sesiones ordinarias del ano de 1954", in *El Més Económico y Financiero*, March 1, 1954; *El Imparcial*, Dec. 15, 1951, "Situacion de la escuela Guatemateca y su orientación", undated

notice in GD.

[42] *El Imparcial,* Dec. 5, 6 and 12, 1950, for official results. This assessment of the fairness of the elections comes from a thorough study of the Guatemalan newspapers, the reports of the various political parties and unions, both nationally and locally, and the records of the U.S. embassy and the Canadian Trade Mission to Guatemala. See also Wells to Edward Clark, Guatemalan Desk Officer, State Department, May 22, 1950; Kenedon Steins, to State, May 24, 1950, SDA. For Arbenz's support among various political parties see *El Imparcial,* Feb. 6, 1950, Feb. 20, 1950. See also J. Handy, "Civil Rights and Central American Revolutions".

[43] Silvert, *A Study,* p. 41.

[44] J. Handy, "Revolution and Reaction: Village Politics and National Policy, Guatemala 1945-1954", paper presented to Graduate History Colloquium, University of Toronto, March 19, 1984.

[45] *Ibid.* See also Handy, "Civil Rights" and Silvert, *A Study,* pp. 92-94.

[46] Cited in Bishop, "Guatemalan Labor", p. 12.

[47] *Ibid.,* p. 21; see also report of the FSG second annual convention enclosed in J. Winsor Ives, commercial attaché, to State, Feb. 5, 1948, SDA.

[48] Bishop, "Guatemalan Labor", p. 136.

[49] Schneider, *Communism,* p. 49.

[50] Aybar de Soto, *Dependency,* p. 90.

[51] Schneider, *Communism,* p. 49.

[52] Arbenz cited in Silvert, *A Study,* p. 58. The notable exception when the PGT and other "communist" organizers stepped outside of the bounds of the constitution and went farther than the government intended in policy implementation is the application of the agrarian reform. CGTG and peasant league organizers, most notably Carlos Manuel Pellecer, inspired land invasions of *fincas* which would not have been subject to the law or where the organizers thought that the process of expropriation was proceeding too slowly. See Handy, "Revolution and Reaction" and next chapter for further discussion.

[53] Silvert, *A Study,* p. 58.

[54] *Diario de la Manana* (Guatemala City), April 6, 1951, on the first appearance of the Communist Party. *Octubre,* June 21, 1950 was the first issue of the paper. "Manifesto a la clase obrera al pueblo de Guatemala del comite organizador del Partido Revolucionario Obrero de Guatemala", June 1, 1950, GD, box 8. *El Imparcial,* Jan. 25, 1952 on the dissolving of PROG. "Boletin para la prensa" of PGT, Dec. 15, 1952, GD, box 9; on the formation of the PGT.

Notes to chapter 6

[1] Jacobo Arbenz, *Informe al congreso, 1953,* p. 8.

[2] Cited in *El Libertador* (Guatemala City), June 20, 1951; organ of the PAR.

[3] M. Siegel, "Perspective on Guatemala", *New Republic,* July 19, 1954, pp. 11-13, See also Harry McArthur and Roland Ebel, *Cambios políticos in tres comunidades indígenas de Guatemala* (Guatemala City, 1969); R. Adams (ed.), *Political Changes in Guatemalan Indian Communities* (New Orleans, 1972); R. Wasserstrom, "Revolution in Guatemala", *Comparative Studies in Society and History* (October, 1975); and J. Handy, "Peasant Politics and the Revolution: Caste and Class in Guatemala, 1945-1954" (Ph.D. diss., Univ. of Toronto, 1985).

[4] *El Imparcial,* Oct. 5, 1945; for the CTG agreement to stop rural organization. "Report on Farm Labour", Endrew Donavan to State, March 16, 1946, SDA. Stines to State, Dec. 9, 1946, SDA. *El Imparcial,* June 23, 1948, for extension of labour code to allow organization of peasant leagues. See also *El Imparcial,* June 28, 1948, for discussion in congress of the extensions.

[5] Torres Moss to Felipe Gonzalez, Sept. 2, 1952, GD. See also K. Steins to State, June 2, 1950, SDA; M. Wells to State, May 18, 1951, SDA; Castillo Flores to Florentin López Hernández, sec. gen. of Unión campesina of Quiriqua, Sept. 10, 1951; letter from president of PRG, San Marcos, to Castillo Flores, July 20, 1952, GT; *El Imparcial,* Aug. 16, 1952; *El Imparcial,* July 6, 1951.

[6] See also R. Ebel, "Political change in Guatemalan Indian Communities", *Journal of Inter-American Affairs,* Vol. 6, (1964).

[7] See, for example, E.M. Mendelson, "Religion and World View in Santiago Atitlán", Microfilm Collection of Manuscripts in Cultural Anthropology, No. 52, 1957; G.A. Moore Jr., "Social and Ritual Change in a Guatemalan Community" (Ph.D. diss., Univ. of Michigan, 1954).

[8] R. Reina, "Chinautla, A Guatemalan Indian Community" (Ph.D. diss., Univ. of North Carolina, 1957), p. 78; M. Nash, *Machine Age Maya* (Glencoe, 1958); P.V. McDowell, "Political Change and Religious Change in a Guatemalan Community" (Ph.D. diss., Univ. of British Columbia, 1974); and K. Silvert, *A Study,* pp. 66-67.

[9] The relationship between political parties and the CNCG changed from village to village. Most often the CNCG was in alliance with PAR. However, in other villages union members denounced the local PAR members as "agents of reaction". See letter from sec. gen. of Unión campesina of San Juan Tecuaco, Santa Rosa to Castillo Flores, Sept. 28, 1953; and from Manuel Monroy Flores, sec. gen. of the federación campesina of Sacatepequez, to Castillo Flores, April 12, 1954. The PRG and PAR, as the most active parties in the villages, were often at loggerheads, but the most common complaint was against the RN. See telegram from Oscar Bautista González, sec. of finances of the CNCG Nuevo Progesso to Max Salazar, May 21, 1954; telegram to sec. gen. of the CGTG from the alcalde municipal, Barberena, May 2, 1953; all in GD. See also *Octubre,* Feb. 26, 1953.

[10] Examples of conflict between the CNCG and the urban union federations abound. Initially the CTG resented the formation of the CGTG, calling it a divisionist tactic, and was obviously worried that it would interfere with its rural worker unions. *Octubre,* June 21, 1950. See also letter from Gutíerrez to Amor Velasco, on the founding of CNCG, reprinted in *El Imparcial,* May 31, 1950. The two national federations soon reached a type of accord and agreed to a pact that would allow co-operation, but in rural areas there was still conflict. Gutíerrez to Flores, Sept. 9, 1952, GD, telegram from sec. gen. of Unión campesina, el Sargento, San Martin Jilotepeque, to CNCG, and others, March 3, 1954, GD; letter to CGTG from sec. de sindicato de la finca Nacional Santa Sofia, Yepocapa, Chimaltenango, Sept. 17, 1952, GD. On battles between neighbouring communities and the peasant unions in these see Morales to Flores, April 12, 1953; letters from Max Salazar to governor of Escuintla, May 18, and June 1, 1954, in GD.

[11] This is the basic argument of Wasserstrom in "Revolution" and is evident in some of the anthropological reports from villages during the revolution, for example, Mendelson and Reina. The type of bias mentioned by Wasserstrom

was evident in the report by Silvert, which concentrated on the number of Indian *alcaldes* who had won office since the revolution rather than being more concerned with the political affiliation of the *alcaldes*. However, by 1953 and 1954, the strength of the peasant unions in the villages meant that national political parties were able to keep better informed of the activities of their affiliates in the villages, and the parties and the unions appear to have quickly withdrawn their support from people who did not have the confidence of the bulk of the poorer peasantry.

[12] Moore, "Social and Ritual", pp. 322-323, 331.

[13] The Indian Institute was formed in 1946 under the direction of the Guatemalan anthropologist Antonio Goubaud Carrera. It immediately began a series of anthropological investigations into various communities with the intent of determining the specific problems of the Indian. See Publicaciones Especiales de Instituto Indígenista Nacional. Also Dennis Casey, "Indígenismo: the Guatemalan Experience" (Ph.D. diss., Univ. of Kansas, 1979).

[14] Dirección General de Estadisticas, *VI Censo General de Guatemala* (Guatemala City, 1953).

[15] M. Monteforte Toledo, "La Reforma Agraria en Guatemala", *El Trimestre Económico,* 19 (julio-sept., 1952), pp. 387-407. Augustin Acosta and Ignacio Acosta, "La Reforma Agraria en Guatemala", *Revista de Economía, 15* (dic. 1952), pp. 374-379.

[16] Jacobo Arbenz, in *Hacía Una Reforma Agraria* (Guatemala City, 1951), p. 15.

[17] Ley de Reforma Agraria, Decreto 900.

[18] "Informe del Ciudadano Presidente de la Republica, correspondente a la gestión administrativa del ano de 1953 y el estado de la situación politíca al 1 de marzo de 1954"; see also J.L. Paredes. *Reforma Agraria* (Guatemala City, 1963), p. 121.

[19] "Informe", see also *El més económico y financiero,* March 1954.

[20] Paredes, *Reforma,* p. 55, pp. 60-62. Arbenz, "Discurso, I de mayo de 1954", pp. 10-11.

[21] Schoenfeld to State, Feb. 10, 1953, SDA; *El Imparcial,* Jan. 20, 1953; *El Imparcial,* Jan. 31, 1952.

[22] Paredes, *Reforma,* p. 58; *El Imparcial,* Aug. 1, 1952; Clodoveo Torres Moss said in October 1952 that there were more than 3,000 Local Agrarian Committees in the country, but this number seems to be somewhat exaggerated. Torres Moss to sec. gen. of Unión campesina, San Vicente Pacaya, Escuintla, Oct. 14, 1952, GD.

[23] There is no consensus on the number of *uniones campesinas* that actually functioned in Guatemala by 1954. Neale Pearson argues that there were slightly more than 1,600 while Brian Murphy states that he found evidence of only 300. Pearson "Confederación Nacional de Campesina de Guatemala and Peasant Unionism in Guatemala" (M.A. thesis, Georgetown, 1964), p. 41; Murphy, "The Stunted Growth of Campesino Organizations" in Adams (ed.), *Crucifixion by Power* (Austin, 1972), p. 418. My own study of the records of the CNCG indicates that there is no reason to doubt the CNCG claims, although many of these unions would be very small and others would be inactive.

[24] See Mendelson, *Los Escandolos del Maxímon* (Guatemala City, 1965); John Gillin, *The Culture of Security in San Carlos* (New Orleans, 1951), p. 48, pp. 73-74.

[25] José Domingo Segura, labour inspector for the department of Retalhuleu, wrote to Manuel Gutíerrez in June 1953, accusing Castillo Flores of bribing the local *Inspector Agrario* to have a *finca* divided up among members of the union rather than the *finca* workers (letter undated, in GD, box 1); on the other hand, the sec. gen. of the union in el Sargento, San Martin Jilotépeque, informed Castillo Flores that the *sindicato* of workers was dividing up land on the *finca* without any consideration for the union members (telegram, March 3, 1954, GD); see also letter from Otilio Marroquin Ruano to Gutíerrez, March 2, 1954; Max Salazar to Florencio Méndez, April 12, 1954; letter from Mario Sosa N., inspector general of DAN to Gutíerrez, Nov. 6, 1952, GD, reel 3); *El Imparcial*, Aug. 3, 1948; *Octubre*, Feb. 28, 1952.

[26] *Harper's Magazine*, July 1955, pp. 60-65, cited in N. Lacharité, *Case Study in Insurgency and Revolutionary Warfare: Guatemala, 1944-1954* (Washington, 1964), p. 59.

[27] Letters to Castillo Flores, March 29, 1954, June 10, 1954, GD, box 10. Castillo to Minister of gobernación, Jan. 16, 1952, GD, box 10. Letter to Castillo from sec. de cultura, Unión campesina, Pontezuel, San José del Golfo, Jan. 6, 1952; Castillo in return, Jan. 10, and to Jefe del departamento de educación rural, Jan. 12, 1952, GD, box 10.

[28] Cited in R. Schneider, *Communism in Guatemala* (New York, 1958), p. 194.

[29] See *El Imparcial*, Jan. 23, 24 and 29, 1953; for reaction from landowners and Guatemalan politicians to the first wave of land invasions, a movement the *Imparcial* editorialized "No one knows where they will end." See also Kreig to State, Jan. 22, 1954, SDA. Arbenz himself blames Carlos Manuel Pellecer, Castillo Flores and Waldemar Barrios Klee, the vice-president of DAN, for the invasions and much of the unrest that accompanied them (Cehelsky, "Habla Arbenz"). While it is clear that many of these organizers did make a conscious decision to hurry the expropriation process along by approving land invasions, they were often pulled into it by their local committees, peasants who had waited long enough for land they had denounced a year earlier. This was particularly the case in early 1953, as peasants were desperate to get the land divided and worked in time to sow for the harvest. By later in 1953, the CNCG was being dragged into land invasions by its peasant affiliates, trying to walk a thin line between abiding by the law and not discouraging peasant organization. See telegram from Flores to president of CAL, Escuintla, Oct. 5, 1953, GD. Flores to Jefe del departamento agrario nacional, Feb. 24, 1954, asking for action on land which was denounced two years ago, Feb. 24, 1954, GD.

[30] For a fuller discussion of the application of the law see Paredes, *Reforma*, pp. 56-75.

[31] Stokes Newbold (R. Adams), "Receptivity to Communist Fomented Agitation in Rural Guatemala", *Economic Development and Cultural Change*, 5 (1957), p. 360.

[32] Martínez, the head of DAN, had been out of the country for a period in late 1953 and early 1954. It was during this period that the worst of the land seizures ocurred. Upon his return there was an announcement that the law would applied strictly and that no land invasions would be tolerated. (Kreig to State, March 12, 1954, SDA).

[33] The Guatemalan Growers' Association was the most consistent voice in opposition to the agrarian reform and paid for numerous full-page advertise-

ments in Guatemalan newspapers denouncing the law. But the president's gravest concern was the heightened level of unrest and the rumours of impending coups that accompanied the reform. When an electrical station was dynamited in June 1952, Arbenz laid the blame squarely on the shoulders of "those who oppose agrarian reform". (Schoenfeld to State, June 25, 1952.) Beginning immediately after the passage of the agrarian reform, the CNCG and CGTG received numerous reports of their organizers being attacked by landlords and their agents in the countryside. There were also reports of caches of arms hidden on *fincas,* letter to sec. gen. of CGTG from the CAL in fincas Las Delicias, San Ignacio, and el Recreo, Villa Canales, Oct. 26, 1952, GD, reel 3; *Octubre*, July 3, July 17, 1952.

[34] A. Frankel, "Political Development in Guatemala, 1944-1954: the impact of Foreign, Military and Religious Elite" (Ph.D. Diss., Univ. of Connecticut, 1969), p. 183.

[35] Cited in G. Toriello Garrido, *Tras la cortina de banano* (Mexico City, 1976), p. 233; and Frankel, "Pol. Dev.", p. 195.

[36] *Acción Social Cristiana* (July 19, Aug. 19, 1945); pastoral letters May 25, 1950, reprinted in *El Imparcial*, May 26, 1950; and a pastoral letter of April 14, 1954, enclosed in W. Kreig to State, April 14, 1954, SDA.

[37] Tulio Benites, *Meditaciones de un católico ante la Reforma Agraria* (Guatemala City, 1952); letter cited in Frankel, "Pol. Dev.", pp. 233-234.

[38] Schoenfeld to State, Aug. 21, 1953, SDA, for the formation of the Department of Military Welfare. *Tribuna Popular,* Aug. 15, 1953, on soldiers getting land under agrarian reform. Spokesmen for the army repeatedly made speeches in 1953 and 1954, praising the government and reiterating the army's loyalty. Col. Díaz, "Discurso al congreso, 13 de marzo 1954", in GD, box 3; see also *El Imparcial,* March 15, 1952. These led a number of observers to suggest that Arbenz still maintained the loyalty of the majority of the officers. The Costa Rican ambassador to Guatemala informed the embassy, "Nothing can happen in Guatemala without the Army's help. However ... the troops are apathetic and all the high officers are affiliated with and loyal to the present regime." (Memorandum of conversation, Clark to Mann, Sept. 4 1952, SDA). See also J. Fisher to Holland, April 14, 1954, SDA; and the Canadian ambassador to the United States summed up U.S. State Department thinking by saying, "There is no sign of disaffection to President Arbenz among the army. President Arbenz' regime is very generous towards the officers of the army who enjoy high salaries and special privileges. ... It is not expected in present circumstances that any large number of troops belonging to [the] regular army will join the rebels." (Memo to sec. of state for external affairs, June 22, 1954, Political and Economic Conditions in Guatemala, Vol. 1, Public Archives of Canada.)

[39] Toriello, *Tras,* p. 221.

[40] Constitution of 1945, Article 145; see also Silvert, *A Study,* p. 29.

[41] Tómas Sierra Roldán, *Dialogos con el coronel Monzón* (Guatemala City, 1958), p. 23; for a description of the coup attempt see Arévalo, Informe al congreso, 1950, pp. 30-32.

[42] Anales de la Escuela Politécnica, 1941-1950, and F. Samayoa C., *La Escuela Politécnica a traves de su história* (Guatemala City, 1964), Vol. II, pp. 113-116; and "Curriculum del Coronel Jacobo Arbenz", Guatemala City, 1952, in GD, box 6, for Arbenz's career in the academy. Colonel Paz Tejada talks about the army being divided into "young" and "line" officers in his "un

militar honesto" in C. Carceres (ed.), *Aproximación a Guatemala* (Mexico, 1980), pp. 36-51; as did Schneider, *Communism,* p. 31; and R. Baker, *A Study of Military Status and Status Deprivation in Three Latin American Armies* (Washington, 1967), p. 41.

[43] M. Monteforte Toledo, *Guatemala: Monografia Sociológica* (Mexico City, 1965), pp. 364-374; see Adams, *Crucifixion,* p. 257, for an argument against this division.

[44] Castillo Flores to Jefe de las Fuerzas Armadas, Feb. 3, 1954, Colonel Díaz to Flores, Jan. 25, 1951, both in GD. Also see circular from Rogelio Cruz Wer, Chief of the Guardia Civil, warning that the Guardia Civil would be disciplined if they disrupted the work of the "proletarian masses", in Schoenfeld to State, Aug. 14, 1953, SDA. On increase in the number of military commissioners, see Cehelsky, "Habla Arbenz", p. 119. Also see Plan presented by the Consejo Superior de la Defensa Nacional, May 19, 1954, citing the disorganization of the militias, GD, box 1.

[45] *El Impacto,* July 25, 1954, p. 3 on Consejo Superior asking Arbenz to account for communists; Arbenz says they met to thank him for the arms sent on the Alfhem (Cehelsky, "Habla Arbenz") and that the matter of the communists came up almost incidentally. S. Schlesinger and S. Kinzer, *Bitter Fruit: the Untold Story of the American Coup in Guatemala* (New York, 1983), p. 165; for Arbenz quote.

[46] There were some attempts to broaden the lessons in the Escuela with the formation of a Department of Political Economy after Arbenz became president. *Anales, 1941-1950.* However, the academy remained in the hands of rather unsympathetic officers for much of the time, including Castillo Armas during the late 1940s and Colonel Paiz Novales in the 1950s.

[47] There have been numerous studies of the intervention from an American foreign policy point of view. The most complete is R. Immerman, *The CIA in Guatemala: the Foreign Policy of Intervention* (Austin, 1982). See also Schlesinger and Kinzer, *Bitter Fruit;* Susanne Jonas-Bodenheimer, *Plan piloto para el continente* (Costa Rica, 1981); José Aybar de Soto, *Dependency and Intervention* (Boulder, Colorado, 1975); B. Wiessen Cook, *Declassified Eisenhower: A Divided Legacy* (New York, 1981); Edelberto Torres-Rivas, "Crisis y conyuntura critica: La caida de Arbenz y los contratiempos de la revolución burguesa", *Revista Mexicana de Sociologia,* Ano XLI, Vol. XLI, Num. 1 (enero-marzo, 1979), pp. 297-323.

[48] Immerman, "Cold War", pp. 3-6, 154.

[49] *El Imparcial,* March 15, 1951.

[50] See Foreign Service of the United States, *Annual Economic Report,* Guatemala, 1950; "Principios de la Acción Económica del Estado", *Revista de Económia,* Ministerio de Económia y Trabajo, Ano. 2, Epoca 11, no. 5-6 (enero-marzo, 1950), pp. 7-10; W. Kyle, *Comentarios sobre la agricultura en Guatemala,* Ministerio de Agricultura, No. 31, Vol. 11, Dec. 1946; "La verdera funcion del congreso de económia", *El Més Económico y financiero* (Jan. 1, 1947), p. 5; J. Bishop, "Arévalo and Central American Unification," (Ph.D. diss., Lousiana State Univ., 1971).

[51] Arévalo, *Discurso en la presidencia, 1945-1948* (Guatemala City, 1948), p. 122.

[52] Boaz Long to State, Jan. 16 and Jan. 26, 1945; M.K. Wells to State, Oct. 31, 1947, all commented on strikes against the railroad. K. Steins to State, Dec. 29 and 30, 1949, on strikes against electric company. W. Turnbull to Patterson,

Jan. 29, 1949, on Puerto Barrios dock workers' strike, all in SDA.

53 Foreign Relations of the United States, 1950, Vol. 11, pp. 880-884, p. 903; see also memorandum of conversation between Kyle and Arévalo, Aug. 8 1947, Foreign Relations of the United States, 1947, Vol. VII, p. 710; memorandum of conversation between Spruille Braden and J. García Granados, May 29, 1947, SDA.

54 Patterson to State, Feb. 26, 1949, SDA; El Imparcial, Sept. 17, 1951; Octubre, Sept. 13, 1951; El Imparcial, Jan. 2, March 10, 1952.

55 El Imparcial, June 12, 1951, April 14, 1952; Schoenfeld to State, Oct. 14 1953, SDA.

56 M.K. Wells to State, Oct. 31, 1947; K. Steins to State, Dec. 30, 1949, R. Patterson to State, Jan. 6, 1950, all in SDA.

57 Cited in Immerman, "Cold War", p. 157.

58 V. Perlo, The Administration of High Finance (New York, 1957), p. 279.

59 Noted in Immerman, "Cold War", pp. 225-238. For a discussion of the dynamics between Eisenhower and Dulles see Cook, Declassified, and Immerman, "Eisenhower and Dulles: Who Made the Decisions?", Political Psychology 1 (Autumn, 1979), pp. 21-38.

60 L. Mosely, Dulles: A Biography of Eleanor, Allen and John Foster Dulles and Their Family Network (New York, 1978), p. 92.

61 See Schlesinger and Kinzer, Bitter Fruit, pp. 80-87.

62 Newsweek, cited in Jonas, Plan, pp. 47-51; G.A. Geiger, Communism vs. Progress in Guatemala (Washington, 1953), p. 162.

63 Time, May 31, 1954; Harper's, July 1955. The deputy chief of mission at the American embassy through the years 1951-1954, W. Kreig, suggested that the U.S. State Department had decided to wait until after the elections scheduled in 1956, to see if the military "would let a communist win", to decide on direct military intervention. According to Kreig, the shipment of arms on the Alfhem was the deciding factor in prompting the State Department and the CIA to go ahead with Operation Success. (Interview with William Kreig, Feb. 1983, Antigua Guatemala.) On the other hand, B. Cook has argued that the State Department knew of the shipment of arms well in advance and could have stopped the ship if it had wished. That it did not indicates that it was prepared to accept the arrival of the arms and use it as a further excuse for the intervention already in progress. (Peurifoy to State, Jan. 5, 1954, SDA; and Cook, Declassified, p. 266.)

64 New York Times, March 5, 1954.

65 S.G. Inman, A New Day in Guatemala: A Study of the Present Social Revolution (Wilton, Conn., 1951), pp. 47-48.

66 El Imparcial, April 11, 1950; memorandum of Chief of Division Security to Director of Office of Middle American Affairs, April 5, 1950: Foreign Relations of the United States, 1950, Vol. 11, p. 876; see also Immerman, "Cold War", p. 177.

67 J. José Arévalo, Guatemala, la democracia y el imperio (Mexico City, 1954), p. 111.

68 Memorandum of conversation between R. Welch and J. Ohmans, March 11, 1953, SDA; cited by Cook, Declassified, pp. 226-227.

69 Paredes, Reforma, pp. 69-70.

70 Leddy to Cabot and Mann, Feb. 26, 1953; Schoenfeld to State, Sept. 4, Sept. 17, 1953, Guatemalan ambassador to Asst. Sec. of State for Inter-American Affairs, June 26, 1953; Schoenfeld to State, Aug. 14, 1953; all in SDA.

Arbenz, *Informe al congreso, 1954.*

[71] Schoenfeld to State, April 12, 1953, SDA.

[72] *Ibid.,* p. 132; Peurifoy's appointment was roundly condemned in Guatemala. The *Diario del Pueblo* headline read, "Promoter of Greek Massacre Coming as Yankee Ambassador", and called it "a new imperialist intervention in our internal affairs". Schoenfeld to State, Oct. 9, 1953, SDA.

[73] K. Roosevelt, *Counter-Coup* (New York, 1979), p. 210.

[74] Peurifoy to State, memorandum of conversation, Dec. 17, 1953, SDA.

[75] Immerman, "Cold War", p. 190; Schlesinger and Kinzer, *Bitter Fruit,* p. 146.

[76] Toriello, *Tras,* pp. 100-140.

[77] Cited in Immerman, "Cold War", p. 272.

[78] Toriello, *Tras,* pp. 114-115.

[79] *Ibid.,* pp. 107-144; N. Ronning (ed.), *Intervention in Latin America* (New York, 1970), p. 79.

[80] Cited in Immerman, "Cold War", p. 272.

[81] Schlesinger and Kinzer, *Bitter Fruit,* pp. 105-115; Immerman, "Cold War", pp. 270-290.

[82] M. Ydígoras Fuentes, *My War with Communism* (Englewood Cliffs, New Jersey, 1963).

[83] Letter from the ambassador to Honduras, Marroquin Orellano, to Raul Osequeda, Minister of External Relations, Nov. 7, 1953, GD, box 7; letter from the Jefe de la Guardia Judicial to Arbenz, June 23, 1954, GD, box 1; "Official statement of government concerning the plot against it", La secretaria de propaganda y divulgacion de la Presidencia to the national and international press, no date, GD, box 3; *Time,* Feb. 1954, cited in *Bitter Fruit,* p. 129.

[84] Report on the debate at the U.N. from the Canadian Permanent Representative to the United Nations, to Sec. of State for External Affairs, June 21 and June 25, 1954, in Pol. and Economic Conditions, PAC.

[85] Cited in Kreig to State, June 29, 1954.

[86] Cehelsky, "Habla Arbenz"; Toriello, *Tras,* p. 226.

[87] Memorandum of phone conversation between Díaz and Peurifoy, in Holland to Dulles, June 28, 1954; Peurifoy to State, June 28, 1954, June 29, 1954, and second June 29, 1954, July 4, 1954 and July 8, 1954, all in SDA.

Notes to chapter 7

[1] The progression through the various juntas is described in ambassador J. Peurifoy's telegrams to the State Department from June 28, 1954 to July 8, 1954, one day after Castillo Armas was named president of the last junta to form; all in State Department Archives (SDA).

[2] Peurifoy to State, Aug. 2, 1954; W. Kreig, chargé at the American embassy to State, Aug. 18, 1954, SDA.

[3] M. Cehelsky, "Guatemala's Frustrated Revolution: The Liberation of 1954", (M.A. thesis, Columbia Univ., 1967), p. 101; N. LaCharite, *Case Studies in Insurgency: Guatemala* (Washington, 1964).

[4] Julio Vielman, "Stabilization of the Post-Revolutionary Government in Guatemala", *Journal of Inter-American Affairs,* (April, 1955).

[5] Milton Jamail, "Guatemala 1944-1972: the Politics of Aborted Revolution" (Ph.D. diss., Univ. of Arizona, 1972), p. 99.

[6] Colonel Castillo Armas, *Informe,* (Guatemala, 1957), p. vii; cited in J. Sloan, "The Electoral Game in Guatemala", (Ph. D. diss., Univ. of Texas at Austin, 1969), p. 86.

[7] J. Peurifoy to State, June 28, 1954; Kreig to State, Aug. 16, 17, 1954; memorandum of conversation, R.F. Woodward with State department, Aug. 6, 1954, all in SDA.

[8] Cited in J. Sloan, "Game", p. 92.

[9] *Ibid.,* p. 93.

[10] J. Weaver, "Administration and Development in Guatemala" (Ph.D. diss., Univ. of Pittsburgh, 1968), p. 24.

[11] *El Imparcial,* Nov. 18, 1961; cited in *ibid.,* p. 40.

[12] E. Torres-Rivas, *El crisis del poder en centroamerica* (Costa Rica, 1981), p. 59; J.H. Petersen, "The Political Role of University Students in Guatemala, 1944-1968" (Ph.D. diss., Univ. of Pittsburgh, 1969), p. 152.

[13] *Hispanic American Report,* (Vol. 13, no. 12, 1960).

[14] M. Monteforte Toledo, *Centro America: subdesarrollo y dependencia,* Vol. 2 (Mexico, 1972), p. 192.

[15] Cited in T. and M. Melville, *Guatemala: the Politics of Land Ownership* (New York, 1971).

[16] C.D. Sereseres, "Military Development and the U.S. Military Assistance Program for Latin America: the Case of Guatemala" (Ph.D. diss., Univ. of California at Riverside, 1971), p. 45.

[17] J. Sloan, "Game", p. 59.

[18] S. Jonas Bodenheimer, *Guatemala: Plan piloto para el continente* (Costa Rica, 1981), p. 295.

[19] Gabriel Aguilera Peralta, "The Process of Militarization in the Guatemalan State", *Latin American Research Unit Studies,* (Sept. 1982), p. 43.

[20] John D. Powell, "Military Assistance and Militarism in Latin America", *Western Political Quarterly,* (June, 1965), pp. 382-392; W.F. Barber and C.N. Ronning, *Internal Security and Military Power, Counter Insurgency and Civic Action in Latin America* (Ohio, 1966), p. 73.

[21] Barber and Ronning, *Internal,* p. 128.

[22] Weaver, "Administration", p. 30.

[23] R. Adams, "The Development of the Guatemalan Military", *Studies in Comparative International Development* (Dec. 1968), p. 92.

[24] *Prensa Libre,* July 18, 1963; cited in Monteforte, *Centro America,* vol. 2, p. 193.

[25] R. James, "Guatemala: The March Coup and the Civil War", *Canadian Forum* (Aug. 1982), p. 12.

[26] J. Sloan, "Electoral Fraud and Social Change", *Science and Society* (Spring, 1970), p. 87.

[27] *Diario Gráfico,* Feb. 5, 1966; cited in Sloan, "Game", p. 159.

[28] Monteforte, *Centro America,* vol. 2, p. 33.

[29] Sloan, "Game", p. 123.

[30] The official results of the election were: PR—201,077; PID—146,085; MLN—110,145. Sloan, "Game", p. 112. But, the PR estimated that the results were actually, PR—156,000; MLN—71,522; PID—66,106; *New York Times,* March 9, 1966.

[31] *New York Times,* March 9, 1966.

[32] Sloan, "Game", p. 123.

[33] Monteforte, *Centro America,* vol. 2, p. 34.

[34] *El Imparcial,* July 11, 1966; cited in Melville, *Guatemala,* p. 193; *New York Times,* June 29, 1966.

[35] Sereseres, "Military Development", p. 71.

[36] Jamail, "Aborted Revolution", pp. 84-85.

[37] B. Jenkins and C.D. Sereseres, "United States Military Assistance and the Guatemalan Armed Forces", *Armed Forces and Society* (Winter, 1977), p. 576.

[38] Méndez to congress, cited in *ibid., p. 581.*

[39] *New York Times,* July 15, 1967.

[40] Jamail, "Aborted", p. 100.

[41] Cited in G. Aguilera P., "Terror and Violence as Weapons of Counter-Insurgency in Guatemala", *Latin American Perspectives* (Spring and Summer, 1980), p. 106.

[42] *New York Times,* Nov. 13, 1966, and July 15, 1967.

[43] *Ibid.,* Nov. 13, 1966.

[44] *Ibid.,* March 21, 1968; *Latin America,* March 22, March 29, and April 5, 1968.

[45] E. Torres-Rivas, *Crisis,* p. 149.

Notes to chapter 8

[1] *Latin America (LA),* Feb. 13, 1970.

[2] Mario Monteforte Toledo, *Centro America: subdesarrollo y dependencia* (Mexico, 1975), vol. 2, p. 35.

[3] *LA,* Jan. 31, 1969.

[4] *New York Times,* May 8, 1971.

[5] Norman Gall, "Slaughter in Guatemala", *New York Times Review of Books,* May 20, 1971; M. Jamail, "Guatemala: 1944-1972: the Politics of Aborted Revolution", (Ph.D. diss., Univ. of Arizona, 1972), pp. 162-163.

[6] K. Johnson, "The 1966 and 1970 Elections in Guatemala: A Comparative Analysis", *World Affairs,* (summer, 1972), p. 42.

[7] Cited in Jamail, "Aborted", p. 166.

[8] *New York Times,* March 2 and 3, 1970.

[9] Arana cited in *New York Times,* July 3, 1970; *LA,* June 12, Dec. 4, 11, and 25, 1970, Jan. 29 and May 21, 1971.

[10] Cited in *LA,* May 21, 1971.

[11] J. Goulden, "Guatemala: Terror in Silence", *The Nation,* March 22, 1971; *New York Times,* Oct. 23, 1971; Senate Committee on Foreign Relations, *Guatemala and the Dominican Republic,* (Washington, 1971), p. 4.

[12] *LA,* June 30, 1972.

[13] Cited in Goulden, "Terror".

[14] Top members of the MLN have openly boasted of the fascist character of their party. Sandoval Alarcón cited in NACLA: report on the Americas, Jan. and Feb. 1983, George Black, "Garrison Guatemala", p. 5.

[15] *LA,* Jan. 19, 1973.

[16] Cited in Susan Jonas and David Tobias (eds.), *Guatemala,* NACLA (Berkeley, 1974), p. 118.

[17] Manuel Colom Arqueta, in *Latin America Political Report,* April 6, 1979.

[18] *LA,* May 4, May 23, Nov. 2, 1973; *New York Times,* March 2, 1974, March 25, 1982; *Latin America Weekly Report,* April 2, 1982.

[19] D. Barillas, *Democracia Crisitana y su posición ante el ejército de Guatemala hoy* (Guatemala, 1974) — pages unnumbered.

[20] *LA*, Feb. 15, 1974.

[21] *New York Times*, March 5, 1974.

[22] *Ibid.*, March 6 and 8, 1974.

[23] Cited in *ibid.*, March 6, 1974.

[24] *LA*, March 22, 1971, May 10, 1974.

[25] Barillas, *Democracia.*

[26] B. Jenkins and C.D. Sereseres, "United States Military Assistance and the Guatemalan Armed Forces", *Armed Forces and Society* (Winter, 1977), p. 589.

[27] *LA*, May 10, July 5, Dec. 13, 1974; Jan. 24, 1975; June 11, 1976.

[28] Barillas, *Democracia.*

[29] *New York Times*, Oct. 2, Nov. 2, 1977.

[30] *LA*, April 1, 1977.

[31] *LA*, July 7, 1978; Amnesty International, Guatemala Campaign Circular, number 5, 1979; R. James, "Guatemala, the March Coup and the Civil War", *Canadian Forum*, (August, 1982), p. 13.

[32] *New York Times*, March 9, 1978; Amnesty International, Cam. Cir. number 5.

[33] *New York Times*, March 9 to 11, 1978.

[34] *LA*, March 17, 1978.

[35] *Central America Report*, Oct. 9, 1978; *Latin America Economic Report*, Oct. 19, 1979.

[36] Amnesty International, number 5; *New York Times*, March 11, 1978.

[37] *LA*, Feb. 2, 1978; *Labor News*, Aug. 1980; "We Will Neither Go Nor be Driven Out", A Special Report by the IUF Trade Delegation on the Occupation of the Coca-Cola Bottling Plant in Guatemala, undated; and discussion on Embotelladora Guatemalteca, at the Canadian Association of Latin American and Caribbean Studies, Oct. 16, 1984, Toronto, Canada.

[38] Information on repression in Guatemala during the Lucas administration has been taken from a variety of sources. Amnesty International reports and "urgent actions" have been relied upon most heavily.

[39] Conversation with member of the Guatemalan Committee for Justice and Peace, in Toronto, Canada, July 1981.

[40] *Noticias de Guatemala*, July 14, 1979; Amnesty International Campaign Circular, number 10, and A.I., special bulletin, Sept. 15, 1980.

[41] *Newsweek*, June 19, 1978; G. Agilera Peralta, "The Massacre at Panzos", *Monthly Review*, (Dec. 1979).

[42] Observations by author in winter of 1980/81 in the highlands; interviews conducted throughout Guatemala in the winter and spring of 1983.

[43] Cited in *LA*, March 30, 1979; *Latin America Political Report*, April 6, 1979.

[44] *Washington Post*, May 14, 1981; *Latin America Regional Report, Mexico and Central America*, Aug. 14, 1981.

[45] Cited in A.I. Campaign Circular, number 5.

[46] *Noticias de Guatemala*, Jan. 26, 1981.

[47] Amnesty International, *Guatemala: A Government Program of Political Murder* (London, 1981); *Latin America Political Report*, April 6, 1979.

[48] Cited in *Latin America Weekly Report*, Jan. 8, 1982, Oct. 23, 1981.

[49] Gabriel Aguilera Peralta, "The Process of Militarization in the Guatemalan

State", *Latin American Research Unit Studies,* (Sept. 1982), p. 48; see also his *Dialecta del Terror en Guatemala* (Costa Rica, 1981).

[50] Aguilera, "Process", p. 46.

[51] *LA,* June 29, 1979.

[52] *Latin America Weekly Report,* Nov. 6, Dec. 11, 1981; March 5, 1982; *New York Times,* March 14, 1982; *Washington Post,* March 28, 1980.

[53] *Uno mas Uno,* July 31, 1981.

[54] *Latin America Weekly Report,* March 19, March 22, 1982; *Globe and Mail* (Toronto), March 25, 1982. For background on the election see E. Torres Lezama, *La construcción de una alterantiva para la reproducción del sistema capitalista en Guatemala: El proceso del recambio de personal que controla el apartada del estado* (CSUCA number 7, Costa Rica, undated).

[55] Cited in *Latin America Weekly Report,* March 26, 1982; *New York Times,* March 26, 27, 1982.

Notes to chapter 9

[1] Julio Vielman, "Stabilization of the Post-Revolutionary Government in Guatemala", *Journal of Inter-American Affairs* (Vol. 9, no. 1, 1955).

[2] T. and M. Melville, *Guatemala: The Politics of Land Ownership* (New York, 1971), pp. 87-103. See also S. Jonas Bodenheimer, *Guatemala: Plan piloto para el continente* (Costa Rica, 1981), p. 252.

[3] J.L. Paredes M., *Reforma Agraria: Una experiencia guatemalteca* (Guatemala City, 1963), pp. 141-146; Kreig to State, July 29, 1954, State Department Archives, Guatemalan correspondence; Inspectors from the Dirección General de Asuntos Agrarios estimated that by January of 1956 only .4 per cent of those who had benefited from the Agrarian Reform remained on their land. CIDA, *Tenencia de la tierra y desarrollo socioeconomico del sector agricola, Guatemala* (Washington, 1965); see also Enrique Torres Lezama, "Estructura interna basica del desarrollo de Guatemala", in *El reto de desarrollo en Guatemala: un enfoque multidisciplinario* (Guatemala City, 1970).

[4] Cited in Bodenheimer, *Plan,* p. 148.

[5] K. Silvert and J. Gillin, "Ambiguities in Guatemala", *Foreign Affairs* (April 1, 1956), pp. 469-482.

[6] Cited in Jonas Bodenheimer, *Plan,* p. 219.

[7] *Ibid.,* p. 206.

[8] NACLA, *Guatemala* (Berkeley, 1974), p. 81.

[9] Cited in Jonas Bodenheimer, *Plan,* p. 209.

[10] *Ibid.,* p. 154.

[11] Cited in Melville, *Politics,* p. 127.

[12] Cited in *ibid.,* p. 131.

[13] Cited in *El Imparcial,* Oct. 30, 1964, in Melville, *Politics,* p. 162.

[14] *El Imparcial,* May 27, 1965, in Melville, *Politics,* p. 160.

[15] *El Imparcial,* Oct. 9, 1965, in Melville, *Politics,* p. 167.

[16] L.B. Fletcher, Eric Graber, W.C. Merrill, E. Thorbecke, *Guatemala's Economic Development: the Role of Agriculture* (Iowa, 1970), pp. 18-23.

[17] *Ibid.*

[18] G. Wynia, *Politics and Planners* (Madison, 1972), pp. 90-94; J. Dombrowski, *et al., Area Handbook for Guatemala* (Washington, 1970); and NACLA, *Guatemala,* p. 105.

[19] *New York Times,* Nov. 14, 1966.

[20] Cited in *ibid.,* Jan. 22, 1968.

[21] Cited in Wynia, *Politics,* p. 71.

[22] *New York Times,* March 30, 1968.

[23] Cited in *Latin America (LA),* March 7, 1969.

[24] *Ibid.,* April 19, 1968; *New York Times,* Oct. 15, 1966; A. Bauer Paiz, "The Third Government of the Revolution and Imperialism in Guatemala", *Science and Society* (Summer, 1970), p. 159.

[25] D. McClelland, *The Central American Common Market* (London, 1972); CEPAL, "Alcance y requisitos de una politica de integración y reciprocidad economicos", pp. 29-39 in Eduardo Lizano F. (ed.), *La integración económica centroamericana;* Vol. 1 (Mexico City, 1975); Alberto Fuentes Mohr, "Surgimiento y orientación del programa multilateral" pp. 82-102, in *ibid.*

[26] Phillippe Schmitter, *Autonomy or Dependence as Regional Integration Outcomes* (Berkeley, 1972), p. 24; S. Jonas Bodenheimer, "La ayuda externa no favorece la integración económica centroamericana", pp. 306-347, in *La integración económica centroamericana,* Vol. II.

[27] NACLA, *Guatemala,* pp. 91-98. D. Browning, "The Rise and Fall of the Central American Common Market", *Journal of Latin American Studies,* (Vol. 6, Number 1), p. 161.

[28] Economist Intelligence Unit Reports, Annual Supplement, 1982, p. 14; NACLA, *Report on the Americas,* June 1981; Marta Ortiz Buonafina, *The Impact of Import Substitution Policies on Marketing Activities: A Case Study of the Guatemalan Commercial Sector* (Washington, 1981), p. 57.

[29] Cited in Ortiz-Buonafina, *Impact,* p. 1.

[30] Browning, "The Rise and Fall", p. 168.

[31] M. Monteforte Toledo, *Centro-america: subdesarrollo y dependencia,* Vol. 1 (Mexico City, 1972), p. 80; A. Guerra Borges, *Geografia Economica de Guatemala* (Guatemala City, 1969); VII Censo de poblacion (Guatemala City, 1964); Agency for International Development, *Guatemala Farm Policy Analysis* (Washington, 1975), p. 11; Fletcher, *et al, Role,* pp. 47-49.

[32] K. Griffin, *Land Concentration and Rural Poverty* (Hong Kong, 1976), p. 155; P. Dorner and R. Quirois, "Institutional Dualism in Central America's Agricultural Development", *Journal of Latin American Studies* (Vol. 5, number 2), p. 225; R. Plant, *Guatemala: Unnatural Disaster* (London, 1978), p. 80.

[33] Cited in B. Villaneuva T., *An Approach to the Study of Industrial Surplus: the Case of the United Fruit Company in Central America* (Land Tenure Centre, Univ. of Wisconsin, Research Paper number 40, 1969), pp. 20-21.

[34] Cited in R. Burbach and P. Flynn, *Agribusiness in the Americas* (New York, 1980), p. 207.

[35] *Ibid.,* pp. 208-211.

[36] *LA,* April 26, 1974.

[37] *Latin America Economic Review,* March 17, 1978.

[38] *LA,* June 25, 1971.

[39] J.J. Parsons, "Cotton and Cattle in the Pacific Lowlands of Central America", *Journal of Inter-American Studies* (Vol. 7, 1965), p. 155.

[40] AID, *Farm,* pp. 25-41. Fletcher, *Role,* pp. 135-136.

[41] Fletcher, *Role,* pp. 56-72.

[42] CIDA, *Tenencia,* pp. 79-80.

[43] Cited in *New York Times,* March 27, 1978.

[44] Villaneuva, *Approach to Industrial Surplus,* p. 57.
[45] Cited in *New York Times,* Aug. 24, 1980.
[46] Roland Ebel, "Political Instability in Central America", *Current History* (Feb. 1982), p. 51.
[47] Richard Millet, "Central American Cauldron", *Current History* (Feb. 1983), p. 72.
[48] *Latin America Weekly Report,* Feb. 6, 1981; July 2, 1983.
[49] *Ibid.,* July 24, 1981, June 25, 1982.
[50] *Ibid.,* Nov. 6, 1981, Jan. 15, 1982; EIU supplement, 1982 and Third Quarter Report, 1982.

Notes to chapter 10

[1] L. Fletcher, Eric Graber, W.C. Merrill, E. Thorbecke, *Guatemala's Economic Development: the Role of Agriculture* (Iowa, 1970), p. 23, 39, 43.
[2] H. Flores Alvarado, *Proletarización del campesina de Guatemala* (Guatemala City, 1970), pp. 134-135; L. Schmid, *The Role of Migratory Labor in the Economic Development of Guatemala* (Land Tenure Centre, Univ. of Wisconsin, Research Paper, no. 22, 1967).
[3] R. Plant, *Guatemala: Unnatural Disaster* (London, 1978), p. 8.
[4] *El Imparcial,* April 21, 1964; cited in T. and M. Melville, *Guatemala: The Politics of Land Ownership* (New York, 1971), p. 174, p. 176.
[5] *El Imparcial,* Aug. 16, 1965; cited in *ibid.,* p. 175; also M. Gollas-Quintero, "History and Economic Theory in the Analysis of the Development of Guatemalan Indian Agriculture" (Ph.D. diss., Univ. of Wisconsin, 1969), pp. 170-171.
[6] *Sugar World Report,* April, 1980; during the early spring of 1983 the author observed workers being hired for the coffee harvest for one quetzal per day on numerous occasions.
[7] *New York Times,* March 27, 1978.
[8] See Gollas-Quintero, "History", E.M. Mendleson, "Religion and World View in Santiago Atitlan", Microfilm collection of manuscripts on Middle American Cultural Anthropology, no. 52, 1957; R. Hinshaw, *Panajachel* (Pittsburgh, 1975); R. Reina, "Chinautla: A Guatemalan Indian Community" (Ph.D. diss., Univ. of North Carolina, 1957); G.W. Hill and M. Gollas, *Minifundia Economy and Society of the Guatemalan Highland Indian* (Land Tenure Centre, Univ. of Wisconsin, 1968); Gollas-Quintero, "History", pp. 170-171; Flores, *Proletarización,* p. 134.
[9] E. Galeano, *Guatemala: Occupied Country* (New York, 1969).
[10] VII Censo de poblacion, 1964 (Guatemala City, dirección general de estadistica); CIDA, *Tenencia de la tierra y desarrollo socio-economico del sector agricola* (Washington, 1965); 1979 figures taken from Isaac Cohen and Gert Rosenthal, "The Dimensions of Economic Policy Space in Central America", pp. 15-34, in R. Fagan and O. Pellicer, (eds.), *The Future of Central America: Policy Choices for the U.S. and Mexico* (Stanford, 1983), p. 27.
[11] *Economist Intelligence Unit Reports,1982 supplement: VI Censo de Poblacion, 1950* (Guatemala City, dirección general de estadistica); IX Censo de poblacion, 1981, cifras preliminares (Guatemala City, dirección general de estadistica).
[12] The figures are: Guatemala — 13.8 per cent, El Salvador — 13.5, Costa Rica — 6.5, Nicaragua — 5.3, Honduras — 4.4; in M. Monteforte Toledo,

Centroamerica: Subdesarrollo y dependencia, Vol. 1 (Mexico, 1972), p. 174.
[13] All cited in M. Ortiz-Buonafina, *The Impact of Import Substitution Policies on Marketing Activities: A Case Study of the Guatemalan Commercial Sector* (Washington, 1971), p. 114.
[14] AID, *Small Farm Policy Analysis* (Washington, 1975), p. 8.
[15] *Latin America (LA),* Jan. 29, 1971. Gollas-Quintero, "History", pp. 164-171.
[16] Sol Tax, *Penny Capitalism* (Washington, 1953), p. 11; also see T.D. Johnston, "Income Potential of Small Farms in Guatemala" (Ph.D. diss., Iowa, 1974), pp. 26-28.
[17] AID, *Farm,* p. 8.
[18] *Ibid.,* p. 24, p. 2.
[19] G.H. Smith, "Income and Nutrition in the Guatemalan Highlands" (Ph.D. diss., Univ. of Oregon, 1972), p. 30; AID, *Farm,* p. 38.
[20] AID, *Farm,* p. 28; CIDA, *Tenencia.*
[21] ECLA, *Desarrollo y política social en Centro-America* (Mexico City, 1978), cited in E. Torres-Rivas, *Crisis del poder in centroamerica* (Costa Rica, 1981), p. 25.

[22] G. Hill and Gollas, *Minifundia,* p. 16; Monteforte, *Centroamerica,* Vol. 1, p. 119.
[23] Cited in *New York Times,* Nov. 14, 1966.
[24] A. Guerra Borges, *Geografia economica de Guatemala* (Guatemala City, 1969), p. 242.
[25] VII Censo de poblacion, 1964, VIII Censo de poblacion, 1973; Hill and Gollas, *Minifundia;* AID, *Farm;* also see the discussion of the VII Censo in *Pensamiento Economica Latina* (1967, number 215).
[26] *Latin American Economic Report (LAER),* Dec. 3, 1976; *LA,* April 9, 1976.
[27] Cited in Melville, *Politics.*
[28] See *ibid.;* AID, *Farm;* R. Adams, *Crucifixion by Power* (Austin, 1970).
[29] Cited in Melville, *Politics,* p. 209.
[30] Cited in Monteforte, *Centroamerica,* Vol. 1, p. 120.
[31] S. Jonas Bodenheimer, *Guatemala: Plan piloto para el continente* (Costa Rica, 1981), p. 302. Guerra Borges, *Geografía económica,* p. 278.
[32] J. Hildebrand, "Guatemalan Rural Development Program: An Economists's Recommendations", *Inter-American Economic Affairs* (1963), p. 68.
[33] J. Hildebrand, "Farm Size and Agrarian Reform in Guatemala", *Inter-American Economic Affairs* (1962-1963), p. 52; also see Hildebrand, "Colonization Projects", *Inter-American Economic Affairs* (1965-66).
[34] George Fisher, "Frontier Settlement Patterns in Northern Guatemala" (Ph.D. diss., Univ. of Florida, 1974).
[35] Artimus Millet, "The Agricultural Colonization of the West Central Petén, Guatemala: A Case Study of Frontier Settlement by Cooperatives" (Ph.D. diss., Univ. of Oregon, 1974).
[36] Cited in Melville, *Politics,* p. 223.
[37] *Grandezas y miserias del Petén,* cited in Melville, *Politics,* p. 224.
[38] Millet, "Colonization", pp. 66-67.
[39] *LA,* June 25, 1971.
[40] *LAER,* June 26, 1979; G. Aquilera Peralta, "The Massacre at Panzos", *Monthly Review,* (Dec. 1979).
[41] Cited in Millet, "Colonization", p. 49.

[42] Cited in N. Peckenham, "Land Settlement in the Petén", *Latin American Perspectives* (Vol. 7, number 2), p. 171.

[43] Cited in J. Swift, *Inco: At Home and Abroad* (Kitchener, 1977), p. 77; also see NACLA, *Guatemala* (Berkeley, 1974); Latin American Working Group, *Letter*, (Vol. 5, number 1).

[44] Cited in NACLA, *Guatemala* p. 156.

[45] *LAER*, March 2, 1975, Aug. 18, 1978, Oct. 30, 1981; EIU 1982 supplement, pp. 13-14.

[46] EIU 1982 supplement; *Latin American Weekly Report*, July 2, 1982.

[47] *LA*, Dec. 11, 1973.

[48] Cited in *LAER*, Jan. 26, 1979.

[49] Mensaje del Episcopado Guatemalteco, *Unidos en la esperanza* (Guatemala City, July 1976).

[50] See R. James, "Guatemala: The Terror Continues", *Ontario Indian*, (May, 1982); Aquilera P. "The Massacre", *Newsweek*, June 19, 1978; Amnesty International, *A Calendar of Abuses.*

Notes to chapter 11

[1] *New York Times*, Oct. 10, 1971.

[2] Shelton Davis and J. Hodson, *Witness to Political Violence in Guatemala: The Suppression of a Rural Development Movement*, Oxfam America Impact Audit p. 2 (1982); also see R. James, "Guatemala: the Terror Continues, the Death of Kai Yutah Clouds", *Ontario Indian* (April, 1982).

[3] Cited in R. Plant, *Guatemala: Unnatural Disaster* (London, 1978), p. 12.

[4] A. Bauer Paiz, *Catalogación de leyes y disposiciones de trabajo de Guatemala del periodo 1872 a 1930* (Guatemala City, 1965); M. Angel Albizurez, "Struggles and Experiences of the Guatemalan Trade Union Movement", *Latin American Perspectives* (Spring, 1980), p. 145.

[5] R. Adams, *Crucifixion by Power* (Austin, 1970), p. 459.

[6] M. Monteforte Toledo, *Centro-America: subdesarrollo y dependencia,* Vol. 2 (Mexico, 1972), p. 132.

[7] M. Monteforte Toledo, *Centro-america*, vol. 2, p. 133; Norma Chinchilla, "Class struggle in Central America", *Latin American Perspectives* (Spring and Summer 1980); *La Clase obrera en la revolución Centroamericana, Cuadernos de Cidamo,* p. 3 (Mexico, 1980).

[8] *Latin America (L.A.)*, Oct. 19, 1973; G. Aguilera Peralta, "The Process of Militarization in the Guatemala State", *Latin American Research Unit Studies* (Sept. 1982).

[9] Angel Albizurez, "Struggles", p. 145; interview with CNUS director in *La Clase Obrera.*

[10] *L.A.*, Oct. 16, 1978; *Latin American Economic Report, (LAER),* Oct. 6, 1978.

[11] Chinchilla, "Class", interview with CNUS director in *La Clase Obrera; Sugar World Special Report* (April, 1980); *Prensa Libre* (Guatemala City), March 7, 1980; *La Nación* (Guatemala City) April 16, 1980.

[12] Marco Antonio Yon Sosa, "Breves apuntes sobre el movimiento revolucionario, 13 de noviembre", in *Revolución Socialista,* cited in NACLA, *Guatemala* (Berkeley, 1974), p. 179.

[13] Adolfo Gilly, "The Guerilla Movement in Guatemala", Part 1, *Monthly Review,* (May, 1965), p. 14.

[14] Yon Sosa, "Breves".

[15] Alan Howard, "With the Guerrillas in Guatemala", *New York Times Magazine,* June 26, 1966.

[16] Cited in R. Gott, *Rural Guerrillas in Latin America* (London, 1973), p. 100.

[17] For a discussion of these developments see A. Gilly, "Guerrilla", Gott, *Rural;* D. Crain, "Guatemala Revolutionaries and Havana's Ideological Offensive of 1966-68", *Journal of Inter-American Studies and World Affairs* (May, 1975); and Leonidas Reyes, "Un bosquejo historico" in Carlos Cáceres (ed.), *Aproximación a Guatemala* (Mexico, 1980).

[18] Cited in Howard, "With".

[19] *Ibid.*

[20] Cited in *New York Times,* July 28, 1966.

[21] Cited in "El hombre en el Socialismo", *Estrategía: Revista del MIR* (Chile, 1966, p. 5.

[22] Cited in *Ramparts,* (1968), p. 56.

[23] See for example R. Reina, "Chinautla: A Guatemalan Indian Community" (Ph.D. diss., Univ. of North Carolina, 1957).

[24] The leaders of the peasant league, union federation, and the revolutionary political parties were swamped with letters from local affiliates pledging support for Arbenz and expressing their willingness to fight for the revolution. These national leaders invariably told their members to place themselves at the disposal of the local military commander where they were to await orders to fight; the orders never came. See for example Castillo Flores to sec. gen. of the Unión Campesina, Naveja, Morales (June 23, 1954); sec. gen. of PAR, Fuentes de Oco to PAR national executive (June 19, 1954); and Castillo Flores to all sec. gen. of uniones campesinas (June 19, 1954), all in Guatemalan Documents, Records of CNCG, available in Manuscript Division, Library of Congress, Washington, D.C.

[25] R. Reina, "Chinautla".

[26] *Ibid.*

[27] Cited in *New York Times,* May 9, 1981.

[28] Cited in K. Warren, *Symbolism of Subordination* (Austin, 1978), p. 89.

[29] *Ibid.*

[30] For example, the Catholic Action newspaper, *Acción social Cristiana,* constantly published articles attacking virtually all aspects of the government's program of reform. See July 19, and Aug. 19, 1945. Also see pastoral letter of Archbishop Rossell of May 25, 1950, in *El Imparcial* (Guatemala City), May 26, 1950; and pastoral letter of April 14, 1954, enclosed in W. Krieg, first secretary of the U.S. embassy in Guatemala to State Department (April 14, 1954) in State Department Archives, Guatemalan Records.

[31] See for example E.M. Mendelson, "Religion and World View in Santiago Atitlan", Univ. of Chicaco, Microfilm collection of manuscripts on Middle American Cultural Anthropology, p. 52, 1957; and his *Los Escandolos del Maximon* (Guatemala City, 1965).

[32] F. Turner, *Catholicism and Political Development in Latin America* (North Carolina, 1971), pp. 135-136; and B.J. Calder, *Crecimiento y cambio de la iglesia católica Guatemalteca: 1944-1966* (Guatemala City, 1970).

[33] R. Adams, *Crucifixion,* p. 294; see also Calder, *Crecimiento,* pp. 148-149.

[34] Cited in Adams, p. 294.

[35] Blase Bonpane, "The Church and the Revolutionary Struggle in Central America", *Latin American Perspectives* (Spring 1980).

[36] Cited in *New York Times,* Jan. 19, Jan. 22, 1968.

[37] *Ibid.,* Sept. 14, 1975.

[38] Cited in *ibid.,* May 9, 1981.

[39] Warren, *Symbolism,* p. 107, 165. The most complete study of the effects of Catholic Action in Indians in the highlands is R. Falla, *Quiché Rebelde: Estudio de un movimiento de conversión religiosa, rebelde a las creencias tradicionales, en San Antonio Ilotenango, Quiché (1948-1970),* (Guatemala City, 1978).

[40] D. Brintnall, *Revolt Against the Dead,* (New York, 1976), p. 141. Also see P. Dierner, "The Tears of St. Anthony", *Latin America Perspectives* (Summer, 1978) for a somewhat unconvincing argument concerning the manner in which Indians are forced to continue with local celebrations by *ladino* merchants.

[41] Brintnall, *Revolt,* pp. 150-161.

[42] Cited in *Noticias de Guatemala* (Costa Rica), July 28, 1980.

[43] Notes taken from Kai's letters to friends in Canada and the U.S.; also see James, "Guatemala".

[44] Davis and Hodson, *Witness,* p. 15.

[45] M. Payeres, *Los dias de la selva* (Mexico, 1980); this has been translated and appears in *Monthly Review* (July-August, 1984).

[46] Davis and Hodson, *Witness,* p. 47; *L.A.,* July 25, 1975, July 23, 1976.

[47] Interview in Amnesty International Bulletin, Feb. 8, 1980.

[48] *Frénte,* Vol. 1, p. 1.

[49] Cited in *Noticias de Guatemala,* Feb. 4, 1980.

[50] Interview with CNUS director in *La Clase Obrera.*

[51] Sean McKenna, cited in article by Tommie Sue Montgomery, for *Network News,* reprinted in the *Toronto Star,* Oct. 16, 1982.

[52] Historia de ORPA, reprinted in *Guatemala: Un pueblo en lucha,* ed. by José Gonzalez and Antonio Campos (Spain, 1983), pp. 178-187. Also see FAR bulletin, edición internacional, p. 29, ano. 3, febrero 1983.

[53] Davis and Hodson, *Witness;* author visited Comolapa in January of 1981; the military had killed three people in the village the evening before, and a number of people were making hasty plans to leave the area.

[54] Declaration of Rolando Morán, made in 1981 and reprinted in *Guatemala: Un pueblo en lucha,* pp. 154-167.

[55] The Nation, Aug. 2, 1972; cited in NACLA, *Guatemala,* p. 203.

[56] *New York Times,* Dec. 14, 1980.

[57] Akwesasne Notes, Emergency Response International Network bulletin, March 1982; author visited Todos Santos in January 1981, shortly after the first visit to the community of the EGP, and again in April of 1983, shortly after the village had just been repopulated after being deserted for seven months.

[58] Amnesty International, *Guatemala: A Government Program of Political Murder,* 1981; also see *L.A., Latin America Weekly Report, Noticias de Guatemala,* and *Uno* más *Uno,* for the most frequent reports of this kind of violence.

[59] For example, only 2 of the 115 respondents to the Oxfam Study thought that the increase in rural violence could be traced to the presence of guerrillas, p. 2.

[60] Cited in *Frénte,* vol. 1, no. 1.

[61] See "Declaration of Revolutionary Unity", *Latin America Perspectives*

(Summer 1982); interview with FAR director, *Uno más Uno*, Oct. 12, 1982; and "Proclama unitaria de las organizaciones revolucionarias EGP, FAR, ORPA, y PGT al Pueblo de Guatemala" in *Guatemala: Un pueblo en lucha*, pp. 201-214.

Notes to chapter 12

[1] Cited in *Time*, Aug. 22, 1983.
[2] Cited by Allen Nairn, "Guatemala Bleeds", *New Republic*, April 11, 1983.
[3] Cited in *New York Times*, Oct. 17, 1982.
[4] Cited by Allen Nairn, "Guatemala".
[5] The Mexican government officially recognized the presence of 35,000 refugees in 32 camps. But, others suggested there were closer to 100,000 in 60 camps. See Ignacio Ramirez, "Tropas Mexicanos forman un cordon de seguridad tras el ataque Guatemaltecos", *Proceso*, Feb. 7, 1983, cited in Grupo de apoyo a refugiados Guatemaltecos, *La contra-insurgencia y los refugiados Guatemaltecos* (Mexico, 1983), pp. 9-10, p. 71. The new archbishop of Guatemala, Prospero Penados, estimated there were 500,000 internal refugees in Guatemala; Enfoprensa, *Guatemala Faces 1984*, p. 34. The Human Rights Commission of Guatemala estimated in September 1982 that there were one million refugees. *Noticias de Guatemala*, Oct. 12, 1982, p. 10.
[6] Report cited in *New York Times*, May 20, 1982.
[7] See, for example, *Los Angeles Times*, Oct. 14, 1982; Shelton Davis and Julie Hodson, "Witness to Political Violence in Guatemala: the Suppression of a Rural Development Movement", *(Oxfam America Study;) El Gráfico* Guatemala City), Oct. 8, 1982.
[8] *Uno más Uno*, Jan. 10, 1983, cited in Grupo, *La contra-insurgencia*, p. 27. Also see *Informe de un genocido — los refugiados Guatemaltecos* (Mexico, 1982).
[9] Cited in *Proceso*, Oct. 4, 1982, in Grupo, *La contra-insurgencia*, p. 27.
[10] One example is the report of a massacre carried out in the village of Parraxtut, El Quiché, which appeared first in *Uno más Uno* in December, 1982 and was subsequently picked up by other newspapers. In a visit months after, Michael Shawcross and two other witnesses, reported that the residents of the town repeatedly denied that any such incident occurred. (Letter from Michael Shawcross with a transcript of their conversation in my possession.) Another widely publicized story concerning the village of San Martin Jilotepeque in Chimaltenango was refuted by members of the diplomatic corps in Guatemala. (Conversation with political officer of the Canadian Embassy, Alexander Graham, Dec. 29, 1982.)

[11] Cited in *Miami Herald*, Aug. 23, 1983.
[12] Cited in *Prensa Libre* (Guatemala City), Jan. 29, 1983.
[13] Address reprinted in *Prensa Libre*, April 18, 1983.
[14] *Miami Herald*, Aug. 23, 1983; conversation with villagers in department of Huehuetenango, April 1983.
[15] Enfoprensa, *Guatemala faces 1984*, p. 9.
[16] Cited in *Noticias de Guatemala*, Oct. 15, 1982. See also *El Dia*, (Mexico City), Aug. 27, 1982; and *Excelsior* (Mexico City), Aug. 2, 1982.
[17] Comite Pro Justicia y Paz de Guatemala, *Human Rights in Guatemala* (Feb. 1984), pp. 10-11.

314 GIFT OF THE DEVIL

[18] *Ibid.*
[19] *Miami Herald,* Oct. 2, 1982; Enfoprensa, *Faces,* p. 9.
[20] Enfoprensa, *Faces,* pp. 10-11; discussion with Alexander Graham, Dec. 29, 1982.
[21] *El Dia,* Aug. 4, 1982.
[22] Cited in *Los Angeles Times,* Sept. 19, 1982.
[23] *Guatemala Update,* April-May, 1984; *Toronto Star,* July 15, 1984.
[24] For example, in Chiché, El Quiché, through the month of January 1983 there was increasing friction between the civil patrols in the town — primarily *ladino* — and the Indian patrols in the cantons surrounding it. This friction erupted in a number of pitched battles in which 25 Indian peasants were killed; *Prensa Libre,* Feb. 4, 5, 1983. Similar tension was also apparent between patrols near the Mam village of Todos Santos; conversation with patrolmen in April 1983.
[25] *Why Don't They Hear Us?,* Report of the Canadian Inter-Church Fact-Finding Mission to Guatemala and Mexico, Aug. 22, 1983 to Sept. 8, 1983, p. 10.
[26] Cited in *Los Angeles Times,* Feb. 11, 1983.
[27] Reports of the military distributing food and offering other services occurred frequently in Guatemala newspapers throughout 1982 and 1983; see for example, *Prensa Libre,* Jan. 11, Jan. 15, 1983.
[28] Cited in *Latin American Regional Report, Mexico and Central America* (LARR), May 6, 1983.
[29] *Newsweek,* Dec. 13, 1982.
[30] Radio broadcast, March 20, 1983.
[31] El Gráfico (Guatemala City) and *Prensa Libre*, April 9, 1983; *Prensa Libre*, April 20, 1982; author observed soldiers and civil patrols distributing notices of amnesty in Spanish and Ixil along paths in the hotly contested area around Nebáj and Chajól in April 1983.
[32] While the Guatemalan government routinely released the figures of the number of "subversives" who had accepted amnesty, they were seldom able to produce any known guerrillas who had turned themselves in. On the rare occasions in which that happened, the government publicized the fact extensively. The guerrilla organizations repeatedly denied that they were losing a significant number of their fighters. See for example the FAR bulletin, February 1983.
[33] Conversation with Mexican relief worker in refugee camp near Comitán, Mexico, April 29, 1983.
[34] Conversation with one of the people sent by the government to help negotiate the return of refugees, in Guatemala, Feb. 17-18, 1983; Jorge Serrano Elias, the head of the Guatemalan Council of State, visited the camps in early May 1983 to try to convince refugees to return; *El Excelsior,* April 26, 1983.
[35] Cited in *Latin America Weekly Report,* March 26, 1982.
[36] *LARR,* April 30, 1982; *El Dia,* Aug. 17, 1982; *Uno más Uno,* Aug. 15, 18, 1982.
[37] *LARR,* April 30, 1982.
[38] *Economist Intelligence Report,* third-quarter report, 1982.
[39] *El Gráfico,* Feb. 22, March 20, 1983; *Prensa Libre,* April 20, 1983.
[40] Cited in *LARR, Sept.* 24, 1982.
[41] *LARR,* June 10, 1983.

42 Cited in *LARR*, Aug. 13, 1982.
43 *Guatenoticias*, (Guatemala City), Jan. 15, 1983.
44 *Prensa Libre*, March 3, 1983.
45 *Prensa Libre*, March 25, 1983.
46 *Los Angeles Times*, Sept. 30, 1982; *Houston Chronicle*, July 30, 1982.
47 *New York Times*, July 18, 1982.
48 *Why Don't They Hear Us?*, pp. 14-15.
49 Cited in *LARR*, Sept. 24, 1982.
50 *El Gráfico*, Feb. 18, 1983.
51 *LARR*, Oct. 29, 1982.
52 *Ibid.*, June 10, 1983.
53 *New York Times*, Sept. 11, 1983.
54 Francis Pisani, "L'eviction du General Ríos Montt fuite en avant au Guatemala", *Le Monde Diplomatique*, Sept. 30, 1983; *LARR*, July 15, 1983. See also *Prensa Libre*, March 21, 24 and 26, 1983; and *Guatenoticias*, Jan. 15, 1983.
55 Cited in *Washington Post*, Sept. 22, 1983. See also Inter-Church Committee on Human Rights in Latin America, Toronto, News Release, Nov. 8, 1983; Guatemalan Human Rights Commission, news release, May 15, 1984.
56 Cited in *LARR*, Aug. 19, 1983.
57 Enfoprensa, April 27-May 3, May 25-May 31, 1984.
58 Cited in *New York Times*, Aug. 13, 1983.
59 Cited in *LARR*, Aug. 19, 1983.
60 *LARR*, Jan. 13, 1984.
61 *El Dia*, Aug. 31, 1982; *Uno* más *Uno*, June 6, 1984; *Guatemala in Struggle*, publication of the URNG, Feb. 1983, "The Tecun Uman Guerilla Front is Born in the Central Highlands".
62 Unpublished survey of communities in Chimaltenango, copy in my possession.
63 *Globe and Mail*, July 15, 16 1984; *El Dia*, May 30, 1984. For an insightful discussion of Mexico's relationship with the Guatemalan government and how this has affected refugees, see Adolfo Aguilar Zinser, "Mexico and the Guatemalan Crisis", in Richard Fagan and Olga Pellicer (eds.), *The Future of Central America: Policy choices for the U.S. and Mexico* (Stanford, 1983), pp. 161-186.
64 Davis and Hodson, Oxfam America Study, pp. 45-46.

Index